Space, Narrative, and Historical Imagination in Livy's *Ab Urbe Condita*

Historiography of Rome and Its Empire

Series Editors

Carsten Hjort Lange, *Aalborg, Denmark*
Jesper Majbom Madsen, *SDU, Denmark*

Editorial Board

Rhiannon Ash, *Oxford, UK*
Christopher Baron, *Notre Dame, USA*
Henning Börm, *Rostock, Germany*
Jessica H. Clark, *Florida State University, USA*
Cynthia Damon, *University of Pennsylvania, USA*
Alain Gowing, *University of Washington, USA*
Lisa Irene Hau, *Glasgow, UK*
Adam Kemezis, *Alberta, Canada*
Christina S. Kraus, *Yale, USA*
J.E. Lendon, *University of Virginia, USA*
David Levene, *New York University, USA*
Christopher Mallan, *The University of Western Australia*
Steve Mason, *Groningen, Netherlands*
Josiah Osgood, *Georgetown, USA*
John Rich, *Nottingham, UK*
Cristina Rosillo-López, *Sevilla, Spain*
Federico Santangelo, *Newcastle, UK*
Andrew G. Scott, *Villanova University, USA*
Christopher Smith, *St Andrews, UK*
Catherine *Steel, Glasgow, UK*
Frederik J. Vervaet, *Melbourne, Australia*
David Wardle, *Cape Town, South Africa*
Kathryn Welch, *Sydney, Australia*
Johannes Wienand, *Braunschweig, Germany*

VOLUME 21

The titles published in this series are listed at *brill.com/hre*

Space, Narrative, and Historical Imagination in Livy's *Ab Urbe Condita*

By

Virginia Fabrizi

BRILL

LEIDEN | BOSTON

Cover illustration: *The Triumph of Aemilius Paulus* by Carle (Antoine Charles Horace) Vernet, 1789. Metropolitan Museum of Art in New York. Public Domain.

The Library of Congress Cataloging-in-Publication Data is available online at https://catalog.loc.gov
LC record available at https://lccn.loc.gov/2025013157

Typeface for the Latin, Greek, and Cyrillic scripts: "Brill". See and download: brill.com/brill-typeface.

ISSN 2468-2314
ISBN 978-90-04-73319-0 (hardback)
ISBN 978-90-04-73321-3 (e-book)
DOI 10.1163/9789004733213

Copyright 2025 by Virginia Fabrizi. Published by Koninklijke Brill BV, Plantijnstraat 2, 2321 JC Leiden, The Netherlands.
Koninklijke Brill BV incorporates the imprints Brill, Brill Nijhoff, Brill Schöningh, Brill Fink, Brill mentis, Brill Wageningen Academic, Vandenhoeck & Ruprecht, Böhlau and V&R unipress.
Koninklijke Brill BV reserves the right to protect this publication against unauthorized use. Requests for re-use and/or translations must be addressed to Koninklijke Brill BV via brill.com or copyright.com. For more information: info@brill.com.

This book is printed on acid-free paper and produced in a sustainable manner.

For Sergio

Contents

Historiography of Rome and Its Empire Series   IX
   Carsten H. Lange and Jesper M. Madsen
Acknowledgements   X
Abbreviations, Texts, and Translations   XII

Introduction: Space, Narrative, and Livy's *Ab Urbe Condita*   1
1   The City, the World, and the Space of Livy's *Ab Urbe Condita*   1
2   Space, Human Experience, and Narrative   4
3   Space, Roman Historiography, and the *Ab Urbe Condita*   6
4   Space in the *Ab Urbe Condita*: State of the Art and
     Open Questions   13
5   A Narratology of Space   15
     5.1   *A Basic Framework*   15
     5.2   *Description and Narration*   19
     5.3   *Focalisation*   26
6   An Outline of This Book   29

1   Strife, Reconciliation, and Change in the Forum Romanum   32
1   Writing the City   32
2   Setting the Scene: Livy's Forum   36
3   A Space Torn Apart: the Forum in Livy's Struggle of the Orders   47
     3.1   *Framing the Struggle*   47
     3.2   *Book 3: Disrupting the Forum*   52
     3.3   *Reconciliation, Crisis, and Refoundation*   62
     3.4   *Shifting Boundaries*   65
4   Forum and Curia in an Expanding World   71
5   Permanence, Change, and Political Symbolism in Livy's Forum   78

2   The Space of the City   82
1   Founding the City: Book 1   82
2   The Capitol   87
     2.1   *History and Archaeology*   87
     2.2   *The Pivot of Roman Space and Time*   91
     2.3   *The Object of Gazes and Words: Verticality, Hierarchy, and
              Authority Struggles*   100
     2.4   *The Core of Roman Identity*   111

    3   Other Hills   119
        3.1   *Viminal, Quirinal, Caelian, and Esquiline*   119
        3.2   *The Aventine*   121
        3.3   *The Palatine*   126
    4   The Campus Martius   133
    5   Boundaries: Tiber, Walls, Gates, and Janiculum   139
    6   Synthetic Views of the City Space   142
    7   Rome in the *Ab Urbe Condita*   146

3   The Space of Battle   150
    1   Shaping Military Space in the *Ab Urbe Condita*   150
    2   Standard Military Space   154
        2.1   *Camps and Sectors of Armies as Spaces*   154
        2.2   *Order and Disorder*   159
        2.3   *Army and Political Community*   165
    3   Topography   170
        3.1   *Introduction*   170
        3.2   *Topographic Features and Their Functions*   171
        3.3   *Locus,* virtus, *and* arma: *Landscape and Military Ethics*   179
        3.4   *Basic and Complex Topographies*   184
    4   The Spatial Vocabulary of Battle: War, Conquest, and Control   192

4   The Semantics of Space and Gender   197
    1   Space, Gender, and Narrative   197
    2   Spatial Transgressions I: Men in (Other Men's) Private Spaces   201
    3   Spatial Transgressions II: Women in Public Space   215
    4   Liminal Spaces   223
    5   Subverting Roman Space I: Verginia and the Decemvirate   228
    6   Subverting Roman Space II: the Bacchanalian Scandal   235
    7   Gender, Power, and Space in the *Ab Urbe Condita*   241

Conclusions: Livy's Vocabulary of Space   245
    1   Space, Semantics, and Historical Imagination   245
    2   Relational Space, Control, and Emotion   246
    3   How to Make the State Function: Space and Livy's Political Vision   249

Referenced Works   253
Index of Places   277
Index of Ancient People   282
Index of Ancient Sources   287

Historiography of Rome and Its Empire Series

Carsten H. Lange and Jesper M. Madsen

The *Historiography of Rome and Its Empire* series (*HRE*) aims to gather innovative and outstanding contributions that identify debates and trends, in order to help provide a better understanding of ancient historiography, as well as to identify fruitful approaches to Roman history and historiography. The series welcomes proposals that look at both Roman and Greek writers as well as manuscripts which focus on individual writers, or individuals in the same tradition. It is timely and valuable to bring these trends and historical sources together in the series, focusing on the whole of the Roman period, from the Republic to the Later Roman Empire.

Historical writing about Rome in both Latin and Greek forms an integrated topic. There are two strands in ancient writing about the Romans and their empire: (a) the Romans' own tradition of histories of the deeds of the Roman people at home and at war, including the fragmentary early Roman historiographical tradition and (b) historical responses in Greek, written by Greeks and Romans alike, some developing their own models and others building upon the writings of earlier historians. Whereas older scholarship tended to privilege a small group of 'great historians' (the likes of Sallust, Livy, Tacitus), recent work has rightly brought out the diversity of the traditions and recognized that even 'minor' writers are worth exploring not just as sources, but for their own concerns and reinterpretation of their material, as well as their place within the tradition. The study of these historiographical traditions is essential as a counterbalance to the outmoded use of ancient authors as a handy resource, with scholars looking at isolated sections of their structure. This use of the ancient evidence makes us forget to reflect on their works in their textual and contextual entirety. Recent years have also witnessed an expansion of what is understood as 'historiography' to include *memorabilia* and antiquarian studies. With the widening of a previously narrow definition to encompass other traditions, the horizon of historiography expands beyond the limits of a fixed genre to include a range of approaches to the past.

Acknowledgements

> I feel like someone who wades out into the sea after being initially attracted to the water by the shallows next to the shore; and I foresee any advance only taking me into even more enormous, indeed bottomless, depths, and that this undertaking of mine, which seemed to be diminishing as I was completing the earliest sections, is now almost increasing in size.[1]

With these words at the beginning of Book 31 of his *Ab Urbe Condita*, Livy expresses his frustration at the magnitude of his undertaking, writing the history of Rome from the foundation of the city to his own times. While the scope of my own project has been much more limited than his, I have shared Livy's feeling at several points while writing this book.

The *Ab Urbe Condita* is, due to its vividness and variety, a fascinating work to wade out into, but one soon becomes aware of the complexity of the cultural, historical, and literary layers that make up Livy's narrative. For this reason, the plan and scope of this book has gone through several changes since I started writing it about a decade ago. Some years away from academia also slowed my work on it significantly. I have to thank the numerous people and institutions who supported me throughout the years for the fact that I have, at last, reached the further shore.

I owe a special debt of gratitude to Elisa Romano, who first awakened my interest in Livy, several years ago, and then repeatedly spurred me to complete this book – even (and especially) at times when the sea voyage looked particularly stormy.

The first ideas from which the book originated were developed during my time as a post-doctoral fellow at the Freie Universität Berlin (2013–2014). During those months, I had the chance to deepen my understanding of space as a social and cultural category by attending numerous seminars, conferences, and having fruitful discussions in the framework of the Excellence Cluster Topoi. I am grateful to Ernst Baltrusch, who was my post-doc supervisor, for discussing my early thoughts about space in Livy.

---

1 (…) *iam provideo animo, velut qui proximis litori vadis inducti mare pedibus ingrediuntur, quidquid progredior, in vastiorem me altitudinem ac velut profundum invehi, et crescere paene opus, quod prima quaeque perficiendo minui videbatur*, Livy 31.1.5. Translation by J.C. Yardley (from Yardley and Heckel 2000).

The book itself was conceived during a second post-doctoral fellowship, at the Ludwig-Maximilians-University of Munich and in the Graduate School 'Distant Worlds' (2014–2017). Therese Fuhrer, my mentor during that time, kindly read and helped improve some parts of this monograph. I also wish to thank all the members of the former Focus Area 'Organisation of Memory and Forgetting' for many stimulating and friendly discussions.

A five-month research stay at the Technische Universität Dresden, in 2018, allowed me to write substantial sections of the book. I am grateful to Dennis Pausch for inviting me there and for giving me the opportunity to discuss some of my ideas about military space in Livy in a stimulating environment.

The last stages of the writing process took place in the first years of my appointment at the Università di Napoli 'L'Orientale'. Here, I have found a very supporting and inspiring environment, which has provided me with the necessary stability and peace of mind to work on the final manuscript; I wish to thank my colleagues for that.

I am deeply grateful to the editors of the HRE series, Carsten Hjort Lange and Jesper Majbom Madsen, for their patience and understanding throughout the publishing process. The anonymous Brill reader deserves my most sincere thanks for helping me improve the monograph in a substantial way. For attentive proofreading of my English text I am grateful to John Perchard.

Finally, I owe a special debt to my family and friends, who supported, encouraged, and helped me in ways beyond recounting. I wish to thank my parents and brother, who never stopped making their support truly felt, even from far away. And I am deeply grateful to my partner, Sergio, for his patient and loving encouragement, and for many hours spent talking about this book; his steadfast presence made any complication I encountered along the way much easier to face.

Abbreviations, Texts, and Translations

ANRW	Temporini, W. and Haase, W. (eds.) (1972–) *Aufstieg und Niedergang der römischen Welt*. Berlin: De Gruyter.
CIL	*Corpus Inscriptionum Latinarum* (1862–). Berlin.
FRHist	Cornell, T.J. *et al.* (ed.) (2013) *The Fragments of the Roman Historians*. Volumes 1–3. Oxford: Oxford University Press.
LTUR	Steinby, E.V. (ed.) (1993–2000) *Lexicon Topographicum Urbis Romae*. Volumes 1–6. Roma: Quasar.
OCD	Hornblower, S., Spawforth, A. and Eidinow, E. (eds.) (2012) *The Oxford Classical Dictionary*, 4th ed. Oxford: Oxford University Press.
OLD	*Oxford Latin Dictionary* (2012) 2nd ed. Oxford: Oxford University Press.
TLL	*Thesaurus linguae Latinae* (1900–). Stuttgart and Leipzig: Teubner / München: Saur / Berlin and New York: De Gruyter.

Abbreviations of journal titles are according to the *Année Philologique*. Abbreviations of ancient authors and works according to *OCD*.

I quote the text of the *Ab Urbe Condita* from the following editions: Ogilvie (1974) for Books 1–5; Conway and Walters (1919) for Books 6–10; Briscoe (2016) for Books 21–25; Walsh (1989) for Books 26–27; Walsh (1986) for Books 28–30; Briscoe (1991) for Books 31–40; Briscoe (1986) for Books 41–45. Unless specified, the translation of Greek and Latin texts in my own.

Introduction: Space, Narrative, and Livy's *Ab Urbe Condita*

1 The City, the World, and the Space of Livy's *Ab Urbe Condita*

Livy's *Ab Urbe Condita* is the history of a city, Rome.[1] Its narrative starts with the fall of another city, Troy,[2] and goes on to report how the Trojan refugee Aeneas came to Italy[3] and how his descendant Romulus founded Rome about 350 years later.[4] The first segment of Livy's work, the so-called First Pentad (i.e. Books 1–5),[5] ends with the rebuilding of Rome after its destruction during the Gallic invasion of 390 BCE.[6]

The city of Rome, however, is more than just a location in space. The text emphasizes its imperial future from the very beginning. When introducing the tale of Romulus and Remus' birth, at 1.4.1, the narrator attributes it to the will of Fate, responsible for 'the origin of so great a city and the founding of the most powerful *imperium* of all next to the gods'.[7] Throughout the narrative of the city's origins, the theme of Rome's greatness comes repeatedly to the fore. At 1.16.7, for example, a man named Iulius Proculus tells the Roman people, who are mourning Romulus' recent disappearance, how the king miraculously appeared to him, revealing his own new divine status. Romulus, Proculus states, instructed him to announce to his fellow Romans that the gods wanted 'his Rome' (*mea Roma*) to be the 'capital of the world' (*caput orbis terrarum*).[8]

---

1 For the *Ab Urbe Condita* as a written city, overlapping the physical *urbs*, see Kraus (1994).
2 *Iam primum omnium satis constat Troia capta in ceteros saevitum esse Troianos, duobus, Aeneae Antenorique (…) omne ius belli Achivos abstinuisse*, 1.1.1.
3 1.1.4–2.6. Aeneas' story is preceded by a brief mention of the voyage of another Trojan refugee, Antenor, who reached the region by the Adriatic Sea where Livy's own town, Padua, was located (1.1.2–3).
4 The legend concerning the foundation of Rome is told at 1.4.1–8.3. On the relationship between Troy and Rome, and the dynamics of destruction and (re)foundation, see e.g. Kraus (1994); Edwards (1996, p. 51).
5 For unitary design and internal symmetry in the First Pentad, see e.g. Vasaly (2002). Some scholars have interpreted this section of Livy's work as narrating a first life-cycle of the city, from birth to destruction and rebirth (see in particular Miles, 1995; Mineo, 2006). For the composition and publication dates of books and book groups of the *Ab Urbe Condita*, cf. below, n. 42.
6 Livy 5.55.
7 *Sed debebatur, ut opinor, fatis tantae origo urbis maximique secundum deorum opes imperii principium.*
8 For other examples, see e.g. 1.9.1; 1.45.1, 3; 1.55.6, with Ogilvie (1965, p. 30).

This is, of course, an anticipation of what the reader sees happening in the following books, which show Rome gradually broadening the reach of its power, since the theme of universal empire receives more and more emphasis as the narrative proceeds towards more recent times. At 36.17, for example, the Roman general Manius Acilius Glabrio harangues his soldiers before fighting a battle against King Antiochus of Syria at Thermopylae in 191 BCE. Among other things, Glabrio shows his men that a Roman victory would mean opening up the East to Roman conquest (36.17.14). 'What shall then prevent us' he goes on to ask, 'from having the Ocean, which delimits the world with its embrace (*qui orbem terrarum amplexu finit*), as the boundary of our territory (*fines*) from Gades to the Red Sea? and what shall prevent the entire human race from honouring the name of Rome as the greatest next to the gods (*secundum deos*)?' (36.17.15).[9] The mention of the Ocean, the boundary of the world *par excellence*, and of two locations epitomising the west (Gades) and the East (the Red Sea),[10] stresses the universality of Roman power through the language of geography. At the same time, Glabrio's rhetoric picks up earlier statements from the foundation story – both the narrator's remark about Rome's *imperium* being the greatest 'next to the gods' might' (*secundum deorum opes*, 1.4.1) and Iulius Proculus' announcement about Rome as *caput orbis terrarum* (1.16.7).[11]

The history of the city that the *Ab Urbe Condita* represents is also, therefore, a history of the world – or rather, it is a history of how the city extended its power to dominate over 'the world'. The problems posed by this lengthy historical process are well defined in the Preface to Livy's work. Here the historian explains the difficulty of his enterprise, exacerbated by, among other things, the greatness of his subject matter (*praef.* 4):[12]

> Res est praeterea et immensi operis, ut quae supra septingentesimum annum repetatur et quae ab exiguis profecta initiis eo creverit, ut iam magnitudine laboret sua; et legentium plerisque haud dubito quin

---

9 *Quid deinde aberit quin ab Gadibus ad mare rubrum Oceano fines terminemus, qui orbem terrarum amplexu finit, et omne humanum genus secundum deos nomen Romanum veneretur?*
10 For this geographical inaccuracy see Briscoe (1981, p. 247).
11 For the latter parallel see Clark (2014, p. 180, with a full analysis of Glabrio's statement). For universal themes in Livy and a comparison with the contemporary discourse of universal empire cf. Fabrizi (2015, esp. pp. 129–136). Briscoe (1981, p. 247) highlights the similarity between Glabrio's wording and *Mon. Anc.* 26.2.
12 As Ogilvie (1965, p. 24) stresses, 'Livy's emphasis on the magnitude of his task' is a 'distinctive feature' of his preface and his work. Cf. the historian's remarks about the effort required to write Roman history at 31.1.1–5.

primae origines proximaque originibus minus praebitura voluptatis sint, festinantibus ad haec nova, quibus iam pridem praevalentis populi vires se ipsae conficiunt.

The topic, moreover, requires immense effort, because it goes further back than seven hundred years and, starting from humble beginnings, has grown so much that it now suffers from its very greatness. And I do not doubt that most readers will not find much pleasure in the origins and the events closest to the origins, as they rush forward to these recent events, through which the forces of a long dominating people destroy themselves.

This programmatic statement casts the *Ab Urbe Condita* as a narrative about a city extending its power to unsustainable dimensions. The *res* mentioned in section 4 is at the same time the 'topic' of Livy's narrative (the history of Rome) and the *res publica* (the Roman state) itself.[13] Both start from 'humble beginnings' – the history of Rome's origins with its limited geographic focus and the small town of the monarchic age – and grow into something far greater – the history of a complex, geographically far-reaching world power and the 'leading people of the world' (*principis terrarum populi*, praef. 3; cf. *praevalentis populi*, 4). Rome's greatness (*magnitudo*) relies on both its vastness (space) and its dominance (power); it is precisely the vast extension of Rome's dominance that, in Livy's interpretation, leads to moral decay, which in turn causes civil wars and the near ruin of the city.

As these observations suggest, a concern with space – the space of the city, the space of the world, and how such spaces interact with each other – lies at the heart of Livy's historiographical project. While every history entails a spatial dimension, in the *Ab Urbe Condita* space plays such a large role as to become an interpretive category. Thus, understanding how Livy's narrative of Roman history uses space can shed light on the historian's representation of historical change, power, and expansion.

This book examines how the *Ab Urbe Condita* constructs the space it narrates, and what the resultant narrated space reveals about the interpretation of Roman history that the work proposes. In the following sections of this introduction, I lay the groundwork for such an investigation. In section 2, I refer to existing sociological scholarship to outline my idea of the relationship between space, human experience, and narrative. In section 3, I locate Livy's *Ab Urbe*

---

13   Cf. Moles (1993, p. 146 and n. 23), with further bibliography.

Condita within the traditions of Roman historiographical thought about space and Roman expansion. In section 4, I briefly discuss existing scholarship about space in Livy's history. Section 5 exposes my narratological approach to space as a narrative category in the *Ab Urbe Condita* and clarifies some terms and issues that will be central to my investigation. Finally, section 6 provides an outline of this book.

2 Space, Human Experience, and Narrative

I start from the assumption that space is socially constructed: social relationships shape space and space, in turn, shapes social relationships. This fundamental concept goes back to a body of work in the fields of sociology and geography, which, starting from the 1970s, substantially changed scholars' ways of thinking about space. The resulting wave of scholarly interest in space and spatiality is usually known as the 'spatial turn' of the humanities.[14]

In a seminal study, French sociologist Henri Lefèbvre (1991)[15] argued that space is not a fixed, objective container of human action but is produced through social practice. More precisely, Lefèbvre distinguished between three different dimensions of what he named 'the production of space': 'spatial practice', that is, the set of practices concerning reproduction and the division of labour, and their shaping of space; 'representations of space', that is, space as conceived on an intellectual level by urban planners and technocrats; and 'lived space' (or 'representational spaces'), that is, the space of everyday human experience with its web of symbolic associations.

These ideas were taken up and further developed, in the following decades, by geographers influenced by the Marxist tradition (e.g. Soja, 1989; Massey, 2005; Harvey, 2006 and 2009). Crucial to their work is the notion of relational space, that is, of space not as a pre-given and unchangeable container of entities and processes but as something resulting from multiple interactions between entities and processes.[16] As a consequence, space is, to use Massey's

---

14   The definition 'spatial turn' was introduced by Soja (1989); for a synthetic history of the phenomenon see Soja (2009); and, for current gaps in sociological research on space Fuller and Löw (2017) and Bartmanski and Füller (2024, p. 4).

15   The original French edition of the work was published in 1974.

16   Harvey distinguishes between an absolute, a relative, and a relational view of space. Absolute space is the space postulated by Newton, Descartes, and Kant, 'a pre-existing and immoveable grid' (2006, p. 121) functioning as a container for objects and actions. The relative view, finding its main reference point in Einstein's Relativity Theory, holds that space is not fixed, because its measurement changes depending on the position of

(2005, p. 9) words, 'always under construction' and, as such, is the realm of complexity and multiplicity.

Within this context, sociologist Martina Löw (2016) has attempted a systematic theorisation of space as a key concept for the study of society. Löw defines space as 'a relational arrangement of living beings and social goods' (p. 188 and *passim*) and argues that it is constituted in action[17] by two processes she calls 'spacing' and 'the operation of synthesis' (p. 135). Spacing is the process by which humans place or move objects, or move themselves (p. 134); by the process of synthesis 'goods and people are amalgamated by way of processes and perception, imagination, and memory' (p. 135). In this interpretation, space has a material and a symbolic component.

Of the utmost importance for my purposes is the idea, which all these approaches share, that the way people think of space, the meanings they attribute to it, and their experiences of it are integral parts of the social production of space. These perceptions, in turn, are inextricably intertwined with action and practice, and with the economic and power structures at work in a society.[18]

These observations lead me to stress a second crucial point of my approach, namely the role of narratives as constitutive elements of both the social construction and the individual experience of space. Research in the neurosciences has shown that narrative is a basic means though which human beings organise their bodily perceptions into a consistent interpretation of the world[19] and that the human experience of space can be thought of as part of such a narrative process. Phenomenological studies suggest that space is experienced by human beings through motion, and that motion can be apprehended narratively.[20]

At the most basic level, when we tell stories about our everyday lives, we shape our notion of ourselves as we speak about the places we have been to and the paths we have taken to get from one point to the other. There are also

---

the observer; moreover, space is an element of space-time, and is affected by objects and processes. Finally, the relational view 'holds that there is no such thing as space and time outside of the processes that define them. (...) The concept of space is embedded in or internal to process' (2006, p. 123). Harvey considers these three views as different ways to think about space, which can all be fruitful in different contexts.

17   More precisely, Löw argues that space is constituted in the interplay of action and structures.
18   On these concepts cf. also Bartmanski (2024).
19   Cf. e.g. Jääskeläinen *et al.* (2020, with further bibliography).
20   Cf. Tilley (1994, esp. pp. 31–33, from whom I draw some of the observations in the following paragraph); Thalmann (2011, pp. 18–19).

stories, however, which concern a community as a whole, transmitting memory of its past and shaping its identity in the present. Such stories, too, involve narratives about space: about the geographical areas felt to be home to the community, about mythical journeys, expansion, or the place that the community occupies in the world. Narratives about space current within a community can be crucial in imagining its possible relationships with other communities in terms of coexistence, conflict, or dominance.[21]

Such narratives are, of course, of various kinds. There are orally transmitted legends and folktales, which are often a primary means for shaping a society's view of the world. There are the stories involved in ritual, which itself often entails some movement through space and thus charges space and spaces with meanings. In literate societies, an important role is played by literary texts, which can work with the spatial semantics of societies to express new meanings.[22] In our contemporary world, conflicting narratives play out on television, in newspapers, on social media, or even in everyday conversation. Finally, there can be intellectual discourses which claim a scientific status, such the writings of professional geographers and historians. All these narratives, though with varying degrees of authority and pervasiveness, contribute to shaping people's perceptions of the space they live in and their imagination of the spaces they have not directly experienced.

I argue that it can be fruitful to approach the writings of Roman historians as narratives of this kind: as narratives, that is, which both reflect and shape spatial experiences and spatial imagination, and thus contribute to the complex set of processes that one may designate as the construction of space in Roman society. It is from this perspective that I read Livy's *Ab Urbe Condita* in this book.

3   Space, Roman Historiography, and the *Ab Urbe Condita*

Born at a time when Rome was emerging as a leading power in the Mediterranean world, from its origins Roman historiography was concerned with the topics of territorial expansion and Rome's identity vis-à-vis foreign spaces and peoples. The earliest contributions came from Roman aristocrats writing in

---

21 See e.g. Said (2000) on the importance of narratives about the past in the Israeli-Palestinian conflict.
22 The bibliography on space in literary texts is vast, especially since the spatial turn has come to affect the field of literary studies. For some recent contributions, see e.g. Hallet and Neumann (2009); Tally (2021); Acharya and Panda (2022).

Greek at the time of the Second Punic War (218–201 BCE) and probably had the purpose of presenting a favourable image of Rome to an international audience.[23] Their works anchored the origins of Rome in the world of Greek myth, connecting the foundation of the city with the wanderings of the Trojan hero Aeneas. At the same time, they provided accounts of the Hannibalic war that countered contemporary pro-Carthaginian writings and supported Rome's claims to hegemony in the Western Mediterranean.[24]

About half a century later, after Rome had established her power in the East by defeating the Hellenistic kingdoms of Syria and Macedon, the first historical narrative in Latin, Cato's *Origines*,[25] emphasised the Italic roots of the city. The first book of the work narrated the foundation of Rome and the deeds of the Roman kings; the second and third recounted the origins of other communities on the Italian peninsula. The remaining four books provided a synthetic account of recent events from the First Punic War to 149 BCE (i.e. to shortly before Cato's own death in the same year);[26] these also included at least some

---

[23] The first Roman historian was Q. Fabius Pictor (cf. e.g. Livy 1.44.2 = *FRHist*. 1 T11a; 2.40.10 = T11c; Dion. Hal. *Ant. Rom.* 7.71.1 = T11d), a senator who lived during the Second Punic War (cf. e.g. Polyb. 3.9.4 = *FRHist*. 1 T6). Our sources record that, in the aftermath of Cannae, the Senate sent him as an envoy to Delphi, to consult the oracle of Apollo on how to win back the gods' benevolence (cf. Livy 22.57.4–5 = *FRHist*. 1 T3a; 23.11.1–6 = T4; Plut. *Vit. Fab.* 18.3 = T3b; App. *Hann*. 27.116 = T3c). This episode points to Fabius' familiarity with the Greek language, which he also displayed in composing a history of Rome in Greek (Cic. *Div.* 1.43 = *FRHist*. 1 T10 speaks of *Graeci annales*) recounting events from the origins to his own age. L. Cincius Alimentus, a contemporary of Fabius' who fought in the Second Punic War and was taken prisoner by the Carthaginians wrote a history with a similar objective, also in Greek (cf. Dion. Hal. *Ant. Rom.* 1.6.2 = *FRHist*. 2 T2; Livy 21.38.2–5 = T1). On Fabius and Cincius' works see e.g. Beck (2003); Beck and Walter (2005, pp. 55–61 and 137–138); Chassignet (1996, pp. LIV–LIX and LXXV–LXXVIII); *FRHist*. I, pp. 160–183 (with further bibliography). We only have scanty information about other Roman historians writing in Greek in the first half of the second century BCE (on Publius Cornelius Scipo, Africanus' son, cf. Briscoe in *FRHist*. I, p. 184; on Aulus Postumius Albinus, Northwood in *FRHist*. I, pp. 85–190; on Gaius Acilius, Bispham and Northwood in *FRHist*. I, pp. 224–226).

[24] On Fabius and Cincius' intended audiences and purposes see e.g. Chassignet (1996, pp. L–LIII); Gotter, Luraghi and Walter (2003, pp. 13–14); Dillery (2009, pp. 77–90); Cornell in *FRHist*. I, pp. 168–169 (with further bibliography).

[25] The last known event Cato narrated was the trial of Servius Sulpicius Galba, who had been prosecuted for his cruel treatment of the Lusitanians, in the same year; Cato inserted his own accusatory speech in his account of the events (cf. *FRHist*. 5 FF104–107). For the various issues connected to the dating and composition of the *Origines* and a summary of previous scholarship see Cornell in *FRHist*. I, pp. 196–198.

[26] For the structure of the *Origines* see Nep. *Cato* 3.3–4; Cugusi and Sblendorio Cugusi (2001, pp. 43–54); Cornell in *FRHist*. I, pp. 198–205.

geo-ethnographic material.[27] Although the fragmentary state of the work prevents us from attaining any certain conclusions about the relationship between the 'origins' and the 'recent history' section, about the exact structuring of the material within each book, and about the features of Cato's treatment of the peninsula, it seems clear that concern for the place of Rome in the world was central to the *Origines*. It seems likely that Cato's history represented Italy as a geographic unity in which different ethnic groups were connected by multiple ties of kinship, while, on the other hand, firmly establishing Rome's hegemonic position within it.[28]

In the about 120 years that passed between Cato's *Origines* and the beginning of Livy's *Ab Urbe Condita*, Roman historiography developed into a rich literary tradition embracing various narrative forms and subgenres:[29] alongside comprehensive histories from the foundation,[30] one could find year-by-year

---

[27] Nep. *Cato* 3.4 writes that Cato 'set forth wondrous events or sights in Italy and the Spanish provinces' (*exposuit quae in Italia Hispanisque aut fierent aud viderentur admiranda*; transl. T.J. Cornell). Fragments are preserved e.g. on Carthaginian houses (*FRHist*. 5 F84), on the river Ebro (F111), and on the climate and natural resources of the region around the Ebro (F116).

[28] Cf. Letta (1984, arguing that the *Origines* displayed two different notions of Italy: a geographic-strategic one, from the Alps to the South; and a political-moral one, which only included the non-Greek peoples of Central and Southern Italy) and (2008); Gotter (2009, pp. 113–115); Cornell in *FRHist*. I, pp. 211–213. The apparent gap between the 'origins' section and post-264-BCE history, too, has been explained as part of a project which stressed the bonds between Rome and its neighbouring communities. Cato might, in this view, have skipped Rome's wars of expansion in Italy in the fifth, fourth, and early third centuries, starting with the clash between an Italian alliance under Rome's lead and a transmarine enemy, Carthage. See Gotter (2009, p. 115). Perhaps the 'origins' section might have played a similar role as the first part of Timaeus' work on the peoples of the Western Mediterranean: see Cugusi and Sblendorio Cugusi (2001, p. 48 and n. 226); Cornell in *FRHist*. I, p. 201.

[29] On these developments, which started around the end of the 2nd or the beginning of the 1st century BCE, see e.g. Walter (2003, pp. 135–137).

[30] This seems to have been the most common structure for historical works in the 2nd century BCE (as exemplified by the writings of, among other, Lucius Cassius Hemina, Lucius Calpurnius Piso Frugi, and Gnaeus Gellius) and was still practised in the 1st by, among others, Valerius Antias, a major source for Livy, and perhaps Aelius Tubero (whose fragments show his treatment of Roman history from the origins to at least 255 BCE: cf. Oakley in *FRHist*. I, pp. 364–365). Another historian consulted by Livy, Claudius Quadrigarius, started his account not with the foundation but with the Gallic conquest of 390 BCE: cf. Briscoe in *FRHist*. I, pp. 289–290.

accounts of more limited historical periods,[31] monographs,[32] biographies, and autobiographies.[33] Yet, with few exceptions, the principal shared focus of this vast output was the political and military history of Rome. This means that the topics of history were the debates within the city and the wars abroad (*political and military* history). After all, most mid-republican historians were members of the elite who personally took part in government and military command; their works often supported their political struggles or celebrated the deeds of their ancestors.[34] When, in the 1st century, historiography came to be also practised by intellectuals who did not belong to the *nobilitas*, with few exceptions, such writers inherited the political and military focus of their predecessors.[35]

31 Lucius Cornelius Sisenna, writing in the first decades of the 1st century BCE, started his account with the year 91, which might have been the ending point of a previous historian, Sempronius Asellio. Sisenna's ending point was perhaps Sulla's death in 78 BCE and Sallust's *Historiae*, narrating events from 78 to 67 BCE, might have continued Sisenna's work. See *FRHist*. 1, pp. 308 (with further bibliography). Cicero's correspondent Lucceius, too, seems to have started his work with the Social War of 91–89 BCE (cf. Cic. *Fam*. 5.12, esp. 2 = *FRHist*. 30 T1); and, at the same time that Livy was composing the early decades of his *Ab Urbe Condita*, Asinius Pollio wrote a work focusing mainly on the civil wars, probably starting in 60 BCE.

32 The late second century historian Coelius Antipater is credited with writing the first Roman monograph, a work on the Hannibalic War (cf. Cic. *Orat*. 230 = *FRHist*. 15 F1; Briscoe in *FRHist*. 1, pp. 256–263), which is an important source for Livy in the Third Decade. Sallust's *Bellum Catilinae* and *Bellum Iugurthinum* are the best-known examples of this sub-genre.

33 For biography, one may mention Nepos' *De viris illustribus*; Tiro's lost life of Cicero; the life of Cato the Younger written by his friend Munatius Rufus (cf. Smith, Levick and Cornell in *FRHist*. 1, pp. 358–360). Autobiographical works (whether full biographies or accounts of specific events in the author's life) are attributed e.g. to Marcus Aemilius Scaurus, a leading politician between the end of the 2nd and the beginning of the 1st century BCE (cf. Cic. *Brut*. 112 = *FRHist*. 18 T1a; Val. Max. 4.4.11 = T2; Plin. *HN* 33.21 = T3; Tac. *Agr*. 1.3 = T4); Lutatius Catulus, consul in 102 BCE (cf. Cic. *Brut*. 132 = *FRHist*. 19, T1); Sulla the dictator (cf. e.g. Plut. *Vit. Luc*. 1.4 = *FRHist*. 22, T1a; Plut. *Vit. Luc*. 4.5. = T1b; Plut. *Vit. Sull*. 6.10 = T1c; Suet. *Gram. et Rhet*. 12 = T4); Cicero (who wrote a Greek *commentarius* on his consulate: cf. e.g. Cic. *Att*. 1.19.10 = *FRHist*. 39 T1; 1.20.6 = T2); and Augustus (who published his autobiography around 23 BCE). A common Latin term to indicate a work of this kind was *commentarius*, and Caesar's *commentarii* (*de bello Gallico* and *de bello civili*) can be seen as belonging to this tradition.

34 Cf. Gotter, Luraghi and Walter (2003, pp. 13–14).

35 Exceptions are few and generally belong to subgenres rather than to 'major' genres of history writing. Cornelius Nepos' *De viris illustribus*, for example, includes the lives of poets, historians, grammarians, and orators alongside those of kings and generals (both Romans and foreigners). This seems to have been an exception even within the panorama of Roman biographical writing, which mostly consisted in the lives of political figures written by their friends and supporters or, in the case of autobiographies, by themselves;

Moreover, historians' focus on the history *of Rome* meant that foreign countries and peoples entered their historical narratives inasmuch as they came into contact with Rome. Here, as well, some exceptions seem to confirm the rule. Cato's *Origines*, as I have mentioned, was peculiar in its interest in Italian communities; but, even in this text, the concern with Italy was probably motivated by the role played by the peninsula in defining Roman identity. Some later authors experimented with universal histories.[36] The bulk of the Roman historical tradition, however, was constituted by histories of Rome and its empire, in which foreign countries appeared exclusively in military contexts, and often as objects of conquest. Even the frequent geo-ethnographic digressions in Roman historical narratives belong within this context: they can be interpreted as part of an intellectual effort to map, define, and express control of the lands falling under the influence of Roman power.[37]

The Romanocentric quality of Roman historiography results in a paradox. On the one hand, the topic of most Roman historiography is the history of one specific city, Rome; on the other, Roman history tends more and more towards universality as the extension of the Roman *imperium* broadens towards the boundaries of the known world.[38] Such ambivalence is especially visible in annalistic history of the kind practised by Livy.[39] This structural pattern involves the sequential account of each consular year with a narrative of its main events both in Rome (*domi*) and abroad, that is, in various theatres of war (*militiae*). In Roman historiography, an annalistic structure is attested

---

cf. e.g. Gotter, Luraghi and Walter (2003, p. 37); Smith and Powell (2009). Nepos also composed a work entitled *Chronica*, a sketch of universal chronology that contained references to at least some literary figures such as Homer and Hesiod (cf. *FRHist*. 45 F1a–b).

36 For Nepos' *Chronica* see above, n. 34. A Lutatius wrote a *Communis Historia*, which might have been a κοινὴ ἱστορία after the Greek fashion; for questions concerning his identity of and the features of his work, see Smith in *FRHist*. I, p. 343. A later specimen of universal history was Pompeius Trogus' *Historiae Philippicae*, dating from the Augustan period and narrating the succession of world empires, with special emphasis on the deeds of the Macedonian king Philip the Second. On universal history see e.g. Momigliano (1987, pp. 31–57); Clarke (1999, pp. 249–79); Alonso-Nuñez (2002); Yarrow (2006, pp. 124–133); Liddel and Fear (2010).

37 Cf. e.g. Riggsby (2006, esp. pp. 21–45), on Caesar's *Bellum Gallicum*.

38 Thus, the Greek historian Polybius, writing in the central decades of the 2nd century BCE, could argue that by his time the history of the world had become interconnected due to the extension of Roman power. For universalism in Polybius see e.g. Momigliano (1987, pp. 39–42); Alonso-Nuñez (2002, pp. 69–80); Hartog (2010); Sheridan (2010).

39 On the definition and characteristics of 'annalistic' history see e.g. Chassignet (1996); Walter (2003).

from the mid-2nd-century at the latest[40] and by Livy's time it was the most common both for *ab urbe condita* history and for non-monographic treatments of more limited periods (such as Sallust's *Historiae*). While a monograph concentrates on one episode (usually a military campaign), annalistic history requires all events of major import in the life of the Roman State to be treated in the account of each year; and this, in turn, means that the narrative spotlight moves between several geographic areas involved in the process of Roman expansion.

At the same time, this chronological pattern sets Rome as the logical centre of the narrated world.[41] First, all events, including foreign history, are subjected to Roman time, that is, to the time structure produced by the annual succession of Roman magistrates. Secondly, Rome is the place where decisions are made, whence generals depart for campaigns and whither they return, where the consuls of each year are elected and take up office. In a way, while universal histories incorporate the history of individual countries into the history of the world, annalistic history incorporates the world into the history of Rome.

Thus, when Livy set to writing his *Ab Urbe Condita*, he had a well-established tradition of Roman history-writing and Roman meditation on space, history, and power behind him. He also wrote at a time when space – both Roman and imperial – was being restructured and subjected to new forms of control.[42] In the city of Rome, the dynasts of the Late Republic had launched ambitious

---

40 For the origins of 'annalistic' historiography see e.g. (with different reconstructions) Wiseman (1979a, pp. 9–26); Walter (2003, p. 135); Beck (2007, p. 297); Rich (2011, esp. pp. 14–21).

41 Cf. Timpe (1979, pp. 101–102); Walter (2003, p. 145); Pausch (2011, pp. 130–131).

42 The date of the *Ab Urbe Condita* is a well-known matter of contention in Livian scholarship. It was once common to date the First Pentad to the years 27–25 BCE (see e.g. the studies quoted by Burton, 2008, p. 72 n.5). 25 BCE is a safe *terminus ante quem* because at 1.19.3 Livy states that the Temple of Janus was closed only twice after the time of King Numa Pompilius: once after the end of the First Punic War and once 'after the Actian War by Imperator Caesar Augustus, after he had established peace on land and sea' (*post bellum Actiacum ab imperatore Caesare Augusto pace terra marique parta*). Here, Livy refers to Octavian's closure of the temple in 29 BCE, but he does not mention the second Augustan closure in 25 BCE; therefore, the passage must have been written before that date. 27 BCE has been thought to be a *terminus post quem* because in the above-mentioned passage and at 4.20.7, Livy uses the name Augustus, which Octavian took on in that year. However, following Bayet (Bayet and Baillet 1940, pp. xvi–xxii) and Syme (1959), Luce (1965) convincingly demonstrates that the two passages are later revisions, and that the composition of the First Pentad should be moved to before 27 BCE. According to Luce, Livy began writing around or before 31 BCE. Burton (2000 and 2008) proposes a date of 33 BCE for Book 1. Syme (1959), for his part, suggests a starting date in the years immediately following Actium; he is followed e.g. by Levick (2015).

building projects. However, starting from the 30s BCE, Octavian[43] and his entourage started even greater interventions on the fabric of the city. Such urbanistic activity would go on throughout Augustus' principate; building programmes inspired by Hellenistic models transformed the disorderly Republican Rome into a city of splendid temples, gardens, and leisure buildings.[44] Moreover, the division of Rome into regions (*regiones*) and quarters (*vici*) in 7 BCE turned the city into a well-defined, controllable, and governable space.[45] At the same time, Augustus re-organised the space of the Empire, facilitating efficient governance by the division of Italy into eleven regions (*regiones*) and by restructuring the provincial system.[46] Poets and artists promoted the idea of a world pacified by Rome's benign rule; later Augustus himself would proclaim his own empire-building achievements in his *Res Gestae*.[47]

The structure of Livy's work highlights the theme of spatial growth. Rather than focusing his attention upon a limited period in Roman history (as was the most usual formula for historians at his time), he takes the whole of Roman history into account, even if it means retelling those ancient (and often fabulous) events that historians before him had already narrated many times.[48] Such a framework has two effects on the narrative's treatment of space. By setting the origins of the city as the starting point, it sets the city, in its material dimension, at the centre of the narrative. The reader sees Romulus found the city by building its first wall, then sees more and more new areas being urbanised as the ages go by. Moreover, the reader can appreciate the whole process of territorial expansion from the city-state to world power and use it as a guiding principle and an interpretative key to Roman history. In both respects, space as a topic emerges at the very heart of Livy's project.

---

43   For practical reasons I use the name 'Octavian' to designate the young Caesar in the period ranging from the moment of his posthumous adoption by Julius Caesar in 44 BCE to his taking the name Augustus in January 27 BCE. His full name after the adoption would have been Gaius Iulius Caesar Octavianus, and the form Octavianus is attested in Cicero, but the young man was reluctant to adopt the cognomen that reminded him of his origins. See e.g. Rubincam (1992).
44   See e.g. Favro (2005); Wallace-Hadrill (2005, pp. 78–80); Eck (2014, pp. 99–106); Flower (2017, esp. pp. 258–270); and cf. the studies quoted in Chapters 1 and 2 on individual sites and monuments in Augustan Rome.
45   See e.g. Nicolet (1991, pp. 189–204); Wallace-Hadrill (2005, pp. 76–78).
46   On Augustus' imperial politics, his reforms in the administration of the provincial system, and the interplay of expansionist policy and Augustus' self-representation as the bringer of peace see e.g. Wallace-Hadrill (2005, pp. 80–81); Nicolet (1991, esp. pp. 123–170); Eck (2014, pp. 81–98); Morrell (2019, with further bibliography).
47   *Mon. Anc.* 25–33; cf. Nicolet (1991, pp. 15–27).
48   Cf. Livy *praef.* 1.

4 Space in the *Ab Urbe Condita*: State of the Art and Open Questions

My observations up to this point suggest that investigating how the *Ab Urbe Condita* constructs space can shed significant light on Livy's interpretations of the Roman past and present. It is not surprising, therefore, that 'space in Livy' has become a popular topic of scholarly investigation.

The ways in which the *Ab Urbe Condita* works as a textual *monumentum* of the Roman past was the topic of Mary Jaeger' seminal 1997 book. Jaeger's analysis focuses above all on the representation of the city of Rome, and of sites of memory within it, in Livy's narrative; her broader argument, namely that the spatial settings in *Ab Urbe Condita* are not mere backdrops to the narrated events but can play important symbolic roles, has opened the way to a varied and rich output of studies about space in Livy.

The connections between monuments, narrative, and memory in Livy's representation of the city of Rome have continued to be a preferred focus of scholarly interest over the last two and a half decades. Such an interest rests on the awareness of the strong spatial dimension of Roman memorial practice. Republican magistrates commemorated their military victories and political achievements by erecting monuments of various kinds (often funded through booty from their campaigns) and, from the mid-Republican period, competition within the *nobilitas* led to an increase in building activities. By the end of the Republic, the city space was a complex web of memories, which its inhabitants would repeatedly stumble upon in their daily lives, and which orators could conveniently reactivate as suited their aims.[49] Scholars have shown how Livy engages with those materialized memories by arranging some narratives around specific sites or monuments, or by playing on the connotations of a certain site at different points of his work.[50]

Another focus of scholarly attention has been Livy's representations of topography and landscape in military accounts. Research of this kind has often taken its cue from the gap between Livy's ways to approach topography and those which prevail in modern scientific approaches to history. In the past, Livy was often accused of superficiality due to the inaccuracy of his geographic and topographic details – a well-known difficulty for modern historians trying to reconstruct the location of a battle, or the itinerary followed by an army. More recently, however, scholars have pointed to the different aims

---

49   See e.g. Vasaly (1993); Hölscher (2009); Hölkeskamp (2012); Muth (2012).
50   See e.g. Edwards (1996, esp. pp. 45–52); Spencer (2007); Jaeger (2015); Pausch (2018a and 2018b). For a different approach to Livy's Rome, underplaying the significance of individual monuments, see Levene (2019).

of a narrative such as the *Ab Urbe Condita* compared to modern historical research. First, ancient writers and readers did not normally use maps as supports for understanding a text; thus, what, for us, is a blatant geographic inaccuracy might have passed unnoticed by an ancient historian and his readers. Moreover, when transmitted topographical information was scanty, an ancient historian would, in most cases, flesh it out with details drawn on rhetorical convention, which, far from making his account less plausible, would enhance its credibility.[51] Based on these premises, scholars have investigated Livy's use of *topoi* of landscape representation, space as an aspect in the narrative design of military episodes, and the symbolic roles that space and landscape may play in Livy's military accounts.[52]

Awareness of the role of spatial symbolism in the *Ab Urbe Condita* has also led to an examination of the role of abstract spatial concepts and broader semantic patterns in Livy's work: for example, the notions of 'public' and 'private' space, the relationships between space and time, and ideas about conquest and power.[53] Moreover, space is often a relevant topic to studies about vision in Livy.[54]

Despite such a remarkable scholarly output, very few attempts have been made to study space and spatiality in the *Ab Urbe Condita* systematically. This is hardly surprising; even in the fragmentary state in which it has come down to us, the *Ab Urbe Condita* is such a monumental work and 'space' is such a wide-ranging – and often underdefined – term that scholars have naturally tended to concentrate on close readings of individual episodes.[55] The time is ripe, I believe, for a thorough reconsideration of the role of space in the *Ab Urbe Condita*.

In my analysis, I look for patterns and recurring techniques or modes of representation in Livy's history. This includes the way in which important settings, or recurrent kinds of settings, are constructed throughout the *Ab Urbe Condita*, as well as aspects of the work's overarching spatial semantics. While I often

---

51   See e.g. Horsfall (1982 and 1985); Oakley (2005, p. 53).
52   See e.g. Horsfall (1982 and 1985); Morello (2003); Jaeger (2007); Clark (2014); Biggs (2016); Fabrizi (2015, 2017a, and 2021a); van Gils (2019).
53   See e.g. the notions of public and private space in Milnor (2005, pp. 141–179, and 2007); Riggsby (2009) and the relationship between the spatial and temporal arrangements of events in Pausch (2011, pp. 129–136). On geography and conquest, see Clark (2014).
54   See e.g. Feldherr (1998 and 2021); Fabrizi (2016).
55   Two notable exceptions are Clark (2014), on the representation of foreign landscapes and geography in Books 21–45, and the excellent synthesis of the main features of Livy's narrated Rome in Jaeger (2015), which is, however, necessarily highly selective due to its limited length.

provide close readings of specific episodes, my aim is to understand whether those episodes contribute to broader patterns of representation. Ultimately, I aim at showing that narrated space is an integral part of the historical imagination in the *Ab Urbe Condita*, and that it should be understood as a crucial element in Livy's construction of the meaning of Roman history. In particular, my investigation of the narrative construction and semantic values of space will allow me to shed light on some aspects of Livy's representation of politics, power, and expansion.

Since I tackle space in the *Ab Urbe Condita* as a narrative category, my inquiry largely rests on theoretical work by narratologists concerning the analysis of space in narratives. In what follows, I provide an overview of their studies, and I then clarify some of the main narratological notions I shall be using in this book.

5 A Narratology of Space

5.1 *A Basic Framework*

A widely accepted tenet of narratology holds that space is, alongside time, a basic dimension of any narrative (just as it is a basic dimension of any human action or experience). Scholars have investigated the techniques through which narratives shape the spaces where narrated events take place, and the functions that space can fulfil within a narrative.[56] For my own purposes, the following approaches are the most fruitful and they should be considered as the underpinnings of my analysis.

Following Dennerlein (2009, p. 239 and 2011, pp. 138–139), I assume that every narrative shapes a 'space of the narrated world', consisting of all the spaces that can act as surroundings for characters within the narrative. This includes not just the settings where events take place but also spaces that characters see or speak about. As Dennerlein suggests, the narrated world is a mental model of an ideal reader. In other words, readers, based on the information a narrative provides, construct a consistent mental image of the world implied by the narrative. Let it be noted that, in the case of a historical narrative, the narrated world aims at reproducing the real, historical world of the past but is not identical with it, just as the narrator of a historical narrative,

---

[56] See e.g. Lotman (1973 and 1974); Hoffmann (1978); Chatman (1978, pp. 96–107); van Baak (1983); Zoran (1984); Bal (1997, pp. 132–142 and 214–217); Ronen (1986); Herman (2002); Buchholz and Jahn (2005); Bridgeman (2007); Ryan (2009); Nünning (2009); Dennerlein (2009 and 2011); de Jong (2012 and 2014, pp. 105–133, with a focus on ancient literature).

while being a projection of the historian, is distinct from the historian as a historical personality.

To understand how narratives shape the space of the narrated world, I draw on Nünning's (2009, especially pp. 33–35 and 39–44) three dimensions of the 'literary representation of space'. The first level is the 'selection' of spaces and objects from historical reality and literary tradition. Selection happens at different levels. First, in any narrative, the action takes place at a limited number of locations (which can exist in the real world or, as is the case of fictional narratives, be the author's own invention); even spaces that characters within the story talk or think about are only a selection among the spaces that exist or can exist. Moreover, even when representing a single space (e.g. a room) it is virtually impossible to provide information about every single feature of it (e.g. the orientation and material of the walls, the floor, all objects, their characteristics, their relative positions, the smells, the temperature or humidity of the air, etc.), because the acts of speaking or writing, and of listening or reading, require some time to unfold, whereas space entails the simultaneous presence of many different elements.

The second level is the 'configuration', into which the spatial elements are organised as a consistent world model. In the case of narratives concerning events in different places or geographical regions, configuration includes the way shifts from one place to another are effected, the amount of narrative time devoted to each, or the information about the relative position and distance of different localities.

The third level is 'perspective' in which the selected and organised spatial information is conveyed through focalisation and spatial standpoints. Any space in any narrative is presented through someone's eyes or experience, whether the narrator's or that of one or more characters; this involves the focaliser's relative position as well as their perception, feelings, and thoughts. In turn, focalisation can significantly affect the reader's imagination of a narrated space. If, for example, a forest is presented through the focalisation of a character who is scared, the reader will tend to visualise that forest as dangerous and menacing; if, on the contrary, the focaliser is serene, the reader will probably imagine the beauty of the forest, birds singing, green grass, etc.

The construction of space at the three levels identified here is also constitutive of the spatial semantics of a text. As Lotman's (1973 and 1974) seminal studies show, space can take on nonspatial connotations in a narrative and thus play an essential role in shaping its meaning. More recently, De Jong (2012, pp. 13–17) distinguishes between different functions of space in narratives: the thematic function, when a space is the main theme of a narrative; the characterising or psychologising function, when a space reflects the nature of a character or their state of mind respectively; and the symbolic function, when a space is charged with symbolic meaning.[57]

The model I have just sketched works not only for fictional narratives but also for historical ones. The latter, however, are subject to more rigid constraints, because historians must base their accounts on evidence of some sort (autopsy, oral witnesses, previous written accounts). In order to account for this basic difference, some narratologists have introduced the notion of *material* as a fourth level alongside those of *fabula*, *story*, and *text*.[58] While the fabula is the chronological sequence of events, the story is the events told in a certain order and from a certain perspective, and the text is the actual wording of a narrative, the material is the set of (written, oral, and material) sources a historian uses. For the *Ab Urbe Condita*, the material level is largely constituted by the writings of previous historians, but also by oral traditions and material traces (especially for what concerns events in the city of Rome).

However, even within the limits set by the evidence ancient historians enjoyed a certain degree of freedom in composing their narratives, which was related to the literary nature of their works. Historians could, for example, describe a character's feelings in detail, or put fictional speeches into their characters' mouths, or imagine lively dialogues between them.[59] One can observe something similar with respect to the portrayal of space, especially of those spaces that historians had no personal experience of. In such cases, they could draw on standardised ways of thinking about specific types of spaces (e.g. the inhospitable mountain) and employ conventional elements that they had learnt as part of their rhetorical training (e.g. high ragged peaks, roaring streams, narrow valleys);[60] or, they might stress features of a place which could resonate with their characters' psychology, or with the overarching themes of their narrative. Following Nünning (cf. above, p. 16), one may say that a

---

[57] As I have mentioned above, this process of meaning-attribution is by no means an exclusive feature of (literary) narratives. Indeed, spatial semantics is constitutive of the everyday perception and the social construction of space; human beings attribute meanings to space in the very process of perceiving it.

[58] For a recent summary of narratological reflections on historical narratives, see van Gils, de Jong and Kroon (2019, pp. 6–8, with further bibliography).

[59] For speeches in ancient historiography see e.g. Luce (1993); Laird (1999); Marincola (2007b); Leidl (2010); Pausch (2010a, 2010c, and 2010d); Adler (2011); O'Gorman (2023).

[60] Cf. above, p. 14.

conventional place of this kind is selected not from historical reality but rather from literary (or rhetorical) tradition.[61]

The representation of space at the level of configuration, on the other hand, works in a very similar way in historical and purely fictional accounts. Spatial information is always arranged in some way or other within a narrative, even when the arrangement appears 'natural' or 'objective'. The *Ab Urbe Condita* provides a fine example. At least in Books 21–45, each year's narrative begins in Rome, where the newly elected consuls enter office; it then turns to events in other geographical areas, which become more numerous and distant from Rome as the account proceeds; finally, it returns to Rome with an 'end of year' section consisting of prodigy lists and notices about building activities, fires, floods, and other events of this kind.[62] As Pausch (2011, pp. 129–136) observes, this structure has important consequences for the narrative organisation of both time and space in the work. By using Rome as the beginning and end of each year's narrative, the *Ab Urbe Condita* establishes the city as the idealised centre of the narrated world. Thus, the elements of the narrated world are not merely juxtaposed but placed into a 'centre vs. periphery' relationship.

Finally, some thoughts are needed concerning the use of perspective in historical and in fictional accounts. It is usually claimed that a distinctive characteristic of history writing is the fact that it does not, as a rule, use embedded focalisation, i.e. the internal focalisation of characters within the story.[63] Modern historians, for example, usually provide information about characters' feelings when they have evidence about them (e.g. an extant letter written by a historical character), and even then only by referencing the source. This, however, is not true of ancient historical accounts: information about the psychological state of characters is a frequent, indeed a standard feature of Graeco-Roman history writing, which accounts for lively, dramatic, or pathetic accounts of historical events. In works like the *Ab Urbe Condita*, spatial information is often conveyed to the reader through the eyes (and ears, and psychological mood) of characters; and, as my analysis shall repeatedly show, such a technique is often crucial for the semantics of narrated space.

These observations provide a basic framework within which to understand and examine space in the *Ab Urbe Condita*. It is now necessary to devote some

---

61   One can think of settings of this kind as what Dennerlein (2009, pp. 178–179) calls a 'Raummodell' ('space model'). A 'Raummodell' is composed of two sets of knowledge, which the ideal reader is assumed to share: on the one hand, knowledge about the material shape and arrangement of a certain spatial element; on the other, knowledge about the typical sequences of events that take place there.
62   For the structure of consular years in the *Ab Urbe Condita*, see Rich (2011).
63   On focalisation see below, pp. 26–29.

more attention to some specific narratological concepts which shall be important in my analysis: namely, the distinction between description and narration, and the concept of focalisation. In the following sub-sections, I examine the role these concepts play in Livy's history.

5.2 *Description and Narration*

One of the issues modern narratologists most often discuss when tackling space in narratives is the distinction between description and narration as the two main techniques for presenting information about space. Unfortunately, the issue is far from simple. Although any reader probably has an intuitive notion of what 'description' and 'narration' are, providing exact definitions of those concepts has proved challenging for scholars.

According to Genette's (1976) famous formulation, narration concerns actions and events, while description concerns objects and beings; moreover, narration has to do with time, whereas description has to do with space; thirdly, description implies a pause in the temporal flow of the narrative.[64] However, such a distinction does not seem to account for cases such as those in which there is a description of an object being produced or those in which the features of a place are presented to the reader as a character walks through it. In such instances one can hardly recognise a pause in the narrative flow.

The central problem with defining description and narration is that, in practice, they often appear intrinsically mixed. Bal (1981 and 1997, pp. 36–43), building on Hamon (1972), defines description as consisting of a theme (the described object), and several subthemes (the parts of the object), to which predicates (i.e. adjectives) can be attached and which can be, in their turn, divided into further sub-themes. An important facet of Bal's analysis concerns the different kinds of motivation for descriptions, that is, how descriptions are incorporated into a text. She distinguishes (Bal, 1997, pp. 37–29) between motivation 'by looking' when a character sees something, and this provides the cue for the description, 'by speaking' when a character describes what they see, and 'by acting' when the actor 'carries out an action with an object' and 'the description is then made fully narrative' (p. 38; the classic example is the description of the shield of Achilles in *Iliad* 18). Thus, a description can

---

64 'The narration links itself to actions or events considered as pure processes, and by this it puts emphasis on the temporal and dramatic aspects of narrative. On the other hand, description, because it lingers over objects and beings considered in their simultaneity and because it envisages the actions themselves as scenes, seems to suspend the flow of time and to contribute to spreading out the narrative in space' (p. 7). Moreover, for Genette description fulfills two main functions, which he defines as 'ornamental', and 'explicative and symbolic' respectively (p. 6).

involve movement.[65] Bal (1981, pp. 134–135) also emphasises the importance of focalisation in descriptions, not only in making descriptions dynamic but also in conveying an interpretation of what is described. Thus, rather than providing a mere 'effet de réel,'[66] description can also represent and develop specific themes, which may be crucial to the narrative (Bal, 1981, pp. 135–137).

Several other attempts have been made to account for the interweaving of narration and description in narratives: from the distinction between the level of sentence and that of narrative 'block' (Lopes, 1995, pp. 3–27) to the development of intermediate categories such as 'narrativised description' or 'descriptive narration' (Mosher, 1991), to the claim that the distinction between description and narration should be abandoned altogether (Ronen, 1997), to a so-called 'prototypical approach' to narration and description (Herman, 2009; Koopman, 2018).

According to the latter, a text can be more or less narrative, depending on the degree to which it possesses the features of 'prototypical' or 'standard' description or of 'prototypical' or 'standard' narration. Herman (2009, p. xvi) singles out the following elements of prototypical narration: 1. 'Situatedness' (a narrative is 'situated in ... a specific context or occasion for telling'); 2. 'Event sequencing' ('a structured time-course of particularised events'); 3. 'World-making' / 'world-disruption' (the events told introduce 'some sort of disruption or disequilibrium into a storyworld'); 4. 'What it's like' ('The representation also conveys the *experience* of living through the storyworld in flux').[67] Koopman (2018, p. 40) establishes some elements of prototypical description: 1) the attribution of qualities to persons, objects, or places; 2) the multiplicity of details; 3) a focus on sensory appearances and impressions.

It is not my aim to review this body of literature in detail, let alone offer a new definition of narration and description. For my analysis, Herman and Koopman's prototypical approach provides a reasonable framework that allows both distinguishing between narration and description and recognising their frequent coexistence in practice. Within such a framework, and as a premise to my analysis in following chapters, I shall briefly outline some crucial features of Livy's writing technique.

---

65   Cf. Bal (1981, pp. 33–35: description 'in motion'). In Bal (1997, pp. 36–38), however, she speaks, rather, of 'a mixture of description and narration' or of a 'narrative' description when examining passages that imply motion.

66   According to Barthes' (1968) famous formulation.

67   For description, Herman (2009, p. 90) gives the following definition: 'representations and discourses that are central instances of this text type category entail the ascription of properties to entities within a mental model of the world (whatever the modality status of that mentally projected world – e.g. real, fictional, dreamed, etc.)'.

The *Ab Urbe Condita* rarely conveys spatial information through extensive description; more often, spatial information is inserted directly into the narrative of events. Let us consider a famous example of such a 'narrative' presentation of space, namely the account of King Philip of Macedon's ascent to Mount Haemus at 40.21–22.[68] Livy relates that in 181 BCE, Philip was filled with a desire to reach the summit of Haemus because, according to a commonly held (if inaccurate) opinion, one could see both the Adriatic and the Black Sea, as well as the Alps and the river Hister, from there. Since the king was preparing a new war against Rome, he thought such a view would give him precious strategic information. However, the expedition proved a failure, and Philip was unable to enjoy the desired view because of both its physical impossibility and a persistent fog. The episode is rich in symbolism since Philip's failure to observe the lands he intended to conquer stands for his failure as a leader (cf. Jaeger, 2007; Clark, 2014, pp. 207–209).

Here is how the historian narrates Philip's march up the mountain (40.22.1–4):

> 1. Philippus, Maedicam primum deinde solitudines interiacentes Maedicae atque Haemo transgressus, septimis demum castris ad radices montis pervenit. Ibi unum moratus diem ad deligendos quod duceret secum, tertio die iter est ingressus. 2. Modicus primo labor in imis collibus fuit. Quantum in alitudinem egrediebantur, magis magisque silvestria et pleraque invia loca excipiebant; 3. pervenere deinde in tam opacum iter ut prae densitate arborum immissorumque aliorum in alios ramorum perspici caelum vix posset. 4. Ut vero iugis appropinquabant, quod rarum in altis locis est, adeo omnia contecta nebula ut haud secus quam nocturno itinere impedirentur. Tertio demum die ad verticem perventum.

> 1. Philip reached Maedica first, then crossed the uninhabited places that lie between Maedica and Haemus and reached the foot of the mountain in six days. He lingered there one day to select the men he would take along and on the third day he started his journey. 2. At the beginning, in the lowest hills, the effort was limited. The more they went up, the more they found woodland, which was mostly impenetrable; 3. then they came to such a shadowy path that one could hardly see the sky due to the thickness of the trees and of their interlocking branches. 4. In truth, as

---

68 On this passage see Luce (1977, p. 11); Jaeger (2007); Pausch (2010, pp. 96, 230); Clark (2014, pp. 207–209); Falcone (2019).

they came closer to the top, everything was so covered in fog – which is unusual on heights – that they were hindered as if they travelled by night. In the end, on the third day they reached the summit.

While information about space accounts for most of the passage, the few properly descriptive remarks are dynamically woven into the narration. Before Philip reaches Haemus proper, the reader learns that there are deserts between Maedica and the mountain and that the king went through them. Then they learn that Philip started his way up the mountain, beginning with the lowest hill; they surmise that the latter must have been gentle and not heavily forested since the party made no great effort to ascend. The text conveys all this information through sentences that portray actions (*transgressus, pervenit, labor ... fuit*). Then the reader sees the landscape of Mount Haemus as it presents itself to Philip and his companions on their march. The remark *magis magisque silvestria et pleraque invia loca excipiebant* has elements of prototypical description (the attribution of qualities to objects) but also involves the sequencing of events, which is typical of narration: the increasing harshness of the landscape corresponds to Philip's progress up the mountain. In the following sentence, *prae densitate arborum immissorumque aliorum in alios ramorum perspici caelum vix posset*[69] is a properly descriptive remark, but the fact that it is a consecutive sub-clause ties it strongly to the narration in the main clause. Finally, the expression *adeo omnia contecta nebula* introduces the impact of the fog on the effort of the people climbing the mountain flank. In other words, this passage is narrative and descriptive, but narration and description are so closely intertwined that it is virtually impossible to separate them.

Of course, such a dynamic presentation of space is also very frequent in accounts of events in Rome. Solely descriptive passages are generally unnecessary in such cases for two rather obvious reasons. First, Livy assumes at least part of his readers have some pre-existing knowledge of the city of Rome (cf. Chapter 1). Secondly, since some settings recur with a particular frequency, each narrative builds upon previous ones. The Forum is a particularly fitting example since, as I show in Chapter 1, the reader of the *Ab Urbe Condita* sees it taking form and developing as the narrative of Roman history proceeds from the origins of the city to more recent times. Thus, a passing remark is often sufficient to evoke a pre-existing mental model in the reader's mind.

---

69   Falcone (2019, p. 237) stresses the 'notevole *evidentia* retorica' of this sentence ('la densità dei rami, infatti, è rappresentata dall'abbinamento di iperbato e poliptoto ed è sinesteticamente percepibile per mezzo del suono dell'omeoteleuto -*orum*').

INTRODUCTION

Another frequent way of presenting a setting consists in a short descriptive section, which sets the scene for the following action. As an instance, let us consider how Livy introduces the battle place at the river Trebia (217 BCE, 21.54.1):

> Erat in medio rivus prealtis utrimque clausus ripis et circa obsitus palustribus herbis et quibus inculta ferme vestiuntur, virgultis vepribusque.
>
> In the middle there was a river, which was protected on both sides by very tall banks; the terrain all around was overgrown with plants that are typical of marshlands and, as is usually the case with uncultivated land, underbrush and brambles.

This short description is followed by the remark that Hannibal found a 'hidden enough place' to hide the cavalry and by Hannibal's instruction to his brother Mago and some of his soldiers in *oratio recta*. In the narrative of the ensuing battle, the river Trebia is the main reference point, and the narrative doubles back, again and again, to the few elements that the descriptive section highlighted at the outset. Apart from being essential for understanding the development of the fighting, however, these elements play another important role: they draw the reader's attention to the contrast between Hannibal's strategic planning – which, coherently with Livy's representation of his character, involves deceit – and the Roman commander Sempronius' rashness in starting the fight.[70]

Based on what I have observed up to this point, it will be clear that Livy's techniques for representing space might not correspond to some modern expectations about what a historical narrative should look like. Modern readers might expect a historian to provide detailed information about the places where events happened through extended descriptive passages, which should be as objective as possible. Instead, the *Ab Urbe Condita* mostly conveys information by inserting some details into the narration of events or by interweaving description and narration. Such techniques produce engaging narratives: readers get to know the setting through the characters' movements and actions and often perceive it through their perceptions (i.e. through the characters' embedded focalisation).

---

70 For the 'rash commander' stereotype in Books 21–22 see e.g. Levene (2010, pp. 170–172); on the theme of Hannibalic deceit, see e.g. Levene (2010, pp. 228–235); Fabrizi (2017a).

This does not mean that extensive descriptive passages do not exist in the *Ab Urbe Condita*. They are, however, less frequent than one might expect, and their function is, at least in some cases, more complex than what might appear at a superficial reading. I consider one example here.

At 36.15–19, Livy narrates the battle the Romans victoriously fought in 191 BCE at Thermopylae against King Antiochus the Third of Syria. As Luce (1977, p. 81) points out, the historian turns this battle into 'a central and prominent feature' of Book 36. Immediately after relating that Antiochus took up a position at the pass and before the account of the battle, Livy introduces an unusually long description of not only Thermopylae but continental Greece (36.15.6–12). It will be worth quoting in full:

> 6. Id iugum, sicut Appennini dorso Italia dividitur, ita mediam Graeciam dirimit. 7. Ante saltum Thermopylarum in septentrionem versa Epirus et Perrhaebia et Magnesia et Thessalia est, et Phthiotae Achaei et sinus Maliacus; 8. intra fauces ad meridiem vergunt Aetoliae pars maior et Acarnania, et cum Locride Phocis, et Boeotia, adiunctaque insula Euboea et excurrente in altum velut promunturio Attica terra, sita ab tergo, et Peloponnesus. 9. Hoc iugum, ab Leucade et mari ad occidentem verso per Aetoliam ad alterum mare orienti obiectum tendens, ea aspreta rupesque interiectas habet ut non modo exercitus sed ne expediti quidem facile ullas ad transitum calles inveniant. 10. Extremos ad orientem montes Oetam vocant, quorum quod altissimum est Callidromon appellatur, in cuius valle ad Maliacum sinum vergente iter est non latius quam sexaginta passus. 11. Haec una militaris via est, qua traduci exercitus, si non prohibeantur, possint. 12. Ideo Pylae et ab aliis, quia calidae aquae in ipsis faucibus sunt, Thermopylae locus appellatur, nobilis Lacedaemoniorum adversus Persas morte magis memorabili quam pugna.

> 6. That ridge divides Greece in its middle, just like the Apennine range divides Italy. 7. Beyond the gorge of Thermopylae, to the North, are Epirus, Perrhaebia, Magnesia, Thessaly, Achaea Phthiotis and the Malian Gulf; 8. within the pass, to the South, are the greatest part of Aetolia, Acarnania, Locris with Phocis, Boeotia and the island of Euboea which is connected to it, the land of Attica, which is located in the rear like a promontory extending into the sea, and the Peloponnese. 9. This mountain range, as it extends from Leucas and the sea in the West, by way of Aetolia, to the other sea in the East, has such rough ground and scattered cliffs that not only an army but even lightly armed men could not easily find a way to cross it. 10. The last mountains to the East are called Oeta; the highest among them is named Callidromon; in its valley, which extends down to

the Malian Gulf, there is a path, not larger than sixty paces. 11. This is the only road fit for military purposes by which an army can cross, if it is not hindered. 12. Therefore, the place is called Pylae ('gates'), and by others Thermopylae ('hot gates'), because there are hot springs in the defile; it is well-known because of the death of the Spartans against the Persian, which is more memorable than the battle itself.

As Briscoe (1981, p. 242) notes, *id iugum* in section 6 does not designate the pass of Thermopylae (even though section 5 ends with the remark that 'Antiochus retreated into the pass of Thermopylae', *intra saltum Thermopylarum sese recepit*) but the whole mountain range which extends from the Malian Gulf to the Ionian Sea. Thermopylae is, after all, not a *iugum* ('summit', 'ridge', or 'mountain range')[71] but a *saltus* ('defile', 7) or *fauces* ('narrow passage', 8). Thermopylae and the mountain range, however, share a crucial military function: they 'divide', as Livy writes, the North from the South of Greece and thus enable or hinder the penetration of armies.[72] This is the main point around which the whole geographical description revolves. As Luce (1977, pp. 81–82) points out, the excursus does not provide much information about the topography of the pass; the only relevant element in understanding the course of the battle is the mention of the narrow path in sections 10–11. Luce compares Livy's topography with the more detailed one in Appian (*Syr.* 17), whose account probably derives from Polybius and expresses doubts over the idea that Polybius is Livy's source for this digression (as he very probably is for the battle). It is probable that at the very least Livy has reworked his source(s), making his own description appealing to a Roman audience through comparison with the more familiar Apennine and focusing on elements important to his narrative.

Such elements are the quality of Thermopylae as a passage or 'gate' (as the etymological explanation in section 12 further stresses) to the core regions of Greece and its role as the theatre for one of the most illustrious feats of bravery in Greek history, the sacrifice of three hundred Spartans who faced the Persian invaders in 480 BCE. As Clark (2014, pp. 169–174) points out, the latter episode is a crucial intertext in Livy's account of the battle.[73] First, it provides a negative

---

71 *Iugum* can mean both a single 'pass, summit' and a mountain 'ridge' or 'range' (*OLD* p. 981 s.v. *iugum* 8.b, 'a long narrow stretch of rising ground').
72 Of course, such an affirmation, as well as the comparison with the Apennine, is an exaggeration: cf. Clark (2014, p. 203).
73 Chaplin (2010a) argues, on the contrary, that Livy downplays the Greek Thermopylae (and especially Herodotus' account of that battle) as an intertext in his narrative and rather encourages readers to compare the battle at Thermopylae in 191 BCE with another battle he relates at 32.11–12, that against Philip of Macedon at the river Aous in 198 BCE.

point of comparison for the behaviour of Antiochus, who is not as brave as the Spartans of old and sets all of his hopes on an advantageous position (36.16.1). Secondly, by evoking implicit associations between Romans and Persians, it plays into the rhetoric of world conquest, which is a *Leitmotiv* of the episode, subtly reminding the reader of what the negative consequences that Rome's Eastern victories entailed for Roman morality (Clark, 2014, p. 174, pp. 178–180). Of course, the theme of world dominion is closely linked to the metaphor of Thermopylae as a gate that can 'open' or 'close' the path to conquest.

The description of Thermopylae is not simply an exposition of geographical or topographical information relevant to the historical account. Rather, it anticipates some of the main interpretive aspects of the later narrative.

This is not to say that every extensive description in the *Ab Urbe Condita* responds to the same need. It suggests, however, that the primary goal of extended descriptions might not always be providing objective information. The slowing down of the narrative pace before a major event (a technique for producing suspense), or the highlighting of location significant for its historical resonances, or a location's potential for providing a visual representation of historical issues might each be just as important.

5.3   *Focalisation*

De Jong (2014, p. 47) defines focalisation as follows:

> The viewing of the events of the fabula is called focalisation: there is the seeing or recalling of events, their emotional filtering and temporal ordering, and the fleshing out of space into scenery and persons into characters.[74]

In other words, focalisation concerns the experience that the reader has of the events of the fabula. The relevant question is: Through whose perception does the reader experience the events?

De Jong distinguishes between the focalisation of a primary or secondary narrator and embedded focalisation. The narrator-focaliser can be internal, when they are characters in the story, or external, when they do not participate

---

However, Livy recalls the ancient Thermopylae more than once in his account (36.15.12; 16.1, 7; 17.10–11) and this very use to highlight the differences between the Spartans and Antiochus (which Chaplin interprets as a downplaying of the ancient battle) is part of its function as an intertext. See also Clark's remarks on this point.

74   The term 'focalisation' was introduced by Genette (1972) to replace categories such 'point of view' or 'perspective', and since then has become a current notion in narrative theory. For a history of the concept, see Niederhoff (2014).

INTRODUCTION   27

in the narrated events. Apart from the primary narrator, a narrative can feature secondary narrators, too: this happens when a character is made to speak and narrate something. Secondary narrators, too, can be focalisers. On the other hand, embedded focalisation is found when the narrator follows the perspective of a character; in such cases, the reader only receives the information that the character possesses and only acquires new information as the character does. In other words, the reader 'sees' with the eyes or the mind's eye of the character-focaliser.

Livy uses all these types of focalisations at different points of his work. The focalisation of the primary narrator is the most frequent case. The narrator of the *Ab Urbe Condita* is, of course, a projection of Livy, the historian: he occasionally intervenes in the first person to discuss alternative versions of facts or to express his thoughts about history, politics, and morals. This 'Livy' is – at least in the surviving books of the *Ab Urbe Condita* – an external narrator who reports the events of Roman history from a chronological distance. Nonetheless, the focalisation of the primary narrator is by no means a neutral one.[75] As Pausch (2011, pp. 129–136) argues, for example, it is generally slanted towards a Roman perspective, as one can see in the Romanocentric annalistic structure, in the more extensive information that the narrator provides about the Roman side than about other peoples, in his explicit commentaries about his lack of interest for conflicts that do not directly involve Rome, and in his adopting of a value system that his Roman readers shared.

Apart from a general pro-Roman bias, the focalisation of the external narrator can also give a tinge to individual scenes. At 1.48.5, for instance, Livy narrates how Tullia hails her husband Tarquinius as the new king of Rome after the murder of the previous king – and her father – Servius Tullius:[76]

> Carpento certe, id quod satis constat, in forum invecta nec reverita coetum virorum evocavit virum e curia regemque prima appellavit.
>
> What is certain is that she rode into the Forum on a carriage – this is well attested – and, in no awe of the crowd of men, she called her husband out of the Curia and was the first to hail him as king.

Through the words *nec reverita coetum virorum*, the narrator implicitly conveys that the Forum (or at least the section of the Forum where the Senate house is

---

[75] In fact, as argued by de Jong (2014), no focalisation is really neutral: the narrator always filters, if covertly, the events of the fabula.
[76] For a full analysis of this passage see Chapter 4, pp. 220–223.

located) is no place for a woman and that Tullia's behaviour is exceptional and subversive. Thus, he reinforces a gendered spatial pattern which, as I argue in Chapter 4, is pervasive in the *Ab Urbe Condita* and is part and parcel of the idea of Roman society that Livy's history proposes.

The focalisation of the primary narrator often yields to the embedded focalisation of characters. The above quoted account of Philip's ascent to Mount Haemus provides a good example, since it is focalised through the king and his men. Another famous instance of embedded focalisation is the account of Hannibal's crossing the Alps in 218 BCE, which constitutes a highlight of Book 21. At 21.32 the threatening Alpine landscape is presented through the eyes of Hannibal's soldiers: focalisation here contributes to the pathos of the narrative and thus to the involvement of readers and the casting of Hannibal's march as an exceptional enterprise within an exceptional conflict.[77]

On various occasions, embedded focalisation rests not with one or more specific characters but with an anonymous or generic observer or listener, whose presence is suggested through an impersonal or passive verb of perception. Consider, for instance, 26.9.7:

> Ploratus mulierum non ex privatis solum domibus exaudiebatur, sed undique matronae in publicum effusae circa deum delubra discurrunt.
>
> The wailing of women was heard not only from private houses, but everywhere matrons threw themselves into public space and ran here and there around the shrines of the gods.

The focalisers are the people in Rome, who hear the women's anxious weeping at the news of Hannibal's approach in 216 BCE. However, the passive form conveys an even stronger notion of the turmoil everywhere in the city. Using generic focalisers is a powerful means of conveying collective emotions or reactions.[78]

Focalisation, however, is not always straightforward; in some cases, it is ambiguous. One such case is the description of the terrain of the battle at

---

[77] Cf. Pausch (2011, p. 150; cf. pp. 149–152 for a detailed analysis of Livy's use of focalisation in the whole narrative of Hannibal's march); de Jong (2014, p. 51). For various other examples of embedded focalisation (if not necessarily concerning space) see Tsitsiou-Chelidoni (2009, pp. 531–534).

[78] For further examples see e.g. 3.52.5, 7 (the second time within a direct speech, of a secondary narrator-focaliser, who however embeds a generic focalisation); 5.55.2; 10.7.10 (also in a direct speech).

Lake Trasimene (22.4.2); when the narrator remarks that the Carthaginians reached 'a place that was naturally suited to an ambush' and that it looked like 'space had been left' between the lake and the mountain 'specifically for that purpose',[79] we may ask whether it is his own interpretation of the landscape, or if he is conveying Hannibal's view of it. Since Hannibal is, in the *Ab Urbe Condita*, the master of ambush and deceit, it is a logical assumption that his perception might be tinging the representation of the landscape here.

One last type of focalisation is frequent in Livy's work, that of a secondary narrator-focaliser. Often the primary narrator of the *Ab Urbe Condita* reports the words of a character through direct or indirect speech. In such cases the thoughts and words of characters can introduce or develop key concepts, reveal the nature and motivations of characters themselves, and allow the reader to recognise the existence of different possible interpretations of the same events.

A technique of special significance in *Ab Urbe Condita* is the interweaving of different types of focalisations within the same passage or sentence.[80] Such a technique can underpin the representation of narrated space in different ways. On several occasions, the *Ab Ube Condita* presents the embedded focalisation of two or more characters in contrast to each other in order to convey different views of the same place or similar places.[81] An even more complex type of interweaving emerges when the narrative alternates between the focalisation of the external narrator, the embedded focalisation of characters, and the focalisation of one or more secondary narrators. As will be evident in this book, interweaving focalisations, together with Livy's subtle use of description and narration, are often keys to shaping spatial semantics in the *Ab Urbe Condita*.

6   An Outline of This Book

The body of my investigation extends over four chapters. In Chapters 1 and 2, I examine the image of the city that emerges from Livy's work: which locations within the city appear in the narrative, which serve as settings for historical events, which the narrative highlights and what functions they fulfil in the narrative. Given the symbolic importance of the Roman Forum and how frequently it is used as a setting, Chapter 1 is entirely devoted to this crucial

---

79   *Via tantum interest perangusta, velut ad ⟨id⟩ ipsum de industria relicto spatio.*
80   On Livy's use of this technique see Tsitsiou-Chelidoni (2009, pp. 531–534).
81   For a striking instance of this technique cf. Chapter 1, pp. 57–60.

space, while Chapter 2 analyses the other major elements of the city. These chapters should be read as a diptych, that is, as two parts of one and the same investigation.

Chapter 1 devotes significant attention to the role of the Forum in Livy's narrative of the Struggle of the Orders in Books 1–10. I argue that the Forum is fundamental not just as a setting but also as an embodiment of the tensions tearing the *res publica* apart. I then examine the representation of the Forum in Livy's later books: I show that it undergoes significant changes while at the same time retaining its basic function as a place where the Roman populace and individuals within it compete, reconcile, and recognise themselves as members of one community.

Chapter 2 starts by investigating how Book 1 of the *Ab Urbe Condita* builds the fundamental layout of the city. I then analyse how the narrative constructs and represents some of the most frequent settings, and most significant places, within the city: the Capitol; the other hills; the Campus Martius; boundary features such as the city walls and gates, the Tiber River, and the Janiculum. I then examine several narratives that feature different locations within the city in order to enquire after the overall image of the city they convey.

After investigating the city space, I turn my attention to the space of war and conquest outside the city. Chapter 3 is an analysis of the narrative construction of battlefields in the *Ab Urbe Condita*: what kinds of topographic information the narrative conveys, what the role of topography vis-à-vis other kinds of spatial reference is, how realistic or conventional descriptions of topography and landscapes are and what role space plays in the narrative of battlefields. Tackling these questions allows me to shed some light on Livy's discourse about war, military ethics, and the control of nature.

In Chapter 4, I turn from the analysis of specific spatial settings to the investigation of an overarching spatial semantics, which, I argue, is fundamental to the *Ab Urbe Condita*. I examine how the narrative uses space to express ideas about gender and its role in upholding the socio-political order of the *res publica*. I argue that the text constructs the opposition of 'public' and 'private' spaces (an opposition which was probably much less active in reality) as gendered opposition and portrays political crises as the consequences of trespassing over the boundary between those two spaces.

In a concluding chapter, I make some final observations about the role of spatial semantics in historical interpretation and identify patterns involving space, politics, and conquest in Livy's history.

My analysis is, by necessity, selective. Some types of settings (e.g. cities other than Rome) and some aspects or features of narrated space (e.g. the 'strategic space'[82] through which armies move from one location to the next, or the narrative techniques used to shift from one setting to another) are not treated extensively in this book. Instead, I have chosen to focus on a limited number of settings and features, but to look at them with a comprehensive approach, aimed at showing how they recur and are transformed throughout Livy's surviving books.

---

82   For this definition, see Chapter 3, p. 150 and p. 153.

CHAPTER 1

Strife, Reconciliation, and Change in the Forum Romanum

1 Writing the City

The city of Rome, in its physical dimension, is a crucial presence throughout the narrative. The city is where political and religious events take place; the reader sees it growing and changing through time, as new buildings are erected, and old ones are destroyed. At the same time, the narrated city of the *Ab Urbe Condita* is not exactly the real, historical city of Rome. Like every narrated space, Livy's Rome is a narrative construct and a mental model, which is shaped in readers' minds as the narrative unfolds.[1]

The shaping of the narrated city, or cityscaping,[2] involves the active participation of readers, who are invited to fill in the gaps using their knowledge of the real urban space of Rome.[3] This is a complex operation, especially because the city of the *Ab Urbe Condita* is – at least in the extant books – substantially different from the Rome of Livy's days. The narrated Rome is a city of the past, which features certain places and monuments that were no longer present in Late Republican and Augustan times and where other places and monuments known to Livy's contemporaries had not yet come into existence. A reader could, in some cases, reconstruct the appearance of lost monuments from remains still visible in the urban fabric or from the stories told by parents and grandparents; in other cases, the reader had to mentally strip well-known sites of the buildings and monuments they currently hosted. In other cases

---

1 The classic study of Rome's urban landscape in the *Ab Urbe Condita* is Jaeger (1997); more recently, Jaeger (2015) and Levene (2019) provide syntheses of the main features of Livy's narrated Rome. For monuments and memory in Livy see also Bonfante (1998); Spencer (2007); Pausch (2008, 2018a, and 2018b); for the significance of the city for Roman identity in the *Ab Urbe Condita* Edwards (1996, esp. pp. 45–52). For Livy's use of abstract spatial categories (e.g. 'public' vs. 'private', on which cf. Chapter 4), cf. Milnor (2005, pp. 141–179, and 2007); Riggsby (2009); Fabrizi (2018).

2 For the concept of 'cityscaping' see Fuhrer, Mundt, and Stenger (2015). They define the term as 'the process through which an image of a city or an urban landscape is imaginatively constructed' (Fuhrer, Mundt, and Stenger 2015, p. 1). For a more comprehensive concept of cityscaping, as the set of processes through which city spaces are formed in the interplay of material and normative processes, see Thiersch (2021).

3 Cf. Fuhrer, Mundt, and Stenger (2015, p. 2).

still, readers could recognize continuity between past and present, for example in the case of ancient monuments still extant in their own time. All such processes are hardly without consequences: the past and the present city constantly interact within the text, projecting their meanings upon each other.[4]

Livy repeatedly (and explicitly) invites readers to think about the effects of time on the physical space of Rome, as, for example, when he locates events of the past by way of current topography. In some cases, he refers to a monument existing 'now' as being a trace or reminder of the event he is narrating. A good example is found in the trial of Horatius, the victor in the duel against the Curiatii, who kills his own sister because she was mourning her defeated fiancée.[5] When Horatius' father pleads with the people for his son, he shows them 'the spoils of the Curiatii affixed in that place which is now called *pila Horatia*' (1.26.10).[6] The latter was, in fact, a small pillar located at the entrance to a portico of the Forum, but the spoils of the Curiatii no longer existed in Livy's time.[7] Shortly afterwards, Livy narrates how Horatius, acquitted by the people in admiration of his deeds, had to pass under a beam (*tigillus*) with his head covered, as if under a yoke, in a sort of expiation ritual (1.26.13). He then adds: 'That beam is extant today, too, and is constantly restored at public expense; they call it *tigillum sororium*'.[8] Clearly, Livy connects *sororius* with the noun *soror, -ris* 'sister', and thus uses the story of Horatius as the aition for a monument which probably had a very different origin.[9]

By mentioning the *pila Horatia* and the *tigillum sororium* in his narration of Horatius' trial, Livy achieves two objectives: first, he locates events of the distant past within the topography of the contemporary city, making it possible for readers to recognize the exact spot where those events took place; secondly, he provides an aition for two existing monuments, thus making the distant

---

4 See Jaeger (2015, p. 76).
5 The duel of the Horatii and the Curiatii is told at 1.25; for Horatius killing his sister see 1.26.2–4. For the trial see Della Calce (2023, pp. 36–38 and 63–66, with further bibliography).
6 [*S*]*polia Curiatiorum fixa eo loco qui nunc Pila Horatia appellatur*. Livy seems to understand *pila* as the plural of *pilum, -i*, and thus the toponym as meaning 'Horatius' spears', from the spears of the Curiatii that Horatius had allegedly affixed there (cf. 1.26.11; for *Horatia pila* as a neutral plural see also Prop. 3.3.7.). Others, among them Dionysius of Halicarnassus (3.32.9), understood pila as the nominative singular of *pila, -ae* ('pillar') and the toponym as 'Horatius' pillar'.
7 Cf. Dion. Hal. *Ant. Rom.* 3.32.9. For discussion of the precise location of the *pila Horatia*, see e.g. Ogilvie (1965, p. 116); Coarelli (1983, pp. 201–202, p. 208, and s.v. *Pila Horatia* in *LTUR* 4, 1999, pp. 89–90).
8 *Id hodie quoque publice semper refectum manet; sororium tigillum vocant*.
9 See e.g. Ogilvie (1965, p. 118, with further bibliography); Coarelli s.v. *Tigillum sororium* in *LTUR* 5 (1999) pp. 74–75.

past relevant to the present.[10] At the same time, his references to the 'now' point to the changes the passage of time has produced in the physical fabric of Rome: while the two monuments were still there in Livy's day, everything around them had changed (and the spoils of the Curiatii, the Roman reader knew, were no longer present).

In other cases, the place the historian mentions with reference to an ancient event is not a direct product or a trace of that event, but simply serves to clarify where it took place. When, for instance, he tells the story of Valerius Publicola, the consul of 509 BCE who the people suspected of monarchic ambitions for building his house at the top of the Velia, and who consequently moved to a less elevated location (2.7.5–12), Livy states that the new house was erected 'where the temple of Vica Pota now is' (*ubi nunc Vicae Potae ⟨aedes⟩ est*, 2.7.12).

A later episode provides a more complex example of how the text can explain an ancient event by means of contemporary topography. In Book 3, Livy narrates how the centurion Lucius Verginius killed his own daughter to save her from the Decemvir Appius Claudius' lust in 449 BCE.[11] The historian specifies that the murder took place 'by the shrine of Cloacina, near the shops that are now called "new"' (*prope Cloacinae ad tabernas, quibus nunc Novis est nomen*, 3.48.5). Two toponyms are at work here. The (*sacrum*) *Cloacinae* was an open-air shrine of a local goddess identified at some point with Venus.[12] Livy's phrasing seems to presuppose the existence of the shrine at the time of the events; this building, therefore, creates continuity between the time Verginia died and the readers' own time. On the contrary, the second toponym, together with the use of the adverb *nunc*, stresses urban change. The *tabernae novae* were shops on the northern side of the Forum; originally *lanienae* ('butchers' shops'), they had later been turned into *argentariae* ('bankers' shops'), then destroyed by a fire in 210 BCE and subsequently rebuilt – hence the designation *novae* ('new'), contrasting them with the *tabernae veteres* ('old shops') on the southern side of the Forum.[13]

Livy himself reports the fire at 26.27.2, a passage rich in references to time and change. The first buildings to burn, he writes, were 'the seven shops which would later be five, and the bankers' shops now called "new"' (*septem tabernae*

---

10   For similar uses of ancient events as aitia of extant monuments or toponyms, and of extant monuments or toponyms as traces of ancient events, see e.g. 1.4.5 (the Ficus Ruminalis); 3.26.8 (the prata Quinctia, where, according to Livy, Lucius Quinctius Cincinnatus lived); 5.32.6 (the shrine of Aius Locutius).
11   For a full analysis of this episode in the *Ab Urbe Condita* see Chapter 4, pp. 228–235.
12   Cf. Coarelli s.v. *Cloacinae, sacrum* in *LTUR* 1 (1993) pp. 290–291; Freyberger (2012, pp. 57–58).
13   See Papi s.vv. *tabernae Argentariae, tabernae circa forum, tabernae Lanienae, tabernae Novae, tabernae Veteres* in *LTUR* 5 (1999) pp. 10–15; Russell (2016a, pp. 79–81).

quae postea quinque, et argentariae quae nunc novae appellantur). Then, he adds, the private buildings caught fire, 'for there were no basilicas at that time' (*neque enim tum basilicae erant*). In the first part, he refers to something that had changed in time (the *tabernae*, which are 'now' called 'new'); in the second, he mentions a kind of building (the *basilica*) that did not exist 'back then'.[14]

There are several other references to contemporary topography in the *Ab Urbe Condita* (a full list can be found in von Haeling, 1989, pp. 80–158). Interestingly, however, remarks of this kind become much rarer after Book 6.[15] A notable exception (apart from the above-mentioned passage from Book 26) might be the discussion of Scipio Africanus' tomb at 38.56.3–4. Here Livy first testifies the existence in Liternum of a funerary monument with a statue, which he claims to have personally seen (Livy's only statement of autopsy in all the *Ab Urbe Condita*);[16] then he speaks of three statues – of Publius and Lucius Scipio and of the poet Ennius – which were 'in Rome outside the Porta Capena' (*Romae extra portam Capenam*). This, however, is not a topographic reference aimed at clarifying the location of an event based on what is known of the contemporary city, but rather the discussion of two alternatives as to the unknown resting place of a historical figure.

It seems, therefore, that the *Ab Urbe Condita* lays great stress on continuity and change in the city when narrating events of the distant past. How, then, do such references to contemporary topography work as a means of cityscaping in Livy's account? First, they enhance the historian's authority: since he claims to know exactly where the events took place, his account appears credible. Secondly, they explain the origin of certain sites, monuments, or toponyms: this is the function of an aition. Most importantly, they anchor the 'then' in the 'now' – or rather, they anchor events, often of a semi-legendary nature, in the materiality of the city that readers know. In so doing, they provide a direct link between past and present: the city many Roman readers walk through is the same city where ancient characters acted, and what characters did in the past is still relevant to the present. At the same time, however, they also point to the fact that the city is not *exactly* the same as before. Readers are reminded time and again that the city has changed. Thus, they are also invited to think about how the city once was, and to conjure up in their minds an image of the older

---

14   For the building of basilicas cf. 39.44.6 (Porcia); 44.16.9 (Sempronia); and below, p. 41.

15   The five topographic references from Books 7–10 listed by von Haeling (1989, p. 41: 7.39.16; 8.22.5; 8.30.4; 9.36.1; 10.9.8) are a different story, in that they refer to locations outside of Rome and do so with a much lower degree of detail. A statement, for example, like *Palaepolis fuit haud procul inde ubi nunc Neapolis sita est* (Palaepolis lay not far from where Neapolis now is, 8.22.5) calls on readers knowledge of Neapolis' geographical position but not of its topography.

16   Cf. von Haeling (1989, p. 44, n. 91); Briscoe (2008, p. 197).

city. The narrated Rome of the *Ab Urbe Condita* unfolds within this dynamic of change and continuity – or, rather, of continuity in change.

This chapter and the next investigate Livy's Rome and its complex web of change, continuity, and memory. I start by focusing on the Forum, by far the most frequent location for events in the city of Rome in the *Ab Urbe Condita*, which shall be the subject of this chapter. In section 2, I provide some basic information about the history and archaeology of the Forum and illustrate some general tendencies in Livy's representation of it. In section 3, I analyse its role in Livy's narrative of the so-called Struggle of the Orders in the First Decade. In section 4, I examine the transformations of Livy's Forum in the later books. In section 5, I draw some conclusions about the semantics of the Forum in the *Ab Urbe Condita*.

2   Setting the Scene: Livy's Forum

Archaeological remains confirm that the Forum – originally a swampy valley stretching between the Palatine Hill to the south-east and the Capitoline Hill to the west – existed as a public square from the mid-7th century BCE.[17] Throughout the Republican period, it was a multifunctional space in which some of the most crucial political, economic, and religious interactions of the city took place.

The original political core of the Forum was its northwestern side, which featured the Comitium, the assembly place of the Roman people, and the adjoining Curia, the Senate House. Both seem to be coeval with the first paving of the Forum[18] and ancient Romans credited King Tullus Hostilius with building the Senate House, as its original name, Curia Hostilia, suggests.[19]

---

17   The Forum is the object of a vast critical literature, which cannot be properly summarised here. For the history and archaeology of the Forum, see e.g. Coarelli (1983, 1985, and 2020); Tagliamonte s.v. *Forum Romanum (fino alla prima età repubblicana)* in *LTUR* 2 (1995) pp. 313–325; Purcell s.v. *Forum Romanum (the Republican period)* in *LTUR* 2 (1995) pp. 325–336; Köb (2000); Kissel (2004); Freyberger (2009a and 2012); Muth (2012 and 2014). For discussions of its socio-political functions and its memorial significance, e.g. Döbler (1999, pp. 22–141); Hölkeskamp (2012); Russell (2016a, pp. 43–95); Hölscher (2020).

18   For the Comitium, see Coarelli (1983, pp. 119–138); Carafa (1998, with a different chronology); Kissel (2004, pp. 79–98); Freyberger (2009a, p. 21, pp. 27–30); Humm (2014). For the Curia e.g. Tagliamonte s.v. *Forum Romanum (fino alla prima età repubblicana)* in *LTUR* 2 (1995) p. 320. On their functions in political communication, Döbler (1999, pp. 27–33).

19   Cf. Cic. *Rep.* 2.17.31 (who indicates Tullus Hostilius as responsible for building both the Curia and the Comitium); Varro *Ling.* 5.155; Livy 1.30.2.

The Curia Hostilia was the main (although not the only) meeting place of the Roman Senate until the first century BCE; with its south-eastern orientation, it loomed above the adjacent Comitium, separated from it by a flight of steps. The Comitium was the seat of the ancient *comitia curiata*,[20] and later (from the 4th century BCE onwards) a frequent location for *comitia tributa*, which elected minor magistrates and voted on some laws, and *concilia plebis*, which also voted on laws and elected the tribunes of the plebs; until the mid-2nd century BCE, trials also took place there.[21]

According to one interpretation, it was originally a square area, befitting its quality as a *templum* (inaugurated space), but, at some point during the 3rd century BCE, it was turned into a circular space surrounded by stairways after the model of Greek *ekklesiasteria* (assembly places).[22] A platform for speakers (*tribunal*), from which magistrates could address the people, was built in the southern area of the Comitium in the early 5th century. In 338 BCE, the platform was embellished by the rams (*rostra*) of the ships from the defeated town of Antium,[23] and Rostra was the name by which Romans called the platform from then on. Close to the Rostra, on the South-West, was the Graecostasis, where ambassadors from foreign cities waited to be admitted into the Curia.[24] The North-Western side hosted the *tribunal* of the praetor and the seats of the tribunes of the Plebs.[25] Moreover, the Comitium was adorned with statues of heroes from the past, who had been so honoured for their services to the state.[26]

Despite progressive enlargements in the 4th and 3rd centuries BCE, the steady growth of the Roman population made the Comitium inadequate for containing the tribes assembled for the *comitia tributa* or for the audiences of public speeches. So, around the mid-2nd century BCE, the *comitia tributa* (Varro *Rust.* 1.2.9; Cic. *Amic.* 96) and the *tribunal* of the praetor seem to have been moved to the Eastern side of the Forum.[27] At about the same time, the

---

20 In historical times, the main function of *comitia curiata* was to pass the law which, each year, defined the powers of the magistrates (*lex curiata*): see e.g. Nicholls (1967); Develin (1977).
21 It could also function as a location for the enrolment of troops, since Livy places enrolment procedures in the Comitium on at least one occasion, at 3.11.1–2.
22 Coarelli (1983, pp. 146–157, and 1985, pp. 11–21); Freyberger (2009a, p. 29). *Contra* Carafa (1998, pp. 117–118, 135–147).
23 Livy 8.14.12.
24 Cf. Coarelli (1985, pp. 138–160).
25 For the monuments on this site of the Comitium see Coarelli (1985, pp. 22–59); Döbler (1999, pp. 26–40).
26 Cf. e.g. Coarelli (1985, pp. 87–123); Freyberger (2009a, pp. 32–37); Hölkeskamp (2012).
27 Cf. Freyberger (2009a, p. 47).

comitia tributa lost some of their judicial functions, which were taken over by permanent boards of judges (*quaestiones perpetuae*), whose seats were also in the same area.

The Rostra of the Comitium continued to be an important location for public speeches, but if one is to believe Plutarch (*Vit. C. Gracch.* 5.4), Gaius Gracchus was the first to face the open Forum, rather than the Comitium and the Curia, while addressing the people from the Rostra.[28] Moreover the area around the temple of Castor[29] on the south-eastern side of the Forum, became an important location for political activity in the 1st century BCE. The temple was a frequent location for Senate meetings and its steps were used as a platform for speakers addressing the people, thus playing the same function as the Rostra of the Comitium. We also know of honorary statues adorning the temple steps, just as monuments of the same type had been placed in the Comitium and the Rostra from olden times.[30]

The erosion of the political and judicial functions of the Comitium intensified during the 1st century BCE. Sulla's enlargement of the Senate House in 81 BCE – which led to its renaming as Curia Cornelia – caused downsizing of the old assembly place and the destruction of some of its ancient monuments.[31] Later, in 52 BCE, an angry crowd burnt the Curia to the ground during Publius Clodius' funeral. Faustus Sulla, the dictator's son, had it rebuilt shortly thereafter, but after 46 BCE Caesar had it destroyed so as to be substituted with a new Curia, which would now be aligned with his new Forum Iulium.[32] The building of the Curia Iulia, as Caesar's Senate House came to be known, started in 44 BCE and was completed years after his death, in 29 BCE, on Octavian's order.

Caesar's building activities also marked the end of the old Comitium, since the Curia Iulia occupied the area previously belonging to the assembly square. Consequently, Caesar had the Rostra relocated to the short Western side of the Forum, where they remained afterwards. The speaker's platform underwent

---

28 Cf. Coarelli (1985, pp. 157–199).
29 Cf. below, p. 39.
30 On the shift of political activity from the northwestern edge to the area of the temple of Castor in the late 2nd and 1st centuries BCE see e.g. Coarelli (1985, p. 199).
31 Cf. Coarelli (1983, pp. 159–170, and 1985, pp. 196–197).
32 For Caesar's building activities in the Forum, see Coarelli (1985, pp. 233–257, with discussion of the ancient sources); for possible interpretations of his displacement of the Rostra, Muth (2014, pp. 305–315).

structural changes under Augustus and, in that form, remained in use throughout the imperial age.[33]

During Augustus' principate, moreover, another Rostra was built on the eastern side of the Forum, in front of the Temple of Divus Iulius, which Augustus dedicated in 29 BCE. Our sources demonstrate its use, among other things, as a speakers' platform during the funerals of members of the imperial house, such as Octavia and later Augustus himself. As the years went by, the eastern section of the Forum became especially rich in monuments celebrating the *princeps*' family, thus acquiring a strong 'Augustan', or 'Julian' connotation. It thus counterbalanced the western side, where the Curia and the Rostra still represented the traditional role of the Senate and people in the *res publica*.[34]

Already before its Augustan restructuring, the eastern area of the Forum had been a location of profound religious and political significance. The temple of Vesta, on the lower slopes of the Palatine facing the Forum, with the adjoining house of the Vestal Virgins, was one of the oldest and most venerable cult places in Rome, hosting the sacred fire on which Rome's welfare allegedly depended;[35] close to it was the *regia*, connected with the sacral activities of various priests and priestesses.[36]

The religious connotations of the Forum (often inextricably intertwined with its political functions) were also visible in a variety of other temples and shrines. The temple of Castor – which, as mentioned above, was to become an important centre of political activity in the Late Republic – was connected to a miraculous apparition of the Dioscuri in support of the Roman army at the battle of Lake Regillus in 499 BCE.[37] The temple of Saturn at the foot of the Capitol, also dating back to the 5th century BCE, hosted the *aerarium* (the state

---

33 On Augustus' restructuring of the Forum see e.g. Coarelli (1985, pp. 239–257, 258–324); Zanker (1987, pp. 85–87); Purcell s.v. *Forum Romanum* (*The Imperial Period*) in *LTUR* 2 (1995) pp. 338–339; Hölscher (2020, pp. 113–116).

34 Cf. Coarelli (1985, pp. 320–324). On the memorial associations of the 'Republican' Rostra see e.g. Biggs (2019).

35 On the temple of Vesta see e.g. Scott s.v. *Vesta, aedes* in *LTUR* 5 (1999) pp. 125–130.; Kissel (2004, pp. 68–79).

36 For the *regia* see e.g. (with different reconstructions) Carandini (2004); Scott s.v. *Regia* in *LTUR* 4 (1999) pp. 189–192; DiLuzio (2024).

37 The temple was, in fact, dedicated to the Dioscuri, Castor and Pollux, though our sources often mention it simply as *aedes Castoris*. The fabulous tale about its founding occurs in its fullest form in Dion. Hal. *Ant. Rom.* 6.13; cf. also Cic. *Nat. D.* 2.2.6; Val. Max. 1.8.1. Livy 2.20.12, 42.5 provides a much soberer version. On its history and archaeology see e.g. Freyberger (2009a, pp. 31–32); Köb (2000, pp. 41–56).

treasure) and an official archive.[38] The temple of Concordia, on the lower slopes of the Capitol and close to the Comitium, is reported to have been dedicated by Marcus Furius Camillus in 367 BCE to celebrate the re-establishment of concord between patricians and plebeian after the Licinio-Sextian Legislation had been passed.[39] While scholars have raised doubts about the veracity of this tale,[40] a tradition concerning a later dedication appears more trustworthy: in 121 BCE, the consul Lucius Opimius, a bitter enemy of the Gracchi, built (or, if one accepts the earlier foundation by Camillus, restored) it after the repression of the popular unrest which had ended in Gaius Gracchus' death. The Augustan renovation which started in 7 BCE aimed at erasing the controversial implications of Opimius's act; therefore, in 10 CE, the future emperor Tiberius dedicated the temple of Concordia Augusta – a celebration of the era of peace and concord inaugurated by the *princeps*.[41]

The presence of religious buildings suggests the Forum functioned as the setting for a variety of cult activities, many of which are now lost to us. Processions of various kinds passed though the Forum, too: most notably, triumphal processions traversed the Forum before ending at the temple of Jupiter Optimus Maximus on the Capitol.[42] A special type of ceremony was constituted by funerals of the elite – complex pageants, which each featured a parade of people who impersonated the illustrious ancestors of the deceased and culminated in a laudatory speech (*laudatio*) delivered by one of the deceased's close relatives from the Rostra.[43] Augustus continued that tradition by turning the Forum into the setting for funerals of the imperial family, with both Rostra – on the western and eastern sides of the square – as speakers' platforms for *laudationes*.[44]

The Forum was also a centre of economic and financial activity. From an early period, it had hosted shops and banker' stalls (*tabernae*), the history of which I have briefly mentioned above. Over time, most of them were moved

---

38 On the temple of Saturn see e.g. Coarelli s.v. *Saturnus, aedes* in LTUR 4 (1999) pp. 234–236; Köb (2000, pp. 70–83).
39 Ov. *Fast.* 1.637–648; Plut. *Vit. Cam.* 42.2.
40 See e.g. Momigliano (1942); Akar (2002).
41 On the temple of Concordia, its implications, and its history in the Republican and Augustan ages, see e.g. Momigliano (1942); Ferroni s.v. *Concordia, aedes*, in *LTUR* 1 (1993) pp. 316–320; Döbler (1999, pp. 48–60); Köb (2000, pp. 56–70); Akar (2002); Humm (2005, pp. 541–600); Coarelli (2020, pp. 73–78).
42 On triumphs cf. Chapter 2, pp. 88–89.
43 The main source for aristocratic funerals in Republican Rome is Polyb. 6.53–54; cf. Flower (1996, pp. 91–127 and 2004b, pp. 331–336).
44 Cf. e.g. Köb (2000, pp. 168–173).

away from the Forum and financial activities came to gravitate around the basilicas that prominent aristocrats built in the area from the 2nd century BCE onwards.[45] In imperial times, basilicas were also the seats for some judicial courts; moreover, they seemed to have functioned, throughout their history, as places where people enjoying their leisure could stroll and meet. The building of basilicas substantially changed the appearance of the Forum, turning it into a closed piazza with a more consistent (though never truly unified) appearance. Moreover, the increasing magnificence of the Forum's architecture came to reflect Rome's new role as a leading international power.[46]

Finally, private residences were also part of the Forum landscape. Aristocratic houses were built all around the Forum, especially on the lower slopes of the Palatine and the Velia, from ancient times. It is hard to neatly distinguish the private, residential function of the Forum from its political one. Living close to the Forum meant public visibility and easy access to the spaces of politics. One can well imagine *nobiles* leaving their houses in the morning followed by throngs of supporters, to take part in senatorial debates or to deliver public speeches in the Forum.[47]

Thus, the Forum was, in several ways, the centre of Roman civic life. It was also a space rich in memories – perhaps more than any other location in the city.[48] Sometimes legendary *aitia* existed for ancient monuments, and sometimes more than one legendary tradition developed around one and the same monument.[49] In Republican times, the Forum became a contested ground in much political competition. Members of the *nobilitas* promoted the building of edifices which would not only provide the growing Roman population with

---

45 On basilicas see e.g. Nünnerich-Asmus (1994); the entries in *LTUR* 1 (1993) pp. 167–190; Freyberger (2009b, pp. 37–44, and 2009b). Cato the Elder had the Basilica Porcia built during his censorship in 184 BCE, close to the Curia and the Comitium. The Basilica Fulvia, built by the censors of 179 BCE, Marcus Aemilius Lepidus and Marcus Fulvius Nobilior, on the northern side would later come to be known as basilica Aemilia after restorations by members of that *gens*. Tiberius Sempronius Gracchus, censor in 169 BCE, had the Basilica Sempronia built on the southern side: Caesar's Basilica Iulia later took its place. The Basilica Opimia, was built by Lucius Opimius in 121 BCE close to his temple of Concordia.

46 Cf. Coarelli (1985, pp. 199–209); Nünnerich-Asmus (1994, pp. 7–10); Russell (2016a, pp. 69–70).

47 Cf. e.g. Carandini and Carafa (1995); Carandini and Papi (1999); Purcell s.v. *Forum Romanum (The Republican Period)* in *LTUR* 2 (1995), p. 329; Freyberger (2009a, pp. 36–37); Russell (2016a, pp. 77–95, with in depth discussion of the relationship between public and private space in the Forum).

48 Cf. Hölkeskamp (2012).

49 The Lacus Curtius provides a famous example: cf. below, pp. 42–43 and Chapter 2, pp. 100–101.

more functional public spaces but also immortalise the names and achievements of their founders;[50] honorary statues were placed at several locations within the Forum. Later, Augustus would turn the Forum Romanum into a space of 'regulated memory',[51] where the traces of the glorious past and the celebration of the *princeps* would work in tandem to promote the ideas of restoration, concord, and peace.

This was the Forum Livy knew. It had lost part of its political functions, but still served as a place where members of the imperial family could speak to the people from the Rostra, and where senators could meet in the Curia Iulia.[52] It was not quite as central as in previous times, due to the competition of the new Caesarian and Augustan Fora[53] and to Augustus' improvements to other districts in the city. Yet, it was a space where one could still recognise the various layers of memory upon which the identity of the city's inhabitants rested. How, then, does Livy's narrative engage with such a rich web of memory, politics, religion, and everyday practice?

A first, partial answer to this question might be: the narrative consistently emphasises the Forum as a centre of action and as a symbolically laden space. The Forum is among the first sites to appear in Livy's account of Roman history. Its space is shaped in and through the battle between Romans and Sabines which follows the abduction of the Sabine maidens by Romulus and his men at 1.12–13. In Livy's narrative the Sabines, led by their king Titus Tatius, occupy the Capitol (1.11.5–9), while the inhabitants of the newborn city of Rome settle on the Palatine; the battle takes place in the valley between the two hills, the future Forum Romanum. During the fight, the Sabines first force the Romans back to 'the old gate of the Palatine' (*ad veterem portam Palatii*, 1.12.3, i.e. the Porta Mugonia). Then Romulus utters a vow to Jupiter, promising to build him a temple if the god stays his men's flight; the Romans take courage and push back the Sabines. This is Livy's aition for the temple of Jupiter Stator ('Jupiter Who Stays the Flight'), which would later rise on the lower slopes of the Palatine.[54] Another aition soon follows. A Sabine knight, Mettius Curtius, pursued by the Romans, throws himself into a swamp with his horse and manages to come out unscathed. After the battle, the swamp receives the name Lacus Curtius in memory of his deed. In Livy's time, the only trace of the original swamp was

---

50   Cf. Nünnerich-Asmus (1994, pp. 10–11).
51   Cf. Muth (2012).
52   On the functions of the Forum in the Augustan age, see e.g. Purcell s.v. *Forum Romanum (Imperial Period)* in *LTUR* 2 (1995) pp. 338–339.
53   For the transfer of some functions to the Forum Augustum cf. e.g. Köb (2000, p. 152).
54   For the story of this temple see Chapter 2, p. 130.

a *puteal* within a monumental enclosure in the middle of the Forum, but the significance of the place persisted.[55]

The narration of the battle ends with a stirring scene: the Sabine women, now wives of the Romans, throw themselves between the warring armies of their respective fathers and husbands and plead for the end of the hostilities. The men, touched by their words, stop fighting; the two kings stipulate a pact and unite the two people into one.

Such a dramatic foundation story, which relates how the first core of the Roman people came from the union of different elements, introduces the Forum as the central place in the city – as a place of encounter, strife, and reconciliation. The back and forth movement of the two armies during the battle shapes the space of the Forum textually; the naming of monuments within it or at its borders (*vetus porta Palatii*, the temple of Jupiter Stator, and the Lacus Curtius) sanctions its entry into Livy's history as an urban space and alerts the readers to its memorial depth.[56]

At the same time, the text handles the Forum very selectively – even surprisingly so. There is no mention, for example, of the shrine of Cloacina, which a tradition singled out as the place where Romans and Sabines had purified themselves after the battle;[57] nor of the location of Romulus and Titus Tatius' peace-making, which other ancient authors identify as the Comitium.[58] Instead of mapping his account of the battle onto the various sites that resonate with its memory, Livy weaves it around a few landmarks and even fewer monuments.

A similar tendency to selectivity characterises the narrative construction of the Forum in Livy's subsequent books. It is not that the monuments and buildings of the Forum are absent from his historical account: in fact, almost all major structures appear at some point or other.[59] Mostly, however, Livy only

---

55   On the Lacus Curtius cf. e.g. Coarelli (1983 and 1985, pp. 226–229); Giuliani s.v. *Lacus Curtius* in *LTUR* 3 (1996) pp. 166–167; Köb (2000, pp. 25–35); Spencer (2007).
56   For full analyses of the narrative of the battle in the Forum and its topography, see Jaeger (1997, pp. 30–56); Pausch (2008, 2018a and 2018b); Fabrizi (2021, pp. 250–256).
57   Cf. Plin. *HN* 15.119.
58   Plut. *Vit. Rom.* 19.7 (Plutarch also mentions the temple of Vesta and the *regia* as standing in the locations where the Romans once pushed back the Sabines after Romulus' prayer to Jupiter had turned the tide); Dio Cass. fr. 5.7. Festus, *Gloss. Lat.* 372 and Serv. *Aen.* 8.641 speak more generally of the Sacra Via (the ancient street traversing the Forum) as the location for the pact.
59   Some examples: the *carcer*, the state prison (cf. e.g. 1.33.8; 3.57.4; 6.16.4; 30.21.5; 34.44.6–8; 38.57.4; 39.41.7); the statue of Cloelia *in summa sacra via* (2.13.11); the temple of Saturn (2.21.1; 22.1.19; 41.12.21; 41.27.7; specifically the *aerarium* at e.g. 4.22.1; 10.36.5–6, 13; 41.28.6; 45.4.1.); the temple of Castor (8.11.16); the equestrian statue of Quintus Marcius Tremulus, which

mentions buildings, sites, or monuments within the Forum very briefly: typically, in prodigy lists, in notices about floods or fires, or in the sections of his work that report the building activities of magistrates. In some cases, a monument serves to locate an event of the past, as in the cases the *tabernae*, the *pila Horatia*, and the shrine of Cloacina, which I have discussed above. The role of such topographic references should not be underestimated, since they convey the complexity of the Forum landscape and the significance of individual monuments as reminders of the past. However, they rarely result in a building or monument functioning as the setting for a fully-fledged narrative.

In fact, most narratives of events in the Forum develop around two poles: the Curia, on the hand, and the Comitium, or, more generally, the open space of the Forum, on the other. In the remaining part of my chapter, I argue that such an opposition between Curia and Comitium/Forum is semantically charged and functions as a crucial component of Livy's political discourse. Before I embark on that discussion, however, let me briefly analyse the vocabulary Livy uses to designate those places.

The historian uses the word *comitium* nineteen times in the surviving books (four times in Books 1–5, three times in Books 6–10, seven times in Books 21–30, three times in Books 31–40, and twice in Books 41–45).[60] Among these occurrences, two are typical 'annalistic' material, reporting the first time the Comitium was covered since Hannibal's invasion (27.36.8) and a prodigy (34.45.6). Two further passages concern the placing of honorary statues of Attus Navius (1.36.5) and Horatius Cocles (2.10.12) *in comitio*; and at 38.56.11 Livy elaborates on Scipio's refusal to have statues of him set up in the most symbolically laden sites of Rome (*in comitio, in rostris, in curia, in Capitolio, in cella Iovis*). In four cases, moreover, the Comitium is mentioned as the location for public executions (9.9.2; 22.57.3; 24.20.6; 25.7.14): here one notes the recurrences of quasi-formulaic expressions which are variations on *in comitio virgis caedere*, 'to kill (someone) with the rods (i.e. by scourging) in the Comitium'. In other cases, the toponym occurs in narratives of high symbolic significance (5.55.1; 6.15.1; 22.7.7; 40.29.13, 14) or stresses the processes of communication embodied in the complex of Comitium and Curia (5.7.8; 10.24.18; 22.59.18;

---

was placed in front of the temple of Castor (9.44.22); Basilica Porcia (39.44.6); Basilica Fulvia (quoted simply as *basilicam post argentarias novas* at 40.51.4); Basilica Sempronia, on the spot previously occupied by Africanus's house *pone Veteres ad Vortumni signum* (44.16.9).

60 Obviously, this only applies to *comitium*, used in the singular to designate the assembly square; *comitia*, in the plural, indicates the elections of magistrates and is frequent in the *Ab Urbe Condita*.

26.16.9; 45.20.5, 11); I shall examine most of these narratives more closely in the following sections of this chapter.

Livy frequently indicates the Comitium through expressions containing the word *contio*, 'public assembly' (*ad contionem, in contione* etc.),[61] or by mentioning the speakers' platform (*Rostra*).[62] Occasionally, the Comitium is designated by the word *templum*, 'inaugurated space'.[63] In some cases, the text refers to the *tribunal* of the praetor or the *subsellia* of the tribunes of the plebs, both located in the Northern part of the Comitium.[64]

Contio designates an assembly of the people, which could also be held in places other than the Comitium, although the latter was one of the most frequent locations.[65] In the surviving books of the *Ab Urbe Condita*, most *contiones* seem to take place in the Comitium, with the presiding magistrate speaking from the speaker's platform. In some cases, the meaning of *contio* appears to lie between that of 'assembly' and that of 'Comitium' or 'the speakers' platform'. At 2.56.10, for example, Livy describes the patricians' obstruction of the tribes' voting procedure: *postero die consules nobilitasque ad impediendam legem in contione subsistunt*. This would mean that the patricians 'made a stand in the assembly' preceding the formal division of the plebs into their tribes for voting,[66] but also that they occupied the Comitium, where the assembly and the voting are presumed to have taken place.[67] Sometimes it is unclear whether assemblies (or other procedures) are set in the Comitium or the wider space of the Forum.[68] Conversely, the *Ab Urbe Condita* rarely mentions locations for

---

61   E.g. 2.7.7; 3.64.6; 4.6.1; 5.2.2; 5.50.8; 8.33.9; 23.48.10; 27.51.5; 33.24.4; 36.21.8; 41.7.5; 42.33.2; 44.22.1; 45.2.6.
62   Cf. e.g. 8.33.9; 23.23.1; 27.50.9; 30.17.3; 34.56.3; 38.51.6, 12; 38.52.11; 38.54.9; 39.15.1.
63   Cf. 3.17.2; 8.35.8.
64   *Tribunal* of the praetor or other magistrates: 3.57.2; 6.15.2 (the judging magistrate is here a dictator, who has placed his seat *in comitio*, 6.15.1); 27.50.9; 29.16.6 (here, too, alongside an explicit mention of the Comitium); 39.32.11; 43.15.5; 45.44.5.
65   On *contiones* in republican Rome, see e.g. Taylor (1966, pp. 15–33); Millar (1985); Hölkeskamp (1995, esp. pp. 27–35); Pina Polo (1989 and 1995); Mouritsen (2001, esp. pp. 38–62, and 2011, pp. 83–98); Morstein-Marx (2004). Among the most frequent locations for *contiones* other than the Comitium were the *area Capitolina* in front of the temple of Jupiter (until the second century BCE), the circus Flaminius (for *contiones* summoned by tribunes of the plebs) and, especially in the Late Republic, the temple of Castor in the Forum.
66   That it was a *concilium plebis* is stated at 2.57.1.
67   Cf. Hölkeskamp (1995, p. 27).
68   See e.g. 2.29.6, where, after narrating various debates and brawls that developed on and around the *tribunal*, Livy has the consuls complaining with the Senate that *nihilo plus sanitatis in curia quam in foro esse*; 2.56, where the consul Appius Claudius' obstruction of the *contio* preceding the *concilium plebis*, which takes place in the Comitium, is

contiones outside the Forum, with the obvious exceptions of *contiones* that took place immediately before elections in the Campus Martius or military *contiones* outside the city.

As for the Senate House, Livy usually refers to it through the noun *curia*; in the entire work he only designates it as *curia Hostilia* three times.[69] This complicates things because, in Latin, the term *curia* can apply to any building where Senate meetings took place – and ancient sources report several locations (mostly temples) that could fulfil that function.[70] In several accounts in the *Ab Urbe Condita*, the narrative contexts suggest that the term *curia* designates the Curia Hostilia, but in other cases, a different location is theoretically possible. As far as I have been able to discern, however, there are only five occurrences in the *Ab Urbe Condita* where the term *curia* undoubtedly designates a building other than the Curia Hostilia:[71] at 30.22.6–23.1, where the noun occurs twice, it designates the temple of Bellona; at 22.1.14, 37.1.3, and 44.19.7, it indicates the Temple of Jupiter Optimus Maximus on the Capitol.[72]

The only locations for Senate meetings other than the Curia Hostilia that the *Ab Urbe Condita* mentions explicitly are the temple of Jupiter on the Capitol, and the temples of Bellona and Apollo in the Campus Martius.[73] All these locations hosted meetings of special kinds. The Temple of Jupiter Optimus Maximus (to which Livy refers, in such cases, by the expression *in Capitolio*) held the first Senate meeting of each year on the day the consuls entered office: the allotment of provinces and the distribution of troops to the magistrates of the year normally took place on that occasion. The temples of Apollo and Bellona, which lay outside the *pomerium*, were frequent locations when the Senate decided on a triumph or received embassies from enemy peoples.[74] All

---

followed by the rushing of people from the whole city to the Forum (14) and the other consul T. Quinctius invites the *consulares* to bring his colleague away 'from the Forum' (*de foro*, 15).

69 Cf. Jaeger (2015, pp. 72–75) for an interpretation of Livy's use of the name *curia Hostilia*.
70 Cf. Bonnefond-Coudry (1989, pp. 49–50; and, for a comprehensive discussion of the locations for Senate meetings in Rome, pp. 26–197).
71 All three passages report the first Senate meeting of a year: 217 BCE (22.1.5–16), 190 BCE (37.1.1–6), and 169 BCE (44.19.1–14).
72 Cf. Bonnefond-Coudry (1989, pp. 65–68).
73 Campus Martius: 3.63.6. Capitol: 3.21.1; 8.5.1–6.7; 23.31.1; 24.10.1; 26.1.1; 28.38.14; 30.27.1; 32.8.1; 42.47.1. Temple of Bellona: 28.9.5; 28.38.2; 30.21.11; 30.40.1; 31.47.7; 33.22.1; 33.24.5; 36.39.5; 38.44.9; 39.29.4; 42.21.6; 42.28.2; 42.36.2. Temple of Apollo: 37.58.3; 39.4.2.
74 Cf. e.g. Rüpke (2019, p. 37). On returning from campaign, it was forbidden for a general to cross the *pomerium* with his army; therefore, the request for a triumph had to be presented and debated outside the *pomerium* itself. On this and other aspects of the triumphal ritual, cf. Chapter 2, pp. 88–89.

the instances in which the *Ab Urbe Condita* mentions them in relation to a Senate meeting belong to these categories. The same is true for the mention of the Campus Martius (without further specification) at 3.63.6.

In other words, Livy only mentions a location other than Curia Hostilia for a meeting of the Senate in cases in which that location is closely associated with the particular type of meeting he is relating. In all other cases, he designates the location, if at all, as *curia*. This has, in my opinion, an important consequence: the reader will imagine the Curia Hostilia as the setting for a Senate meeting when the text provides no further specification, even if that might not have been the case in reality (and in Livy's source). In a similar manner, the historian tends to speak of *contiones* either as taking place in the Comitium or without a specific location, so the reader will be inclined to think of the Comitium even in the absence of a more precise indication.

In what follows, I investigate how such a selective representation of the Forum is part of Livy's reflections on the forces at work within the Roman state, and on the right course to follow in governing the *res publica*.

3 A Space Torn Apart: the Forum in Livy's Struggle of the Orders

3.1 Framing the Struggle

One of the main narrative threads in the First Pentad and the first half of the Second is the so-called Struggle of the Orders, the series of conflicts through which, in the 5th and the 4th centuries BCE, the plebeians gradually obtained admission to the highest magistracies and the abolition of debt bondage. Such a process led to the rise of a mixed patricio-plebeian *nobilitas* to rule the Republic until its fall.[75]

Two narratives frame the long history of the Struggle of the Orders in the *Ab Urbe Condita*: the story of the first plebeian revolt against debt bondage (*nexum*) at 2.23–24 and the story of its abolition at 8.28.[76] As I argue, the two accounts and their spatial settings are symmetrical: they represent two different ways of using the space of the Forum and dealing with social tensions.

The former narrative, which relates to the breakout of the patricio-plebeian conflict in 495 BCE, may be summarised as follows. One day, an elderly former centurion rushed into the Forum to lament his misfortunes before the

---

[75] On the creation of the patricio-plebeian *nobilitas* cf. e.g. Cornell (1995, pp. 340–344); Humm (2015).
[76] For attempts to reconstruct the historical facts concerning *nexum*, see e.g. Cornell (1995, pp. 265–268); Oakley (1998, pp. 688–691), with further bibliography.

crowd. He told them that, while he was away fighting the Sabines, the enemy had burnt his farm and plundered his fields, leaving him no choice but to take on debts to pay the tribute. When he could not repay his debts, he had to sell everything, first his house, then the rest of his goods, and finally, become a bondsman to his creditor. Outrage filled the plebs on seeing the old centurion's miserable state and the marks of floggings on his body. Unrest ensued, during which the crowd all but forced the Senate to meet and deliberate over the abolition of debt bondage. Precisely at that point, news reached Rome that the Volscians were moving against the city. The plebeians refused to take arms against the enemy: since the patricians were the only ones to reap the fruits of military victory, let them fight alone! Then the consul Publius Servilius spoke to the people, exhorting them to turn their minds to the common good, and decreed that no one should keep a Roman citizen willing to enrol in the army in chains. This changed the plebeians' minds: men, and *nexi* in particular, rushed *en masse* to enrol. The army defeated the enemy.

The Forum acts as an almost theatrical stage throughout the narrative. Its beginning coincides with the entrance of its main character into the Forum (2.23.3),[77] which is also the starting point and end point of the people's movement through the city (2.23.7–8):

> Non iam foro se tumultus tenet, sed passim totam urbem pervadit. 8. Nexi, vincti solutique, se undique in publicum proripiunt, implorant Quiritium fidem. Nullo loco deest seditionis voluntarius comes; multis passim agminibus per omnes vias cum clamore in forum curritur.
>
> The unrest no longer remained in the Forum but spread throughout the entire city. 8. The bondsmen, some in chains, some unchained, rushed everywhere into the open and pleaded for the Quirites' mercy. Nowhere was there a lack of willing participants in the rebellion; many throngs of people ran shouting through all the streets to the Forum.

In the Forum, the first spark is lit; from the Forum, the fire of revolt spreads to the rest of the city. The text here insists on the ubiquity of the uprising (*totam urbem*; *undique*; *nullo loco deest*). Eventually, however, the people return from the whole city (*per omnes vias*; *passim*) to the Forum. Such a double movement (from the Forum outward and from the city back to the Forum) sets the Forum as the centre of the city, of the events, and of the narrative.

---

77 *Magno natu quidam cum omnium malorum suorum insignibus se in forum proiecit.*

The Forum is also, of course, the space of communication between plebs and patricians, but such communication is strained from the very beginning. While political communication presupposes speakers and an audience ready to listen, at 2.23.9–11 the people express their protest with violence; later (2.23.12–13), they misinterpret the absence of most senators, who fear keeps away from Curia and Forum, and the behaviour of the consuls as stalling tactics. The space of the Forum bears the marks of such miscommunication. While normally the magistrates speak to the people from the speakers' platform or the stairs of the Senate House, the people now surround the Curia as if they were the leaders of public debate (2.23.11). It comes as no surprise that the senators themselves appear unable to agree upon a course of action, as the two consuls propose contrasting solutions for the crisis (2.23.13).

Even if the text does not explicitly state when the news of the Volscian attack arrives, the reader has the impression it happens while the senators are debating in the Curia (2.24.1). The reaction of the *patres* is described through metonymy (2.24.3):

> At vero curia, maesta ac trepida ancipiti metu et ab cive et ab hoste, Servilium consulem (...) orare, ut tantis circumventam terroribus expediret rem publicam.

> But the Curia, grim and anxious for the twofold fear which came both from the citizens and from the enemy, prayed (...) the consul Servilius to help the State as it was surrounded by so many terrors.

This particular metonymy is, of course, frequent in Latin literature.[78] However, its use in this context emphasises the close connection between the physical building and the political body it hosts. The physical Forum comes to represent the state: the plebs surround the Curia, just as the State is 'surrounded by terrors' (and might soon be surrounded by enemies).

Servilius' summoning of an assembly of the people (*in contionem prodit*, 2.24.4) restores political and spatial order. One can safely assume that the *contio* occurs in the Comitium and that Servilius goes out of the Curia to step onto the speakers' platform. Now a magistrate is directing the meeting of the people; this time, communication is successful. The episode ends with the plebeians rushing once more from the entire city to the Forum (*undique ex tota*

---

78 Cf. *TLL* 4, coll. 1484–1485. Cic. *De or.* 3.167 uses this metonymy as an example when explaining what metonymy (*traductio atque immutatio*) is (*ex quo genere haec sunt, ...* 'Cererem' pro frugibus ... 'curiam' pro senatu, etc.).

urbe ... proripientium se ex privato ... concursus in forum ... fieri, 2.24.7) – but, this time, to take the military oath.

The episode anticipates some crucial features of the representation of the Forum in the First and Second Pentads. Firstly, the Forum is where anything and everything important to the city's life converges, a space of strife and reconciliation. Secondly, the text uses Forum and Curia to represent the relationship between patricians and plebeians; successful communication involves the correct use of space, while the dysfunctional use of space epitomises miscommunication and violence.

The parallel episode at 8.28 brings out the same spatial patterns, but with significant changes in the communication dynamics. The story is set in 326 BCE, well after the Licinian-Sextian Laws (367 BCE) have sanctioned the plebeians' access to the consulship. The latter episode is the object of an extended and dramatic narrative in Book 6, befitting the main political turning point in the process of patricio-plebeian integration; it does not, however, mark the final act in the history of the plebeian struggles. The *Ab Urbe Condita*, instead, presents the shift from the duality of patricians and plebeians to the rule of the *nobilitas* as a gradual progression, made manifest in several steps.

The importance of the episode from Book 8 within the overall narrative design of Livy's work is signalled by its opening words (8.28.1):

> Eo anno plebi Romanae velut aliud initium libertatis factum est quod necti desierunt.
>
> In that year the freedom of the Roman plebs experienced, so to say, a second beginning, because they stopped being enslaved for debts.

Such an emphatic incipit hints, of course, at the initial tenor of Book 2, where the historian introduces his account of Republican history as 'the deeds of the free Roman people' (*Liberi ... populi Romani res ... gestas*, 2.1.1). While the fall of the kings is presented as an initial step towards freedom for all the Roman people, the abolition of *nexum* is the 'second beginning' for the plebs. The later statement at 8.28.1 reinforces the parallel between the establishment of the Republic and the abolition of *nexum*: the latter, Livy writes, occurred due to 'the notorious lust and cruelty of one creditor' (*ob unius feneratoris simul libidinem, simul crudelitatem insignem*).[79] The reader cannot but be reminded of the lust

---

79 Cf. 8.28.8 (*ob impotentem iniuriam unius*).

and cruelty of Tarquinius Superbus' son Sextus, whose rape of Lucretia brings about the fall of the monarchy (1.57–60).[80]

The story that follows is simple. A young man, Gaius Publilius, gives himself to his father's creditor, Lucius Papirius, in bondage (8.28.1). Instead of showing mercy in favour of Publilius' youth and beauty, Papirius first attempts to seduce him, then, when the young man refuses to give in, has him flogged (8.28.2–3). Publilius rushes into the streets to display his injuries; the people join him in indignation, go down to the Forum and the Curia, and all but force the consuls to convene the Senate (8.28.4–6). As soon as the senators enter the Curia, the people throw themselves at their feet and plead for mercy, showing the marks of flogging on Publilius' back (8.28.7). The Senate heeds their prayers and order the consuls to bring a bill for the abolition of debt bondage before the people; this marks the end of *nexum* (8.28.8–9).

As at 2.23–24 (the story about the beginning of the struggles in 494 BCE), the Forum is what I would like to call a 'meaningful setting' for the events. By this definition I mean a setting that resonates with the narrative's main themes and is fundamental to the narrative's meaning. The symmetry between the two narratives arises not only from their basic outline (mistreatment of a bondsman stirs the people's unrest), but also from the spatial dynamics at work and the vocabulary used to describe the events.

In both cases, an abused bondsman makes an ostentatious public display of his wounds (*magnus natu quidam ... se in forum proiecit*, 2.23.3; he is followed by other *nexi* who *in publicum proripiunt* at 2.23.8; *iuvenis cum se in publicum proripuisset*, 8.28.5). In both cases, the people, aroused by the sight, rush to the Forum (*multis passim agminibus per omnes vias cum clamore in forum curritur*, 2.23.8; *ingens vis hominum ... in forum atque inde agmine facto ad curiam concurrit*, 8.28.6–7). In both cases, the enraged people press the consuls to convene the Senate (*postulare multo minaciter magis quam suppliciter ut senatum vocarent* 2.23.11; *cum consules tumultu repentino coacti senatum vocarent*, 8.28.7).

At this point, however, an important difference between the two episodes emerges. At 2.23.11, the plebs threaten the consuls and surrounds the Curia as if to take control of Senate proceedings. At 8.28.7, on the other hand, the plebeians throw themselves at the senators' feet while these are entering the Curia (*introeuntibus in curiam patribus ... procumbentes ad singulorum pedes*). Similarly, at 2.23.12–15, the Senate cannot, at first, be summoned because of the *patres*' fears, and even after the Senate meeting begins, the senators

---

80   Cf. Chapter 4, pp. 201–202.

cannot find an agreement. Only an external threat brings temporary pacification (2.24.6–7). At 8.28.8–9, on the contrary, the senators reach their decision swiftly, moved – one seems to understand – by the plebeians' prayers.

Thus, while in Book 2 the struggles over *nexum* break out around a besieged Curia, in Book 8 the ending of the same struggles happens through the plebeians' movement toward the Curia – not in war, but in pleading.[81] What remains the same is the role of the Forum as the space where people go to express their discontent, and where strife is averted (temporarily, in Book 2; for good, in Book 8).

As I argue in what follows, the uses of the Forum space that characters undertake is crucial in Livy's representation of the Struggle of the Orders throughout the First Pentad and part of the Second.

3.2 Book 3: Disrupting the Forum

Book 3, a peak of Livy's artistry, can be read as a story of increasing strife leading to the near-implosion of the city and a partial (and temporary) recovery. As I intend to show in the following pages, it is also a story of the city space being subverted and partially recomposed.

Scholars have stressed the careful design of Book 3 as well as its prominent position within the First Pentad as a whole. The long and dramatic account of the Decemvirate of 451–449 BCE (3.33–58) is placed at the centre of both Book 3 and the Pentad, and in the chronological middle of Books 2–4, which contain events from 510 to 404 BCE.[82] Book 3 itself is then divided into three parts: 1) the struggles between patricians and plebeians over the Terentilian bill,[83] a proposal that a board of five be elected to regulate consular power (1–32); 2) the Decemvirate (33–58); 3) the aftermath of the Decemvirate, culminating in the great speech of Titus Quinctius Capitolinus (59–72). Speeches are important means for effecting structural symmetry within the book: in particular, as Vasaly (2002) shows, Capitolinus' speech, calling his fellow citizens to concord (3.67–68), is anticipated by the speech of another Quinctius, Cincinnatus, at 3.19.4–12. The Quinctii, two paradigms of the stern but just patrician leader,

---

81 In the account of the same events in Dion. Hal. *Ant. Rom.* 16.5.1–3, there is nothing comparable to the scene in the Senate house. After Publilius displays his wounds in the Forum and the people are filled with indignation, the tribunes prosecute the creditor, who is sentenced to death; Dionysius adds that a law for the abolition of *nexum* was passed. For other parallel sources and variants in the tradition, see Oakley (1998, pp. 688–691).

82 Cf. e.g. Ogilvie (1965, p. 390); Vasaly (2002, p. 278, p. 281).

83 The bill was named after Gaius Terentilius Harsa, the tribune of the plebs who was its first proponent in 462 BCE (3.9.2–5).

provide a counterpart to the character of the tyrannical Decemvir Appius Claudius, whose appalling behaviour brings about the fall of the Decemvirate.

Vasaly also points out that the whole First Pentad is built according to similar principles of symmetry and variation: Book 3 is connected to both Book 1 and Book 5 through the idea of the re-foundation of *libertas*, and the rebellion that overthrows the Decemvirs can be seen as a central refoundation, logically related to the two re-foundations of Book 1 (the establishment of the Republic) and 5 (the rebuilding of the city after the Gallic invasion). Or, perhaps, one might see the Decemvirate itself as a failed re-foundation of the city through the Decemviral laws, as opposed to the two successful foundations at the beginning (Romulus' founding of Rome) and the end (the rebuilding of the city).[84] Be that as it may, there is no doubt that the Decemvirate marks a crucial point in the development of Livy's archaic Rome; and the space of the city, and the Forum in particular, plays an essential role in Rome's (failed) re-foundation, just as it does in Book 1 and Book 5.

First, the narrative increasingly applies military imagery to the Forum. Such imagery is prominent, for example, in the account of the brawls over the Terentilian Bill and in the story of the young patrician Caeso Quinctius (3.11–13), who is represented in a way strongly reminiscent of the warriors of epic.[85] Secondly, the text repeatedly uses the duality of Forum and Curia to represent the fractures within the citizen body.

An example of this is the account of a slave uprising in 460 BCE (3.15.4–18.11). One night, as Livy writes, a host of slaves and exiles, led by a Sabine named Appius Herdonius, takes control of the Capitol and the *arx* (3.15.5). Turmoil in the city ensues and survivors from the assault rush down into the Forum to bring news of the attack (3.15.6). The scene is now firmly set in the Forum.[86] Confusion reigns during the night; the consuls are not even sure whether they are dealing with an external or an internal threat (3.15.7). Only the next morning do they realise who their enemy is (3.15.9). To make things worse, the tribunes of the plebs convince the people that the slave revolt is but a sham, which the patricians have instigated to prevent them from voting on the Terentilian bill; the people consequently refuse to answer the call to arms (3.15.8–16.6).

When news of this reaches the senators assembled in the Curia, the consul Publius Valerius rushes out into the adjacent Comitium (here referred to as *templum*, 3.17.1), where he rebukes the plebeians for their selfish behaviour.

---

84   In fact, the *Ab Urbe Condita* presents the Decemvirate, at 3.33.1, as a change in the form of government and compares it to the shift from Monarchy to Republic.
85   For a full analysis of such similarities see Fabrizi (2021b, pp. 256–270).
86   Cf. Fabrizi (2021b, p. 265).

The space of the Forum, which constitutes the setting for this scene, also works as a major prop for Valerius' rhetorical strategy. The consul starts by addressing the tribunes through a series of rhetorical questions (3.17.2):

> 'Quid hoc rei est', inquit, 'tribuni? Appi Herdoni ductu et auspicio rem publicam eversuri estis? Tam felix vobis corrumpendis fuit qui servitia non commovit auctor? Cum hostes supra caput sint, discedi ab armis legesque ferri placet?'

> 'What is this, tribunes?' he said. 'Are you going to subvert the state under the command and auspices of Appius Herdonius? Was he who did not stir the slaves so fortunate in corrupting you? While the enemies are upon our heads, do you want to avoid arms and vote on laws?'

Supra caput esse is an idiomatic expression that means 'to be upon someone, to be an imminent threat' (as such, it is used by other Roman authors).[87] In the episode we are considering, however, the enemies are literally 'above the heads' of the citizens assembled in the Forum – *viz.* on the Capitol, which Valerius and his listeners have before their eyes. Such a remark brings the physical reality of the threat – war penetrating the political and religious heart of the city – vividly and effectively before the audience's (and the reader's) eyes.

In the next sections (3.17.3–8), Valerius addresses the whole of the people assembled in the Comitium. In sections 3–4, he paints a dramatic scene of a city where none of the main elements of public space works as it should:

> Iuppiter optimus maximus, Iuno Regina et Minerva, alii di deaeque obsidentur; castra servorum publicos vestros penates tenent; haec vobis forma sanae civitatis videtur? 4. Tantum hostium non solum intra muros est sed in arce supra forum curiamque; comitia interim in foro sunt, senatus in curia est; velut cum otium superat, senator sententiam dicit, alii Quirites suffragium ineunt.

> Jupiter Optimus Maximus, Juno Regina and Minerva, and the other gods and goddesses are besieged; a camp of slaves holds your public *penates* captive; does this seem to you the image of a healthy community? 4. So many enemies are not just within the walls, but on the citadel, above the Forum and the Curia; meanwhile, assemblies take place in the Forum,

---

87   Cf. again Ogilvie (1965, p. 426).

the Senate is in the Curia; as when there is peace, the senator speaks his opinion and the other Quirites vote.

The speaker stresses the boundaries (the city walls) and the city's centre (the citadel and the Forum).[88] The Forum area is split into its main components, the Forum proper and the Curia, which function as discrete spaces without collaboration or communication between them. In its turn, the citadel lies *supra forum curiamque* ('above the Forum and the Senate House', an expression which somehow recalls *supra caput* in section 2). Here Valerius is pointing up to the Capitol and reminding his audience that the enemies are above them, yet the Roman citizens are doing nothing. At the same time, however, he also suggests that the citadel, the seat of Roman national cults, occupies a higher position than Forum and Curia (i.e. people and senate) in the ideal hierarchy that underpins civic life.

Valerius construes the Forum as the mirror and symbol of political relationships within the citizen-body by drawing attention to the space where his listeners stand. Instead of functioning as elements within a harmonious city model, the Curia and the open space of the Forum work as the seats of two distinct political communities, each going about its own affairs. Consequently, the order of the city space along the vertical axis is subverted, too, and the citadel itself can be conquered by enemies who come from the very 'bottom' of the social hierarchy.

The consul's fiery rhetoric produces no immediate effect. Indeed, things might have turned into a civil war had the night not put an end to the tribunes' and consuls' disagreement (3.17.9). Only the following morning do the plebeians finally agree to comply with their military duties. While Valerius is deploying his army in the Forum, a second army comes with help from the allied city of Tusculum; the allies march to the Forum and join the Romans in a victorious attack on the Capitol (3.18).

In the *Ab Urbe Condita* (as well as in other ancient historical narratives), speeches that have little effect on their internal audience are usually aimed at the external audience (i.e. the readers).[89] Thus, Valerius' speech, as ineffectual as it might be in appealing to the plebeians' sense of duty, fulfils an important narrative function: it puts the powerful image of a Forum torn apart by civil discord before the reader's eyes and thus represents the *forma civitatis* (the set of political relationships and tensions within the citizen community) through

---

88 This way of thinking of the city is frequent in the *Ab Urbe Condita*: cf. e.g. Jaeger (1997, p. 10).
89 Cf. e.g. Leidl (2010).

the medium of what one might call the *forma urbis* (the physical shape of the city). This is a fine example of Livy's telling history through space, that is, expressing abstract concepts concerning politics and society by embodying them in the material fabric of the city of Rome.

The disruption of the space of the Forum (and of the whole city) reaches one of its high points with the narrative of the Decemvirate (3.33–58). The events may be summarised as follows.

In 451 BCE, the people elect a board of ten patricians and plebeians who are charged with the writing of laws. The Decemvirs rule justly, are loved by the people, and produce ten tables containing laws by the end of their one-year term (33.1–6). Then, however, rumours spread that two more tables need to be added to complete the work, and the people elect a second board of Decemvirs for the next year. Using his demagogic campaign and irregular handling of the elections, Appius Claudius, the leading Decemvir, gets himself re-elected together with the men more favourable to him, all of them patricians (33.7–35.11). Now Appius reveals his true, tyrannical nature. The new Decemvirs rule without consulting the Senate, use violence against their fellow citizens and are especially cruel towards the plebeians (36–37). When their term of office is concluded, they refuse to give up power; the discontent of both the plebs and the majority of the *patres* only gets worse after two harsh military defeats (38–43). The final straw is Appius' attempted rape of the plebeian maiden Verginia, whose account is the climax of Livy's narrative. Using a staged trial, Appius adjudicates the girl to one of his clients as a slave, but before she can be brought away, Verginia's own father stabs her to death. The outraged plebeians revolt and, with the help of the Senate, overthrow the Decemvirs.[90]

Throughout this narrative, the Forum plays a crucial role as a setting for events and a symbol for the subversion of Republican legality caused by the Decemvirate. In the Forum, the second board of Decemvirs makes its formidable appearance on its first day of office, escorted by one hundred and twenty lictors (3.36.3–4).[91] Such an unusual number – twelve lictors for each Decemvir – signals the shift from legitimate rulers to tyrants. In the Forum, the Decemvirs parade surrounded by patrician youths, who 'besiege the tribunes' seats' (*eorum catervae tribunalia obsiderant*, 3.37.6), thus turning the heart of Roman space once more into a space of war. The Forum also loses its function

---

90   For a historical commentary on Livy's narrative, see Ogilvie (1965, pp. 451–454), who points out the fictitious nature of the account of the second Decemvirate.

91   The Decemvirs of the first board had taken turns in being accompanied by lictors: each of them enjoyed that mark of power every tenth day, this being the same day that he also administered justice (3.34.8).

as the space of public justice since the Decemvirs start holding private meetings to decide on the outcome of trials (*Iudicia domi conflabant, pronuntiabant in foro*, 3.36.8).

Two episodes, which, as I argue, one should read in parallel, epitomise the crisis in the Roman community in the image of an empty Forum. The first passage relates how the aggressions of the Sabines and Aequians forced the Decemvirs to summon the Senate. Livy describes the reaction of the plebeians as follows (3.38.8–11):

> 8. Postquam audita vox in foro est praeconis patres in curiam ad decemviros vocantis, velut nova res, quia intermiserant iam diu morem consulendi senatus, mirabundam plebem convertit quidnam incidisset cur ex tanto intervallo rem desuetam usurparent; 9. hostibus belloque gratiam habendam quod solitum quicquam liberae civitati fieret. Circumspectare omnibus fori partibus senatorem, raroque usquam noscitare; curiam inde ac solitudinem circa decemviros intueri, 10. cum et ipsi consensu invisum imperium, et plebs, quia privatis ius non esset vocandi senatum, non convenire patres interpretarentur; iam caput fieri libertatem repetentium, si se plebs comitem senatui det et quemadmodum patres vocati non coeant in senatum, sic plebs abnuat dilectum. Haec fremunt. 11. Patres haud fere quisquam in foro, in urbe rari erant. Indignitate rerum cesserant in agros, suarumque rerum erant amissa publica, tantum ab iniuria se abesse rati quantum a coetu congressuque impotentium dominorum se amovissent.

> 8. The herald's voice was heard in the Forum, summoning the senators to the Decemvirs in the Curia. This novelty – because they had long since stopped summoning the Senate – attracted the attention of the plebs. They wondered what on earth had happened to make the Decemvirs do something they were not used to anymore after such a long time. 9. One had to thank the enemies and the war if something happened that was normal for a free state! The plebeians looked for a senator throughout the Forum, but they seldom saw any in any place; then they looked at the Curia and the desert around the Decemvirs. 10. The latter understood that their own power was hated by everybody, and the plebs guessed that the senators did not answer the summons because private citizens did not have the right to summon the Senate. There was already an opportunity for those who wanted to take freedom back – they said –, if the plebs joined the Senate and refused to answer the levy, just as the senators did not assemble into the Senate. So did they murmur among

themselves. 11. Among the senators almost no one was in the Forum; few were in the city. They had retired to the countryside because of the indignity of the situation, and they were devoting themselves to their own affairs since the state was lost. They believed that they were the farther removed from violence the more they kept away from the company of those intemperate masters.

The Latin passage begins with a temporal sub-clause featuring a verb of perception in the impersonal form, *audita est*. The reader does not yet know who 'heard' the herald's voice,[92] but it soon becomes clear that the scene is focused on the plebeians. The adjective *mirabundam* (8), which refers to *plebem*, provides access to their thoughts and feelings. Section 9 starts with a sentence in *oratio obliqua* in which – as is often the case in the *Ab Urbe Condita* – it is not clear whether the words that plebeians exchange with one another or merely their thoughts are reported. With the verb *circumspectare*, followed by *noscitare* and *intueri*, attention is focused once more upon the Forum. Through the eyes of the plebeians, who observe the Forum and the adjacent places, the reader is granted an effective view of an almost empty Curia and of the Decemvirs alone in that desert. At that point, focalisation briefly shifts onto the tyrants themselves (10), only to return to the plebeians, whose reasonings are once again reported in *oratio obliqua*.

The vision of the empty Curia graphically conveys the idea of a state where political life has been emptied from the inside and, simultaneously, the idea of the Decemvirs' (spatial and political) isolation (*solitudo*).[93]

Embedded focalisation is essential here: the plebeians interpret as they watch, and the reader, too, shares in their interpretation. Such an interpretation contains some misunderstanding. The plebeians see the senators' absence from the Forum and the Curia as an act of rebellion. The shift in focalisation in section 11 proves them wrong: in fact, the senators have retired into their country estates out of fear of the Decemvirs. The plebeians cannot fully understand the implications of what they are seeing.

---

92   For this kind of passive construction cf. Introduction, p. 28.
93   As Ogilvie (1965, p. 467) notes, Livy's passage might be reminiscent of evens of 49 BCE (when 'Caesar was reluctant to call the Senate to secure authority for the prosecution of the war against Pompey … because of the large number of senators who had left the city and were either with Pompey or *in agris*') and in the 80's BCE (Rome empty during the civil war between Marius and Sulla).

STRIFE, RECONCILIATION, AND CHANGE IN THE FORUM ROMANUM   59

A similar vision of emptiness at the heart of Rome occurs later in the book, in the account of the revolt which follows Verginia's death. After the plebeians have left the city to occupy the Sacred Mount, the senators are left with an unusual spectacle (3.52.5–7):

> 5. Cum vasta Romae omnia insueta solitudo fecisset, in foro praeter paucos seniorum nemo esset, vocatis utique in senatum patribus desertum apparuisset forum, plures iam quam Horatius ac Valerius vociferabantur: 6. 'Quid expectabitis, patres conscripti? Si decemviri finem pertinaciae non faciunt, ruere ac deflagrare omnia passuri estis? Quod autem istud imperium est, decemviri, quod amplexi tenetis? Tectis ac parietibus iura dicturi estis? 7. Non pudet lictorum vestrorum maiorem prope numerum in foro conspici quam togatorum aliorum? Quid si hostes ad urbem veniant facturi estis? Quid si plebs mox, ubi parum secessione moveatur, armata veniat? Occasune urbis voltis finire imperium?'

> 5. As the emptiness had made a desert out of every place in Rome, as no one was in the Forum expect few elderly men, and the Forum had appeared deserted to the senators who had been summoned to the Senate, not only Horatius and Valerius, but a number of senators were already crying out: 6. 'What are you waiting for, senators? If the Decemvirs do not put an end to their own stubbornness, are you going to let everything collapse and burn? But what is this power that you hold so tight, Decemvirs? Are you going to administer justice to roofs and walls? 7. Are you not ashamed that one can almost see more of your lictors than of other toga-clad citizens in the Forum? What are you going to do if enemies come to the city? What, if the plebs come in arms, when little is achieved through secession? Do you want to end your power with the fall of the city?'

The symmetry between this passage and the previous one is evident. In chapter 38, the plebeians watch the empty Curia from the Forum; in chapter 52, the senators watch the empty Forum from the Curia. The noun *solitudo*, which recurs in both scenes, stresses their similarity. In both cases, the text displays the effects of a situation in which one part of the citizen body leaves the community. Such effects are portrayed through the eyes of the other party, which realises the impossibility of the State functioning without all its elements.

In sections 6–7, the direct speech of the senators emphasises the fundamental vulnerability of the tyrannical power of the Decemvirs – and, possibly, of any tyrannical power – which empties itself by emptying the space over which it is supposed to rule. Moreover, tyrannical power endangers the crucial distinction between the inner space of the city and outer military space. External enemies – the senators say – might attack Rome, or even the plebs might turn into an external enemy and come back in arms to attack the city.

Here, again, a partial misunderstanding seems to be at work. It is true that, at one point, the plebeians seem intentioned to take arms against Rome (3.50.11, 15), and the army that is stationed against the Sabines marches through the city in military array to reach the Aventine (3.51.10). Livy, however, emphasises that the plebeians avoided violence, just as their ancestors had done during the First Secession of 494 BCE (3.52.3). Indeed, the narrative stresses both the moderation of the Roman plebs and the openness of some patricians to the plebs' requests as the basis for the re-establishment of Republican legitimacy. Thus, the two symmetrical passages convey incommunicability between patricians and plebeians, who misunderstand each other's intentions and motives. At the same time, however, the dramatic events of the Decemvirate lead both patricians and plebeians to be aware that the State cannot properly function without the cooperation of its components.

Framed by these two visions of the empty Forum is the real climax of Livy's narrative of the Decemvirate, *viz.*, the tale of Verginia (3.44–49). The Forum is the setting for both Verginia's trial and her death; it plays a fundamental role in Livy's meditation on the nature of tyranny.

As Feldherr (1998, pp. 203–212) shows, Appius Claudius' attempted rape marks, among other things, a blurring of the boundary between public and private space, between the space of politics and the space of the home. This can be related to a recurring pattern in the *Ab Urbe Condita*, in which men who abuse their power violate the domestic space of other male citizens.[94] Verginia is, in Livy's account, an element or an extension of her father's home; by attempting to violate her, Appius Claudius is attempting to violate Verginius' private space – and thus his dignity as a freeborn citizen.[95] But one further aspect of the Decemvir's spatial subversion is that his assault on the Verginia's freedom takes place in the Forum: a young maiden whose place is her father's house is forcibly exposed in the Forum.

This endangers, once more, the fundamental distinction between internal and external space, between the space of the city and the space of war. In his accusatory speech during the trial of Appius Claudius, Verginius uses the space of the Forum to remind his audience of the Decemvir's crimes (3.57.2–4). In inviting them to look at Appius' *tribunal* (2), he reminds them of how the

---

[94] For a detailed treatment of Verginia's tale see Chapter 4, pp. 228–235.
[95] Cf. Joshel (1992, p. 122).

Decemvir took a freeborn girl away from her father 'as if she had been conquered in war' (*velut bello capta*, 3). Virginia receives the treatment that victors usually reserve for the conquered; her father, a centurion who normally fought against the enemies of Rome on the battlefield, had to take arms against his daughter (cf. 3.57.4, *dextram patris in filiam armaverit*).[96] The presence of military violence in the Forum parallels the Romans' inability to defeat their actual enemies (the Sabines and the Aequians) in battle under the Decemvirs' leadership (3.42.1–5).

Thus, Livy's narrative of the decemvirate portrays the tyranny of the Decemvirs as disrupting all the main spatial relationships on which the life of Rome rests. The space of collective decision-making is emptied, while actual decision-making happens in the private space of the Decemvirs' homes; senators leave the public space of the forum and Curia to follow their private concerns, and the plebeians leave the city; the plebeians might turn against the city and behave like external enemies; external enemies defeat the Romans; and the distinction between public and private space collapses.

The space of the Forum, in both its material and its symbolic dimensions, comes once more to the fore in the last major piece of Book 3, the speech by which the consul of 446 BCE, Titus Quinctius Capitolinus, addresses the plebeians who are once more refusing to fight against Aequians and Volscians. Scholars have stressed the importance of the speech as a retrospective view of the events narrated in Book 3 and, more generally, as a lesson in politics.[97] In Capitolinus' words, 'discord between the orders, the poison of this city' (*discordia ordinum et venenum urbis huius*, 3.67.6) is caused by the inability of patricians to set limits to their power and of plebeians to set limits to their freedom (*dum nec nobis imperii nec vobis libertatis est modus, ibid.*). Significantly, Capitolinus does not blame the plebs but recognises that each part of the citizen body must give up something for the greater good of the community.

Capitolinus uses the space of the city, and the space of the Forum in particular, to epitomise the effects of strife on the community.[98] Thus, for example, he casts the Forum as 'hostile' (*infestum*, 3.68.1) and the Curia as 'besieged' by the plebeians (*ubi hic curiam circumsederitis, ibid.*). Moreover, he argues that precisely the plebeians' unwillingness to fight against the external enemies, and willingness to fight in the Forum against the patricians, is endangering the very distinction between 'internal' and 'external' space so that the enemies themselves are now attacking the city (3.68.6–7). Capitolinus' speech, different

---

96 Cf. e.g. Joplin (1990, p. 67).
97 See e.g. Ogilvie (1965, pp. 516–517) and Vasaly (2015, pp. 86–91).
98 Cf. Fabrizi (2021b, pp. 267–269).

from Valerius' speech at 3.17, reaches the goal: the plebeians accept to fight, the citizen-body finds unity, and the enemies are beaten.

If Capitolinus' speech is a retrospective view of the events of the Struggle of the Orders till 446 BCE, it is also a retrospective interpretation of Roman space during that period. It depicts civic strife as endangering the spatial order of the city – indeed, her existence as one unitary city;[99] and it proposes a way in which that order can be reconstituted. In the next section, I focus on the specific spatial dynamics of reconciliation.

3.3 Reconciliation, Crisis, and Refoundation

While disconnection between the open Forum and the Curia functions as a physical embodiment of discord in the citizen-body, the *Ab Urbe Condita* represents the re-establishment of concord as the re-establishment of a connection between those two sites. Two accounts, one from the end of Book 4 and the other from the beginning of Book 5, are especially significant.

The first account relates to the Senate's decision to grant a *stipendium* to soldiers by drawing on the public treasury during the war against Veii (4.59.11–60.9; 406 BCE). The plebs reacts with joy and gratitude (4.60.1):

> Concursum itaque ad curiam esse prensatasque exeuntium manus et patres vere appellatos, effectum esse fatentibus ut nemo pro tam munifica patria, donec quicquam virium superesset, corpori aut sanguini suo parceret.

> Everyone ran to the Curia, clasped the hands of those who were going out and called them verily 'fathers'; it had been achieved, they declared, that no one would spare his own body or blood for so generous a fatherland, as long as he had any strength left.

In this short passage, the reconciliation between plebeians and senators is performed through the physical act of moving from the Forum to the entrance of the Curia, whence the *patres* come out into the Forum.

---

99 Cf. 3.67.3: *Qui finis erit discordiarum? ecquando unam urbem habere, ecquando communem hanc esse patriam licebit?* ('When will there be an end to strife? When will it ever be possible for us to have one city and for this to be our common fatherland?'). For the topos of the two cities in one cf. Ogilvie (1965, p. 509); Vasaly (2015, p. 89). Note, however, that Livy generally uses the noun *civitas* (community, State) in such cases (cf. *res publica* in Sall. [*Ad Caes. sen.*] 1.10.8), whereas Capitolinus speaks of one *urbs* (city) – thus laying a heavier stress up on the effects of strife on the material city. Dion. Hal. *Ant. Rom.* 6.36.1 and 6.88.1 also uses πόλις.

A more extensive account of a similar occurrence is found at 5.7, an episode related to the former in several ways. Due to the protracted siege of Veii, some senators propose that the Roman soldiers spend the winter in a camp near the city since the *stipendium* allows the plebeians to stay away for Rome over a longer period. The tribunes forcefully oppose the proposal, while Appius Claudius delivers a long speech in the Senate in favour. Amidst such tensions, news of a setback in Veii reaches Rome and fills the senators with foreboding.

At this point, some men who belong to the *census equester* but have not been assigned horses at public expense declare in the Senate that they will carry out their military service on their own horses.[100] Their decision elicits gratitude and relief from the senators. The news spreads through the city (*famaque ea forum et urbem pervasisset*, 5.7.6), and the plebeians rush *en masse* to the Curia. Now they are filled with the desire to match the knights' generosity: they promise they will serve as infantry and will not abandon their service until Veii be taken.

The senators are overwhelmed with joy (5.7.9–10):

> 9. non enim, sicut equites, dato magistratibus negotio laudari iussi, neque aut in curiam vocati quibus responsum daretur, aut limine curiae continebatur senatus; sed pro se quisque ex superiore loco ad multitudinem in comitio stantem voce manibusque significare publicam laetitiam.

> 9. The task of praising them was not left to the magistrates, as it had happened with the knights, nor were they called into the Curia, so that they could receive a reply, nor did the senators keep to the threshold of the Curia, but each one individually, with his voice and hands, expressed the common joy to the crowd standing in the Comitium from their higher ground.

The spatial structure that the text delineates is harmonious here. The senators go out of the Curia to address the people – one seems to understand – from the top of the stairs leading down to the Comitium. Their elevated position still sets them apart from the people standing below, but their movement toward the people mirrors that of the people toward the Curia. Thus, individuals from both spaces move toward each other instead of acting as two separate communities.

---

100   For the problems connected to this episode, see Ogilvie (1965, pp. 641–642).

Let it be noted that here, as well as in Book 3, Livy constructs two episodes as parallel. At 4.60.1, the plebs rush to the Curia in gratitude towards the senate; at 5.7.8–11, the senators rush from the Curia toward the Comitium in gratitude towards the plebs. The spatial structure and the characters' movement in the space represent the dynamics within the citizen body. Concord, Livy suggests, can be achieved when each part of the community steps towards the other, giving up some of its resources for the well-being of the State.

Such harmony, of course, does not last long. The remaining part of Book 5 relates Rome's first great crisis, the Gallic sack, which Livy depicts as the consequence of internal discord and neglect of duties toward gods and men. Only at the end of the book will the Romans be able to drive the enemy away and rebuild the city, thanks to Marcus Furius Camillus' intervention.

The re-establishment of the Roman spatial order is sanctioned by a great speech that Camillus delivers in the Comitium (5.51–54).[101] Camillus speaks forcefully against the tribunes' proposal to leave Rome, destroyed by the Gauls, and move to the conquered city of Veii. His main point is that the physical sites of the city of Rome are inextricably bound up with Roman religion; it would not be possible to carry out the most important religious ceremonies in a different environment. Moreover, people become naturally attached to where they were born and raised.

Throughout his speech, Camillus mentions several sites hallowed by Roman religious tradition and the main physical features that define the city's image. Interestingly, however, he does not mention the Forum, apart from a cursory (and implicit) remark on the space reserved for the *comitia curiata* (5.52.16). This is certainly not because the Forum is unimportant. In fact, there is no need to mention the Forum explicitly because the importance of the Forum is implicit in the narrative. The Forum is not only the place in which Camillus speaks and in which plebs and senate come together for the occasion (*in contionem universo senatu prosequente escendit*, 5.50.8), but is the standpoint, both physical and ideal, from which the citizens of Rome look at the city and the world.

Moreover, the Forum is the space in which the gods sanction the refoundation of the city, and plebs and *patres* once more reunite after their long struggles. After Camillus' speech, an omen decides the matter once and for all (5.55.1–2):

---

101 For detailed analyses of Camillus' speech see e.g. Ogilvie (1965, pp. 541–543, and notes *ad loc.*); Edwards (1996, pp. 44–68).

1. (...) cum senatus post paulo de his rebus in curia Hostilia haberetur cohortesque ex praesidiis revertentes forte agmine forum transirent, centurio in comitio exclamavit: 2. 'Signifer, statue signum; hic manebimus optime'. Qua voce audita, et senatus accipere se omen ex curia egressus conclamavit et plebs circumfusa adprobavit.

1. (...) As shortly afterwards the Senate was deliberating over these issues in the Curia Hostilia and some cohorts, which were returning from their patrol duty, happened by chance to march through the Forum, a centurion cried out in the Comitium: 2. 'Standard-bearer, fix the standard! We will stay here as is best'. As this sentence was heard, the Senate went out of the Curia and cried that they accepted the omen, and the plebs, thronging all around them, confirmed it.

The omen, which manifests in the Comitium while the Senate debates in the Curia, brings about one last converging movement from the Curia to the Forum and from the Forum to the Curia. Significantly, this is one of only three occurrences in the surviving *Ab Urbe Condita* in which the Curia Hostilia is mentioned with its full name,[102] and one of the few in which the Comitium is designated as such. This cannot be by chance in a narrative where topography plays such a crucial role: the names of the time-honoured Curia and Comitium add solemnity to the final act of collective reconciliation marking the city's rebirth.

3.4 *Shifting Boundaries*

The shift of Roman politics from the duality of patricians and plebs to the leadership of the patricio-plebeian *nobilitas* is a major thread within the Second Pentad. At the same time, a gradual shift in emphasis occurs concerning the representation of the Forum in Books 1–6.

First, while most events are still set in the Forum and the Curia, the latter becomes slightly more prominent. Compared to the First Pentad, one finds fewer collective scenes in the Forum or the Comitium and more debates or embassies in the Senate. Secondly, and perhaps most importantly, Forum and Curia function more often as implicit rather than explicit settings. While events such as public speeches are logically set in the Forum, the kind of semantic highlighting of the setting which is frequent in the First Pentad is, in many cases, missing.

---

102   Cf. Jaeger (2015, pp. 72–73).

This does not mean, of course, that episodes in which the Forum fulfils a symbolic function are totally absent from this section of the work. An exemplary case is the narrative about the abolition of debt bondage at 8.28, which I have examined in section 3.1. Another one is the account of the sedition of Marcus Manlius Capitolinus, a patrician and the former hero of the resistance against the Gauls turned demagogue, in Book 6.[103]

The narrative stretches through 6.11–20, with interruptions where Livy inserts sequences about external events. Military imagery recurs repeatedly throughout.[104] At 6.15.2, for example, Manlius, on hearing he has been summoned by the dictator Aulus Cornelius Cossus, '[gives] his men the sign of the impending fight and then [goes] to the *tribunal* with a great army' of supporters (*cum signum suis dedisset adesse certamen, agmine ingenti ad tribunal venit*). In the preceding section (6.15.1), the dictator is said to have placed his curule chair *in comitio* – one of the few occurrences of that substantive to designate the assembly place. The scene is thus set, and it looks more like a battlefield than a place for political debate (6.15.3): 'On one side the senate, on the other the plebs had arrayed as for battle, each looking at their own commander' (*Hinc senatus, hinc plebs, suum quisque intuentes ducem, velut in acie constiterant*). The Comitium works as the meeting point of the two opposing armies, which come from the Curia and the Forum's open space, respectively.

The presence of such a striking scene is no accident if one considers that the story of Manlius Capitolinus is one of the last major episodes in the Struggle of the Orders. Manlius is a patrician who courts the favour of the plebs in his attempt to overthrow the Republican government; and he stirs the plebs against the *patres* in a way not dissimilar from the demagogic tribunes of the previous books. Thus, the first dramatic scene of his story re-activates that set of ideas that the reader is by now accustomed to from the First Pentad: conflict between patricians and plebs brings war into the very heart of the State and the physical fabric of the city.

The rest of the narrative, however, emphasises different ideas. While the episode of Manlius Capitolinus recalls the civil discords of the previous books, it

---

103   The bibliography on the story of Manlius Capitolinus is vast. Scholars have discussed the several problems connected with the historical reconstruction of the events, the different versions emerging from the sources, and the literary aspects of ancient narratives of it (Livy's first of all). See e.g. Gagé (1953); Seager (1997); Wiseman (1979b); Jaeger (1997, 57–9); Oakley (1997, pp. 476–493); Chassignet (2001); Smith (2006); Kaplow (2012); Krebs (2012); Neel (2015); Meunier (2019, with further bibliography). For other ancient accounts of Manlius' story see Diod. Sic. 15.35.3; Plut. *Vit. Cam.* 36.1–9; Gell. *NA* 17.21.24; Zonar. 7.23.1. I provide a fuller analysis of the episode in Chapter 2, pp. 106–111.

104   Cf. Krebs (2012, pp. 148–149).

also marks a shift in Roman politics and in how the narrative constructs space. Manlius is the first patrician to act as a champion of the plebs in an attempt to win tyrannical power. This introduces complexity in a political system that the First Pentad represents as fundamentally based on a duality. Similarly, while most of the plebs support Manlius, the tribunes of the plebs ally themselves with the Senate: their role in Manlius' downfall is decisive because they act as prosecutors in the trial that results in his execution (6.19.6–7). Thus, rather than staging a clear-cut opposition between patricians and plebs, the narrative shows different groups and interests at work within Roman society and, in so doing, anticipates the dangers posed by the ambition of powerful aristocrats later in Roman history.

A consequence of such a shift in the boundaries between different sociopolitical groups is the different spatial semantics that govern the rest of the tale about Manlius. As I shall show in Chapter 2, the narrative does not so much emphasise spatial fractures in the Forum, but rather works with the metaphor of verticality as embodied by the Capitol.[105]

In other cases, however, the new debates animating Roman society find expression in the semantic laden role of the Forum. I shall only consider two examples here.

The first is the narrative of the dispute between Papirius Cursor and Fabius Rullianus at 8.30–36.[106] In 325 BCE, Livy writes, the dictator Lucius Papirius Cursor came very close to executing his young *magister equitum* (second-in-command) Fabius Rullianus, who had successfully engaged in battle against the Samnites in his absence and against his orders. The first part of the episode (8.30.1–33.2) mostly occurs in the Roman camp in Samnium. In the narrative's second half (8.33.3–36.9), however, the contention moves to Rome – more precisely, to the Curia and the Comitium.

Fabius flees to the city at night and convenes the Senate the following morning with the support of his father, Marcus Fabius, a former consul and dictator. While the young Fabius is lamenting the dictator's cruelty in front of the Senate, Papirius enters the Curia (8.33.4). Although the whole senate implores him to spare Fabius, the dictator does not change his mind. Then Fabius' father appeals to the people, and the scene moves from the Curia to the Comitium (*Ex curia in contionem itur*, 8.33.9). Both Papirius and Fabius, who are escorted by an *agmen principum*, make their way to the Rostra, but the dictator has Fabius removed from there; nonetheless, the elder Fabius goes on to address

---

105 See again Chapter 2, pp. 106–111.
106 For analyses of this famous episode cf. Chaplin (2000, pp. 106–136); Oakley (1998, pp. 704–707).

the people from a lower place (8.33.9–22).[107] Papirius also delivers a speech in which he restates his intention to punish Fabius' breach of military discipline (8.34.2–11). Then the people turn from rebellion to prayer, and the two Fabii follow suit, falling on their knees and imploring the dictator's mercy (8.35.1–3). Then, at last, Papirius pardons the young Fabius for the sake of the people: now that the *magister equitum* has admitted his mistake, discipline is restored, and an act of clemency becomes possible (8.35.1–8). The scene ends with Papirius leaving the Rostra (*degressum ... templo*), followed by the rejoicing people and Senate, who congratulate him and Fabius (8.35.9).

Throughout this episode, the reader is invited to imagine the Rostra as a dramatic stage where the two opposing sides clash and eventually reconcile. Once more, the Comitium functions, following the etymology of its name, as the place where opposing groups 'come together' and learn important lessons about communal life. Here, as in similar episodes from the earlier books, each opponent must renounce part of his pride so that both can live in some sort of harmony. Fabius, the young man who calls for a relenting of old discipline, must first admit his trespass to be forgiven; and Papirius, the old dictator acting as a defender of tradition, contents himself with reasserting the value of discipline and gives up punishment.

While in this narrative the contention to be solved in the Forum is between the young and the old, or between traditional severity and modern flexibility, the second episode I shall consider brings us back into the realm of social tensions and enriches the tie between Forum and plebs with new connotations. In Book 9, Livy vividly sketches the character of Gnaeus Flavius, a former scribe and a freedman of Appius Claudius Caecus, who became curule aedile in 304 BCE.[108] As the historian reports, the election of one of such humble origins raised strong opposition in the *nobiles* (likely, both patrician and plebeian); so did Flavius' actions as an aedile (9.46.1–7). He was responsible for publishing the formulae used in judicial proceedings (*ius civile*) and the official calendar of *dies fasti* and *nefasti* – previously known only to the (all patrician) pontifices.

As Livy writes, Flavius had been elected by the *forensis factio* (9.46.10), 'the faction of the Forum', namely, the urban plebs that supported Appius Claudius. The latter had redistributed the humblest citizens among all the tribes, so their

---

107 The elder Fabius comments: *bene agis (...) cum eo nos deduci iussisti unde et privati vocem mittere possemus* (8.33.10). For the possible meaning of these words cf. Oakley (1998, p. 731).

108 On Flavius's historical figure and his relationship with Appius Claudius see e.g. Wolf (1980); D'Ippolito (1986, pp. 1–67); Loreto (1991); Forsythe (1994, pp. 339–347); Cornell (1995, pp. 374–375); Purcell (2001, pp. 635–637).

political weight in the comitia increased (9.46.11). 'From that point', the historian goes on to write in section 13, 'the citizen-community was divided into two factions (*in duas partes discessit civitas*): one was made up of the honest people, who supported and respected the best citizens (*integer populus, fautor et cultor bonorum*), the other of the Forum faction' (*forensis factio*, again). The problem was solved (from Livy's point of view) when the censor Quintus Fabius moved all the humblest citizens, the 'crowd of the Forum' (*forensem turbam*, 9.46.14), into four urban tribes; he did this, in the historian's view, both 'for concord's sake' (*concordiae gratia*) and to avoid the humblest citizens taking control of the comitia.

The influence of late Republican political discourse appears strong here. The idea of the *civitas* being divided into two parts or factions is common in authors from the 1st century BCE (and of course Livy's own portrayal of the duality of patricians and plebs in early Roman history resonates with those discourses).[109] Parallels with Cicero's definition of *populares* and *optimates* at Pro Sestio 45 are especially significant. Cicero speaks of 'two categories' (*duo genera*) of people engaged in politics in the citizen-community (*in hac civitate*). He defines the people who stand for conservation of the social order as *optimates*, since they strive for the approval of 'all the best' (*optimo cuique*). The superlative is in line with Cicero's frequent use of the substantivized adjective *boni* to designate 'the honest, decent people' (that is, people of conservative views).[110] Similarly, Livy's *integer populus* is the *fautor et cultor bonorum*; note that Cicero's *optimates* are also defined as *integri* in the same chapter of the Pro Sestio.[111]

In such a context, the adjective *forensis*, which occurs three times at Livy 9.46 in conjunction with either *factio* or *turba*, appears significant. While the adjective is frequent enough in Latin literature with the meanings of 'related to the Forum', 'common', or 'popular', it does not usually entail the pejorative nuance it possesses in this chapter of the *Ab Urbe Condita*.[112] Livy himself uses it only once more in the surviving books and with a neutral meaning.[113] We do not know if the historian drew the syntagm *forensis factio/turba* from one of his predecessors, let alone from which one, although it is certain that he used

---

109   For parallels cf. above, p. 62 n. 99.
110   Examples in Oakley (2005a, p. 641).
111   For other occurrences of *integer* in a similar meaning in Latin authors, cf. Oakley (2005a, pp. 640–641).
112   Cf. *TLL* 6.1, coll. 1052–1054.
113   At 33.47.10 it relates to *vestitus* and indicates civilian (as opposed to military) attire.

the annalists Piso and Licinius Macer as sources for Gnaeus Flavius' career.[114] However that may be, the repeated use of the adjective at 9.46 once more suggests the importance of location in political struggles.

Spatiality, in fact, looms large in the whole chapter. In sections 10–11, for example, Livy writes that Appius Claudius first tried to co-opt the sons of freedmen into the Senate, but since nobody ratified his act, and he thus did not achieve the influence he hoped for within the Curia (*in curia*), he polluted the Forum and Campus Martius through his enrolment of the humble into all the tribes (*humilibus per omnes tribus divisis forum et campum corrupit*). The three toponyms are, of course, metonymic for the Senate, the *comitia tributa*, and the *comitia centuriata* respectively. Through such metonymies, the text stresses the tie between political activity and specific sites within the city. In particular, the remark about the polluted Forum echoes the emphasis placed on the *forensis factio/turba* as a new negative element in Roman public debate.

The importance of space in this account also emerges in the mention of Gnaeus Flavius' controversial dedication of a shrine to Concordia in the *area Volcani* ('area of Vulcan') in the Comitium (9.46.6). Livy's only states that Flavius dedicated the temple 'with the *nobiles*' opposition' and that the people had to force the *pontifex maximus* Cornelius Barbatus to recite the ritual formulae for the dedication, after he had protested that only a consul or an *imperator* could dedicate a temple (9.46.6). We have some background from Pliny the Elder (32.19): Flavius had vowed to build a temple to Concordia if he should reconcile the people with the *nobilitas* and the equestrian order; when he failed to receive the necessary funding, he had a bronze shrine (*aediculam aeream*) to Concordia built in the Graecostasis from fines paid by moneylenders.

The story about the temple, which Livy presents as part of a larger contention within Roman society, will have reminded any Roman reader of the *Ab Urbe Condita* of another controversial dedication to Concordia, that of Opimius in 121 BCE. The two foundations were probably close to one another: Opimius' temple (later restored by Augustus and Tiberius) at the foot of the Capitol, Flavius's *aedicula* in the Comitium. Most importantly, in both cases the dedication to Concord actually sanctioned the victory of one faction over the other. Livy's text plays on the ambiguity of the notion of concord when, at 9.46.14, it reports Quintus Fabius' reform of the tribes as occurring *concordiae causa*; this time, the *nobiles*' view of concord proves victorious.

---

114   Livy quotes Macer at 9.46.3 about a variant version of the tale. For Piso's account of Gnaeus Flavius' career cf. Gell. *NA* 7.9.1–6 = *FRHist.* 27 F 24. Similarity in wording suggests Livy drew on him in this narrative (cf. Oakley, 2005a, pp. 603–606).

Once more, then, the text of 9.46 uses a location within the Forum (the shrine of Concordia) to activate more recent memories, and to anticipate some features of Late-Republican politics. Overall, the narrative of Flavius' career and controversial acts suggests that the impact of political tensions in the Forum has changed. There is no longer a well-defined opposition between patricians and plebs; there is, instead, a duality of 'the honest people' (patrician and plebeian both) who support the new *nobilitas* and the lower urban plebs championed by the patrician Claudius. The Forum, however, retains both its connection with the humblest and, from the narrator's point of view, most dangerous population strata and its function as the terrain for the difficult negotiation of concord between competing elements of Roman society.

4 Forum and Curia in an Expanding World

As Livy's account proceeds towards the historian's own time and its geographical scope broadens, events in the city alternate with increasingly long sections that feature events abroad. Yet the city, and especially the area of Forum, Curia, and Capitol, remains, throughout the *Ab Urbe Condita*, the clear centre of the narrated world.

While the open space of the Forum gradually loses its predominance as a setting, it continues to be crucial in the mental model of the city of Rome throughout the *Ab urbe Condita*. First, the Forum is, even after Book 10, one of the main seats of political activity. The *Ab Urbe Condita* contains countless accounts of institutional proceedings – voting in the *comitia tributa* for the passing of laws, speeches to the people, and levies; and one should not forget that triumphal processions (many of which appear in the *Ab Urbe Condita*) passed through the Forum before reaching their destination on the Capitol. Livy briefly mentions many such occurrences while developing others into full-fledged scenes – sometimes, into major episodes. In most cases, the Forum-setting remains implicit; in some, however, the narrator mentions the Forum explicitly (and occasionally with emphasis) as the location for certain events.[115]

---

115   Occurrences of this kind are so frequent that an exhaustive list would by far exceed the purposes of this book. Here I give some examples of narratives of institutional proceedings set in the Forum from Books 21–45: 23.23; 25.4.7–11; 34.56.3–5; 38.58.3–59.11; 42.32.5–35.2 (a long narrative, which includes a levy, the ensuing debate, and the speech of the centurion Spurius Ligustinus); 44.22.

In addition, the Forum retains its crucial function as the place where the Roman people fight and reconcile and where they negotiate their identity as a people. While, in the First Pentad and occasionally in the Second, the focus is on strife and reconciliation between patricians and plebeians, in the later books, the groups that communicate, fight, and reconcile in the Forum are now of a different sort.

Some of these episodes receive detailed analysis in Chapter 4. The account of the Bacchanalian scandal, for example, sets the well-ordered space of the city against an alternative space of chaos that threatens to subvert the political order. Significantly, the culminating scene of the whole narrative – the consul Postumius' speech to the Roman people after the unveiling of the conspiracy – takes place in the Forum and on the Rostra.[116] In the story about the Oppian Law, which I also mention in Chapter 4,[117] the Forum and its entrances work as a public or semi-public space in opposition to the private space of the house. They are thus crucial in representing the politics of gender.

Let me here discuss one further example, namely the narrative of Scipio Africanus' trial in Book 38. In this analysis I shall not be delving into the many historical problems raised by Livy's treatment of the trials of the Scipio brothers, which is notorious for its inconsistency and conflation of alternative traditions.[118] Rather, I will focus on the first version of Africanus' trial, which Livy reports at 38.50.5–53.11.

The historian relates how two tribunes of the plebs, named Petillii, summoned Scipio Africanus to trial (38.50.4–51.5) with the allegation of embezzling the war indemnity paid by King Antiochus, of being corrupted by the king himself, and of yielding unlimited power when acting as a *legatus* to his brother Lucius in the Syrian War.[119] On the day of the trial Scipio, rather than

---

116   See Chapter 4, pp. 235–241.
117   See Chapter 4, pp. 218–219.
118   For a long time, the account was held up as an example of Livy's unsatisfactory working methods. See the opinions discussed by Luce (1977, pp. 90–104 and esp. p. 96 n. 35). Luce, on his part, gives credit to Livy for consulting and comparing different sources, and interprets the peculiar structure of the text as the result of Livy's need to provide a main, consistent narrative, while at the same time mentioning the existence of alternate traditions. More recently, some scholars have interpreted such a conflation of contradictory traditions as a conscious choice on Livy's part and as a meditation on the impossibility of attaining certainty (Jaeger, 1997, pp. 132–176) or as an act of self-positioning in the historiographical tradition (Haimson-Lushkov, 2010).
119   38.51.1–2. Livy gives the first allegation as *pecuniae captae* (1), a term which might be anachronistic (see Adam, 1982, 190 n. 3). In McDonald's (1938, p. 163) words, 'the five hundred talents of indemnity paid to the Scipios had been treated as booty, which could be handled by the general, whereas it was strictly public money, for which account should

defending himself, delivered a speech in which he recalled his victory over the Carthaginians on that very same day years earlier and led the people in a procession first to the temple of Capitoline Jupiter, then to all the temples in the city, to give thanks to the gods (51.6–14). The trial was adjourned, and Scipio took this chance to leave Rome and settle at Liternum. When the tribunes summoned him to Rome again, he claimed he could not appear due to his poor health. The Petillii did not intend to accept his excuse, but another tribune, Tiberius Sempronius Gracchus, spoke in his defence; in the end, the Petillii withdrew their accusations (52.1–53.7). Scipio spent the last part of his life in Liternum and died sometime later (53.8–11).

The climax of this account is the scene in which Scipio leads the people to the Capitol to give thanks (51.5–14). Consistent with his overall representation in the *Ab Urbe Condita*, Scipio proves himself a master of public spectacle: through his well-staged performance of victory,[120] he implicitly claims that his extraordinary achievements dispense him from the need to give account for his behaviour as a commander. Hence, this episode brings out all the complexities of Livy's Scipio, whose magnanimity and charisma are counterbalanced by dangerous personal ambition.[121]

As Jaeger (1997, pp. 147–153) points out, the narrative centres on the Rostra and the Capitol and the spatial relationship between the two. The tribunes are on the Rostra (*tribuni in rostris prima luce consederunt*, 5) when Scipio enters the Forum and, passing through the assembly, he reaches the foot of the Rostra (*per mediam contionem ad Rostra subiit*, 6). There he invites the Roman people to follow him to the Capitol to celebrate the anniversary of his victory against Carthage (6–11). Then Scipio 'went up from the Rostra to the Capitol' (*Ab rostris in Capitolium escendit*, 12), followed by the entire assembly; in the end, nobody but their slaves remains with the tribunes and the herald, who 'was summoning the defendant from the Rostra' (*reum ex rostris citabat, ibid.*). Livy adds that Scipio 'went over all the temples of the gods together with the Roman people, not only on the Capitol but across the whole city' (13).

The heavy emphasis the text places on Rostra and Capitol makes it clear that their role is not merely locational but symbolic: what is at stake here is two competing notions of urban space. The tribunes' notion centres on the

---

have been given through the quaestor to the *aerarium*'. The allegation of corruption rested above all on Antiochus' restitution of Scipio's son without ransom (cf. Livy 37.36).
120 For recent studies on performance as an integral element of Roman political culture, cf. e.g. Bell (2004); Hölkeskamp (2011 and 2023); Luke (2014). For performance in Roman historiography, e.g. Feldherr (1998); Pelikan Pittenger (2008); O' Gorman (2023).
121 On Livy's ambiguous characterisation of Scipio see e.g. Rossi (2004); Levene (2010, pp. 231–235); de Franchis (2013); Beltramini and Rocco (2020); Beltramini (2023).

Rostra and interprets Scipio's procession to the Capitol as either a triumph over the Roman people or a secession; Scipio's notion centres on the Capitol as the core of both Rome and the world and as the symbol of the gods' power and the community's concord. Of course, these spatial models imply two competing views of authority within the city. The tribunes think of a community in which nobody is allowed to 'tower upon' others (cf. Livy 38.50.6–9 and 51.3–4), Scipio sees himself as the centre of authority, just as the Capitol (a height) is the centre of Roman space. To quote Jaeger (1997, p. 151), 'the narrative links Africanus' ability to create concord among citizens to his leading them away from the centre of civic power to the centre of aristocratic and divine power instead'. The Capitol is also closely associated with Scipio's personal authority; as Livy writes in 26.19.4–5, Scipio spent time in the temple of Jupiter Optimus Maximus before beginning any important enterprise and often presented his actions as inspired by the gods.

At this point there is something worth noting. While in the other accounts I have examined throughout this chapter, reconciliation between opposing factions takes place in the Forum, Scipio unites the people by taking them away from the Forum. However, Scipio's re-establishment of concord proves illusory; in the end, the trial resumes, and the great man dies as if exiled from Rome. In other words, this narrative suggests that the Forum is where fractures must be mended. Attempts to deal with conflict in different ways – and in different spaces – are problematic. Just as problematic is the growing power of great individuals – even one with as many positive qualities as Scipio. Even though the account of the trial presents Africanus in an overall favourable light, it also highlights the ambiguity of his authority. Once more, a character's use of the city space reveals a great deal about his positioning himself within the community.

Until now, I have examined the role of the open space of the Forum in the Third, Fourth and Fifth Decades of the *Ab Urbe Condita*. But what about that other focal point of the narrative, central to the early books – the Curia?

While in the First and, to a lesser degree, the Second Pentads, the Curia is, above all, the material embodiment of the patrician order, in the later Decades, this building gradually becomes the real centre of events and the most frequent setting within the city, thus reflecting the increasing importance of the Senate in Roman politics during the Middle Republic. The *Ab Urbe Condita* reports many senatorial debates and deliberations, some only cursorily sketched, others as fully-fledged scenes and including extended speeches or pairs of speeches. The Curia is also where events from various theatres of war are reported and discussed, and senators make choices that will affect various areas of the world.

And yet, this space of deliberation remains, in most cases, an implicit setting with its physical features never mentioned by the narrator or the characters that appear there. Indeed, the text often provides no clue as to whether a Senate meeting occurred in the Curia Hostilia or another building. As mentioned above (pp. 46–47), the noun *curia* could apply to any place where the Senate met; often, even that noun is absent from the narrative. However, as I also showed above, the way the narrative talks about Senate meetings leads the reader to think of them as taking place in the Curia Hostilia when no other location is explicitly stated – with the obvious exception of the first meeting of each year, which took place on the Capitol, and of meetings concerning the awarding of triumphs, which had to be convened outside the *pomerium*.

As a result, the Curia, as a physical space, appears less significant to this part of Livy's history than the 'Senate' as an underdefined and omnipresent 'place'. And yet, the space in and around the Curia occasionally takes on a more direct symbolic role. One significant instance is the account of the Rhodian embassy in 167 BCE (45.20.4–25.6).

Book 45 is devoted to the aftermath of the Roman victory against King Perseus of Macedon, beginning with the announcement of the news in Rome and culminating in Aemilius Paullus' triumph. Among other things, it reports the embassies of various foreign kings and states, which offer the reader a vivid representation of the impact of Rome's success throughout the world. The account of the Rhodian embassy of 167 BCE, which had the goal of avoiding the Roman retaliation against the Rhodians' ambiguous conduct during the Macedonian War, is the longest and most dramatic one, including a long speech in *oratio recta* by a Rhodian envoy.[122] What is especially relevant to the present discussion is the role that the city space, especially the Curia and the Comitium, plays in the episode.

When the Rhodians arrive in the Comitium (*viz.* in the *Graecostasis*, the section of the Comitium reserved for foreign envoys)[123] and ask to be received in the Curia, the Senate denies their request on the grounds that the Rhodians cannot be considered allies of the Roman people (45.20.4–9). During the next few days, however, the Rhodians visit the homes of the most prominent citizens dressed as suppliants (20.10). Meanwhile, the praetor Marcus Iuventius Thalna urges the people to declare war on Rhodes, but two tribunes of the plebs oppose his initiative (21.1–8). At this point, a lacuna occurs, but the lost

---

122 The historian seems to have 'combined material from Polybius, Cato and his usual annalistic sources, while the speech of the Rhodian envoy, partly or wholly, is almost certainly his own composition' (Briscoe, 2012, p. 669).
123 Cf. Briscoe (2012, p. 670).

text must have reported that the Rhodians were finally given an audience because the account resumes with the direct speech of a Rhodian envoy in the Senate.

Although its beginning is lost, the speech is the longest one in the surviving books of the Fifth Decade. As suggested by Briscoe (2012, p. 672), this might serve the purpose of characterisation, stressing the speaker's 'Asiatic loquacity', or it might compensate for Livy's omission of Cato's famous speech in defence of the Rhodians, which the Censor pronounced during the ensuing senatorial debate and then included in his *Origines*.[124]

The beginning of the transmitted speech laments the Rhodians' fall from grace by directly referring to Rome's city space (45.22.1–2). More to the point, the Rhodians depict their relationship with the Romans in terms of their access to Roman space. The passage is divided into two parallel sentences, describing the Rhodians' movement within the city as it used to be (*antea*) and now (*nunc*). When they enjoyed Roman favour, they set out from the accommodation they obtained at public expenses (*ex publico hospitio*) to go first to the Curia to congratulate the Senate (*in curiam gratulatum*), then from the Curia to the Capitol, to bring gifts to the gods (*ex curia in Capitolium ad deos vestros dona ferentes*). In other words, they had access to the two places that embodied Roman power over the world: the seat of political decision-making and that of the national cults. Now, on the other hand, they leave their squalid accommodation (*ex sordido deversorio*), which is not even within the city (i.e. outside the *pomerium*), as is the norm with enemies of Rome. And, while they eventually get into the Curia (*venimus in curiam Romanam*), they do so dressed as suppliants (*in hoc squalore*) and there is certainly no chance of their being admitted to the Capitol.

At the end of their long speech, the Rhodians once more stress the importance of spatiality in their relationship with Rome. If the Senate perseveres in its wrath – they announce – they will first go back to their city to report the bad news (*hanc funestam legationem domum referamus*, 45.24.11); then they will transport the whole Rhodian population and their riches to Rome by ship, leaving the tutelary gods of their homes and fatherland behind (*relictis penatibus publicis privatisque Romam veniemus*, 45.24.12). In Rome they will amass all their public and private goods 'in the Comitium, in the vestibule of your Curia' (*in comitio in vestibulo curiae vestrae*, ibid.) and put themselves, together

---

124 As Livy explains at 45.25.2–3, he chose not to write a speech for Cato because that would have been but a shadow of Cato's own speech as published in the *Origines* (*non inseram simulacrum viri copiosi, quae dixerit referendo; ipsius oratio scripta exstat, Originum quinto libro inclusa*, 3). For the fragments of Cato's speech cf. *FRHist.* 5 F87–93.

with their wives and children, at the Romans' mercy. Let their city, Rhodes, be destroyed far away from their eyes! (*procul ab oculis nostris urbs nostra diripiatur incendiatur, ibid.*).

The image is rhetorically inflated, consistent with the Rhodian envoys' tendency to exaggerate. At the same time, it graphically portrays the role of the Forum in a new topography of the world. Rome is by now the centre of things, where Rhodes' destiny is decided; and the Curia and Comitium are the centre of the centre, the new place of communication between the city and the world.

The Curia appears again in the account of another embassy, that of Prusias, King of Pontus, which closes the *Ab Urbe Condita*'s surviving section and directly relates to the Romans' Macedonian victory.[125] Prusias states that he has come to Rome 'in order to salute and congratulate the gods who inhabited the city of Rome, the Senate, and the Roman people for defeating kings Perseus and Gentius and broadening their dominions through the submission of the Macedonians and the Illyrians'.[126] From the outset, the narrative lingers on the spatial dimension of the embassy. At 45.44.4, the narrator describes Prusias and his son Nicomedes' entrance in Rome by specifying that they went 'from the gate to the Forum and the dais of the praetor Q. Cassius'.[127] As in so many other narratives in the *Ab Urbe Condita*, the Forum functions as a sort of stage for a play where characters enter and recite their part before an audience (in this case, the throng of people who escort the royals to the Forum). Prusias asks for two days to 'see the temples of the gods, the city, and his friends and hosts' (45.44.6).[128] On the third day, he is admitted into the Senate, where he congratulates the Romans, reminds them of his own merits during the war, introduces his son to the Senate, asks for permission to perform sacrifices on the Capitol and in Praeneste, and requests that part of Antiochus' former territory be assigned to him (45.44.7–9). The Senate accepts most of his requests but announces they will send envoys to inquire after the territorial issue. Prusias leaves the city (45.44.10–18).

At this point, the narrator specifies that what he has only reported is 'the account of our (i.e. the Roman) historians' (45.44.19: *Haec de Prusia nostri scriptores*). Then he adds Polybius' version of the events, which is much less

---

125 A lacuna breaks the text at 45.44.21 but, since Prusias' embassy is the last event recorded by the *Periocha* of Book 45, one can assume that not much text was lost.
126 (...) *deos qui urbem Romam incolerent senatumque et populum Romanum salutatum se dixit venisse, et gratulatum quod Persea Gentiumque reges vicissent, Macedonibusque et Illyriis in dicionem redactis auxissent imperium*, 45.44.5.
127 *Is magno comitatu urbem ingressus ad forum a porta tribunalque ⟨Q.⟩ Cassi praetoris perrexit* (...).
128 *Biduum petit quo templa deum urbemque et hospites amicosque videret.*

favourable to Prusias. According to the Greek historian, Prusias acted in a way unworthy of a king because of his slavishness (45.44.20):

> Romae quoque, cum veniret in curiam, summisisse se et osculo limen curiae contigisse, et deos servatores suos senatum appellasse, aliamque orationem non tam honorificam audientibus quam sibi deformem habuisse.

> In Rome, too, as he went to the Curia, he bent and kissed the threshold of the Curia and called the Senate his saviour gods and said other things that did not bring as much honour to the audience as disgrace upon him.

In both versions, the *Ab Urbe Condita* dwells on Prusias' use of the city's space. In the former version, the king walks to the Forum and wishes to visit and honour 'the gods who inhabit the city'. In the latter, he stoops to kiss the entrance to the Curia. What emerges is the significance of those sites within the city: political action, including the action of ambassadors and visiting kings, is a spatial performance.

The embassies in Book 45 present the reader with an array of reactions to the Roman victory over Macedon. How Livy develops his narration of them suggests the centrality of the city of Rome in the world. When describing the beginning of the conflict, at 42.29.1–30.7, the historian conveyed such centrality by describing the attitudes of kings and free peoples in Europe and Asia in the face of the imminent war. After the war's end, the historian shows its impact on the world by displaying how those same kings and peoples (or their envoys) converge to the Roman Curia. The Curia thus emerges as the place par excellence where the world's destinies are decided upon and as the very heart of Roman power.

5 Permanence, Change, and Political Symbolism in Livy's Forum

The Forum, as I have argued in this chapter, is a space of both permanence and change in the *Ab Urbe Condita*. Its permanence is apparent in its retaining, throughout the surviving books, some basic features. The Forum of the *Ab Urbe Condita* is the space where Roman citizens unite to fight, reconcile, and debate. It is a space of multiple encounters (some of them peaceful, some of them not): between patricians and plebs, between magistrates and common people, between old and young. It is the space where people recognise themselves as members of one community. Most importantly, it is the ideal standpoint from which events inside and outside the city are observed, discussed, and evaluated.

Change, on the other hand, concerns both the material fabric of the Forum and the functions of its elements. The narrative stresses the transformations in the material fabric at different points, reporting the founding of new buildings and the disappearance of once extant monuments. Moreover, the emphasis shifts, as the account proceeds toward the Middle Republic, from the open space of the Forum to the Curia as the place where events not just in the city but also in the world converge.

One is left wondering how Livy's lost books treated the transformations of the Forum from the mid-2nd century BCE to Augustan times. One would profit from knowing, for example, whether in the account of the Late Republic the area around the temple of Castor played a comparable role as the Comitium and Curia in the earlier books, and how the narrative constructed episodes of political violence in the Forum. The *Periochae* provide only occasional glimpses.[129] *Periocha* 74, for example, reports the killing of the praetor Sempronius Asellio in the Forum by moneylenders, whom he had displeased by passing judgements in favour of debtors; in *Periocha* 89 Sulla the dictator is said to have ordered the murder, in the Forum, of a political adversary who had applied for the consulate against his will. *In foro* is the expression used in both cases, but there is no way of knowing whether Livy's original text was more precise.[130]

Periocha 58 presents a former consul, Titus Annius, delivering speeches against Tiberius Gracchus first in the Senate, then, after the angry people had dragged him out of there, 'before the Rostra' (*pro rostris*). The Rostra are also, in *Periocha* 80, where Marius and Cinna have the heads of their enemies on display after their conquest of Rome. *Periocha* 107 reports the burning of Clodius' body in the Curia (but makes no mention of the burning of the Curia itself); in *Periocha* 116, the plebs have Caesar's body cremated before the Rostra (*ante rostra*).

These scattered pieces of information suggest that a concern with the Forum as a meaningful setting for episodes of political violence characterised Livy's lost books, too. A fragment from Book 120, transmitted by Seneca the Elder and portraying Cicero's death in 43 BCE during the proscriptions of the

---

129 On the *Periochae*, their relationships with the Livian original, and their status as a literary work, see e.g. Jal (1984a–b); Chaplin (2010b); Ricchieri (2022); Levene (2023b).

130 For topographical simplification cf. e.g. *Per.* 5, where the omen which persuaded the Romans not to move to Veii after the Gallic sack (cf. above, pp. 64–65) is said to have occurred *in foro*; Livy 5.55.1 speaks of the Comitium and features a more complex and symbolic construction of space.

so-called Second Triumvirate,[131] may provide the most significant insights, in that Livy narrates Mark Antony's defilement of the orator's body in highly pathetic terms:

> Ita relatum caput ad Antonium iussuque eius inter duas manus in rostris positum, ubi ille consul, ubi saepe consularis, ubi eo ipso anno adversus Antonium quanta nulla umquam humana vox cum admiratione eloquentiae auditus fuerat.

> The head was thus brought to Antony and, per his command, placed between Cicero's two hands on the Rostra, where Cicero – as consul, as former consul, and even that very year, as he had spoken against Antony – had often been heard amid such admiration for his eloquence as no human voice had ever elicited.

As Biggs (2019, esp. pp. 35–37) notes, the characterisation of the Rostra as the very same place where Cicero had so many times spoken entails imprecision: the Rostra where Antony had his hands and head affixed were the Caesarian ones, not the old Rostra of the Comitium where Cicero had harangued the people as a consul.[132] By conflating the old and the new monument, the narrative brings reader's attention away from the Rostra as a material structure to the Rostra as a symbolic place of communication and strife. This can be compared with what I have observed about Livy's construction of Comitium and Curia in the account of Mid-Republican history: the Curia, in particular, gradually becomes more an ideal place than a material one, just as its centrality to Roman events increases.

Livy's Forum results from the interplay between physical structure and symbolic significance. Precisely for this reason, the narrative can use its space to map power relationships within the Roman citizen body. Whereas, in the earlier books, the Forum acts as a powerful symbol for the social struggles tearing the *res publica* apart, as Livy's history goes on, it becomes a collective space where different groups negotiate their positioning within the community.

---

131 Sen. *Suas.* 6.17 = Livy F 61 Levene. For detailed analyses of the fragment see Woodman (2015, pp. 75–89); Levene (2023b, pp. 254–256). The death of Cicero and the display of his body parts on the Rostra is also mentioned in *Per.* 120: see, however, Woodman (2015, p. 75 n. 167) for the differences between the two texts.

132 Biggs (2019, p. 36) points out how such a 'flattening of change' is found not only in Livy but also in various early-imperial account of Cicero's death. On the displaying of political opponents' heads on the Rostra see also Lange (2020).

One may surmise that later, in the missing books, fractures in the space of the Forum once more became evident.

These observations allow me to stress one final point, on which I shall expand in the next chapter: Livy's narrative reveals an underlying notion of the city as an embodiment of the community it hosts. Locations are often significant as material correspondents to elements or aspects of the Roman citizen body, and relationships among citizens shape the space of the Forum. The narrative construction of the Forum in the *Ab Urbe Condita* emerges as an integral part of Livy's reflections on how a political community can grow, thrive, or fall.

CHAPTER 2

The Space of the City

1   Founding the City: Book 1

Like other Roman writers, Livy imagined the history of the monarchic period as the gradual shaping of the Roman State through the addition of one element after the other.[1] According to such a view, each of the seven kings had been responsible for some of the institutions, laws, and customs that characterised Rome's political and religious life. Moreover, various ethnic groups had been absorbed into the community of Roman citizens at different points during the monarchic period. The rape of the Sabine women led to the mixing of Roman and Sabine blood, and, after the reconciliation of Romulus and Titus Tatius, the two kings ruling together;[2] the population of Alba Longa was transplanted to Rome after the destruction of their city under Tullus Hostilius[3] and the inhabitants of various Latin towns were accepted as new citizens by Ancus Marcius.[4] Tarquinius Priscus, who established a new dynasty at Rome, was himself an Etruscan immigrant, and his successor Servius Tullius was, according to the version of the story that Livy prefers, the son of a prisoner of war from Latin Corniculum.[5]

In Livy's history, this gradual addition and incorporation process is also a spatial one. At 1.8.4, immediately after reporting the foundation of Rome and the first laws instituted by Romulus, he writes that the new-born city grew 'as one area after another was annexed' (*alia atque alia adpetendo loca*). As Pausch (2008) points out, the narrative of Romulus' reign introduces the essential features of Roman topography: the Palatine, at the foot of which Romulus and Remus are suckled by the wolf, and where Rome is eventually founded; the Aventine, where Remus takes the auspice that indicates his brother shall be the king of the city; the Forum Boarium, the setting for the story of Hercules and Cacus to which Livy devotes a long flashback; the Capitol, where the king establishes his asylum and which the Sabines will conquer later on; the Circus

---

1 Cf. e.g. Cic. *Rep.* 2.1.1–2.
2 Livy 1.9–13.
3 Livy. 1.29.1–30.3.
4 Livy 1.33.1–5.
5 The story of Tarquinius Priscus' arrival in Rome is told in Livy 1.34. For Servius Tullius' origins and his succession to Tarquinius, see Livy 1.39–41.

Maximus, the location for the Consualia during which the Romans kidnap the Sabine maidens; the Forum, which serves as the location for the battle between Romans and Sabines. One may add that the narrative of Romulus' reign also introduces the boundary between Rome and the external world, in the form of the wall that the king builds at the very same time as founding the city (1.7.1–3) and of the *vetus porta Palati* (the later Porta Mugonia), a gate of the Romulean city, mentioned at 1.12.3.[6] Moreover, the narrative emphasises the Tiber as a defining element of Roman topography and identity:[7] the river is the first feature of Roman topography to enter Livy's narrative (1.4.4). Finally, the last act of Romulus' life, his mysterious disappearance in front of his army, takes place in the Campus Martius and thus allows the introduction of the space outside the *pomerium* (and the later Servian Walls).

This narrative pattern – the shaping of an urban image through mention of the city's main topographic features, alongside that of a boundary and of an extension of the city that lies beyond the boundary – is at work in the rest of Book 1. Here the narrative introduces all the remaining hills of Rome, one by one, as they are the most distinctive natural features of the city alongside the Tiber. Livy writes that, when the population of Alba Longa migrated to Rome, the Caelian Hill was added to the city to provide space for the new inhabitants and that Tullus Hostilius established his palace there (1.30.1). Later, after his victory against the Latin town of Politorium, Ancus Marcius transferred its inhabitants to Rome (1.33.2):

> Et cum circa Palatium, sedem veterum Romanorum, Sabini Capitolium atque arcem, Caelium montem Albani implessent, Aventinum novae multitudini datum.

> And since in the areas around of the Palatine (which was the seat of the original Romans) the Sabines had filled the Capitol and the citadel, and the Albans the Caelian Hill, the Aventine was given to the new crowd.

Shortly afterwards, the historian reports that further victories against Latin towns led to new migrants, who were assigned a place in the valley between the Aventine and the Palatine in the area known as *ad Murciae* or *Admurciae* (1.33.5).[8] It is significant that Livy explicitly remarks on the correspondence between each hill and each ethnic component of the city. In other words, he

---

6   Cf. Plin. *HN*. 3.5.66.
7   Cf. Jaeger (2015, p. 66).
8   For the origins of the name and the history of the place see Ogilvie (1965, p. 137).

uses a schematic topography to think about the structure of Roman society: Rome's mixed origins and her readiness to incorporate external elements[9] are part of the very landscape of the city.

Ancus Marcius was also responsible for annexing the Janiculum, which was joined to the city through a wall and a bridge (the Pons Sublicius) – the first (as Livy remarks) to be built across the Tiber (1.33.6). In this way, the city space is again extended beyond its boundary (in this case, the natural one constituted by the river). The historian states that this was not any need for more room (*inopia loci*) but the preoccupation that the hill might be used by enemies for military purposes (*ne quando ea arx hostium esset*). By adding the hill and building the bridge, Rome looks out beyond her natural boundaries, thus setting the stage for her future expansion.

Under the reign of Servius Tullius, the steady growth of the Roman population led the king to enlarge the city once more (*urbs ... amplificanda*, 1.44.3) by incorporating two more hills, the Quirinal and the Viminal, and by 'extend[ing] the area of the Esquiline' (*auget Esquilias*),[10] where the king also went to live.

As the previous summary makes clear, Livy accepts the Varronian list of the seven *montes* that one can infer from *De lingua Latina* 5.41–54: Capitol, Aventine, Caelius, Esquiline, Viminal, Quirinal, and Palatine. To these seven hills, he adds the Janiculum as a military outpost, providing the link to the space outside the Servian Walls. The 'canon' of those seven hills seems to have been an innovation of Varro and to have originated from his attempt to make sense of the name Septimontium: this designated a long-standing festival, which the scholar connected with the seven *montes* that *postea urbs muris comprehendit* (5.41).[11] Although Varro's selection of those seven hills appears partly arbitrary,[12] it originated the image of Rome as 'the city of the seven hills', which was popular from the Augustan age[13] (although alternative lists continued to exist until Late Antiquity).[14]

Besides the hills, the other fundamental elements of the city space are also laid out one after another in Book 1. First, the walls: after those of Romulus,

---

9   For this topos in Livy, cf. e.g. 4.3.10–13.
10 As Ogilvie (1965, p. 179) notes, this probably means that part of the Esquiline was already included in the city and that Servius Tullius added other areas of the hill.
11 For the 'seven hills' of Rome, the Septimontium, and Varro's list, see e.g. Fraschetti s.v. *montes* in *LTUR* 3 (1996) pp. 282–287 (with further bibliography); Vout (2012).
12 For example, he subsumes two distinct *montes*, the Cispius and the Oppius, under the name Esquiliae and includes the Velia and the Cermalus in the Palatium; cf. Fraschetti s.v. *montes* in *LTUR* 3 (1996) p. 286.
13 Cf. Vout (2012).
14 Cf. e.g. Festus, *Gloss. Lat.* 474–476; Paul. Fest. 459; Serv. *Aen.* 6.783.

the building of walls is attributed to Tarquinius Priscus (1.36.1; 1.38.6) and Servius Tullius (1.44.3). The latter is also credited with enlarging the *pomerium*, which, as a consequence, is mentioned in the *Ab Urbe Condita* for the first time (1.44.4).[15] Porta Capena, one of the city gates, is where Horatius meets and kills his sister while returning from the duel against the Curiatii (1.26.2–4).[16]

Moreover, the narrative gradually introduces all the main sites within the city. The battle between Romans and Sabines in the valley between the Palatine and Capitoline hills that would soon become the Forum Romanum marks the entrance of this space into Roman history as well as the aition of the first monument within it, the Lacus Curtius (1.12.9–10; 13.5). Other buildings rise within the space of the Forum later on: Tullus Hostilius built the first Senate House, the Curia Hostilia (1.30.2), Ancus Marcius the *carcer*, which is located 'in the middle of the city, overlooking the Forum' (*media urbe imminens foro*, 1.33.8). Tarquinius Priscus has private buildings, shops and porticoes built around the Forum. The Campus Martius, which had been the setting for Romulus' disappearance, occurs again at 1.44.1–2, where, for the very first time, Servius Tullius summons the Roman people divided into their *centuriae* and performs the *lustrum*.

The religious topography of the city gradually develops, too. Numa Pompilius is responsible for various religious buildings: the shrine of Janus at the bottom of the Argiletum (1.19.2) (i.e. at the entrance of the Forum), which was to be opened in times of war and closed in times of peace – a site of topical significance in the light of Octavian's closing of the shrine in 29 BCE;[17] the temple of Vesta adjacent to the Forum (1.20.3); the altar of Jupiter Elicius on the Aventine (1.20.7); the shrines of the Argei in various locations across the city (1.20.5).[18] Moreover, Numa consecrates the grove where he allegedly met with his lover and counsellor, the nymph Egeria, to the Camenae (1.21.3).[19] Ancus Marcius enlarges the temple of Jupiter Feretrius, which Romulus had founded (1.33.9); Servius Tullius builds the temple of Diana on the Aventine (1.45.3–7).

Finally, the most important landmark of all, the temple of Jupiter Optimus Maximus on the Capitol, is first vowed by Tarquinius Priscus (1.38.7) and later

---

15　On walls and the *pomerium* in Book 1 cf. Konstan (1986, pp. 198–201).
16　On the significance of the Porta Capena as a boundary feature in this tale see Solodow (1979); Jaeger (2015, p. 67).
17　Livy 1.20.3 emphasises this fact. On the shrine, its implications, and Livy's mention of it see the detailed commentary in Ogilvie (1965, pp. 93–95).
18　On the possible significance of the rituals connected with the Argei see Ogilvie (1965, pp. 104–105).
19　Livy describes the site according to the typical features of the *locus amoenus*: *Lucus erat quem medium ex opaco specu fons perenni rigabat aqua*.

built by his son Tarquinius Superbus (1.55). During the construction works for the temple, the Romans witness two prodigies foretelling the eternity and universal power of Rome. While the temples previously built on the Capitol are being removed to leave room for the new building, the auspices forbid the *exauguratio* of the shrine of Terminus, the god of boundaries; this is taken as an omen for the stability of Rome (1.55.3-4). There is, besides, the discovery of a human head (*caput*) found buried in the ground; this is also interpreted as an omen, designating the hill as *arcem* (...) *imperii caputque rerum* (1.55.5-6; the story also constituted the aition for the name Capitolium).[20]

Thus, there is a circular movement in Book 1: a first, essential city-topography emerges during Romulus' reign, but that topography is enlarged and developed in the remaining part of Book 1. The narrative returns to the first sketch, repeatedly adding to and building on it. Some places first enter the narrative during Romulus' reign but are later mentioned again as later kings add important buildings or functions to them. By the end of Book 1, the reader can shape a basic mental model of the city, which is to be understood as the implicit backdrop to everything narrated in the later books. Such a model includes boundaries (the *pomerium* and the walls), the Tiber and the seven hills – the most characteristic feature of the Roman cityscape – as well as the Janiculum, an outpost in the outer world; a sacred landmark (the Capitol with the temple of Jupiter); a political centre (the Forum); temples; and an undistinguished set of private buildings where people live and work. It is a space that is both fixed – i.e. unmovable, as the Terminus omen makes clear – and temporary since its boundaries are continually extended.

Most importantly, it is a space which is closely connected to the form of the Roman community. Its boundaries set it clearly apart from the external world; at the same time, the Janiculum as a military outpost ensures Rome's ability to extend her reach beyond her own boundaries. The Forum is, from its very birth, the space of clashes and encounters between different groups; linking the Palatine and Capitol, the first two hills from which the new city came into being, it embodies the dynamics by which two become one. More generally, the hills of Rome provide a material counterpart to the ethnic components coming together to form the Roman State. And, by the end of the book (and of the monarchic period), the Capitoline emerges as the core of the (by now) fully formed community, embodying its internal hierarchy of gods and human beings and the stability of the Roman State.

---

20 For further ancient sources on these legends see Ogilvie (1965, pp. 210–212): for an examination of the stories and their significance Thein (2014).

In the following sections, I shall show how the *Ab Urbe Condita* develops this basic city structure in the remaining books, delineating it according to the dynamics of historical change and imbuing it with meanings that are central to Livy's perspective on Roman history.

In section 2, I focus on the Capitol and its multifaceted connotations in Livy's narrative. Section 3 is devoted to the other hills of Rome, with a special emphasis on the Aventine and Palatine. In section 4 I turn to the Campus Martius, and, in section 5, I analyse Livy's representation of boundary features such as the city walls, the gates, the Tiber, and the Janiculum. In section 6, I examine some narratives which involve several places within the city and thus work as synthetic overviews of the city as a whole. Finally, in section 7, I draw some conclusions regarding the image of Rome that the *Ab Urbe Condita* suggests.

2   The Capitol

2.1   *History and Archaeology*

The Capitol,[21] the smallest of the seven hills, is located between the Forum to the south-east and the Campus Martius to the west. Its southern summit, the Capitolium proper, housed the Temple of Jupiter Optimus Maximus; the northern summit was known as the *arx* ('citadel'). Between the two summits lay a depression known as *inter duos lucos* (lit. 'between the two groves')[22] where, according to legend, Romulus had established his Asylum.[23]

Both ancient sources and modern excavations suggest that the Capitol had been Rome's citadel from ancient times.[24] The hill plays a significant role in the Roman foundation legend, particularly in the tradition concerning the war between Romans and the Sabines following the abduction of the Sabine

---

21   On the topography of the Capitol, see e.g. Ashby and Doughill (1927); Tagliamonte s.v. *Capitolium (fino alla prima età repubblicana)* in *LTUR* 1 (1993) pp. 227–231; Danti (2016a); Mazzei (2019).

22   Livy 1.8.5; Vell. Pat. 1.8.5; and cf. Dion. Hal. *Ant. Rom.* 2.15.4 (τὸ γὰρ μεταξὺ χωρίον τοῦ τε Καπιτωλίου καὶ τῆς ἄκρας, ὃ καλεῖται νῦν κατὰ τὴν Ῥωμαίων διάλεκτον μεθόριον δυεῖν δρυμῶν καὶ ἦν τότε τοῦ συμβεβηκότος ἐπώνυμον) and Ov. *Fast.* 3.430 (*templa ... lucos Veiovis ante duos*).

23   Cf. e.g. Verg. *Aen.* 8.342–344; Livy 1.8.5; Dion Hal. *Ant. Rom.* 2.15.4–5; Luc. 7.438; Tac. *Hist.* 3.71.3; Flor. 1.1.9.; Plut. *Vit. Rom.* 9.3; and Wiseman s.v. *Asylum* in *LTUR* 1 (1993) p. 130.

24   See Tagliamonte s.v. *Capitolium (fino alla prima età repubblicana)* in *LTUR* 1 (1993) p. 229.

women: according to ancient writers, the Sabines took hold of the Capitol thanks to the betrayal of Tarpeia, the daughter of the citadel's guardian.[25]

In Republican times, the Capitol had crucial religious and political connotations. The most prominent building on the hill was undoubtedly the temple of Jupiter Optimus Maximus, whose construction Roman writers attributed to Tarquinius Superbus in the late 6th century BCE (a date which seems to be confirmed by modern scholarship). As Dionysius of Halicarnassus, (*Ant. Rom.* 4.61.4) testifies, the temple was rebuilt on the same foundations after a fire in 83 BCE, the new one only differing from the old 'in the costliness of the material'. Dionysius describes the building of his own – and Livy's – age as having three orders of columns on the front (which faced southwards, toward the Forum) and a single order of columns on the sides and as consisting, in fact, of three temples with adjoining walls: the temple of Jupiter in the middle and those of Juno and Minerva on each side of it.

The temple certainly made a great impression, especially for the age in which it was first built,[26] but its role in Roman institutional life was even greater. In the temple, the newly elected consuls took the auspices and were inaugurated at the beginning of each year; in the temple, they presided over the first Senate meeting of the year, in which provinces and armies were allotted to magistrates, and matters of international policy were discussed. The area in front of the temple of Jupiter, the *area Capitolina* or *area Capitoli*, was a frequent location for the voting of the tribes.

The temple was also the end point for triumphal ceremonies (*pompae triumphales*) – those well-staged pageants by which successful commanders celebrated major military victories, paraded the spoils from their campaigns, and gave solemn thanks to the gods.[27] Although the precise route followed by triumphal processions, its degree of flexibility, and the changes it might have undergone through time have been the object of much debate, the

---

25 Livy tells the story at 1.5–9; see, moreover, Varro *Ling.* 5.41; Dion. Hal. *Ant. Rom.* 2.38; Ov. *Fast.* 1.261–262; Val. Max. 9.6.1; Festus, *Gloss. Lat.* 496; and Ogilvie (1965, pp. 74–75).

26 For the debate on the structure and dimensions of the Temple of Jupiter Optimus Maximus, see Ridley (2005); Arata (2010); Danti (2016b); Galluccio (2016). For the impact that the temple had on the perception of the city space cf. Jenkyns (2103, p. 111).

27 On the Roman triumph see e.g. Versnel (1970); Itgenhorst (2005, with detailed analysis of several sources; on Livy see pp. 148–179); Beard (2009); Östenberg (2009); Lange (2016); Rüpke (2019, pp. 229–240); and cf. following note. On triumphs in Livy see also Phillips (1974); Pelikan Pittenger (2008).

following points seem certain.[28] The victorious general and his army waited in the Campus Martius (i.e. outside the *pomerium*) while the Senate debated on the granting of the triumph. After the Senate had granted the general the right to triumph, the procession started in the Circus Flaminius. The spoils and prisoners of war were paraded in the front; then came the triumphant general himself on a chariot drawn by white horses, preceded by the senators and magistrates and accompanied by his children; at the rear of the procession, the victorious soldiers cheered their commander by singing licentious verses. The procession then crossed the *pomerium* through a gate or arch, which ancient sources call *porta triumphalis* and modern scholars have tried to locate without success; it passed through the Forum Boarium, proceeded to the Circus Maximus, reached the Forum, then halted at the foot of the Capitol, where the defeated enemies could be taken away to be executed. Finally, the triumphant general dismounted his chariot and ascended on foot, via the *clivus Capitolinus*, to the Capitol, where he sacrificed in the temple of Jupiter Optimus Maximus.

The latter, however, was not the only building of deep religious significance on the hill. Most notably, the temple of Jupiter Feretrius on the Capitolium, believed to have been founded by Romulus, hosted the *spolia opima* dedicated by generals who had killed an enemy leader in combat;[29] and in 22 BCE Augustus founded a new temple to Jupiter Tonans as a thanksgiving for escaping death by lighting some years earlier. The *arx* hosted, among other things, the temple of Juno Moneta and the *auguraculum*, where auspices were conducted at the *comitia curiata* and on other occasions.[30]

---

[28] On the triumphal route and the many problems connected with it, see e.g. Makin (1921); Coarelli (1968); Versnel (1970, pp. 93–163); Favro (1994); Beard (2009, pp. 92–105); Wiseman (2007); Östenberg (2010); Rüpke (2019, pp. 234–236). The most debated points have been: 1) the location and identification of the *porta triumphalis*; 2) whether the *pompa* made a loop from the Forum Boarium to the Velabrum and back on its way to the Circus Maximus; 3) whether it proceeded all around the Palatine before reaching the Sacra Via and the Forum. Since these questions are not directly relevant to my analysis, I shall not treat them here.

[29] Livy 1.10.5–7 relates that Romulus founded the temple with the *spolia opima* of the king of the Caeninenses. The historian stresses that this was the first temple to be dedicated (*sacratum*, 6) in Rome. On the *spolia opima* see also Livy 4.20.4–11; and cf. e.g. Ogilvie (1965, pp. 563–565); Flower (2000a); Sailor (2006); Polito (2017).

[30] See Coarelli s.v. *Auguraculum (arx)* in LTUR 1 (1993) pp. 142–143.

Livy mentions the hill in its entirety through the syntagm *Capitolium atque arx* (or similar ones),[31] simply through the noun *Capitolium*,[32] or through the expression *Capitolinus mons*.[33] *Capitolium* can also indicate the southern summit more specifically[34] or, metonymically, the *area Capitolina*;[35] Livy also frequently uses the term *Capitolium* to designate the temple of the Capitoline Triad.[36] Of course, the different meanings of *Capitolium* are not always clearly distinguishable from one another: for example, expressions such as *in Capitolium escendere*, which Livy uses when writing about triumphal ceremonies, means both that the triumphing general 'goes up the Capitol' and that he 'goes up to the Capitoline temple'.[37] Finally, on one occasion (1.55.1), the historian designates the southern summit as *mons Tarpeius*, which is how some ancient sources call either the *Capitolium* or the Capitoline Hill in its entirety.[38] Livy's use of that name does not seem random. The passage in question reports Tarquinius Superbus' decision to build the temple of Jupiter Optimus Maximus promised in a vow by his father and thus introduces the narrative of the prodigies concerning Terminus and the finding of a human head during the construction works (cf. above, p. 86). As Varro (*Ling.* 5.41) informs us, the name *Capitolium* was believed to derive from the *caput* (head), and the hill was believed to have been named *Tarpeius* previously. Livy does not make such etymology explicit, but probably alludes to it by using *Tarpeius* in such a context.

In my analysis, I shall use the term 'the Capitol' to designate the hill in its entirety, or when referring to passages in which Livy employs the term *Capitolium* generically (i.e. without specifying which section of the hill he is

---

31 E.g. 1.33.2; 2.7.10 (*in ipsa arce Capitolioque*); 2.49.7 (*Capitolium arcemque*); 3.15.5; 3.18.1 (*de arce capta Capitolioque occupato*); 3.68.7 (*arcem et Capitolium*); 4.2.14; 4.45.1; 5.39.12; (*arx Capitoliumque*); 5.40.1 (*in Capitolium atque in arcem*); 5.44.5 (*ex arce Capitolioque*); 5.52.3 (*arx ... et Capitolium*); 6.11.4; 6.20.9; 8.37.6; 26.10.2,6 (*ex arce Capitolioque*); 38.51.1. As my selection of examples suggests, expressions of this kind are frequent in Books 1–6, while they only occur three times after Book 6.

32 See e.g. 2.10.3; 3.15.9; 3.16.5; 3.17.7; 3.18.6, 10; 3.19.12; 3.20.3; 5.46.2–3; 5.52.10; 5.53.5; 9.4.7; 25.1.7; 34.5.8.

33 See e.g. 1.12.1.

34 See e.g. 1.10.5; 1.38.7; 2.8.6; 3.29.9; 5.54.7; 6.20.10, 11; 7.6.3; 9.44.16; 23.31.9; 23.32.20; 24.10.6; 25.7.7; 26.9.9; 26.31.11; 35.21.6; 37.3.7; 40.45.3; 41.27.7; 45.22.1; 45.39.2.

35 See e.g. 33.25.7; 34.1.4;34.53.2; 34.56.5–6; 43.16.9; 45.36.1, 6–7.

36 See e.g. 2.22.6; 3.21.1; 3.57.7; 4.20.4; 5.52.6; 6.4.2, 12; 6.29.8; 7.38.2; 8.5.1; 9.44.16; 10.23.12; 21.63.7–9; 22.1.6; 22.51.1; 23.22.6; 23.31.1; 24.10.1; 25.39.16; 26.1.1; 28.38.8, 14; 31.14.1; 35.41.10; 36.35.12; 41.10.7; 44.14.3; 45.39.11,13.

37 See e.g. 38.48.13; 42.49.6.

38 See e.g. *Rhet. ad Her.* 4.43; Varro *Ling.* 5.41; Prop. 4.4.93; Suet. *Iul.* 44.

THE SPACE OF THE CITY

indicating); I shall use Capitolium when it is clear that precisely the southern summit, and not the *arx*, is meant; and I shall designate the latter as 'the citadel'.

In what follows, I examine some recurring aspects of Livy's representation of the Capitol. First, I show that the narrative sets the Capitol as the beginning and end point of Roman space and time; secondly, I argue that the Capitol takes part in reflections on hierarchy and authority, and that this often happens by stressing the Capitol as the object of characters' gazes and words; finally, I analyse the role of the Capitol, in the *Ab Urbe Condita*, as the very embodiment of Roman political and religious identity.

2.2   *The Pivot of Roman Space and Time*

Starting from the Third Decade, the narrative of each consular year in the *Ab Urbe Condita* features a 'beginning of year' section, which includes a report on the consuls' entry into office and an account of the first Senate meeting of the year in the temple of Jupiter on the Capitol.[39] As I mentioned in my Introduction, the effect of such recurring narratives on the overall spatial structure of the *Ab Urbe Condita* cannot be underestimated: the annalistic structure is in itself Romanocentric, setting Rome – where the narrative constantly comes back to at the beginning and end of each year – at the centre of the narrated world. If this is true, then the Capitol is the very centre to which Roman space and time converge.

Livy's narrative stresses the importance of magistrates' entry in office on the Capitol, as one can observe in an account that relates a breach of spatial rules. In 217 BCE, one of the two consuls was Gaius Flaminius, who had made himself an enemy of the Senate some years earlier because of his *popularis* policy. Fearing that the Senate would try to delay his departure by alleging negative omens, Flaminius departed from Rome with the intention of entering office in his area of operations, that is, without taking the customary auspices on the Capitol. Livy reports the senators' outraged words at 21.63.7–9 *in oratio obliqua*:

> Nunc conscientia spretorum et Capitolium et sollemnem votorum nuncupationem fugisse, 8. ne die initi magistratus Iovis optimi maximi templum adiret, ne senatum invisus ipse et sibi uni invisum videret consuleretque, ne Latinas indiceret Iovique Latiari sollemne sacrum in monte faceret, 9. ne auspicato profectus in Capitolium ad vota nuncupanda, paludatus inde cum lictoribus in provinciam iret. Lixae

---

39   Among beginning-of-year accounts, the Capitol is mentioned explicitly at 22.31.1 (215 BCE); 24.10.1 (214 BCE); 26.1.1 (211 BCE); 28.38.14 (205 BCE); 30.27.1 (202 BCE); 32.8.2 (198 BCE); 41.27.3 (174 BCE). At 37.1.3 (190 BCE) Livy calls the temple of Jupiter *curia*.

modo sine insignibus, sine lictoribus profectus clam, furtim, haud aliter quam si exsilii causa solum vertisset. 10. Magis pro maiestate videlicet imperii Arimini quam Romae magistratum initurum et in deversorio hospitali quam apud penates suos praetextam sumpturum.

Now, aware as he was of what he had neglected, he had escaped the Capitol and the solemn taking of the vows, 8. that he might not enter the temple of Jupiter Optimus Maximus on the day of his entrance into office; that he, who was hated by the Senate and was in his turn the only one to hate the Senate, might not see and consult the Senate; that he might not proclaim the Latin Festival and perform the solemn sacrifice to Jupiter Latiaris on the Sacred Mount; 9. and that he might not depart for his area of operation dressed in the military mantle, together with his lictors, after taking the auspices and going to the Capitol to formulate his vows. Just like a camp-follower, without military standards, without lictors he has departed secretly, by stealth, as if he had gone away in exile. 10. It was certainly more appropriate to the majesty of the *imperium* that he would enter office in Ariminum rather than in Rome and put on his praetexta in a lodging place rather than in front of his own household gods!

This passage constructs Flaminius' breach in terms of his subversion of the relationship of centre and periphery. Two locations are especially relevant: the Sacred Mount and the Capitol, presented as the seats of rituals which are at the same time religious and political. Especially the Capitol, which is named twice, appears as the core on which other spatial relationships depend. By not entering office on the Capitol, Flaminius has failed to honour his own household gods and has exchanged an external place for Rome, thus putting the majesty of Roman imperium into question; moreover, he has turned himself into an *exul* rather than a magistrate invested with legitimate power.

At the beginning of the following book, when the other consul that year, Gnaeus Servilius Geminus, enters office in Rome, the senators comment once more on Flaminius' irresponsible behaviour (22.1.4–7).[40] This text once more emphasizes the spatial dimension of the ceremonies involved in the conferral of *imperium* and *auspicium* upon a magistrate. First, a magistrate carries the *auspicia* 'from the fatherland' (*a domo*) into the external world; it is not possible to receive them 'in a foreign land' (*in externo ... solo*). In this context, the

---

40   Jaeger (2015, p. 68) points out that the two passages portraying the senators' indignation 'bridge the divide between Books 21 and 22'; the Capitol thus acts once more as a structural end and beginning (this time, of two books).

remark that Servilius entered his office in Rome on the Ides of March, while being a common formula that Livy uses to shift from events abroad to events in the city, produces a stark contrast between the two consuls. Moreover, the text once more stresses the two locations that are essential in the conferral of auspices, namely the Sacred Mount (*in monte*) and the Capitol.[41]

The Capitol's function as a marker of space and time, however, can be observed even before the account of the Middle Republic and from the very beginnings of the city; indeed, the Capitol recurs at some significant points at the beginning and end of several Decades, Pentads, or books.[42] In Romulus' time, the Capitol is the location for the Asylum,[43] the place where the king dedicates the first of all Roman temples, that of Jupiter Feretrius (1.9.5–7) and later, together with Forum and Palatine, for the battle between Romans and Sabines which shapes the heart of Roman political space (1.12.1–13.5).[44] Towards the end of the monarchic period, the Capitol receives its most important temple, that of Jupiter Optimus Maximus, that Tarquinius Priscus began building (1.38.7) and Tarquinius Superbus later brought to conclusion (1.55.1–56.2). The building of the temple takes place at the end of a chronological unit in Roman history, the monarchic period, and, as mentioned above (p. 86), is accompanied by omens that predict the that Roman power in space and time will be limitless.

---

41   Both indirect speeches are followed by accounts of prodigies that suggest divine disfavour as a consequence of Flaminius' actions. At the end of Book 21, Livy reports that, when Flaminius enters office in Ariminum, the sacrificial victim escapes from the hands of sacrificing priests and sprays the audience with its blood; people interpret this as a bad omen (21.63.13–14). At the beginning of Book 22, the senators' worries are followed by a full prodigy list (22.1.8–13). By remarking that *augebant metum prodigia ex pluribus simul locis nuntiata* (prodigies, announced from several places at a time, increased their fear, 8), the text suggests that the negative omens are connected with Flaminius' disregard for the gods. In fact, disaster will soon follow: Flaminius will lead his army into the battle of Lake Trasimene, which will result in a major defeat for the Romans. The narrative of this event that the *Ab Urbe Condita* proposes, with its interweaving of human action and almost supernatural phenomena, strongly suggests that Flaminius' neglect of the gods was one important reason for the Carthaginian victory. Cf. Levene (1993, p. 22 and pp. 32–44).

42   On this point cf. again Jaeger (2015, p. 68).

43   *Locum qui nunc saeptus descendentibus inter duos lucos ⟨ad laevam⟩ est asylum aperit* ('he opened the place which is now enclosed and lies ⟨to the right⟩ for those who descend between the two groves as an asylum', 1.8.5). Livy means here 'the dip between the two peaks of the Capitoline Hill' (Ogilvie, 1965, pp. 62); in ancient times, two groves probably grew on either peak (cf. *OLD* s.v. *lucus*). For the textual and interpretive problems connected to the passage cf. Ogilvie (1965, pp. 62–63).

44   Cf. Chapter 1, pp. 42–43.

The dedication of the temple of Jupiter Optimus Maximus takes place in the new Republic's first year (2.8.6–8). Later, the First Pentad ends with the events connected to the Gallic sack of 390 BCE, in which the Capitol plays a crucial role as the site of the Romans' resistance. Book 6, the first after the 're-foundation' of the city, is connected to the previous one through the figure of Marcus Manlius Capitolinus, the one time rescuer of the Capitol and now demagogue; the Capitol looms large in the account of Manlius' attempt at conquering monarchic power and his consequent death.[45]

The fact that the Capitol was the end point in triumphal processions also has some consequences on the structure of the *Ab Urbe Condita*. Logically, the account of each victorious campaign ends with a report of the triumph, which can be very cursory (in many cases, not more than a passing mention) or extend to a fully-fledged narrative. Consequently, two major structural units of Livy's history end with events set on the Capitol. The first is the Third Decade, which concludes with an account of Scipio's lasting popularity due to his triumph over Carthage in 201 BCE (30.45). Livy does not mention the Capitol explicitly here, but his readers will have imagined the general ascending to the temple of Jupiter to give thanks.

The second unit is constituted by Books 41–45, which focus on the war against King Perseus of Macedon. The triumph of Lucius Aemilius Paullus is not the very last event that the book reports, but it comes close to the end and is certainly its climax.[46] In the narrative concerning the triumph (45.35.4–42.1), the Capitol is crucial as both a setting and a symbol. The account of the triumph itself is preceded by that of the debates concerning Aemilius Paullus' conduct of the war. At 45.35.4–9, Livy writes that the Senate decreed a triumph for Paullus and the other two commanders in the war, Gnaeus Octavius and Lucius Anicius, but Paullus came under heavy fire for his excessively rigid military discipline; a tribune put a bill before the assembly of the plebs, asking that Paullus be denied the triumph (45.36.1).

In the account of the assembly, the name of the Capitol recurs three times within the same chapter. First, Livy states that the tribune presented the bill *in Capitolio* (45.36.1) – that is, on the *area Capitolina*. Then, as he reports the voting of the tribes on the following day, he depicts a vivid scene of political strife.

---

45   See below, pp. 106–111.
46   After Paullus' triumph Livy related the triumphs of Cn. Octavius (45.42.2–3), some senatorial deliberations (45.42.4–12), the triumph of L. Anicius (45.43), the elections for the following year and some annalistic notices (45.44.1–3), and the embassy of Prusias of Bythinia (45.44.4–21, on which cf. Chapter 1, pp. 71–78).

THE SPACE OF THE CITY   95

The soldiers, he writes 'had crowded the Capitol' (*Capitolium compleverant*, 6) and the most prominent citizens 'rushed to the Capitol together' (*concursus in Capitolium principum civitatis factus est*, 7) to support Paullus' claims. Through the repetition of the toponym, the text emphatically sets the scene and alerts the reader to the fact that the Capitol will play a significant role in what follows.

Then Livy introduces a former military tribune, Servius Suplicius Galba, to speak against Paullus, stressing his harsh treatment of his soldiers (45.36.2–5); but, when the assembly is reconvened on the following day (45.36.6–10), the former consul Marcus Servilius delivers a long speech in the commander's defence (45.37–39). A lacuna breaks the continuity of the text, but the reader knows the speech has been successful because, when the text starts again, they find the report of the triumph (45.40).

Servilius mentions the Capitol four times in the surviving portion of the speech. At 45.39.2, he stresses how absurd it would be if the other two generals triumphed for their less important victories and Paullus did not:

> Quod si in curru scandentes Capitolium, auratos purpuratosque, ex inferiore loco L. Paulus, in turba togatorum unus privatus interroget 'L. Anici Cn. Octavi, utrum vos digniores triumpho esse an me censetis?', curru ei cessuri et prae pudore videntur insignia ipsa sua tradituri.

> What? If Lucius Paullus, as a private citizen amidst the throng of toga-wearers, from a position down below, were to ask the ones ascending the Capitol on a chariot and dressed in gold and purple: 'Lucius Anicius, Gnaeus Octavius, who do you believe worthier of a triumph: you or I?', it seems to me that they would descend from the chariot and give him their very insignia out of shame.

Servilius insists upon the vertical opposition between the triumphant generals ascending to the Capitol and the remaining people who stay below. The absurdity of this scenario results from the incongruity of Paullus, the general who has won the 'highest' achievements, occupying a lower position than his less prestigious colleagues.

Later, Servilius states that the triumph is due not only to the victorious general but also to the gods (45.39.10). To prove his point, he emphasises the role of the Capitol as a beginning and an end to Roman enterprises (45.39.10–11):

> Maiores vestri omnium magnarum rerum et principia exorsi a dis sunt, et finem statuerunt. 11. Consul proficiscens praetorve paludatis lictoribus

> in provinciam et ad bellum vota in Capitolio nuncupat: victor perpetrato ⟨...⟩ eodem in Capitolium triumphans ad eosdem deos quibus vota nuncupavit merita † bonaque pr. trans † redit.

> Your ancestors started all great things from the gods and ended them with the gods. 11. The consul or praetor who departs for his area of operation and to war, with his lictors in military attire, takes the vows on the Capitol; after victoriously bringing the war to conclusion, he triumphs on the Capitol and thus comes back to the very same gods he had invoked as he had made his vows.

Beginning and ending on the Capitol is tantamount to beginning and ending with the gods (10). In what follows, Servilius insists once again on the importance of the religious ceremonies connected to a triumph (45.39.12–13). In particular, he mentions the *epulae senatus*, the 'senate's feast' following a triumph,[47] which, as he says, could only take place on the Capitol (*quidem † illae epulae senatus, quae nec privato loco nec publico profano, sed in Capitolio eduntur*, 13). Thus, the Capitol is the embodiment of Roman civic religion and religious observance produces Roman military victories and ensures the stability of the *res publica*.

In a speech that plays so strongly on the circularity of Roman movement through space, one further circular element is the implicit reference to Livy's account of the beginning of the war. When describing the departure of the consul Publius Licinius for the Macedonian campaign in 171 BCE – the act which marks the start of military operations against Perseus – Livy emphasised the circular movement of consuls from and back to the Capitol (42.49.1–6):

> 1. Per hos forte dies P. Licinius consul, votis in Capitolio nuncupatis, paludatus ab urbe profectus est. 2. Semper quidem ea res cum magna dignitate ac maiestate † queritur †; praecipue convertit oculos animosque cum ad magnum nobilemque aut virtute aut fortuna hostem euntem consulem prosequuntur. 3. Contrahit enim non officii modo cura, sed etiam studium spectaculi, ut videant ducem suum, cuius imperio consilioque summam rem publicam tuendam permiserunt. 4. Subit deinde cogitatio animos qui belli casus, quam incertus fortunae eventus communisque Mars belli sit; 5. adversa secundaque, quae inscitia ac temeritate ducum clades saepe acciderint, quae contra bona prudentia et virtus attulerit. 6. Quem scire mortalium utrius mentis utrius fortunae

---

47 Beard (2007, pp. 261–263).

consulem ad bellum mittant? triumphantemne mox cum exercitu victore scandentem in Capitolium ad eosdem deos a quibus proficiscatur visuri, an hostibus eam praebituri laetitiam sint?

1. In those days it happened that the consul Publius Licinius, after making his vows on the Capitol, departed from the city wearing the military mantle. 2. That ceremony is always carried out with great dignity and grandeur; it especially attracts gazes and spirits when people follow a consul who marches against an enemy who is great and famous either for his valour or for his prosperity. 3. They come together not only out of a sense of duty but also out of a desire to watch, in order to see their leader, to whose command and judgment they have entrusted the protection of the whole State. 4. It occurs to them what the events of war are like, how uncertain the outcomes of destiny and the fortunes of war are; 5. they meditate upon favourable and unfavourable events: what defeats have often occurred because of the ignorance and rashness of commanders, and what advantages, on the other hand, are the product of discernment and valour. 6. Who among mortals knows what the spirit and destiny of the consul who they are sending to war will be like? Will they soon see him ascending the Capitol together with the victorious army to the very same gods from whom he departed, or will they offer the enemy such joy?

As Feldherr (1998, pp. 9–12) argues, this passage emphasises the role of the consul's progress as a public spectacle. By watching Licinius departing for the campaign, the people also look at 'a representation of the Republic in microcosm' (p. 10), both spatially (the consul departs from the Capitol, 'the physical and religious centre of the city' to reach the 'periphery and the distant battlefield', *ibid.*) and temporally (the departure is one in a series of similar occurrences, both past and future). At the same time, the spectacle of the consul's departure is parallel with and complementary to Livy's history as a visual spectacle (an *inlustre monumentum*, as the historian states at *praef.* 10) from which readers can learn about their past and gain valuable lessons for the future. Thus, by 'looking' at the consul departing, readers of the *Ab Urbe Condita* can share in the hopes and fears of 2nd-century Romans, reflect upon the historical significance of the war, and meditate on some more general historical facts, such as the fundamental instability of human fortunes. The latter thought appears particularly fitting when reading about a war which marked the end of a once powerful kingdom such as Macedon.

The correspondences between this passage, which marks the start of military operations against Perseus, and the narrative of Paullus' triumph, which sanctions the war's end, are probably stronger than hitherto noticed. First, there are some formal similarities. The phrasing describing Licinius' departure at 42.49.1 (*Per hos forte dies P. Licinius consul, votis in Capitolio nuncupatis, paludatus ab urbe profectus est*) is very similar to Servilius' words at 45.39.11 (*Consul proficiscens praetorve paludatis lictoribus in provinciam et ad bellum vota in Capitolio nuncupat*). One might object that the similarity is simply due to Livy's use of formulaic language;[48] however, the reference to the triumph at 42.49.6 (*triumphantemne mox cum exercitu victore scandentem in Capitolium ad eosdem deos a quibus proficiscatur, visuri ...?*) also finds a correspondence in 45.39.11 (*victor perpetrato ⟨...⟩ eodem in Capitolium triumphans ad eosdem deos quibus vota nuncupavit merita † bonaque pr. trans † redit.*).

Moreover, both the passage from Book 42 and the narrative of Paullus' triumph stress the theme of the instability of fortune. In the account of Licinius' departure, the focus is on the uncertainty of military outcomes; however, the emphasis Livy lays on the power of Macedon and the final sentence, with its alternative between the Roman triumph and the enemy's victory, seems to suggest that the theme has broader implications. The people watching the departing consul are not merely wondering about the outcome of any military campaign. They ask themselves whether Rome will follow in Macedon's footsteps as a leading power, or the war will mark her downfall.

The narrative of Paullus' triumph develops the theme in full. After describing the triumphal procession, Livy expands on the paradoxical destinies of both the victor and the defeated king, defining both as specimens of human fortunes (*documentum humanorum casuum*, 45.40.6). Defeated kings as examples of the instability of fortune were commonplace in ancient historiography from Herodotus.[49] Perseus' fall is, after all, one of the two possibilities that the spectators of Licinius' progress in 171 BCE had contemplated. However, Aemilius Paullus, who lost one son in the days preceding the triumph and one shortly after it,[50] provides even more striking evidence of that historical lesson.

In the speech that Livy has him deliver some days after the triumph to pass a review on his deeds during the campaign, the victorious general ties together his private misfortunes and the fortune of the Roman state (45.41.6–12). Paullus reveals to his listeners that, when he realised that all his military enterprises had met with success, he started to fear for Rome. The underlying idea – and one with a Herodotean tinge[51] – is that too much good fortune is dangerous

---

48 For similar phraseology cf. e.g. 21.63.9; 31.14.1; 41.10.5, 7, 11, 13.
49 Perhaps the most famous example is the story of the Lydian king Croesus in Hdt. 1.86–87.
50 These were, as Livy explains, his only remaining sons who might have carried on his name, since two other sons had been adopted by the *gentes* Fabia (Quintus Fabius Maximus Aemilianus) and Cornelia (Scipio Aemilianus), respectively (Livy 45.41.11–12).
51 See e.g. Hdt. 3.39–43.

because some catastrophe is bound to follow to compensate for it. Thus, following the example of other Livian heroes who put the state's interests before their own,[52] he wished that misfortune would fall on his house rather than on the community (7–8). His wish has been now granted, prompting his hope that 'public fortune' (*fortuna publica*) will be content with his private tragedy (9). The contrast between public and private is emphatically restated in section 12 through the contrast between *hanc cladem domus meae* and *vestra felicitas et secunda fortuna publica*, which is strengthened by the chiastic juxtaposition of *meae vestra*.[53] In inviting his audience to contemplate such a contrast, Paullus insists on the nature of his triumph as a spectacle through the verb *spectemur* in section 10: *Et cum ego et Perseus nunc nobilia maxime sortis mortalium exempla spectemur* ('And while Perseus and I are now observed as the most renowned examples of human destiny ...'). His words reinforce the external narrator's remark at 45.40.6 that Perseus and Paullus provided a *documentum* of human fortunes. The Roman people, one understands, are supposed to watch the spectacle and learn a general truth from it.

What, however, is the *external* audience (i.e. the readers of the *Ab Urbe Condita*) supposed to learn? Probably, a more complex truth. Readers knew Paullus' hopes would not come true and that – at least according to a long-standing interpretive pattern in Roman historiography – the achievement of power and wealth through military successes in the East would bring about a process of moral decay, which was to result in the civil wars of the 1st century BCE.[54] In this respect, the victory over Macedon provides a very effective chance to prompt readers to reflect on that process: the defeat of the glorious kingdom that had been Alexander the Great's invited one to think about the rise and fall of empires as something that had always governed human history.

My argument has led me far from the Capitol, but it is now where I – just as Livy's *imperatores* – now intend to return. How can one understand the stress that Livy lays, in the account of Aemilius Paullus' triumph, on the pivotal role of the Capitol? As I have observed above, the Capitol appears at the end of a very important portion of Livy's Roman history: the victory over Macedon sanctions Rome's role as a leading power in Alexander's footsteps and her embracing the cultural role that Greece had previously fulfilled. In such a context,

---

52   A typical example is Lucius Junius Brutus, the founder of the Republic, who had his own sons executed for treason after discovering that they were part of a monarchic conspiracy (Livy 2.3–5): cf. Feldherr (1998, pp. 200–203).
53   *Sed hanc cladem domus meae vestra felicitas et secunda fortuna publica consolatur* ('But your felicity and public good fortune soothes the calamity of my house').
54   On this explanatory pattern see Introduction, pp. 2–3.

the circularity of history engenders both positive and negative connotations for Roman readers. On the one hand, it points to the fact that Rome has now taken on the hegemonic role of previous empires; on the other, it suggests that Rome itself might, as all previous empires, decay and fall. Within this historical pattern, the Capitol provides a fundamental element of stability: it is the point where, as has already happened in the past, Rome can start anew after each year, military campaign, or cycle of growth and decay.

Servilius stresses the importance of maintaining a good relationship with the gods; in this light, the narrative casts Paullus' triumph as the celebration of the collaboration between gods and human beings for the success of the *res publica*. Such collaboration, the text suggests, is the guarantee of the city's stability. As long as the Romans work in harmony with their gods, there will be no end to Roman power. On the other hand, recognising the hierarchy of gods and human beings, on which the city's prosperity rests, appears closely connected to upholding other kinds of hierarchies at work within the citizen community. The narrative from Book 45 makes this very clear: only when the Romans overcome their inner conflicts and re-establish the hierarchy between soldiers and generals, people and magistrates, can they come together to give the gods their due.

Apart from its being the seat for some of the most important temples in Rome, there is one further feature of the Capitol that makes it especially productive as a symbol of authority and hierarchy: its height. Since the Capitol is a hill, it towers above the adjacent valley – especially above the Forum. In the following paragraph, I show how the *Ab Urbe Condita* works with such metaphorical connotations to develop complex reflections about the relationship between individuals, community, and gods; and it does so by construing the Capitol as something to be looked at and spoken about.

2.3 *The Object of Gazes and Words: Verticality, Hierarchy, and Authority Struggles*

At 7.6, Livy provides a second aition for the Lacus Curtius, after the story about the Sabine warrior Mettius Curtius he reports in Book 1.[55] In 362 BCE, he writes, a vast chasm opened in the Forum because of an earthquake (7.6.1). Since it proved impossible to fill, the Romans enquired after the will of the gods and received the response that they should look for the thing 'in which the Roman people were most powerful' (*quo plurimum populus Romanum posset*, 7.6.2).[56] A young man named Marcus Curtius provided the solution (7.6.3–4):

---

55 On the two stories and their implications for Livy's history, cf. Spencer (2007).
56 In the parallel account of Dion. Hal. *Ant. Rom.* 14.11.1–5, the response is that Rome should sacrifice 'what is most valuable to the Roman people' (τὰ πλείστου ἄξια τῷ Ῥωμαίων

THE SPACE OF THE CITY   101

> Tum M. Curtium, iuvenem bello egregium, castigasse ferunt dubitantes an ullum magis Romanum bonum quam arma virtusque esset; 4. silentio facto templa deorum inmortalium, quae foro imminent, Capitoliumque intuentem et manus nunc in caelum, nunc in patentes terrae hiatus ad deos manes porrigentem, se devovisse.

> It is reported that at that point Marcus Curtius, a young man distinguished in war, reproached the people who doubted whether there were any other more Roman virtue than warlike valour. 4. After asking for silence, he consecrated himself as he looked at the temples of the immortal gods, which loom upon the Forum, and at the Capitol, and stretched his hand now to the sky now to the open chasms of the earth.

Then Curtius threw himself into the chasm; the pond that originated from it was named after him (5–6).

The context is highly symbolic. In describing Curtius' act of self-sacrifice,[57] the text insists on verticality.[58] The elevated position of the temples on the Capitoline Hill, stressed by the verb *inminent*, represents a hierarchy of values: the city's gods – and thus the city itself, the community of citizens as a whole – are more important than any individual. Indeed, an individual must die so that the city lives; Curtius' gaze, which wanders from the depth of the chasm to the height of the Capitol,[59] connects the realm of the heavenly gods to that of the infernal gods (the *di manes*) and thus recomposes the cosmic and political order through sacrifice.

It can be interesting to read this story in parallel with a passage from the speech of Fabius Rullianus' father at 8.33.20–21. The elder Fabius is stirring the people in the Forum against the dictator Papirius Cursor, who has sentenced his son to death for engaging in single combat with an enemy against orders:[60]

δήμῳ, 1). In Varro *Ling.* 5.148, the *di Manes* require that the strongest citizen (*fortissimum civem*) be offered to them. Varro reports three different aitia for the Lacus Curtius at *Ling.* 5.148–150: the story of Marcus Curtius is followed by the one about the Sabine warrior Mettius Curtius – for which he gives credit to the historian Piso Frugi – and then by a third tradition that the site was struck by lightning under the consulate of a Curtius. On these traditions, see Oakley (1998, pp. 96–97).

57   For other ancient tales of 'substitutionary sacrifice', which are very similar to Curtius' story in their basic structure, see Oakley (1998, p. 97).
58   On this point cf. Spencer (2007, p. 87).
59   As Oakley (1998, p. 100) remarks, it is an attested custom that, 'when praying, one pointed in the direction in which one believed the relevant deities were to be found'.
60   Cf. Chapter 1, pp. 67–68.

> 20. Quam conveniens esse (...) 21. eum propter quem deum delubra pateant, arae sacrificiis fument, honore donis cumulentur, nudatum virgis lacerari in conspectu populi Romani, intuentem Capitolium atque arcem deosque ab se duobus proeliis haud frustra advocatos!

> 20. How proper it is (...) 21. that the one because of whom the temples of the gods are open, altars smoke in sacrifices and are overloaded with gifts, is stripped naked and torn to pieces with rods under the eyes of the Roman people, as he looks up at the *Capitolium* and the citadel and at the gods who he successfully called to his aid in two battles!

This passage is very interesting because it presents two kinds of 'visions' of the Capitol: the actual one – the audience is in the Forum and can therefore see the Capitol – and an imagined one (the young Fabius is executed as he looks toward the Capitol, and is, in turn, looked at by the Roman people). When describing the imaginary view of young Fabius' death, his father uses the verb *intueri*, which designated Curtius' 'looking up' at the Capitol. Once again, a young man dies in the Forum as he looks up at the Capitol and its temples. This time, however, his death is not a sacrifice that the gods will appreciate (or, at least, this is what his father wants to persuade his listeners of): Fabius' gazing at the Capitol makes the impiety of his death all the more evident. The actual and the imagined view reinforce each other and recall Fabius' military success and its ties with Roman civic religion. Thus, by contemplating the imaginary view, the Romans can see that Fabius's death would subvert the ideal relationship between gods and city.

In both episodes, the Capitol is invoked as the embodiment of the relationship between gods and men that the Romans are going to strengthen (in the first case) or to defile (in the second).[61] Moreover, both episodes involve a negotiation of hierarchy. In the first case, Curtius' sacrifice affirms the primacy

---

61 The two passages belong in a broader pattern of attention to issues concerning the relationship between gods and men, on the one hand, and between the old and the young, on the other, in Books 7 and 8 (cf. Spencer, 2007, pp. 85–86, who speaks of a 'series of supernatural terrors' in Book 7). One might recall a pestilence and its expiation at 7.1.1–3.4 and the following excursus on the ceremony of hammering a nail on the right side of the temple of Jupiter Optimus Maximus (7.3.6–9); the story of Manlius Torquatus stepping in defence of his father at 7.4–5 and later, at 8.7, executing his own son for fighting an enemy against orders. The latter story finds a correspondence in the episode of Fabius Rullianus at 8.30.1–35.9, where the conflict between an older commander and a younger officer finds a happier solution (on this episode cf. e.g. Chaplin, 2000, pp. 108–119). Moreover, Book 8 contains the *devotio* of Publius Decius Mus (8.9.3–12) in the battle of the Veseris of 340 BCE, which works as a pendant to Curtius' own *devotio* in Book 7.

of the community with respect to the individual. In the second, hierarchy is a more complex issue. The whole story of Fabius Rullianus and Papirius Cursor involves a discussion about the limits of magisterial authority. Since the young Fabius has disobeyed the dictator's orders, Papirius has the authority to put him to death. However, Fabius challenges such authority by first appealing to his fellow-soldiers for protection and then fleeing to Rome to appeal to the people. His father, another authority figure, supports him and thereby challenges the dictator. Father and son argue that the young Fabius' victory makes punishment inappropriate. In doing so, they enlist the supreme authority of the gods to their aid: by inviting his audience to look up at the Capitol, the elder Fabius suggests that their authority should be viewed as even higher than the dictator's – and that the man responsible for the victory which will bring the gods due honour should be spared because of his connection with their authority. The dispute ends when the two Fabii and the people submit to the dictator's authority, pleading with him instead of challenging him, and when the dictator rewards such submission with an act of mercy; Livy's narrative is a lesson in how public concord can be achieved when each side shows moderation. What matters to me at this point is the elder Fabius' rhetorical use of the Capitol within such a struggle over authority. By inviting the people to look at the hill, he proposes his view of the hierarchies within the *res publica*.

There is, however, one further similarity between this narrative and the account about the Lacus Curtius, namely the role the text attributes to gazes and speech in constructing the semantic role of the Capitol. Curtius looks up at the looming Capitol and temples as he utters his *devotio*, thus creating a symbolic association between the hill's height and the depth of the chasm he is going to fill. Fabius, the father, uses the hill as a rhetorical prop, playing on his audience's imaginative power to produce a vivid representation; his words are functional in driving his listeners' gaze towards the Capitol and in eliciting a mental image of it in readers' mind. The Capitol's height, which makes it a convenient symbol for hierarchy, also makes it the ideal object for gazes and an effective rhetorical prop for speakers.

In fact, hardly any other site is so frequently looked at and spoken about, in the *Ab Urbe Condita*, as the Capitol. In the first Pentad, the hill (or one of its parts) is mentioned 30 times in (both direct and reported) speeches (none of them in Book 1),[62] often by speakers standing in the Forum, who can therefore be imagined as pointing to the hill.[63] In the Second Pentad, the Capitol

---

[62] 2.7.10; 3.16.5; 3.17.4, 5, 6, 7, 9, 10; 3.18.6; 3.19.6, 7 (twice), 8, 12; 3.20.3; 3.68.7; 4.2.13; 5.30.5; 5.44.5; 5.51.3 (twice), 9; 5.52.3, 6, 11, 12; 5.53.5, 9; 5.54.7 (twice).

[63] A curious instance of the *arx* as an object of the gaze occurs at 4.18.6–7. Relating the beginning of a battle between Romans and Etruscans in 437 BCE, Livy states that the

appears at least seventeen times in speeches, although these mentions occur in a limited number of episodes.[64] Speakers mention it nine times in the Third Decade,[65] eight in the Fourth – where most of these occurrences comes from Book 38;[66] and twelve in the Fifth Decade.[67]

Speakers use the Capitol in various ways, but one can recognise some frequent rhetorical strategies. First, there are some passages where the Capitol works as a reminder of past events – most often the Gallic sack of 390 BCE, which speakers employ as a historical *exemplum*.[68] Secondly, just like in Servilius' oration from Book 45, speakers use the Capitol as the epitome of the triumphal ceremony and, thus, of the collaboration between the Romans and their gods on which Roman military power rests.

The latter category is especially interesting, because speeches of this kind often feature mentions of the Capitol in discussions about hierarchy and authority. One speaker uses a rhetoric very much like Servilius', and in a similar context. At 38.47–49 (187 BCE), Gnaeus Manlius Vulso speaks in support of his application for a triumph after his victory over the Galatians in 189 BCE. When defending himself from the criticism raised by his political adversaries, at 38.49.14–16, Manlius stresses the role of the Capitol as the beginning and end point of campaigns in words that seem to anticipate Servilius' statements

---

Roman dictator did not start the fight before seeing a sign sent from the augurs on the citadel to inform him that the auspices are favourable. Indeed, Livy presents the dictator Mamercus Aemilius in the act of 'looking back at the Roman citadel' (*arcem Romanam respectante*) while waiting for the sign. As Ogilvie (1965, p. 561) remarks, it would have been impossible to see the Roman *arx* from the plain of Fidenae, where the armies were deployed; one should probably think of some kind of signal which was visible from afar (a 'signal optique' according to Bayet and Baillet, 1954, p. 32 n. 1). Livy's wording, however, emphasises the idea of gazing at the citadel, stressing the dictator's devotion to Rome's gods. This appears significant when one considers the narrative context of the episode. Livy presents the conflict with the Etruscans as the consequence of two impious acts: the defection of Fidenae, a Roman colony, from Rome to Veii; and the murder of the Roman ambassadors who had been sent to Fidenae to enquire after the reason of such a betrayal (4.17.1–6). The account of the battle ends with the dictator's triumph and Aulus Cornelius Cossus' dedication of the *spolia opima* in the temple of Jupiter Feretrius on the Capitoline – the second and last occurrence of this kind in Roman history (4.19–20). Therefore, the whole narrative develops, so to say, under the shadow of the Capitoline Hill, stressing the union of martial valour and piety that makes the Romans victorious.

64 6.11.4–5; 6.14.4; 6.15.11; 6.16.2; 6.17.4 (the Tarpeian Rock); 6.20.9, 13, 16 (all occurrences till here in the narrative concerning Manlius Capitolinus; see below); 6.40.17; 6.41.3; 8.4.11; 8.5.8 (Jupiter temple); 8.33.21; 9.4.7, 9 (L. Lentulus at the Caudine Forks); 10.7.10.

65 21.63.7–9 (twice the Capitol and once the Jupiter temple); 22.1.6; 22.37.11,12; 22.51.2; 23.22.7; 28.39.15 (*Iovi Optimo Maximo ... praesidi Capitolinae arcis ... in Capitolium*), 19.

66 34.5.8; 36.35.12; 38.17.9; 38.48.15; 38.51.8 (twice); 38.56.12; 39.15.11 (*in arce*).

67 41.10.7; 42.49.6; 43.6.6 (twice); 44.14.3; 45.22.1; 45.39.2, 11 (twice), 13; 45.41.10; 45.44.8.

68 Cf. e.g. 6.40.17; 9.4.8–9; 38.17.9.

THE SPACE OF THE CITY

in favour of Aemilius Paullus in Book 45; and, just like Servilius, he argues that a triumphal procession is due not only to the commander but to the gods as well.[69] Here, too, the mention of the Capitol is functional to a contest for authority. Vulso's authority as a commander is put into question and, in order to reaffirm it, Vulso recurs to the fundamental hierarchy of gods and men on which even magisterial authority rests.

In an earlier episode, at 10.6.3–9.2, Livy relates the story of the Ogulnian plebiscite, which, in 300 BCE, decreed access to the pontifical and augural colleges for plebeians. The issues of hierarchy and authority are crucial here. The patricians, in Livy's narrative, oppose the rogation on the ground that only they can take auspices, but Publius Decius Mus effectively counters their points: his main argument is that, since plebeians already hold all main political offices, and have done so with honour, there is no reason why they should not be pontiffs and augurs as well. In this context, he mentions the Capitol as the end point of triumphs (10.7.10): if a plebeian magistrate has triumphed – so goes his argument – and sacrificed to Jupiter on the Capitol,[70] why should the gods not accept his performing of augural or pontifical rites?[71] There is also topographic contiguity between the triumph and the duties of augurs since

---

[69] *14. Sed ego in ea civitate quae ideo omnibus rebus incipiendis gerendisque deos adhibet, quia nullius calumniae subicit ea quae dii comprobaverunt, et in sollemnibus verbis habet, cum supplicationem aut triumphum decernit, 'quod bene ac feliciter rem publicam administrarit', 15. si nollem, si grave ac superbum existimarem virtute gloriari, ⟨si⟩ pro felicitate mea exercitusque mei, quod tantam nationem sine ulla militum iactura devicimus, postularem 16 ut dis immortalibus honos haberetur et ipse triumphans in Capitolium escenderem, unde votis rite nuncupatis profectus sum, negaretis hoc mihi cum dis immortalibus?'* '14. But I live in a state which resorts to the gods in beginning and in carrying out all things: it does not subject what the gods have approved to anybody's calumny and, when it decrees a supplication or a triumph, it uses the ceremonial words "because he administered the State well and successfully." 15. Suppose I did not want to boast my valour, suppose I believed that unpleasant and proud; suppose, however, that, because of my own success and that of my army—since we defeated such a great people without any loss of soldiers—, 16. I asked that honour be given the immortal gods and that I may ascend to the Capitoline, whence I departed after correctly formulating my vows, in triumph. Would you deny that to me and to the immortal gods?'

[70] The implication is that the triumphant general has fought under his own auspices.

[71] *Qui Iovis Optimi Maximi ornatu decoratus, curru aurato per urbem vectus in Capitolium ascenderit, is ⟨non⟩ conspicietur cum capide ac lituo, ⟨non⟩ capite velato victimam caedet auguriumve ex arce capiet?* 'Will the one who has been led through the city in a golden chariot and climbed to the Capitol, adorned with the ornaments of Jupiter the Best and Greatest, not be seen with the votive bowl and the augural staff? Will he not, his head covered, kill the sacrificial victim, or take the augurium from the citadel?' I here print the text as proposed by Oakley (2005b, p. 83, who also discusses the textual problems connected to this passage).

auspices were usually taken, as Livy stresses here, on the *arx*.[72] The Capitol thus appears as the visible symbol of the legitimacy of Roman political and military power as sanctioned by the city's gods.

A different kind of hierarchy is at stake in Maharbal's famous remark to Hannibal after the battle of Cannae: 'In order that you may know what has been achieved with this battle: in four days you will banquet on the Capitol' (*Immo ut quid hac pugna sit actum scias, die quinto (…) victor in Capitolio epulaberis*, 22.51.2). Livy's phrasing significantly differs from Cato's and Coelius Antipater's, who, as we learn from Aulus Gellius (*NA* 10.24.6–7) also transmitted the episode.[73] While in Cato and Coelius, Maharbal spoke of a dinner to be cooked on the Capitol (Cato: *in Capitolio tibi cena cocta erit*; Coelius: *in Capitolium curabo tibi cena sit cocta*), Livy uses the verb *epulari*, which reminds one of the ceremonial banquets on the Capitol; moreover, through the insertion of the substantive *victor*, he further insists on the association between Hannibal and a triumphant general. Thus, he conveys to his Roman readers the idea of a drastic subversion of the ritual of Roman victory, by which the enemy threatens to 'triumph' on the Capitol.[74] This also implies a subversion of the hierarchy (which Livy's readers have in mind) between Romans and others: what Maharbal imagines is an alternative vision of world power, which features Carthage, not Rome as the victor and mistress of other peoples.

The Capitol, however, can work as the terrain for competing interpretations of hierarchy even in contexts where it does not appear in direct connection with a triumph. The narrative of the fall of the hero-turned-demagogue Marcus Manlius Capitolinus in Book 6 provides a striking instance.[75] This account resonates with themes of Late-Republican Roman politics and civil unrest: scholars usually connect it with the similar stories of Spurius Cassius (Livy 2.41; cf. Dion. Hal. *Ant. Rom.* 8.69–79) and Spurius Maelius (Livy 4.13; cf. Dion. Hal. *Ant. Rom.* 12.1–2) and see the three tales as portrayals of 'proto-*populares*' leaders who, in Livy's narrative, ingratiate themselves with the plebs in their attempts to achieve monarchical power and are consequently punished with death.[76]

---

72   For the *arx* as seat of augural observation cf. Oakley (2005b, p. 108).
73   For this episode and the historical problems it poses, cf. Hoyos (2000).
74   Cf. Jaeger (2015, pp. 69–70).
75   For bibliography on this episode, cf. Chapter 1, p. 66 n. 103. Some of the studies quoted there will be cited and discussed in the following footnotes.
76   On the presence of elements pertaining to 1st century agitations in Late-Republican and Augustan portraits of Manlius and other early demagogues (and most notably of similarities between Livy's Manlius and Catiline) see e.g. Seager (1977, esp. pp. 377–384); Oakley (1997, pp. 481–486); Smith (2006); Kaplow (2012). Neel (2015), while recognising the importance of first-century politics in the development of Manlius' tale, argues that the

The reader of the *Ab Urbe Condita* encounters Manlius for the first time at 5.31.2–4, where he is elected consul for 392 BCE and then obtains an ovation for a victory against the Aequians; but his most glorious feat is found in Livy's narrative of the Romans' resistance during the Gallic invasion of 390 BCE. At 5.47.1–5, while the Romans are barricaded on the Capitol, the Gauls attempt a surprise attack by climbing up a rock or cliff (*saxo*, 2) 'near the shrine of Carmenta' (*ad Carmentis*, ibid.) in the night; but the honking of the geese sacred to Juno awakens Manlius, who heroically throws the invaders down the cliff. Since the shrine of Carmenta was located on the south-western flank of the Capitolium, the *saxum* in question must be a rock of the Capitolium itself; consequently, one should assume that the geese of this story were kept in the temple of Juno that was part of the complex of the Capitoline triad.[77]

Some years later, in 385 BCE, Manlius turns *popularis* (6.11.3–10)[78] and begins stirring the plebs, who are angered by increasing debts (6.14.1–10); he hosts secret meetings in his home and goes as far as to accuse the senators of concealing Gallic gold (6.14.11–13). For these reasons, the dictator Aulus Cornelius Cossus has him thrown in jail (6.15.1–16.3); this only exacerbates the plebeians' spirits, so, in the end, Manlius is set free again (6.16.4–17.5). He then starts planning a *seditio* to win monarchic power (6.17). The Senate and tribunes of the plebs act in concert this time (6.19), and the tribunes put Manlius under trial. Manlius delivers a magnificent defensive speech, but even more effective in swaying the plebeians' minds is the sight of the Capitol, a reminder of the defendant's past heroism (6.20.1–10). Only after the trial has been moved to a site where the hill is not visible do the people vote for Manlius' condemnation. So, the former saviour is thrown down the Tarpeian Rock (6.20.11–12). The people decree that no patrician will be allowed to live on the Capitol from that moment onwards, and the *gens* Manlia establishes that none of its members will ever bear the *praenomen* Marcus again (6.20.13–16).

There is, of course, tragic irony in that Manlius, the defender of the Capitol, ultimately dies by falling from the same hill (more precisely from the *arx*, of which the Tarpeian Rock is the northeastern side). His very *cognomen*, Capitolinus,[79] epitomises both aspects of his life. Even more importantly, as Jaeger (1997, pp. 57–93) shows, the Capitol functions as the focus for two

---

association between Manlius, Spurius Cassius, and Spurius Maelius in a trio of so-called *adfectatores regni* is a modern construction.
77   Cf. Oakley (1997, p. 540), with further bibliography.
78   Livy remarks that Capitolinus was the first patrician to do so: *primus omnium ex patribus popularis factus* (7).
79   In fact, the name probably originated from Manlius' house being located on the Capitol: cf. Oakley (1997, p. 476), with further literature.

competing spatial semantics. Manlius identifies with the Capitol and proposes 'a model of the city in which the Capitoline predominates'.[80] His focus on the vertical axis,[81] with the Capitol as the highest point, mirrors his view of the Roman community as one in which one citizen – he – should hold supreme power. Camillus, on the other hand, views the Capitol as the embodiment of a hierarchy in which the highest point is reserved for the community and its gods. In the end, the narrative confirms Camillus' interpretation of the city space, as Manlius is thrown down from the *arx*.

Livy develops the semantics of the Capitol primarily through the words and gazes of characters. Manlius frequently mentions the Capitol and, since he delivers most of his speeches in the Forum, the reader can imagine him pointing to the hill while speaking. When, for example, he frees an enslaved centurion, at 6.14.4, he emphatically states that his rescue of the Capitol will have been in vain, if one of his fellow-citizens is taken captive as if the Gauls had won.[82] The scene has, as so often in Livy, an almost theatrical quality, with the Forum as the stage where people act and speak.[83] If the Forum is the stage and the observation point, then the Capitol is the conspicuous landmark people are invited to look at, and readers are prompted to visualise.

Similarly, at 6.15.11, Manlius evokes the Capitol while standing before the *tribunal* of the dictator, who is questioning him about his allegation that the senators are concealing the Gallic gold. 'But then, why do I alone take care of my fellow-citizens?' he rhetorically asks. 'I have no other answer than if you asked me why I alone saved the Capitolium and the citadel'.[84] Later, at 6.16.2, while Manlius is being led from the *tribunal* to the *carcer*, he does not simply remind his listeners of his rescue of the Capitol, but openly invokes the deities 'who inhabit the Capitolium and the citadel' (*qui Capitolium arcemque incolitis*) and implores them to come to the aid of their 'soldier and protector' (*vestrum militem ac praesidem*). One can imagine him raising his eyes and hands to the temples on the Capitol in his prayer.

---

80 Jaeger (1997, p. 79).
81 For the importance of images of verticality in the tale of Manlius see Krebs (2012, esp. pp. 145–148).
82 *'Tum vero ego' inquit 'nequiquam hac dextra Capitolium arcemque servaverim, si civem commilitonemque meum tamquam Gallis victoribus captum in servitutem ac vincula duci videam'.*
83 The centurion is brought away 'in the middle of the Forum' (*medio foro*, 6.14.3). On the role of the Forum in this scene cf. Kraus (1994, p. 172).
84 *At enim quid ita solus ego civium curam ago? Nihilo magis quod respondeam habeo quam si quaeras quid ita solus Capitolium arcemque servaverim.*

Manlius' supporters, too, evoke the citadel by rhetorically asking the people whether 'the image of the army of Gauls climbing up the Tarpeian Rock' (*speciem agminis Gallorum per Tarpeiam rupem scandentis*) did not occur to them when they let their leader be brought away in chains (6.17.4). These members of the *turba Manliana* ('Manlius' throng', cf. 6.16.8) contradict the external narrator's account of the same event in Book 5 by having the Gauls climb the Tarpeian Rock – that is, the southeastern side of the *arx* – rather than the Capitolium. Such an inconsistency possibly derives from Livy using a different version of the story, one that had the Tarpeian Rock as the location for both the Gallic assault and Manlius' later execution.[85]

On all these occasions, the Capitol works as a visual reminder of Manlius' past heroism; such a reminder is effective because it stands before the eyes of the people in the Forum. The most significant functionalisation of the Capitol as both a reminder and a rhetorical argument, however, comes later, in the account of his trial. In his harangue, Manlius lays special emphasis on the act of looking at the Capitol (6.20.8–9):

> Et cum ea quoque quae bello gesta essent pro fastigio rerum oratione etiam magnifica, facta dictis aequando, memorasset, nudasse pectus insigne cicatricibus bello acceptis 9. et identidem Capitolium spectans Iovem deosque alios devocasse ad auxilium fortunarum suarum precatusque esse ut, quam mentem sibi Capitolinam arcem protegenti ad salutem populi Romani dedissent, eam populo Romano in suo discrimine darent, et orasse singulos universosque ut Capitolium atque arcem intuentes, ut ad deos immortales versi de se iudicarent.

> And after he had also recalled what he had done in war in a splendid speech, as was suited to the loftiness of the subject, by matching facts and words, 9. he bared his breast, which was remarkable for the scars he had received in war. Looking again and again at the Capitol he called to Jupiter and the other gods to help him; he implored them to give the Roman people the same spirit they had given him when he defended the Capitol's citadel for the welfare of the Roman people; and he pleaded that each and everyone of them pass judgement on him while they looked at the Capitolium and the citadel and as they faced the immortal gods.

---

85   On the topography of the Manlius tale, both in Livy and in other sources, see Wiseman (1979b); Oakley (1997, pp. 490–491 and p. 540).

Once more, Manlius looks at and stretches his hands toward the Capitol (*Capitolium spectans*) as he prays to the gods. Moreover, Manlius openly invites his people to look at the Capitolium and the citadel, so that they shall keep his past benefactions in mind while they judge him. The text powerfully stresses the verticality of such gazes, both through the verb *devocare*, in section 9 ('to call *down*') and through the noun *fastigium*, by which the external narrator indicates the 'loftiness' of the speech's subject.[86]

What follows (a famous passage) shows just how effective the view of the Capitol is on Manlius' audience (6.20.10–11). Since the trial takes place in the Campus Martius, that is, in a location where the Capitol is literally before the people's eyes, the tribunes realise that 'unless they freed people's eyes, too, from the memory of so great a glory, there would never be the chance of a proper trial before spirits already won over by Manlius' benefactions' (*nisi oculos quoque hominibus liberassent tanti memoria decoris, numquam fore in praeoccupatis beneficio animis vero crimini locum*, 10). Therefore, after the trial is adjourned, they convene the people 'to the Petelian grove outside the Porta Flumentana, whence the Capitol could not be seen' (*in Petelinum lucum extra portam Flumentanam, unde conspectus in Capitolium non esset, ibid.*). There the accusation was, at last, effective.

The topography of this passage is notorious for its absurdity. In fact, the Capitol *was* visible from the Petelian grove, since the Porta Flumentana, near which the *lucus* lay, seems to have been in the Forum Boarium.[87] It is possible that, as Wiseman (1979b) argues, this mistake originated from Livy's conflation of different sources.[88] Whatever the truth may be, what matters to my

---

[86] On the expression *pro fastigio rerum* see Krebs (2012, pp. 139–140). Krebs also notes the spatial image implicit in *facta dictis aequando*, which he effectively translates as 'his language rising to the level of his exploits'.

[87] For localisation of the Porta Flumentana see Wiseman (1979b, pp. 32–37), with an analysis of ancient sources and further bibliography.

[88] In Wiseman's reconstruction, two versions of the story of Manlius and the geese circulated: one, which Livy follows in his narrative of the Gallic sack in Book 5, had Manlius throw the Gauls down the Capitolium; another one, which, as I have mentioned, might have left a trace in the words of Manlius' supporters at 6.17.4, had the Gauls climb the Tarpeian Rock. Moreover, while in Livy the *comitia centuriata* (which had to be convened outside the *pomerium*) tried Manlius, a previous version of the story might have featured a trial by a council of the plebs in the Forum. There Manlius could have pointed to the Tarpeian Rock as the site of his heroic feat of 390 BCE; this would have led the consuls to move the trial to a place (the *lucus Petelinus* in the Forum Boarium) where the Tarpeian Rock was not visible. Thus, Livy's source might have correctly stated that the Tarpeian Rock (which faced the Forum) was not visible from the Petelian grove; but the historian probably misunderstood this and took the fact as applying to the whole Capitol. Cf. also Oakley (1997, pp. 487–492 and p. 563). If this reconstruction is correct, the imprecision

analysis is the meaning that the act of gazing at the Capitol acquires in the narrative. Livy grants the Capitol a striking power to sway minds. The memories the hill evokes are so effective that the Roman people cannot even consider the accusations against Manlius as long as they see it. As Livy puts it, the people's minds must be 'freed' from the memory of Manlius' glory, just as – one can surmise – the people themselves must be freed from his tyranny. Otherwise, the spirits will be 'seized upon beforehand' (*praeoccupatis*) by their memories of Manlius' benefactions so that there will be no 'place' (*locum*) in them to host the accusations. The metaphors in this passage resonate with the theme of enslavement and freedom that governs the whole episode: the effect of the view of the Capitol is a sort of 'enthrallment' of the people's spirits. At the same time, one cannot help observing the spatial quality of the latter two metaphors: minds are like sites conquered by an enemy, and leave no room for the truth to penetrate.

Thus, the Capitol's functioning as a symbol in the account of Manlius' sedition is inextricably tied with its role as a visual landmark and with interacting with and speaking about it. Of course, when readers of the *Ab Urbe Condita* 'look' at the Capitol through Livy's vivid narrative, they see something different than what Manlius' primary audience sees. For them, the Capitoline is not simply a reminder of recent events but a symbol of the Roman people's unity and the gods' favour. Thus, just by 'looking' at it, they can understand the flaws inherent in Manlius' notion of the Capitol as a spatial appendage of his own 'eminence' within the community of citizens. For the reader, the Capitol embodies a different hierarchy than that proposed by Manlius, one in which the welfare of the State takes precedence over the ambitions of individuals.

2.4　The Core of Roman Identity

In the previous section I have shown that the Capitol plays an important role, in the *Ab Urbe Condita*, in narratives that stage conflicts about hierarchy and authority, and that ultimately it embodies the various hierarchies on which, according to Livy, the Roman State in its healthy form rests: those of gods and men, magistrates and people, generals and soldiers, individuals in their public and private roles. Romans, Livy implies, should look at the hill, looming high above his narrated city, to be reminded that only abiding by such hierarchies will ensure the stability and constant renewal of the Roman State of which the Capitol itself is the seat and symbol. In the present section I argue that the Capitol, precisely because of its function as both a marker of space and time

---

might suggest that Livy was not very familiar with the topography of the area of the Forum Boarium when he wrote Book 6; cf. Levene (2019, p. 20).

and as a symbol for hierarchy, also works as the ultimate embodiment of the identity of the Roman people. Such an identity is not stable: it is constantly redefined, threatened, and reaffirmed.

I would like to start my analysis with the account of the Roman resistance during the Gallic sack in Book 5, where the Capitol, the core of the city, is the location of the Romans' last stand and stays unviolated by foreign invasion. At 5.39.9–13, Livy relates the Romans' decision to move the senate and the men of military age together with their families onto the Capitol. At the same time, the elderly are to stay behind in the city. In section 12, the narrator reports the thoughts and words of the Roman people immediately prior to the attack, explaining the underlying motivation:

> Si arx Capitoliumque, sedes deorum, si senatus, caput publici consilii, si militaris iuventus superfuerit imminenti ruinae urbis, facilem iacturam esse seniorum relictae in urbe utique periturae turbae.

> If the citadel and the Capitolium, seats of the gods, the Senate, the head of public decision-making, and the men of military age survived the imminent ruin of the city, then the loss of the elderly, who would be left in the city as they would die anyway, would be easy to bear.

This passage suggests that Rome, or her essential core, is, according to these Romans, the citadel and Capitolium, the Senate, and the fighting young men. The latter must survive both because they can fight the enemy (and thus avert the utter destruction of the city) and because they will assure the reproduction of Rome in the future; the senators must survive because they are the leaders who will guide and direct the survivors and also because they represent the political institutions of the *res publica*. Significantly, the Capitolium and the citadel are the only places on this list, the other elements of the quintessential Rome being human. The Capitol is included not only because it is the seat *par excellence* of civic religion, but also because it is the unmoveable place around which Roman space itself revolves. If there is no Capitol, there can be no Rome.

This concept comes to the fore in the aftermath the Gallic Sack, when the Romans, who have by now defeated the Gauls thanks to an army under Marcus Furius Camillus' command coming to their rescue, consider the idea of leaving their ravaged city behind and move to Veii.[89] Livy has Camillus deliver a long and impressive speech to persuade the people to vote against the move (5.51–54). His core argument is that the deities who protect Rome have their

---

89 The proposal had been aired for the first time before the Sack (5.24.4–25.3); now, as Livy writes, the tribunes put it forth with more force.

seats in specific sites within the city and, therefore, abandoning the city would amount to an act of impiety.[90] Camillus refers to several places in his speech, but the Capitol has special relevance.

At 5.51.3, he reminds his audience of how 'the Roman gods and men' held the Capitolium and the citadel even when the Gauls had conquered the rest of the city (*Et cum victoribus Gallis capta tota urbe Capitolium tamen atque arcem dique et homines Romani tenuerint et habitaverint, victoribus Romanis reciperata urbe arx quoque et Capitolium deseretur ...?*). The expression *dique et homines Romani* deserves a closer look. Although forms of the syntagm *di hominesque* are frequent in Livy, especially in the first Pentad,[91] this is one of only two occurrences of the syntagm in conjunction with the adjective *Romanus, -a, -um*.[92] The other one is a passage from Book 2 portraying the shock of the Roman people at the execution of a group of patrician youths who had conspired against the Republic in the very first year of its existence: the people contemplate how the young men (among whom is the son of Marcus Junius Brutus, the leader of the rebellion against the Tarquins and first consul of the *res publica*) betrayed 'their liberated fatherland, a liberator father, the consulate born into the Junian House, the patricians, the plebs, every Roman god and man' (*patriam liberatam, patrem liberatorem, consulatum ortum ex domo Iunia, patres, plebem, quidquid deorum hominumque Romanorum esset*, 2.5.7).[93] In both passages, 'Roman gods and men' appear to be elements of an ideal core of the Roman *res publica*. At 5.51.3, such a core once more includes the Capitol as the essential spatial element of Rome, complementing its human and divine elements. For this reason, Camillus presents the idea of abandoning the Capitol, now that there is no longer a Gallic threat, as paradoxical.

---

90   Cf. 5.52.2: *nullus locus in ea non religionum deorumque est plenus; sacrificiis sollemnibus non dies magis stati quam loca sunt in quibus fiant.*

91   I have counted forty-eight occurrences of the syntagm in Livy's extant book, twenty-two of which in the First Pentad. Some examples: 2.9.3; 2.10.9; 3.17.15; 3.25.8; 3.57.3; 4.53.5; 5.21.15; 5.39.9; 5.43.6; 5.49.1 (*diique et homines*); 5.51.8–9; 6.14.5 (*deos atque homines*); 7.5.1; 8.6.5; 10.7.9 (*deorum hominumve*); 21.63.11; 22.44.5; 28.8.2; 34.44.6; 38.52.11; 40.12.18; 45.32.9.

92   The adjective *Romanus* is also rarely attached to the noun *homo, -inis* in Livy. The only two occurrences of this kind are 1.59.9 *Romanos homines, victores omnium circa populorum, opifices ac lapicidas pro bellatoribus factos* and 42.29.4 *regem* (scil. Arthiaratum) *educendum filium Romam misisse, ut iam inde a puero adsuesceret moribus Romanis hominibusque*.

93   In both cases, I take the adjective *Romani/Romanorum* to modify both *di/deorum* and *homines/hominum*. The position of the adjective after two nouns connected through *-que* is not uncommon when it refers to both (e.g. *Senatus populusque Romanus*, 'the Roman Senate and people'); if 'gods and Roman men' were the meaning, one would expect something like *dique et Romani homines*. Moreover, the sense requires that the Roman-ness of men *and* gods is stressed in both passages.

In section 9 of the same chapter, he attributes the Roman defeat by the Gauls at the Allia to the Romans' impiety and recalls how they subsequently 'flew to the gods and the seat of Jupiter Optimus Maximus onto the Capitol' (*confugimus in Capitolium ad deos, ad sedem Iovis Optimi Maximi*) after catastrophe had reminded them of their religious scruples. This is a re-reading of the past that downplays the military rationale of barricading troops on a hill that is also Rome's citadel, representing such a choice as symbolic of a return to piety, which, in turn, brought about the Romans' final victory (cf. 5.51.10).

These reminders (*monumenta*, 5.52.1) of the consequences of piety and impiety must work, as Camillus goes on to say, as indications of the *nefas* that the Romans are going to commit if they leave their city behind. In chapter 52, he mentions various aspects of Roman cult and political activity tied to specific places and among these the Capitol appears once more as the location for the *epulum Iovis* (5.52.6); it is followed by the fire in the temple of Vesta, the *ancilia*, the cults of Mars and Quirinus (5.52.7); the *flamen Dialis*, who is not allowed to spend a night outside the city (5.52.13); the *comitia centuriata* and *curiata* (5.52.16–17). Camillus also reminds his audience of the Romans' readiness to import foreign cults into the city and institute new ones: he remembers the *evocatio* of Juno Regina from Veii to the Aventine, the new shrine of Aius Locutius, a god whose voice had been heard in Nova via, and the institution of the *ludi Capitolini* (5.52.10–11).

In the final part of the speech, in chapter 54, Camillus first strikes a more emotional note, by appealing to the love that one should feel for one's fatherland (*caritas ... patriae*, 5.54.2) and remembering his own longing for the Roman landscape while he was in exile in Veii (5.54.3). He then adopts a rational argument to demonstrate that 'gods and men' chose the site of the city wisely, which is confirmed by Rome's successful growth (5.54.5–7). Finally, at the very end of his oration, he emphasises the close tie between the *fortuna* of the Roman people and the site of Rome, especially with the Capitol as the site of Roman stability (5.54.7):

> Hic Capitolium est, ubi quondam capite humano invento responsum est eo loco caput rerum summamque imperii fore; hic cum augurato liberaretur Capitolium, Iuventas Terminusque maximo gaudio patrum vestrorum moveri se non passi; hic Vestae ignes, hic ancilia caelo demissa, hic omnes propitii manentibus vobis di.

> Here is the Capitol, where once, after the discovery of a human head, the response was given that here would be the head of all things and all the power; here, as the Capitol was made free after taking the *augurium*,

Iuventas and Terminus, to the greatest joy of your forefathers, did not consent to be moved; here are the fires of Vesta, here the shields fallen from the sky, here are all gods who will be favourable as long as you stay.

In this final review of Rome's most sacred places Camillus devotes particular attention to the ancient omens that singled out the hill as the centre (*caput*) of Rome's everlasting power. Indeed, he adds to the external narrator's account in 1.55.3–4, which does not mention Iuventas (Youth). This piece of information is known, among others, from Dionysius of Halicarnassus (*Ant. Rom.* 3.69.4–6), who reports that, since Terminus and Iuventas (Νεότης) were the only deities who refused to be moved elsewhere, one was lodged in the pronaos of Minerva's temple and the other within the temple itself, near the statue of the goddess.[94] The augurs' interpretation, Dionysius goes on the write, was that 'no event would move the boundaries of the Roman city nor change its prime'. When telling the story in Book 1, Livy is, as often, more selective in his exclusive focus on Terminus; but in Camillus' speech – in the context, that is, of a new beginning –, he points both to Rome's permanence in space (Terminus), and to its permanent vitality and constant rebirth (Iuventas).

Thus, in a speech in which space plays such an important role, the Capitol emerges as the quintessence of Roman space. It is the space that remains intact even when the rest of the city falls, the space without which Rome cannot exist, and the ideal core from which Roman power is bound to extend itself again after any crisis. But Camillus also proposes his view of what 'Rome' as a *res publica* is, a view which significantly interacts with the Romans people's previous assessment at 5.39.12. Rome is defined by the interaction of place, people, and gods. The landscape and buildings (especially religious buildings) and the spaces defined through augural procedures are all part of this Roman identity; but the defining core, the one that assures Rome's survival, is the Capitol, inhabited by Roman gods and Roman people. Such a powerful definition of Roman identity, at a moment when Rome undergoes near destruction

---

94   Other sources transmitting the piece of information about Iuventas are Flor. 1.1.7.8; August. *De civ. D.* 4.23.3 (who adds Mars to Terminus ad Iuventas). Plin. *HN* 35.108 writes of a painting 'on the Capitol in the shrine of Minerva above the *aedicula* of Iuventas'. Coarelli s.v. *Iuventas, aedicula* in *LTUR* 3 (1996), p. 164 suggests that one should think of an *ara cum aedicula* placed in the pronaos of the temple of Minerva. This cultic place should not be confused with the temple of Iuventas in the Circus Maximus: cf. Coarelli s.v. *Iuventas, aedes* in *LTUR* 3 (1996), p. 163. The latter was promised to the goddess by Marcus Livius Salinator in 207 BCE during the battle of Metaurus and dedicated in 191 BCE by Gaius Licinius Lucullus (Livy 36.36.5–6). Augustus restored it in 16 BCE: cf. *Mon. Anc.* 19.

and subsequent rebirth, provides an interpretive key for the account of Roman history.

Just as the Gallic sack endangers the existence of Rome, a later episode features the Capitol in an account of the endangering of Roman-ness itself. The context of this narrative is the Latin War of 340–338 BCE, a crucial moment in laying the foundations for Roman expansion, first in Italy and then abroad.[95] The peace treaty of 338 BCE sanctioned the dissolution of the Latin League and thus Rome's prominence in Latium; moreover, to quote Oakley (1998, 538), 'it provided Rome with the secure system of incorporated states and subject allies which was to prove the rock upon which the great expansion in Italy before the First Punic War was based'. In other words, the conflict and the ensuing peace could be seen, in retrospect, as the moment that Rome's identity as the leading power in Latium and as a potentially hegemonic power on a wider scale fully emerged.

In 8.3.8–6.7, Livy provides a dramatic account of the breakout of the war, which can be summarised as follows. In 340 BCE, the Latin praetor Titus Annius from Setia demanded from the Roman Senate, who had given him an audience in the temple of Jupiter Optimus Maximus, that the rights of Romans and Latins be made equal: one consul and half of the Senate should be chosen among the Latins. The request was met with indignation by the senators and especially by the consul Titus Manlius Torquatus. Having been forced to leave the temple in a rush, Annius fell down the temple steps and lost consciousness or – according to some – died. Manlius interpreted the event as the rightful punishment inflicted by Jupiter for Annius' insolent request.

Throughout this narrative, the Capitol is a very important symbol of the Roman *imperium*.[96] In the speech that Annius delivers in a *concilium* of the Latins, he promises that he will make his proposal 'not only for the Roman people and Senate but for Jupiter himself, who dwells on the Capitol, to hear' (*audiente non populo Romano modo senatuque sed Iove ipso, qui Capitolium incolit*, 8.4.11). Through this remark, the narrative introduces the setting of the next scene, the temple of Jupiter on the Capitol. The account of the Senate meeting begins with the explicit mention of the location (*Ubi est Romam ventum, in Capitolio eis senatus datus est*, 8.5.1).[97] Then, when introducing Annius' speech, the narrator states that he delivered it 'as though he had conquered the Capitol as a victor, not as if he spoke as an ambassador protected by universal law' (*tamquam victor armis Capitolium cepisset, non legatus iure*

---

95 Cf. Oakley (1998, pp. 538–559).
96 Cf. Oakley (1998, p. 409).
97 'As soon as he arrived in Rome, the senate received him on the Capitol.'

gentium tutus loqueretur, 8.5.2). The spectre of a conquered Capitol pervades the prayer on which Manlius Torquatus – who belongs to the same *gens* as the former saviour of the Capitol – rounds off his speech (8.5.8):

> Et conversus ad simulacrum Iovis, 'Audi, Iuppiter, haec scelera' inquit; 'audite, Ius Fasque. Peregrinos consules et peregrinum senatum in tuo, Iuppiter, augurato templo captus atque ipse oppressus visurus es?'

> And, turning to the statue of Jupiter, he said: 'Hear, Jupiter, these crimes! Hear them, *Ius* and *Fas*! Are you, Jupiter, going to see foreign consuls and a foreign Senate in your inaugurated temple, while you, too, are captive and defeated?'

Manlius' words emphasise the contrast between the temple of Jupiter as a centre (of civic religion, of the Roman institutions, of Roman time) and the senators and consuls who come from elsewhere. In the consul's view, such an incongruous presence is tantamount to sacrilege.

What follows confirms his interpretation. This is an interesting passage because of how the historian deals with different versions of the event, and it is worth quoting it in full (8.6.1–3):

> 1. Cum consulis vocem subsecuta patrum indignatio esset, proditur memoriae adversus crebram inplorationem deum, quos testes foederum saepius invocabant consules, vocem Anni spernentis numina Iovis Romani auditam. 2. Certe, cum commotus ira se a vestibulo templi citato gradu proriperet, lapsus per gradus capite graviter offensus impactus imo ita est saxo ut sopiretur. 3. Exanimatum auctores quoniam non omnes sunt, mihi quoque in incerto relictum sit, sicut inter foederum ruptorum testationem ingenti fragore caeli procellam effusam; nam et vera esse et apte ad repraesentandam iram deum ficta possunt.

> 1. It is recorded that, after the senators' indignation had followed the consul's words, Annius' voice was heard as he reviled the majesty of the Roman Jupiter amidst the many prayers to the gods, who the consuls repeatedly invoked as witnesses to the treaties. 2. It is certain that, as he rushed, beside himself with rage, out of the entrance of the temple, he fell down from the stairs, hurt his head badly, and hit a stone at the bottom so that he lost consciousness. 3. Since not everyone reports that he died, let me also leave it undecided, just as the tale that, as the senators were calling the gods as witnesses to the breaking of treaties, a storm broke out

with a loud rumble in the sky. These stories might be true, or they might have been fittingly invented to portray the gods' wrath.

As on other occasions, Livy discusses the credibility of different traditions in a way that provides an overall interpretation of the events: even if the traditions about Annius' death and the storm were not true, they would still have been 'fittingly' (*apte*) created to represent the wrath of the gods.[98] Thus, Livy's narrative suggests that Annius was punished for his impiety.

As Manlius comments on the accident, he confirms such an interpretation (8.6.4–5):

> Bene habet; di pium movere bellum. 5. Est caeleste numen; es, magne Iuppiter; haud frustra te patrem deum hominum hac sede sacravimus.

> It is well: the gods have started a pious war. There is a divine power; you exist, great Jupiter: not in vain have we worshipped you in this place as the Father of men and gods.

If one considers the episode in its entirety, one can recognise an effective narrative technique. The external narrator mentions the Capitol explicitly and emphatically at the outset of the main episode as the setting for the Senate meeting. As the events develop, characters within the story speak about the same place in their voices, each projecting his own semantics on it. Such an entwining of voices turns the Capitol into a meaningful setting.[99]

The fact that Annius puts forth his demands in the temple makes their disrupting effect even stronger. Since the temple, and the Capitoline Hill on which it stands, are the core of Roman identity and religion, the advocated presence of foreign magistrates and senators there appears as an impious subversion of the Roman order.[100] In the end, the gods re-establish order as Annius falls and

---

[98] A similar idea is found at *praef.* 7, where Livy explains his method for dealing with legendary (pre-foundation) history: *Datur haec venia antiquitati ut miscendo humana divinis primordia urbium augustiora faciat; et si cui populo licere oportet consecrare origines suas et ad deos referre auctores, ea belli gloria est populo Romano ut cum suum conditorisque sui parentem Martem potissimum ferat, tam et hoc gentes humanae patiantur aequo animo quam imperium patiuntur.*

[99] On the importance of voices in this narrative, see my observations in Fabrizi (2023).

[100] The episode is explicitly recalled at 23.22.1–9, where a Roman senator, Sp. Carvilius proposes admitting the Latins to the Senate in order to compensate for the losses at Cannae. A descendant of Torquatus, Titus Manlius, intervenes to counter his proposal. For a comparison of these episodes, see Fabrizi (2023).

perhaps dies in the very steps of the temple, just as the Gauls had been thrown down from the citadel and Manlius Capitolinus had been thrown down from the Tarpeian Rock. In all these cases, the falling from the Capitol means that a (foreign or internal) threat to Roman stability is removed.

From my observations, it will be clear that the Capitol is a fundamental landmark in the imagined topography of Rome in the *Ab Urbe Condita* – not merely because of its central location in the city or its prominence as a height, but because of the complex of meanings and values which it embodies. Together with the Forum, the Capitol constitutes the political centre of Rome; unlike the Forum, it is not a place of debate, strife, and reconciliation but rather a place of unity and stability. Since it hosts the temples of the gods, the citadel with its augural connections, and the ceremonies that mark the annual renewal of Roman institutions, the Capitol symbolises the union of gods and men and of citizens as members of something greater (or 'higher') than each of them. Precisely for this reason, it can act as a symbol for Roman identity: a symbol to be looked at and spoken about, as the characters of history and the readers are constantly reminded of both change and continuity in Roman history.

3   Other Hills

3.1   *Viminal, Quirinal, Caelian, and Esquiline*

Livy's account of the monarchic period in Book 1 features, as I have shown in section 1, all seven (Varronian) hills in turn, presenting them, together with the Tiber, as the natural features defining the Roman landscape. Yet, in the rest of the surviving books, the importance devoted to each hill varies greatly. The Capitol is, as I have demonstrated in the previous section, the most prominent of all, and the semantic centre of the narrated Rome. But what of the remaining six?

Three of them play a marginal role. Livy does not mention the Viminal after he introduces it together with the Quirinal at 1.44.3. The Quirinal appears at 5.46.2 as the seat of a sacrifice of the *gens* Fabia, which the heroic Gaius Fabius Dorsuo does not fail to perform during the Gallic sack even if it means going from the Capitol to the Quirinal and back at risk of being killed by the Gauls; Furius Camillus later remembers this act of devotion in his speech at 5.52.3. The only other mention of the Quirinal occurs at 34.53.5, where Livy mentions the dedication of an *aedes* to Fortuna Primigenia *in colle Quirinali* within a list of temples dedicated in 194 BCE. The Caelian is mentioned at 2.11.8 as the hill from which the consul Publius Valerius leads his troops down and out of the city to attack the Etruscans; and, at 35.9.3 Livy reports that the Porta Caelimontana (on the slope of the hill) was struck by lightning.

The Esquiline is more relevant to the narrative. After Servius Tullius incorporates it into the city and establishes his abode there (cf. above, p. 92), the hill appears as the place where Tullia, daughter to Servius and wife to Tarquinius Superbus, rides after Tarquinius' murder of her father; it is on her way to the Esquiline (i.e., in all likelihood, to Servius Tullus' palace)[101] that she gives full proof of her impiety by riding over her father's corpse (1.48.5–7).[102] At 2.28.1–3 the Esquiline is, together with the Aventine, the location for clandestine meetings of the plebs. On other occasions, the Esquiline and the Porta Esquilina appear in their quality of bordering areas, involved in the movement of armies or possible enemy attacks. At 3.67.11–68.1, Titus Quinctius Capitolinus reproaches the plebs because, due to their refusal to take up arms, the Volscians have almost conquered the Esquiline, and exhorts them to go out the Porta Esquilina to attack the enemy.[103] At 6.22.8, an army about to march against the Volscians is assembled *ad portam Esquilinam*. The hill and the gate are involved in the security measures the Romans set up in expectation of Hannibal's attack in 211 BCE. The proconsul Fulvius Flaccus enters Rome with his army through the porta Capena, heads for 'the Carinae and the Esquiline', and sets camp between the porta Esquilina and the porta Collina (26.10.1–2). Later, after Hannibal has reached the outskirts of Rome, the consuls order the Numidian deserters, who reside on the Aventine,[104] to pass through the Esquiline 'because they believed nobody would be better suited than them to fighting among the hollows and the buildings of the gardens, the tombs, the streets that passed everywhere through uneven ground' (26.10.5). The consuls take pains to have the Esquiline defended because Hannibal is threatening the north-eastern side of the city.[105] A different kind of threat is reported within a prodigy list at 33.26.9, where Livy writes that in 196 BCE a wolf entered Rome through the porta Esquilina and reached the Forum 'through a very densely inhabited area of the city'.[106]

---

101 Livy 1.48.6 writes that she was going home (*cum domum se reciperet*); this probably means she was going to take possession of her father's palace (cf. Ogilvie, 1965, p. 192).
102 Cf. Chapter 4, pp. 220–223.
103 For this speech see Chapter 1, pp. 61–62.
104 The Numidians are probably on the Aventine because, as members of an enemy people, they cannot enter the pomerium: cf. Beltramini (2020, p. 163).
105 Cf. 26.10.3.
106 To these mentions of the Esquiline Hill, one might add that of the *tribus Esquilina*, one of the four urban tribes, at 45.15.6, where Livy writes that in 168 BCE the disenfranchised slaves were enrolled in that tribe.

3.2 The Aventine

The remaining two hills, the Palatine and Aventine, play a much more substantial role. In this section, I concentrate on the latter.

The Aventine is the southernmost of the seven Varronian hills. Its northwestern side lies close to the Tiber; its northeastern side was divided from the Palatine by the Circus Maximus. Despite its central location, this hill lay outside the *pomerium* until 49 CE, which made it a suitable location for temples of originally foreign deities. The Aventine was also very close to sites involved in commerce, such as the Forum Boarium, the old cattle-market, with its fluvial port on the north, and the Emporium on the south-west. The hill seems to have been densely inhabited by a socially diverse population.[107]

In the *Ab Urbe Condita*, the Aventine appears for the first time in the narrative of the *augurium* of Romulus and Remus, at 1.6.4, where Romulus chooses the Palatine and Remus the Aventine as *templa* for taking the auspice. This tradition is found in various ancient sources and seems to have been the *communis opinio* at least from the Late Republic on,[108] but it was not the only one: Ennius' *Annales* and Servius' commentary to the *Aeneid* preserve an alternative version of the auspice which featured Romulus on the Aventine.[109] The version Livy accepts strengthens the tie between the Palatine, on which Rome would be founded, and the person of Romulus as the one chosen by the gods to lead the new city.

In the monarchic age, the Aventine is also mentioned as the site of the altar of Jupiter Elicius, founded by Numa (1.20.7) and as one of the areas that Ancus Marcius added to the city at 1.33.2–5 (cf. above, pp. 83–84). At 1.45, Livy recounts the founding of the temple of Diana on the Aventine and her cult being common to Romans and Latins. The historian attributes the impulse of its foundation to Servius Tullius after the example of the Ephesian temple of Artemis and presents it as an admission, on the Latins' part, of Roman supremacy. He also reports a story about a cow of exceptional size and beauty born in Sabina, of which it was foretold that whoever sacrificed it would make his city the seat of hegemony (*imperium*, 5); an officer of the temple of Diana sacrificed the cow after tricking her Sabine owner and her horns were affixed for many years to the temple doors (no longer in Livy's age, however) as a *monumentum* of the miraculous occurrence (4). It is interesting that throughout this tale, which takes up a full chapter, Livy never mentions the Aventine; his Roman readers,

---

107 For the Aventine and its history see e.g. Merlin (1906); Andreussi s.v. *Aventinus mons* in *LTUR* 1 (1993) pp. 147–150; Mignone (2016); Prim (2021).
108 Cf. Ogilvie (1965, pp. 55).
109 Cf. Enn. *Ann.* 75–76 Sk.; Serv. *Aen.* 3.46.

of course, will have known that the temple was on that hill, but readers not familiar with the city might have been unaware of this fact.

In Books 2–10, the Aventine appears predominantly as a site connected with the struggles of the plebs. Although it shares this role with other sites within or without the city (most notably with the Sacred Mount, the theatre of the First Secession of 494 BCE[110] and one of the locations for the Second Secession of 449 BCE),[111] its connotations in this sense remain significant. At 2.28.1 the Aventine is, together with the Esquiline, the location for secret meetings of the plebs (cf. above, p. 120). At 3.31.1 the historian reports the passing of the *lex de Aventino publicando* of 456 BCE; although the precise contents of the law are the object of scholarly debate, and although Livy does not give any explanation of what he believed its provisions were, the role the historian gives its author, Lucius Icilius, as a champion of the plebs reinforces the tie between the hill and the plebeian struggles of the fifth century.

Most notably, the Aventine plays a central role in the account of the Second Secession of the plebs, which in 449 BCE brought down the tyrannical rule of the Decemvirs.[112] In Livy's account, a host of Roman soldiers from the camp on Mons Vecilius, stirred against the Decemvirs by Lucius Verginius (Verginia's father and murderer), enter Rome in arms to occupy the Aventine, exhorting the people who they met along the way 'to restore liberty and elect tribunes of the plebs' (*ad repetendam libertatem creandosque tribunos plebis*, 3.50.13). Shortly afterwards, another Roman army, coming from Sabina, enters Rome from the Porta Collina and, marching through the city, joins them on the hill (3.51.6–10). Then, however, the rebels realise the Senate will not grant them their requests – that is, the Decemvirs' resignation and the restoration of the tribunate – unless they leave the city; so they decide to move to the Sacred Mount together with all the plebs (3.52.1–4). Only when they obtain the restoration of freedom, do they go back to the Aventine (3.54.8–11).

The plebeians' occupation of the Aventine bears the features of an enemy attack and evokes comparisons with various other armies assailing Rome through the Porta Collina (including Sulla's attack in 82 BCE).[113] The historian, however, repeatedly stresses how the plebeians abstained from violence, both on the Aventine (3.50.13) and on the Sacred Mount (3.53.3; 3.54.8). Moreover, their final return to the Aventine is presented as a gesture towards the re-establishment of concord. When the legates from the Senate reach the plebeians on the Sacred Mount and announce all their requests have been

---

110 Cf. Livy 2.31.7–33.3.
111 See Mignone (2016, pp. 17–47).
112 For a summary of the events cf. Chapter 1, p. 56.
113 See Mignone (2016, pp. 29–31).

accepted, they also invite them to go back to the city and to the Aventine: in that 'fortunate place', which provided the beginning of their freedom, the plebeians will elect their magistrates (*ibi felici loco, ubi prima initia inchoastis libertatis vestrae, tribunos plebi creabitis*, 3.54.9). Thus, the Aventine emerges in this episode both as a site of plebeian struggle and as the site of plebeian reintegration into the citizen body.[114] Later speakers in Livy mention the Aventine as a site connected to the plebs' rebellion (e.g. at 3.67.11, together with the Sacred Mount and the Esquiline; at 7.40.11 together with the Sacred Mount; and at 9.34.4).

Among the buildings located on the hill, the temple of Juno Regina is particularly prominent in the text. Juno Regina was the tutelary goddess of Veii, the Etruscan city the Romans besieged and captured at the turn of the fifth century (in Livy's account, the siege lasted ten years, from 406 to 396 BCE). The Romans, as ancient sources report, performed the *evocatio* of the goddess, a ritual by which they invited the tutelary deity of an enemy community to move to Rome. This involved offering the foreign deity a new home (i.e. a new temple) in the city: after the Roman victory over Veii, the temple of the Aventine was built to this purpose. Livy, at 5.21.3, has the dictator Marcus Furius Camillus pronounce an *evocatio* formula before launching the final attack on the city.[115] Shortly afterwards, the Roman soldiers enter Veii through a tunnel, which exits in the temple of Juno on Veii's citadel (5.21.5). Livy also reports a miraculous story concerning the transportation of the cult image of Juno away from Veii (5.22.3–7): when the young men chosen for the task entered the temple, one asked the (image of the) goddess whether she wanted to go to Rome and others exclaimed that Juno had nodded her assent. Later, someone went so far as to add that they had heard the goddess' voice. Juno (i.e. her cult image) was then brought to Rome and 'to the Aventine, its eternal seat where the Roman dictator's vows had summoned her, and where Camillus, the person who had vowed to erect it, later dedicated the temple to her' (*in Aventinum aeternam sedem suam quo vota Romani dictatoris vocaverant perlatam, ubi templum ei postea idem qui voverat Camillus dedicavit*, 5.22.7). Livy reports first the stipulation of the contract for the building works (5.23.7), then the dedication of the temple (5.31.3). Later Camillus, in his speech against the move to Veii at the end of Book 5, will recall Juno Regina's arrival in Rome as an example of a foreign cult imported into the city (5.52.10).

---

114 Mignone (2016, p. 32).
115 *Te simul, Iuno regina, quae nunc Veios colis, precor, ut nos victores in nostram tuamque mox futuram urbem sequare, ubi te dignum amplitudine tua templum accipiat.* This seems to be a very free and compressed rendition of the *carmen evocationis* transmitted by Macr. *Sat.* 3.9.6.

The importance the temple on the Aventine has in Book 5 finds a parallel in the emphasis it receives in the account of the Hannibalic War in the Third Decade. There, the temple is a focus of religious activity more than once: it appears in a prodigy list at 21.62.4, 8 and in a list of measures for the *procuratio* of prodigies at 22.1.17.[116] Most famously, at 27.37 the historian describes the ceremonies through which, in 207 BCE, the Roman people appeased Juno Regina. Livy reports how, after the announcement of several worrying prodigies, the pontiffs decreed that twenty-one maidens should go through the city in procession while singing a hymn (*carmen*), which was composed for the occasion by the poet Livius Andronicus (27.37.1–7). However, while the maidens were learning the hymn in the temple of Jupiter Stator, the temple of Juno on the Aventine was struck by lightning. The haruspices concluded that the prodigy concerned the matrons, whom the aediles consequently summoned to the Capitol. The matrons collected money from their dowries to pay for a golden bowl to be dedicated to Juno on the Aventine and performed a sacrifice there (8–10). Moreover, the *decemviri sacris faciundis* established that one further sacrifice be celebrated in the temple of Juno; the chorus of maidens was incorporated into this rite. Livy describes the order and the route of the procession in detail at sections 11–15: from the temple of Apollo (outside the *pomerium*) the victims were led through the Porta Carmentalis, followed by two wooden images of the goddess, by the singing maidens, and by the *decemviri*. Passing through the *vicus Iugarius*, they reached the Forum, where the procession made a halt and the maidens danced at the rhythm of their song. Then the pageant went through the *vicus Tuscus*, the Velabrum, the Forum Boarium and, by the *clivus Publicius*, reached the temple of Juno, where the victims were killed, and where the two images of the goddess were set up.

The presence in the Third Decade of notices about propitiatory ceremonies in honour of Juno is, per se, not surprising. Juno, who was generally identified with the Carthaginian goddess Tanit, seems to have become the object of increased attention during the Punic Wars, especially at times of special danger. One might argue that, in the Third Decade, Livy simply reported information that he found in his sources. However, the unusual amount of attention the historian devotes to the procession of 207 BCE suggests there might be something more than that to Livy's text. Just as, in Book 5, Camillus mentioned

---

116   Prodigies on the Aventine (*in Aventino*) are reported without mention of the temple of Juno at 22.36.7; 35.9.4; 38.36.4; in all three cases, the prodigy is a rain of stones. At 40.2.2 the text mentions a storm tearing away the doorpost of the temple of Luna and sticking it into the rear wall of the temple of Ceres, both on the Aventine (*forem ex aede Lunae quae in Auentino est raptam tulit et in posticis parietibus Cereris templi adfixit*).

the temple of Juno Regina as an example of the Roman custom of incorporating the deities of foreign or even enemy communities into their city, thereby stressing Roman piety as a reason for Rome's success, the emphasis on ceremonies in honour of the same goddess in the Third Decade suggests that piety will once more play a role in Rome's victory against Carthage.

At the same time, both the narrative about the arrival of Juno Regina from Veii in Book 5 and the one concerning the procession of 207 BCE share a deep concern with place. I have shown how the external narrator describes the Aventine, at 5.23.7, as Juno Regina's 'eternal seat', and how Camillus powerfully argues for the non-moveability of Roman cults. Similarly, the account from Book 27 details all the places involved in the events, including the precise itinerary the procession follows to reach the Aventine.

The Aventine thus emerges as a location with profound historical and religious meaning. Just as in the narrative of the struggles of the plebs, such meaning relates to the Aventine being a place where alterity or otherness is incorporated into the city. The temple of Juno Regina, connected as it was with two of Rome's most famous enemies, is a perfect example of incorporated alterity as a guarantee for stability and military success. The memories of the struggles of the Roman plebs provide another, just as potent, example. After all, it is those struggles which, in Livy's interpretation, led to the gradual forming of the political system of the Middle Republic, and of a unitary citizen-body.

One can quote one more instance of integrated alterity connected with the Aventine in the *Ab Urbe Condita*. At 24.14–16, the historian narrates how, in 214 BCE, the proconsul Tiberius Gracchus granted freedom to the slave volunteers (*volones*) who had fought the Carthaginians under his command at Beneventum.[117] The battle was followed by a banquet in the city, in which the former slaves took part wearing the *pilleus* or with their heads veiled by white wool; after Gracchus returned from campaign, he had the scene painted in the temple of Libertas that his father had built and dedicated on the Aventine (*in aede Libertatis, quam pater eius in Aventino ex multaticia pecunia faciendam curavit dedicavitque*, 24.16.19).

My analysis has revealed the recurring presence of the Aventine as a place of both otherness and identity in the *Ab Urbe Condita*. Against this background one can read the role of the Aventine in a famous narrative in which it works as a setting, that of the Bacchanalian scandal in 186 BCE (Livy 39.8–19). Since I examine this account in detail in Chapter 4 – where I focus, in particular, on the subversion of gendered boundaries that the episode thematises –, I shall

---

117 These slaves had been bought with public money and enrolled in the army to obviate the scarcity of soldiers after the disaster at Cannae (cf. 22.57.11–12).

not treat it here; instead, I defer my analysis of the significance of the Aventine as a setting to Chapter 4, where I show that the dynamics of marginalisation, integration, and exclusion is paramount to that narrative.

3.3 *The Palatine*

The Palatine played a prominent role in Roman collective memory: according to the version of the foundation legend that became dominant from at least the 3rd century BCE onwards, the hill was where Romulus and Remus had grown up and Romulus had later founded the city.[118] Romans of Livy's time recognised traces of those ancient events in the urban landscape. One could see the Lupercal, a monumentalised version of the cave where the she-wolf had allegedly retired after suckling the twins, at the southwestern foot of the Palatine not far from the Circus Maximus;[119] on the slopes of the hill, also on the southwest and facing the Circus Maximus, was the so-called 'hut of Romulus' (*casa Romuli*), that Romans identified with the first king's modest dwelling, and which State authorities took care to renovate on a regular basis.[120] In the same area, the *scalae Caci* ('Cacus' stairs') recalled even more ancient times, when Hercules had passed by the Tiber and had been welcomed (according to one tradition) or had had his cattle stolen by a character named Cacus (according to another, which would become more popular).[121]

The Palatine also featured various important temples and cults, among which those of Vesta, Jupiter Stator, Victoria, and Magna Mater (the 'Great Mother', i.e. Cybele),[122] and it was densely inhabited at least from the 2nd

---

118 See e.g. Dion. Hal. *Ant. Rom.* 1.79 and 1.85.6; Vell. Pat. 1.8.4; Val. Max. 2.2.9. For other ancient sources on Romulus' city see Cecamore (2002, pp. 15–54).

119 Dion. Hal. *Ant. Rom.* 1.79.8 locates it 'on the road leading to the Circus' and writes of an adjacent sacred precinct where one could see a bronze statue of the she-wolf suckling two babies; at 1.32.4–5 he states that the cave was originally an Arcadian sanctuary to Pan Lycaeus. Plut. *Vit. Rom.* 3.6 locates it more precisely on the Cermalus, the western part of the Palatine. On the Lupercal see also (with different localisations) Coarelli s.v. *Lupercal* in *LTUR* 3 (1996) pp. 198–199; Coarelli (2012); Carandini and Bruno (2008, pp. 4–29 and 122–137); Carandini and Carafa (2021, pp. 102–107).

120 Cf. Varro *Ling.* 5.54 (who locates it in the Cermalus, an area on the south-western slopes of the Palatine); Dion. Hal. *Ant. Rom.* 1.79.11; Plut. *Vit. Rom.* 20. Solin. 1.18 mentions a hut of Faustulus at the top of the *scalae Caci*, which was probably the same building. Cf. Coarelli s.v. *casa Romuli* (*Cermalus*) in *LTUR* 1 (1993) pp. 241–242 and (2012, pp. 128–132); Pensabene (2017a, pp. 19–23). Other authors, starting from the Thirties BCE, mention a *casa Romuli* on the Capitol: see e.g. Balland (1984); Coarelli s.v. *casa Romuli* (*area Capitolina*) in *LTUR* 1 (1993) p. 241.

121 On the legend of Hercules and Cacus, see below, p. 129 and n. 136.

122 On these and other cults on the Palatine, see e.g. Cecamore (2002, pp. 99–154); Coarelli (2012, pp. 191–285); Pensabene (2017a). I treat the temple of Magna Mater in more detail below, pp. 130–133.

century onwards and notable for the presence of aristocratic mansions (Cicero's house among them).[123]

Starting from the Thirties BCE, the hill had become a major focus of Octavian's urban renewal activity. Octavian, who had been born on the Palatine,[124] had established his new residence on the hill since the late forties, when he had acquired a house that had previously belonged to Quintus Hortensius Hortalus (the son of the famous orator).[125] He later bought some of the adjacent houses to enlarge his own, but sometime after 36 BCE (when construction works were probably under way) lightning struck an area of the property. Acknowledging the divine sign, Octavian promised to make that section of his property public and vowed to build a temple to Apollo, his patron deity, which he then dedicated in 28 BCE.[126] The temple featured, among other things, a portico where statues of the Danaids were on display, and a Greek and Latin library.

The features of Octavian's (and later, of course, Augustus') residence on the Palatine and its relationship with the temple of Apollo have been, and still are, the object of intense critical debate. A major point of contention is whether the *princeps* had a proper 'temple-palace complex' built, or whether he simply went on living in Hortensius' house; moreover, scholars who argue for the existence of a palace disagree as to its structure and history.[127] Some facts, however, are commonly accepted and important for understanding the conditions and connotations of the hill at Livy's time.

First, Augustus' development of the Palatine was closely connected with his own self-representation as a second founder of Rome. As is well known, in 27 BCE he had toyed with taking on *Romulus* as a *cognomen*. He then gave up the idea because of the monarchic implications of that name, but the *cognomen* he eventually chose, *Augustus*, resonated deeply with Romulean associations. The adjective *augustus, -a, -um* (literally 'venerable, blessed, holy') pertained to the field of religion and especially applied to places, people, or objects consecrated by an *augurium*. The *cognomen* thus alluded to the *augurium* through

---

[123] Cf. Coarelli (2012, pp. 287–346).
[124] Cf. Suet. *Aug.* 5.
[125] Suet. *Aug.* 72.1.
[126] Cf. Vell. Pat. 2.81.3; Suet. *Aug.* 29.3; Dio Cass. 49.15.5.
[127] See e.g. Zanker (1983); Cecamore (2002, pp. 2013–218); Iacopi and Tedone (2005–2006); Carandini and Bruno (2008); Carandini (2010); Carandini, Carafa and Ippoliti (2021, pp. 205–250 and *passim*); Wiseman (2009, 2012a, 2012b, 2013, 2014, and 2019); Coarelli (2012, pp. 347–450); Pensabene (2017b, pp. 43–111 and p. 2021); Pensabene and Gallocchio (2011); de Souza and Devillers (2019); Pandey (2020). Specifically on the temple of Apollo Zink (2008 and 2012); Claridge (2014). For analyses of the role of the temple in Augustan propaganda and culture, see e.g. Gurval (1995); Miller (2009); Lange (2009, pp. 166–181); Menichetti (2021, pp. 61–69).

which Romulus, according to legend, had founded Rome – and ensured the gods' protection over the city.[128]

Secondly, the association between the idea of foundation (and re-foundation) and the cult of Apollo, as sanctioned by the building of the temple on the Palatine, was particularly powerful. Octavian/Augustus stressed the god's protection as crucial in his success at Actium. Indeed, it seems Actium partially changed the significance of the temple, which became connected, at least in the minds of contemporary observers, with that victory.[129] At the same time, Apollo, who presided over the arts and intellectual endeavours, could be seen as a bringer of peace.[130] From this the idea emerges of Augustus as a second founder, who, under Apollo's guidance, ensures peace and prosperity for a newly founded Rome after the destructions of the civil wars.

Thirdly, the Palatine became a new fulcrum of political and religious life during the Augustan age, taking on some of the functions (and ideal associations) of other sites. In 18 or 12 BCE, or perhaps even earlier, Augustus transferred the Sibylline Books from the Capitoline temple to the temple of Apollo.[131] When, in 12 BCE, he became *pontifex maximus*, he did not move to the traditional residence of that office, the *domus publica* in the Forum. Instead, he made part of his house on the Palatine public and incorporated a cult of Vesta there.[132] The Palatine thus came to be perceived as a site representative of the political and religious identity of Rome, partly supplanting, or downplaying, even the Capitol as the Roman core.[133]

---

128   Cf. e.g. Suet. *Aug.* 7.2.
129   Lange (2009, pp. 166–181); Menichetti (2021). For the idea of Apollo as central in Octavian's self-representation from the triumviral period see Zanker (1983 and 1987). Contra Gurval (1995), who denies any actual connection between the temple of Apollo and the victory at Actium and argues the idea of such a connection originates in poetical works. For literary representations see e.g. Verg. *Aen.* 8.720 (and cf. 704–605); Prop. 2.31 and 4.6.
130   Cf. Zanker (1983, p. 32); Lange (2009, p. 170).
131   Suet. *Aug.* 31.1 writes that, when Augustus became *pontifex maximus*, he had more than 2,000 prophetic texts burnt but kept the Sibylline Books (but even with these he made a selection) and 'deposited them in two gilded cases under the pedestal of Palatine Apollo' (*condiditque duobus forulis auratis sub Palatini Apollinis basi*, transl. Rolfe). Dio Cass. 54.17.2, on the other hand, reports that, in 18 BCE, Augustus ordered the priests (i.e. the quindecemviri) to copy the Sibylline Books, which had become scarcely legible due to their age (he does not, however, mention the temple of Apollo). Miller (2000, pp. 412–413 and n. 13) argues that Verg. *Aen.* 6.69–73 and Tib. 2.5.17 allude to the presence of the books in the temple; this would indicate the books were already there by 19 BCE, the year both Vergil and Tibullus died.
132   Cf. e.g. Cecamore (2002, pp. 155–159, with further bibliography).
133   Cf. Miller (2000, p. 412).

Not surprisingly, the Palatine plays a major role in the foundation legend in Book 1 of Livy's *Ab Urbe Condita*. Livy writes that the infant twins were exposed 'where the Ficus Ruminalis is now' (*ubi nunc ficus Ruminalis est*, 1.4.5): this probably refers to the fig tree in the Lupercal, which was supposed to go back to the times when the she-wolf had suckled the twins, and of which, according to Ovid (*Fast*. 2. 411–412), only some remains were extant in Augustan times.[134] Later, when introducing the Lupercal festival in which young Romulus and Remus took part, he provides an etymological explanation of the toponym *Palatium* and an *aition* for the festival itself: both went back, in his interpretation, to the Arcadian king Evander, and the hill was named after the Arcadian town of Pallanteum (1.1–2).[135] After narrating the *augurium* – which, as mentioned above, featured the Palatine as the location of the victorious Romulus (1.6.4) – the historian reports the foundation of the city on the Palatine, where Romulus had been reared (*Palatium primum, in quo ipse erat educatus, muniit*, 1.7.3) and provides one more *aition* connected to the hill and the adjacent Forum Boarium: namely, the story of Hercules and Cacus, which accounts for the ceremonies in honour of Hercules at the Ara Maxima (1.7.4–15).[136] Although Livy does not mention the Palatine explicitly in his account of the legend, his Roman readers will have connected it with the *scalae Caci* ('Cacus'

---

[134] On this Ficus Ruminalis and the other Ficus in the Comitium, witnessed e.g. by Plin. *HN* 15.77–78; Tac. *Ann*. 13.58, see Coarelli s.v. *Ficus Navia*; *Ficus Ruminalis* in *LTUR* 2 (1995) pp. 248–249.

[135] This seems to have been the most successful etymology in Antiquity, although alternative explanations existed: cf. Tagliamonte s.v. *Palatium, Palatinus mons (fino alla prima età repubblicana)* in *LTUR* 4 (1999) pp. 14–15.

[136] The story of Hercules and Cacus enjoyed special popularity in Augustan literature, as shown by Verg. *Aen*. 8.185–275; Prop. 4.9.1–20; Dion. Hal. *Ant. Rom*. 1.39–40; Ov. *Fast*. 1.543–586. Livy's account is probably the earlier version of the legend in the form it took in Augustan times (contra Paratore, 1971, who argues for Vergil's priority); earlier testimonies transmit variant versions of the legend (e.g. Hemina *FRHist*. 6 F 3; Cn. Gell. *FRHist*. 14 F 17; Diod. Sic. 4.21.1–4). According to Augustan writers, as Hercules was leading Geryon's cattle back to Greece, he happened to come by the area where Rome would later be founded and halted by the Tiber to rest. While he was sleeping, Cacus, a local shepherd, stole some of his cattle. When he woke up, Hercules went looking for the cattle, found them in Cacus' cave, and killed the shepherd. Evander welcomed Hercules and told him how his mother Carmenta had predicted his deification and the dedication of an altar in his honour, which people from the entire world would call 'greatest' (*maxima*); Hercules himself dedicated the altar. The outline of the story is very similar in Livy, Dionysius, Vergil, Propertius, and Ovid, if with some differences in detail. In Vergil and Ovid, Cacus is a monster, son of Vulcan (cf. Verg. *Aen*. 8.193–199; 251–266; Ov. *Fast*. 1.553–554); in Prop. 4.9.10 he has three faces. For Dion. Hal. *Ant. Rom*. 1.39.2, and also for Livy, Cacus is a human being (a robber); unlike Livy, however, Dionysius considers the whole story a legend (1.40.6). For the relationships between these accounts see e.g. Paratore (1971); Holzberg (2012).

stairs') on the south-west slope of the hill.[137] The Palatine is also involved (as mentioned in Chapter 1, pp. 42–43) in the account of the battle in the Forum following the rape of the Sabine women (1.11–13): the Romans go down from this hill into the valley that would become the Forum to face the Sabines, who have occupied the Capitol. When the Sabines force the Romans to retreat, Romulus vows to build a *templum* to Jupiter Stator if the god stays the Romans' flight. As Livy later explains (10.37.15–16), Romulus had, in fact, founded a *fanum*, that is, a consecrated place (*locus templo effatus*, 15); only in 294 BCE, after the battle of Luceria against the Samnites, was the temple once more promised and acually built (16). For this reason, therefore, Romulus' vow, which changes the fortunes of the battle, works as a legendary *aition* for the historical temple of Jupiter Stator on the lowest slope of the Palatine.

In Livy's post-Romulean history, on the other hand, the Palatine occupies a less conspicuous, but not unimportant, place.[138] The *Ab Urbe Condita* mentions the Palatine by name on only nine occasions after the narrative of Romulus' reign. Two of these occurrences concern Ancus Marcius' enlargement of the city (1.33.2, 5; cf. above, pp. 83–84). The Palatine as an emblem for the very core of the city appears later, at 2.10.4, where Horatius Cocles admonishes his fleeing fellow soldiers that, if they leave the Sublician Bridge to their enemies, there will soon be more of them on the Palatine and the Capitol than on the Janiculum, which the Etruscans have already conquered. At 8.19.4 and 20.8, the historian mentions Vitruvius Vaccus' house on the Palatine. This aristocrat from Fundi was the leader of a rebellion of the Privernates and Fundani; after his defeat, the Romans destroyed his house, and the area came to be known as *Vacci prata* ('Vaccus' meadows'). At 30.38.9, a rain of stones on the Palatine features in a prodigy list.

The context in which the Palatine plays the most important role in Livy's post-Romulean narrative, however, is the episode concerning the arrival of the Idaean Mother (i.e. the goddess Cybele, commonly designated in Latin as the Magna Mater, the 'Great Mother') in Rome during the last years of the Second Punic War. In 205 BCE, as Livy (29.10.4–8) writes, frequent prodigies led to consulting the Sibylline Books. These prophesised that, should a foreign enemy invade Italy, victory would come from bringing the Idaean Mother from Pessinus, a town in Phrygia which hosted a sanctuary of the goddess,

---

137 Cf. Pensabene s.v. *Scalae Caci* in *LTUR* 4 (1999) pp. 239–240 and (2017a, pp. 38–39); Coarelli (2012, pp. 191–192); Carandini, Carafa and Ippoliti (2021, *passim*). Verg. *Aen.* 8.231 and Ov. *Fast.* 1.551 place Cacus' lair on the slopes of the Aventine.

138 Levene (2019) points out the scarcity of references to the Palatine in the *Ab Urbe Condita*.

to Rome.[139] At about the same time, the envoys previously sent to Delphi to donate part of booty from the battle of Metaurus to the sanctuary of Apollo[140] came back with an encouraging response from the Pythian oracle: the Romans would soon experience a greater victory than the one at the Metaurus. The Senate thus sent a delegation to King Attalus of Pergamum to ask him for support in the matter (29.11.1–4).[141] Before going to the king, however, the envoys paid one more visit to Delphi; the oracle predicted that they would obtain what they wanted through Attalus' mediation and gave instructions that, when the Idaean Mother would arrive in Rome, the best man in the city receive her (29.22.5–6). The envoys then proceeded to Pergamum, where Attalus received then in a friendly way. The king led them to Pessinus and arranged for a black stone, an aniconic cult image of the Idaean Mother, to be given to them (29.1.7–8). The embassy returned to Rome the following year and the goddess was welcomed into the city by a great procession which ended at the temple of Victoria on the Palatine (29.14.13–14).[142] Livy also reports the *locatio* of the new temple of the Idaean Mother on the Palatine in the same year at 29.37.2 and its dedication in 191 BCE at 36.36.1–4.

The historian devotes considerable attention to this series of events, which, through the emphasis he lays on prodigies and oracles, he presents as anticipating Scipio's launch of the victorious campaign in Africa in 204 BCE.[143] In particular, his narrative reserves a special role for the Delphic oracle. Livy is one of only three sources (the other two being Val. Max. 8.15.3 and Dio Cass. fr. 57, 61) who record two responses from the oracle; in other versions, the first prophecy is not mentioned and the second is attributed to the Sibylline Books.[144]

Perhaps, it is no accident that the historian explicitly mentions the Palatine first in the account of the procession, then in the reports about the *locatio*

---

139   On the sanctuary of the Great Mother in Pessinus cf. Strabo 12.5.3. On the role of Pessinus in the story see Casapulla (2024, pp. 129–131), with further bibliography.

140   Cf. 28.45.12.

141   Pessinus was not under Pergamum's rule at that time, as it was under the direct authority of the priests of the Great Mother (cf. again Strabo 12.5.3). Attalus' role thus seems to have been one of mediation, since the king had a good relationship with the inhabitants of Pessinus: cf. Casapulla (2024, p. 130, with further bibliography).

142   Livy reports the dedication of the temple of Victoria at 10.33.9 (294 BCE). Cf. e.g. Pensabene s.v. *Victoria, aedes* in *LTUR* 5 (1999) pp. 149–150; Coarelli (2012, pp. 226–234); Carandini, Carafa and Ippoliti (2021, pp. 185–187). Livy later mentions Cato's dedication of a shrine (*aedicula*) to Victoria Virgo by the temple of Victoria in 193 BCE (34.9.6).

143   Cf. above all 29.10.4.

144   For comparison between the different versions see Casapulla (2024, pp. 124–126, with further bibliography).

and the dedication, considering the links between the foreign goddess and the Roman foundation legend. The Trojan connections of the Idaean Mother made her a logical protectress of the people descended from Aeneas. When Livy wrote Book 29 (sometime in the late Twenties BCE), both the Trojan legend and the god of prophecy, Apollo, were prominent elements in Augustus' cultural politics, and both, as I have shown, were implied in his restyling of the Palatine. The *Aeneid* (written between 29 and 19 BCE) also reserves an important role for Cybele, as a Trojan goddess, and for Apollo, the deity who, through his oracles, guides Aeneas in his search for the new homeland. So, it is likely that, in recounting the events of 204 BCE, Livy was responding to contemporary discourses about the Palatine as a site related to the Roman Trojan origins and as the seat of Palatine Apollo.

While the passages I have just listed constitute the only explicit mentions of the Palatine in the *Ab Urbe Condita*, there are also several references to buildings located on the hill. Camillus, for example, in his great speech at the end of Book 5, mentions two Palatine sites among the ones that it would be unthinkable to abandon: the *casa Romuli* (5.53.7, if, indeed, the one on the Palatine rather than the one on the Capitol is implied: cf. above, p. 126 n. 120 and Balland, 1984, p. 62) and the temple of Vesta (three times). The latter receives special emphasis: as I have mentioned above (p. 114), for example, 'the fires of Vesta' appear at the very end of the speech among the most hallowed treasures of Roman religion (5.54.7).[145] The temple also appears in an episode connected with an earlier proposal about moving to Veii, which Livy dates to before the Gallic invasion (393 BCE): here the patricians break off voting in the Forum and plead with the plebeians not to abandon the city, 'showing them the Capitol, the temple of Vesta, the other temples of the gods around there' (5.30.4).[146] In all these occurrences, the temple appears, alongside the Capitol, as the quintessence of Roman piety. Later, in Book 28, the extinction of the fire of Vesta is the climax of the prodigy list of 206 BCE, and the historian presents it as a particularly terrifying one (28.11.6–7).[147] Another site in the vicinity of the temple, the shrine of Aius Locutius, receives an *aition* at 5.32.6 (also in connection with the history of the Gallic invasion). The dedication of the temple of Victoria Virgo, also on the Palatine, is reported at 35.9.6.

Given the importance of the hill in the foundation account and the roles of at least the temples of Vesta and the Idaean Mother in the narrative, it

---

145 The other two occurrences are at 5.52.7 and 5.52.13.
146 *Capitolium, aedem Vestae, cetera circa templa deorum ostentantes.*
147 At 26.27.4, 13 Livy mentions the temple in the report about a fire in the Forum area in 210 BCE.

would be wrong to interpret the role of the Palatine as marginal in the *Ab Urbe Condita*.[148] However, it is certainly true that this hill does not receive the emphasis one would expect considering its Augustan associations and its topicality in the years when Livy was writing Book 1–45. While one might explain this absence through the fact that the Palatine was not, in Republican times, a site for institutional procedure, what is most striking is that speakers (with the only exception of Horatius Cocles on the bridge) do not mention the Palatine by name; comparison with the frequent and multifaceted rhetorical uses of the Capitol is illuminating. One might expect Livy's Roman orators in the Forum to point to the Palatine as the original site of the city, and thus as a symbol of Rome's identity; in fact, they do not.

As I shall now show, the Palatine is not the only 'Augustan' site that the *Ab Urbe Condita* seems to downplay. The examination of another such site, the Campus Martius, will allow me to reflect on the possible reasons behind this narrative tendency.

4 The Campus Martius

The Campus Martius, originally a grassy plain lying outside the *pomerium*, north of the Capitol and east of the Tiber, was the location for the *comitia centuriata*, the assembly of the Roman people which elected the higher magistrates and voted on declarations of war as well as (until Sulla at the latest) on capital charges of a political nature. It was also the location for the census and the place where Roman generals and armies would wait for permission to celebrate a triumph, and whence they would make their way to the Capitol in the triumphal procession.[149]

---

148 Levene (2019) goes too far, in my opinion, in downplaying the role of the hill in Livy's history. More generally, he argues that Livy's construction of the city space is schematic and focuses on very few significant sites. While selectivity is certainly an important part of Livy's narrative construction of space, and while sites such as the Forum and Capitol play a prominent role, I argue that other places play a significant role in Livy's narrated city.

149 On the Campus Martius see e.g. Coarelli (1997); Albers (2013); Jacobs and Conlin (2014). On capital trials see Alexander (2010, p. 243); and *OCD* 3, pp. 833–834 s.v. 'law and procedure, Roman. 3. Criminal law and procedure' for *iudicia populi*, i.e. trials before an assembly. Moreover, the *comitia tributa* also voted in the Campus Martius when they elected the lower officers (aediles, quaestors, tribunes of the plebs). Cf. Taylor (1966, pp. 5–6, pp. 85–106); North (2006, pp. 261–262).

Livy reports the dedication of the Campus to Mars and this being the origin of its name, at 2.5.2; since, as the historian writes, the Campus was previously the Tarquins' land, its consecration sanctions the beginning of the Roman Republic. Livy seems to have stressed the Republican connotations of the area by choosing this tradition over other *aitia* that we know from different ancient authors.[150]

Since Livy's history is annalistic, the names of consuls, or (for part of the fifth and fourth centuries BCE) military tribunes with consular power, are recorded yearly. In Books 2–5, this usually consists in a brief notice that marks the shift from one year to the next; in some cases, the consuls' names are introduced at the beginning of a year without any formal mention of their election,[151] in others their election is briefly reported with words such as *consules facti*.[152] There are few fully-fledged narratives of elections; even there, the text does not usually set the scene: the fact that voting took place in the Campus Martius is left implicit. The same holds true for the notices about triumphs, which started in the Campus Martius, touched several locations within the city, and ended on the Capitol.

There are seven explicit mentions of the Campus in Books 2–5, none in the context of an extended scene.[153] The Campus is also never mentioned in speeches in Books 2–5, although it is alluded to by Furius Camillus at 5.52.16 as the seat for the *comitia centuriata*.

Even in the later books, this general tendency holds. Each year features reports about elections of consuls and other magistrates, but most of them are quite sober. There are three explicit mentions of the Campus Martius in the Second Pentad. The first is the trial mentioned above (pp. 107–111) of Manlius Capitolinus in Book 6 (6.20.10–11). The remaining two are found in the account of the consular *comitia* for 354 BCE, which saw the elections of two patrician consuls. The narrative introduces the event emphatically, it taking place 'in the

---

150 For alternative traditions see Ogilvie (1965, pp. 244–245).
151 See e.g. 4.7.1 (*tribuni militum … consulatum ineunt*); 4.12.2 (*C. Furio Pacilo et M. Papirio Crasso consulibus*); 6.22.1 (*Insequenti anno Sp. et L. Papirii novi tribuni militum consulari potestate Velitras legiones duxere, quattuor collegis Ser. Cornelio Maluginensi tertium Q. Servilio C. Sulpicio L. Aemilio quartum tribunis ad praesidium urbis … relictis*); 6.31.1 (*Insequentis anni principia statim seditione ingenti arsere tribunis militum consulari potestate Sp. Furio Q. Servilio iterum Licinio† Menenio tertium P. Cloelio M. Horatio L. Geganio*); 7.28.1 (*Hos consules secuti sunt M. Fabius Dorsuo Serv. Sulpicius Camerinus*).
152 Cf. e.g. 2.63.1; 4.11.1; 4.13.6–7; 4.23.1; 5.36.11.
153 3.10.1 (a public exposition of booty), 3.27.3 (an enrolment of troops decreed by the dictator Cincinnatus); 3.63.6 (the returning consuls summon the Senate in the Campus Martius); 3.69.6–8 (the enrolment of troops decreed by T. Quinctius Capitolinus; the Campus is mentioned three times, once as *campus Martius*, twice as simply *campus*); 4.22.7 (the building of the *villa publica* and the first census).

four-hundredth year since the foundation of Rome, in the thirty-fifth since her rescue from the Gauls; after eleven years the consulate was taken away from the plebs' (*quadringentesimo anno quam urbs Romana condita erat, quinto tricesimo quam a Gallis reciperata, ablato post undecimum annum a plebe consulatu*, 7.18.1). Through such an accumulation of dates, Livy conveys that the election of two patricians to the consulate, in contrast with the Licinio-Sextian legislation of 367 BCE, may have brought about a historical break.

In the subsequent account of the elections, the expression *in campo* recurs twice in section 9, once in the narrator's voice (*aliquotiens frustra in campum descensum cum esset*, 'after people went down to the Campus several times with no result') and once in the tribunes' words. The latter lament that 'now they must leave not only the Campus but also the city, which had been conquered and subdued by the kingly power of patricians' (*non campum iam solum sed etiam urbem captam atque oppressam regno patriciorum*). In the end, the election of the patricians does not turn out to be as game-changing as the tribunes fear. It is clear, however, that Livy's account stresses the constitutional regularity at stake in those elections: the emphasis on the Campus Martius both in narrative and in speech alerts readers to the importance of the theme.

In the Third Decade, there are three explicit mentions of the Campus Martius. At 21.30.11, the conclusion of Hannibal's famous speech to his soldiers before the crossing of the Alps, the Carthaginian general exhorts his troops to envision 'the field lying between the Tiber and the walls of Rome' as the end point of their march (... *itineris finem sperent campum interiacentem Tiberi ac moenibus Romanis*). This is probably a reference to an imagined triumph since the Campus Martius was the starting point of triumphal processions. 22.36.8 reports a prodigy *in via fornicata, quae ad Campum erat*. Finally, the Campus features in the narrative of the consular elections for 214 BCE (24.7.10–9.4), which, as Livy writes, took an unexpected turn. The presiding magistrate, Quintus Fabius Maximus, invited the members of the *centuria praerogativa* to reconsider their first choice considering the danger the state was facing. The voters heeded him and elected two more experienced commanders – Fabius himself and Marcus Claudius Marcellus.

Explicit mentions of the Campus occur three times in the Fourth Decade and only once in the Fifth.[154] Two of these occurrences belong to contexts in which the Campus as a setting is significant and deserve closer consideration.[155]

---

[154] At 45.42.12, where the Macedonians' ships are transported to the Campus Martius after Paullus' triumph.

[155] The remaining occurrence (38.28.4) is an annalistic notice about the Tiber repeatedly flooding the Campus Martius in 189 BCE.

The first is the account of the *comitia* which sanctioned the declaration of war against Macedon in 200 BCE. At 31.6–7, Livy relates that the consul Publius Sulpicius presented a *rogatio* to the people on whether they wanted to declare war. The *centuriae* first rejected the proposal, but the Senate invited Sulpicius to convene them again. The consul delivered a speech on the necessity of war; this time, the *centuriae* approved the proposal. The external narrator introduces the consul's speech by specifying the location of the assembly (*contio*) convened for the occasion *in campo Martio* (31.7.1).[156]

The second episode belongs to the account of the reconciliation between the censors of 179 BCE, and long-standing enemies, Marcus Fulvius Nobilior and Marcus Aemilius Lepidus (40.45.6–46.16). The whole episode is significant, as Livy presents it as an instance of public interests taking precedence over private ones. At 40.45.8, the narrator specifies that the scene takes place 'in the Campus by the altar of Mars' (*in Campo ad aram Martis*), where the censors have sat down in their curule chairs. The most distinguished senators rush there, followed by a throng of citizens; one of them, Quintus Caecilius Metellus delivers a speech to exhort both men to find concord. A public reconciliation takes place, sanctioned by a spontaneous procession to the Capitol.

As is easy to see, all the episodes that mention the Campus Martius as a setting of *comitia* are concerned with the legality of institutional procedures and/or the prevalence of the public good over private interest. An exception is the passage from Book 6, where mentioning the Campus explains the people's view of the Capitol at Manlius' trial. In Book 7, the tribunes refer to the Campus Martius as the location for the elections which the patricians are endangering. In Book 24, the Campus Martius is the setting for voters' display of regard for an authoritative adviser like Quintus Fabius Maximus – in Livy's account, an example of harmonious interaction between people and aristocracy. At the outset of Book 31, the people must decide on a particularly important matter: the start of a war which (as Livy's readers know in retrospect) would launch Rome's expansion in the East. Once again, the voters accept the guidance of one from their ruling elite and reconsider the original choice. Finally, in Book 40, the reconciliation between Nobilior and Lepidus sanctions the value of the highest magistracy – the censorship – by setting it (and the will of the Roman people who have voted in the *comitia*) as superior to any personal enmity. In all these episodes, as I have observed in Livy's representation of the Forum and Capitol, stressing of the place highlights the general theme of a narrative.

---

156 *Consul in campo Martio comitiis, priusquam centurias in suffragium mitteret, contione advocata* (...).

Apart from these few instances, the Campus Martius appears remarkable for its inconspicuousness in the extant books of the *Ab Urbe Condita*. The narrative, it is true, includes the Campus Martius in the basic sketch of the city from the time of its foundation: it is there, in the *Palus Caprae*, as the site was allegedly called in Romulus' age, that the first king of Rome mysteriously disappears and possibly ascends to heaven; and, as we have seen, Livy does not fail to mention its dedication to Mars in Book 2. However, one can observe, with respect to the Campus Martius, something similar to what is true of Livy's representation of the Palatine: after granting it a significant role in the narrative of origins, the historian seems to downplay this space in his account of early- and mid-republican history.

This is surprising for several reasons. First, although the Campus Martius lay outside the *pomerium* and the Servian walls, and thus had predominantly military connotations at least until Late Republican times, its role as the location for elections made it a major setting for political activity. Secondly, one would think that its connection with Mars, the ancestor of the Roman people and the god of war, would grant him an important symbolic role in the history of Rome. Thirdly, the Campus Martius was also topical when Livy wrote. Few places in Rome could boast such a close association with Augustus and his urban renewal projects. Already in the late Thirties BCE, Agrippa had made the area less subject to floods by building a new aqueduct (the Aqua Virgo); this, in turn, led to the construction of Agrippa's baths near the Theatre of Pompey in the centre of the Campus Martius (which corresponded to the ancient site of Romulus' deification). In the northern part of the Campus, Octavian built his Mausoleum in the early Twenties BCE and would later build the Horologium and the Ara Pacis. Finally, the Circus Flaminius, the southern part of the Campus, hosted porticoes and buildings funded by the *princeps*' family and friends. Gardens turned the Campus Martius into one of the city's most beautiful areas, a place for leisure and imperial self-representation.[157]

Thus, as with the Palatine, the question arises: how should one understand this apparent downplaying of such an important 'Augustan' space?

I suggest that modern expectations that the *Ab Urbe Condita* should directly reflect the Augustan city miss the point. Rather, Livy's attitude to Augustus' intervention on the city space appears more nuanced. His narrative engages in dialogue with Augustus' cultural and urban politics, reflecting and alluding to contemporary developments in the building programmes concerning the Palatine ad the Campus Martius; in a way, Livy's narrative of monarchic and

---

[157] On Augustan architectural projects in the Campus Martius see e.g. Albers (2013, pp. 109–133); Jacobs and Conlin (2014, pp. 138–148).

mid-republican times anticipates some aspects of the Augustan city. This is the case with the role he gives the Palatine Hill and the Campus Martius in his first sketch of the city in Book 1, or with his 'Apollinean' narrative of the arrival of the Idaean Mother. It might well be that such threads were taken up again in the later books of the *Ab Urbe Condita*, which narrated the events of the Late Republic and Augustus' principate.

Once more this accentuates how much of the *Ab Urbe Condita* is lost: it is very likely, in particular, that the role of the Campus Martius became more prominent as the narrative reached more recent times. Caesar's murder, as reported in the *Periocha* to Book 116, took place in the Curia of Pompey (*in Pompeii curia*), which was part of the complex of the temple of Venus Victrix built by Pompey in the Campus Martius; the same *Periocha* also mentions Caesar's funeral *in Campo Martio*. Another *Periocha*, that to Book 138, mentions the Theatre and Porticus of Marcellus, both of which were in the Campus Martius, as memorials (*monumenta*) to Augustus' nephew; and it is hard to think that urbanistic projects such as the Mausoleum and Agrippa's baths would not have elicited Livy's attention, too. Indeed, it seems likely that the role of the Campus Martius in the account of Romulus' disappearance in Book 1 hinted at Caesar's murder, at Augustus' Mausoleum, which was built in the early Twenties BCE, but probably planned earlier, and at Agrippa's Pantheon;[158] and, as with the Apollinean connotations of the Palatine, it may well be that Livy's narrative of recent events took up those earlier references. The historian, as I argued in Chapter 1, proves himself aware of the effects of time and change on the urban landscape; this includes constructing an early- and mid-Republican city space in Books 2–10 ad 21–45, and playing on its relationships with future developments in the city in an implicit way.

That said, the lack of emphasis on the Campus Martius – the place where the Roman people elected their magistrates – might still be surprising because of the significance of elections in the workings of the Republic. A possible explanation lies in the role that spatial semantics plays in shaping the narrated city. It will be clear by now that the historian tends to associate each of the main sites in Rome with a specific set of political meanings. The central core of Forum and Capitol provides the main stage for action, its structure reflecting the struggles and identity of the early and middle Republic. The Campus Martius, on the other hand, comes into play when historical reflections directly focus on elections as a theme. The Campus, just like the Forum, the Curia, or the Capitol, thus seems to fulfil a thematic function within individual

---

158 Cf. e.g. Pausch (2018, n. 40, with further bibliography).

narratives: explicit mentions alert the reader to its role as a meaningful setting, and thus to the main topic that a specific narrative will develop and discuss.

Livy's construction of the city appears both selective, focusing on a central space laden with meaning, and prepared to stress other significant sites when the semantics of his account requires it. At the same time, it interweaves past, present, and future, in a subtle way, suggesting how those very meanings develop and change over time as the political institutions of the *res publica* develop.

5 Boundaries: Tiber, Walls, Gates, and Janiculum

Further recurring elements of the city space are the ones that mark the boundary between Rome and the outside world: the Tiber and the city walls and gates.[159]

The Tiber is especially prominent in the First Pentad. In Book 1, it is crucial to the foundation legend. In Books 2–5, it is mentioned twenty-one times – two of which in speeches – as an element of Roman city space or as related to Rome (for example, as a border or a route for communication).[160] It plays an especially prominent role in the narrative of the war against Porsenna in the first part of Book 2, providing the setting for the heroic feats of Horatius Cocles and Cloelia.[161] Later, it keeps its role as a boundary in military contexts,[162] but also works to bring goods or people to the city.[163]

The role of the Tiber as an essential element of Rome's urban image emerges in the great speech of Marcus Furius Camillus against the plan of moving the Roman population to Veii at the end of Book 5. After expanding on the religious

---

159 See Jaeger (2015, pp. 66–68). Apart from the Tiber, the Janiculum, too, plays a significant role in the early books, as Jaeger points out. It plays a strategic role in the account of the war against Porsenna and in that of an Etruscan attack at 2.51. It then reappears at 5.40.5, as the place where the plebs take refuge from the invading Gauls; and the street leading through the Pons Sublicius to the Janiculum is the path along which the Vestals leave Rome on the same occasion (5.40.8). As I showed in section 1, the Janiculum and the Pons Sublicius are liminal spaces, which connect the space of the city with the outlying space.

160 One occurrence is in the famous speech of Camillus, quoted below; the other is Mucius Scaevola's words at 2.12.5.

161 Cf. 2.5.2–3; 2.10.1–2; 2.10.11; 2.11.1–2; 2.12.5; 2.13.5; 2.16.6.

162 Cf. 2.51.2; 2.51.6–7; 4.19.6. In 3.10.3 and 3.26.8 (both about Cincinnatus) the Tiber works as a boundary, although not in a military context.

163 Cf. 2.34.4; 4.52.6; 5.46.8. At 3.26.11 Cincinnatus, who had been relegated *trans Tiberim* (see previous footnote), is brought back to Rome by ship along the river.

importance of specific sites within the city, toward the end of the speech, Camillus addresses the emotional attachment to one's homeland (5.54.2–3):

> 2. Adeo nihil tenet solum patriae nec haec terra quam matrem appellamus, sed in superficie tignisque caritas nobis patriae pendet? 3. Equidem fatebor vobis, etsi minus iniuriae vestrae quam meae calamitatis meminisse iuvat: cum abessem, quotienscumque patriam in mentem veniret, haec omnia occurrebant, colles campique et Tiberis et adsueta oculis regio et hoc caelum sub quo natus educatusque essem; quae vos, Quirites, nunc moveant potius caritate sua ut maneatis in sede vestra quam postea, cum relinqueritis eam, macerent desiderio.

> 2. Do the soil of our fatherland and this land we call mother have no hold on us? Does our love for our fatherland depend on buildings and beams? 3. Indeed, I will confess to you – although I like remembering the wrong you did me even less than my disgrace – that, while I was away, every time I thought of my fatherland, all these things occurred to me: the hills, the plain, the Tiber, the land that my eyes knew so well, and this sky under which I was born and raised. May these things, Quirites, stir you now with the love they inspire to remain in your homeland, rather than torment you later with regret once you have left it!

Camillus distinguishes between the buildings, that is, the human-made component of the city, and its natural component, the landscape. He argues that both are integral parts of a city. Indeed, the image that came to his mind when he was away had more to do with the landscape than the architecture. The essential elements of the Roman landscape are the hills, the plains lying between them, and the Tiber.

Camillus then goes on to argue, in rational rather than emotional terms, why the position of Rome is convenient (5.54.4). Camillus here employs a topos about Rome's ideal location, which we also find – albeit with different overtones – in Cicero (*Rep.* 2.3–10): the Tiber allows the city to receive goods both from inland and from the sea while not directly exposing her to the dangers of the sea itself.[164] In this way, the river contributes to the city's destiny of imperial domination.

---

164 Livy refers specifically to the 'dangers of foreign fleets' (*pericula classium externarum*), whereas Cicero writes of both military and moral dangers, alleging that cities located by the sea import 'foreign customs', too, alongside foreign goods (*non merces solum adventiciae, sed etiam mores*, 5).

After the First Pentad, the Tiber is – not surprisingly – less present in the narrative, as military campaigns now take place farther and farther from Rome. It is mentioned most frequently in annalistic notices or reports of censors' building activities.[165] Jaeger (2015, 68) singles out two notable exceptions. One is 39.13.12, where the women participating in the Bacchic cults throw torches into the river.[166] The second is Aemilius Paullus' return from the Macedonian campaign at 45.35.3: Paullus sails to Rome up the Tiber (*adverso Tiberi*) in a Macedonian ship of striking size, which transports part of the Macedonian spoils and is greeted by a cheering crowd on the riverbanks. Here, the Tiber regains its functions as a boundary, which the victorious general crosses to return to his people.[167]

However, the most prominent boundary features in the *Ab Urbe Condita* are the city walls and gates.[168] Magistrates strengthen surveillance on the walls and gates each time some danger comes close to the city.[169] Indeed, both Livy and speakers within the narrative often stress situations of danger for Rome by remarking that war – literally or metaphorically – (almost) reached the very walls of Rome.[170] In some cases, the city's inhabitants rush to the walls to watch the enemy approaching or to seek news about events abroad.[171] Gates are places for communication with the external world, through which people or news about events outside Rome reach the city.[172] In several cases, Livy indicates specific gates at which certain military engagements or other events occurred or certain characters left or entered the city, or as local indications in annalistic notices.[173] While in the earlier books, such mentions are frequent in

---

165 See e.g. 7.3.2; 24.9.6; 30.38.10; 35.9.2; 35.40.8; 38.28.4; 40.51.6; 41.27.8.
166 For the narrative of the Bacchanalian scandal of 186 BCE, see Chapter 4, pp. 235–241.
167 Jaeger (2015, p. 68) contrasts this scene, with the emphasis on the Macedonian wealth that Paullus introduces into Rome, with 'the passage identifying the location of Cincinnatus' meager farm "across from the very place where the *navalia* are now" (*contra eum ipsum locum ubi nunc navalia sunt*, 3.26.8)'. According to Jaeger, this reference invites readers to think of the new influx of wealth in opposition to earlier Roman simplicity.
168 For the space within the walls as opposed to the space outside the walls, see. e.g. 39.17.4 (*Contione dimissa magnus terror urbe tota fuit, nec moenibus se tantum urbis aut finibus Romanis continuit, sed passim per totam Italiam ... trepidari coeptum est*).
169 Cf. e.g. 2.39.9; 4.21.9; 5.39.2–3 (where the Gauls are surprised that the Romans have *not* manned their walls); 6.28.3; 7.12.3; 8.37.6; 10.4.2; 22.8.7; 22.55.8; 39.17.4–5 (in this case, surveillance at the gates is not against external enemies, but to prevent the people involved in the Bacchanalian scandal from leaving the city).
170 Cf. e.g. 2.24.5; 2.51.2; 2.64.3; 3.26.1; 3.68.7, 13; 6.28.2–3; 21.16.2, 6; 21.57.1.
171 Cf. e.g. 5.18.11–2; 6.28.3.
172 For news, cf. e.g. 22.7.11 (on which see below, pp. 142–143).
173 *Ad veterem portam Palati*: 1.12.3. Porta Capena: 1.26.2 (on which see Solodow 1979; Jaeger 2015, 67); 3.22.4; 7.23.3; 10.23.12; 26.10.1; 29.11.13; 38.55.2; 38.56.4. Porta Esquilina:

military accounts, in the later ones – where military events tend to take place far away from Rome – gates appear much more often in reports about building activities, prodigies, or events such as floods and fires. The narrative often uses gates to locate specific monuments or buildings; this suggests that gates were important reference points for thinking about the space within the city.

By being present at several levels throughout the narrative, the walls and gates of Rome are part of a mental model of the city characterised by a clear distinction between the city and the outside world. They constitute both boundary features and important reference points for orientation; most significantly, they continue to serve their boundary function even when the space of Roman imperium extends far beyond the confines of the city herself.

6   Synthetic Views of the City Space

I end my analysis by considering some episodes that provide overviews of the city space. Passages of this kind mostly report reactions in the city to events such as military victories and defeats, or to the danger posed by an attacking enemy, and show the impact of such events on the different elements of the city space. By offering comprehensive views of the city and singling out its main elements, such narratives shape an overarching model of the city space.

A striking example is 22.7.6–14, relating how the news of the defeat at Lake Trasimene reaches Rome. The first part of this narrative is set in the open:

> 6. Romae ad primum nuntium cladis eius cum ingenti terrore ac tumultu concursus in forum populi est factum. 7. Matronae, vagae per vias, quae repens clades allata quaeve fortuna exercitus esset obvios percontantur; et cum frequentis contionis modo turba in comitium et curiam versa magistratus vocaret, 8. tandem haud multo ante solis occasum M. Pomponius praetor 'Pugna' inquit 'magna victi sumus'.

> 6. In Rome, at the first announcement of that defeat the people rushed to the Forum in great terror and tumult. 7. The matrons went here and there through the streets and asked those they came upon which sudden

---

2.11.5; 6.22.8; 26.10.1; 33.26.9; 41.9.6. Porta Naevia: 2.11.8–9; Porta Collina; 2.11.7, 9; 2.64.3; 3.51.10; 4.21.8; 4.23.1; 4.31.9; 5.41.4; 6.28.2; 8.15.8; 22.57.2; 23.32.3; 26.10.1, 3; 30.38.10–11; 33.26.9; 40.34.4; 41.9.6. Porta Carmentalis: 2.49.8; 24.47.15; 25.7.6; 27.37.11. Porta Trigemina: 4.16.2; 35.10.12; 35.41.10; 40.51.6: 41.27.8. Porta Flumentana: 6.20.11; 35.9.3; 35.21.5. Porta Caelimontana: 35.9.3. Porta Fontinalis: 35.10.12.

catastrophe had been reported and which was the destiny of the army; and since the crowd, as at a crowded assembly, turned towards the Comitium and the Curia and called the magistrates, 8. in the end the praetor Marcus Pomponius, shortly before sunset, said: 'We have been defeated in a great battle'.

The *populus* assembles in the heart of the political space, the Forum, where events are announced, discussed, and decisions are taken; they turn to the sites that embody the main institutions of the city, the Comitium and the Curia. Women, who Livy tends to present as less organised and more emotional, move through the streets looking for information.

Then attention moves to the private houses and the city gates. After the praetor has announced the defeat, the people take the news home (*domos referunt*, 8). The next day, a crowd of men and women assemble at the gates (*ad portas*, 11), where they anxiously await information about their loved ones in the army. Once more, the narrator insists that the people go home after receiving information (12). He then tells the stories of two women who died of emotion after seeing their sons alive, one at the gate itself (*in ipsa porta*, 13), the other as she sat in her home (*domo, ibid.*). After penetrating the heart of Roman political space and the indefinite space of streets, this defeat in the outside world affects people's most intimate spaces – their homes. In the end, however, the narrative goes back to the Curia, where the Senate debates from sunrise to sunset over the strategy to use against Hannibal (*senatum praetores per dies aliquot ab orto usque ad occidentem solem in curia retinent*, 14).

Good news, too, requires the participation of the whole city in both its human and its physical components. In recounting how news of the victory at the river Metaurus reached Rome in 207 BCE (27.50.1–51.10), Livy constructs a narrative in several stages, each of which brings the people from uncertainty to joy. At 27.50.4–5, he portrays the fear and expectation in the days preceding the arrival of the news in Rome. Once more, he describes the contribution of different elements of the population to the general atmosphere in the city by showing them as acting in specific places: the senators do not leave the Senate House and the people do not leave the Forum (*nusquam ... aut senator quisquam a curia atque a magistratibus abscessit aut populus e foro*, 4); the matrons, 'since they had no power themselves, turned to prayers and invocations and pressed the gods hard with entreaties and vows' (*matronae quia nihil in ipsis opis erat in preces obtestationesque versae per omnia delubra vagae suppliciis votisque fatigavere deos*, 5).

While everyone is feeling both hope and fear, two knights from Narnia enter the city with news of the victory, but, at first, the people are reluctant to fully believe their reports, which sound too good to be true (27.50.6–7). Then a letter from the commander Lucius Manlius Acidinus reaches Rome (8) and stirs excitement in the Forum (9):

> Hae litterae per forum ad tribunal praetoris latae senatum curia exciverunt; tantoque certamine ac tumultu populi ad fores curiae concursum est ut adire nuntius non posset, sed traheretur a percontantibus vociferantibusque ut in rostris prius quam in senatu litterae recitarentur.

> This letter, which was brought through the Forum to the praetor's dais, had the senators go out of the Curia; and the people rushed in such an uproar to the gates of the Curia, struggling with one another to get there, that the messenger could not go in. Instead, he was dragged by people who asked him questions and shouted that the letter should be read first on the Rostra, rather than in the Senate.

The narrative places significant emphasis on the location of events by incorporating precise local information (*per forum ad tribunal praetoris*; *ad fores curiae*). The argument over the place where the letter should be read stresses the participation of both the people and the Senate in the destiny of the Roman army. As Livy writes in section 11, the letter was finally read 'first in the Senate, then in the popular assembly' (*in senatu primum, deinde in contione*). At the same time, the movement of the Senate out of the Senate House and the people toward the gates of the Senate House creates a movement of concentration, further stressed by the verb *concursum est* (9).

The remaining doubts dissolve as the legates arrive. The consequent eruption of collective joy is once more mapped onto the most significant places in the city (27.51.1–7). The people rush out to meet the envoys 'all the way to the Mulvian Bridge' (*ad Mulvium usque pontem*, 2). The envoys reach the Forum (3), where they enter the Curia with some effort because of the crowd all around them; the letter is read in the senate, then the envoys are lead to the popular assembly (that is, in the Comitium, just outside the Senate House, 5).[174] In the end, the people go away, partly to the temples (*circa templa deum*, 7) to give thanks, partly to their houses (*domos, ibid.*) to announce the good news to their wives and children. All essential elements of the city space are present here: the outskirts, that is, the boundaries of the city (the Mulvian Bridge); the political centre where communication between envoys, Senate, and people takes place (the Forum and the Senate House); the temples of

---

174 For the Comitium and the Senate House as meaningful settings see Chapter 2.

the gods throughout the city; the houses, where wives and children wait for the news.[175]

An even more significant example – and the last one I shall examine – of how the elements of the city space participate in defining moments for Rome is the beginning of Book 45, where Livy recounts the reactions in Rome to the news of Aemilius Paullus' victory over Perseus (45.1–2). The progression from rumour to certainty is carefully crafted. The historian starts by reporting two stories, to which he attaches no credibility, about how a hint of the news reached Rome. According to the first (45.1.1–5), during the games in the Circus Maximus (*cum in circo ludi fierent*, 2), a rumour spread among the crowd that the Romans had fought victoriously against Perseus in Macedon. When the presiding magistrate looked for the bringer of the news, he could find no one; but everyone took the strange occurrence as an omen.

According to the second story (45.1.6–10), on the second day of the Roman games, while the consul Licinius was about to give the starting signal for the chariot race, a messenger brought him a letter decorated with laurel. After giving the signal, the consul mounted his chariot and held the letter visible to the people while racing through the Circus back to the seats of honour. The people rush to the racing track. Then the consul summoned the senate on the spot; before the seats of honour in the Circus he announced that Aemilius Paullus had defeated Perseus.

The Circus-setting and the public gestures of the consul provide the scene with a spectacular quality which stresses the collective significance of the event. All the crucial components of the Roman *res publica* – the people, the senate, and the consul – are gathered in one place; the spectacle of the chariot race gives way to a collective spectacle. After the consul's announcement, everyone goes home to bring the news to their wives and children (10).

While these two traditional fables focus on one place – albeit an unusual one as a setting for significant events in the *Ab Urbe Condita* – the next section of the narrative takes place in the heart of political space. The next day, Livy writes, the Senate met in the Senate House (*senatus in curia habitus*) to decree supplications and measures concerning Aemilius' army (45.2.1–2).

Then there is the real highpoint in this sequence of scenes, the messengers' return from Macedon (45.2.3–12). The text stresses the importance of the event by recording the exact date and time of their arrival (*ante diem sextum kalendas Octobres hora fere secunda*, 3). Moreover, the passage is notable for the density of spatial information. The messengers immediately head towards the Forum (*in forum*), where a crowd of people follows them; thence, they are

---

175 Livy goes on to report that the Senate decreed a supplication, which both men and women celebrated in all the temples of the city (27.51.8–10).

admitted to the Senate House, where the senators are gathered (*senatus forte in curia erat*, 4).

After they have reported to the senate (5), the messengers are led to the assembly (*in contionem*, 6), that is, to the Rostra, to report the same news to the people. From the assembly (*e contione*, 6) everyone goes to the temples to give thanks to the gods; both men and women flood the temples all over the city (*tota urbe*, 7). Then the Senate returns to the Senate House once more (*in curiam*, 8) and decrees several measures concerning religious ceremonies and practical matters (9–11). Finally, a *supplicatio* is announced before the popular assembly (*pro contione populi*, 12).

What is especially significant in this kind of episodes is the correspondence between the collective reactions of the Roman population and the external narrator's synthetic overview of the city space. The text presents the entire city's reaction to events, in both human and material terms. The most recurrent elements are boundaries, the Forum and Senate House, streets, temples, and private houses. While the boundaries are the physical expression of the distinction, which war endangers, between the city and the external world, the other recurrent elements are tied to the main components of Roman society: the senate, the people, the matrons – and the gods who protect the city. Collective scenes of this kind remind the reader that Rome is made up of all these elements, both human and material and that human and material elements are inherently bound up with one another.

7   Rome in the *Ab Urbe Condita*

As my analysis has shown, Livy's Rome is dominated by some major elements, each of which has its specific meaning in the spatial and political semantics of the city.

First, it is clearly distinguished from the outside world by boundary elements: the city walls and gates, the Tiber, and the Janiculum. These boundaries – especially the city walls and gates – continue to be significant in the mental model of Rome even when Livy narrates events from a time when wars were generally fought far away from the city. In the *Ab Urbe Condita*, the opposition between the city and the external world is constantly reinforced through the attention devoted to the arrivals and departures of magistrates and messengers, also through the stress the narrative places on walls and gates as ways for the exchange of news from the outside world, and from the metaphors of 'enemies at the gates' in the accounts of foreign wars.

Within the circle of the city walls, the main centre of narrative attention is the complex of Forum and Capitol. The Capitol is a constant reminder of

Rome's highest civic and religious values. While less frequently a setting than the Forum and the Senate House, it is one of the places speakers most frequently refer to, and it is often the object of gazes and speech. Throughout the *Ab Urbe Condita*, the Capitol embodies Rome's identity, her relationship with her gods, and the stability of her power over time.

Among the other hills, the Palatine and the Aventine play a significant role, even if not such a central one as the Capitol. The Palatine is an important setting in the foundation narrative and, later, is given emphasis as the seat of the temples of Magna Mater and Victoria – and, one can surmise, as the future seat of the temple of Palatine Apollo. The Aventine is connected with the struggles of the plebs and with foreign inhabitants and cults. Some of the latter, like that of Diana and Juno Regina are the subjects of detailed narratives.

Another important district is the Campus Martius, which lies outside the city walls and the *pomerium* but is integral to the city's political life as the setting for magisterial elections. The narrative integrates this external space into the overall image of the city from the very beginning, ending the account of Romulus' reign with his disappearance in the *Palus Caprae*. In the subsequent account of Roman history, the Campus Martius rarely plays a prominent role, at least in the extant books. While it is the implicit setting for all accounts of elections and narratives concerning the return of victorious armies from campaigns, it rarely receives the kind of emphasis reserved for symbolically charged locations such as the Capitol or the Forum. However, its enduring presence from foundational times makes it an integral component of Livy's city.

An indefinite space of streets, temples, and private houses is a constant background to Livy's account of Roman history. Of course, some streets, temples, and private houses provide the setting for specific events or are recalled as the location of prodigies or dedications. More often, though, they work as a communal space in which people move, act, and react to events. Streets also provide the paths that orient movement through the city. In the *Ab Urbe Condita*, special attention is devoted to paths leading from the gates to the inner of the city or from the city outward. Another frequent direction for movement is from the Forum outwards into 'the streets', or 'throughout the city', and from the streets into the Forum. Finally, the triumphal route, especially its last portion from the Forum to the temple of Jupiter on the Capitol, is often the focus of attention.

If considered in its entirety, the narrated city reveals three aspects, which constantly interact in Livy's account. First, a schematic city topography,[176] a basic template of the city space dominated by few main features. The narrative,

---

176 Cf. Levene (2019).

as I have argued, works with such features, which take on semantic values, to express ideas about Roman politics and society: thus, for instance, the Capitol embodies Rome's identity and inner hierarchies; the relationship between open Forum and Senate House represents the conflicts within the city; the walls help conceptualise the distinction between Rome and the outside world. What is especially striking is that such features are organically bound up with the image of the Roman civic body. The basic template of the city graphically represents the relationships between the main components of the community of Roman citizens. The relationships between the different ethnic communities of the monarchic period, between people and Senate, between people and their gods, between the community and the outer world, and (as I shall show in more detail in Chapter 4) between women and men are reflected in the spatial order within the city.

Such schematic topography, however, is not the whole story. In several cases, Livy provides more detail of the topographies of specific areas and proves aware of their complex connotations. This is the case with his representation of the Palatine: the stress he lays on the relationships between the temples of Magna Mater and Victoria suggests the connection of the Phrygian goddess with Roman expansion and plays on the contemporary connotations of the site. Moreover, his mention of the cult sites on the slopes of the hill (the temple of Vesta, the shrine of Aius Locutius, etc.) enriches the sacred connotations of the hill in the minds of readers familiar with the area. In addition, his attention for ceremonies related to the temples of Diana and Juno Regina shows awareness of their connection with otherness and Roman victory, even if such sites do not appear as frequently as, for example, the Capitol or the Curia.

There is, however, one more aspect to the city space, one I have not treated explicitly but which will by now have emerged as important from my discussion. I am referring to the many mentions of specific sites or buildings in the context of so-called 'annalistic' material: prodigy lists, records of floods and fires, reports about censors' building activities. Such mentions are usually very brief (in many cases, no more than a name) but they convey the impression of a city composed of a multiplicity of sites, each with its own significance and history – one, moreover, which grows and changes over time, all the while incorporating ancient memories.

The realisation of the interaction of these three aspects, or modes, of Livy's representation of the city leads me to stress two final points. The first concerns the ways the narrative represents the passage of time in the urban fabric. One can observe an interplay of stability and change, which is crucial to the ideology of the *Ab Urbe Condita*. What I have called the basic template remains very similar throughout early-and mid-republican history, though with some shifts in focus and emphasis (for example, from the open Forum to the Senate House as the centre of events). Specific topographies, however, change constantly. Magistrates have temples, public facilities, and monuments built; some areas are destroyed and then rebuilt or renovated; some monuments no longer exist; others preserve the memory of specific events. Thus, the narrated city invites readers to consider it diachronically, while assuming that there is a core that will remain unchanged or unmoveable.

Secondly, Livy's narrative meant different things to different readers. Some of his readers were Romans, or familiar with Rome; Livy certainly knew this and appealed to their everyday experience to hint at some connotations of specific places. Other readers, however, did not know the city as well, or at all; and it is likely that the historian knew his work would be read far from Rome.

When, for example, the historian narrates how the self-immolating Marcus Curtius 'looked at the temples of the immortal gods, which loom upon the Forum, and at the Capitol' before throwing himself into the chasm (7.6.4; cf. above, pp. 100–101) a reader unfamiliar with the city will have thought of the Capitol – in an image they will have by now formed in their mind – and of an indeterminate set of other temples looming above the city. A Roman reader, however, will have pictured those temples in their specificities; for instance, they will have thought of the temple of Vesta and automatically brought all its connotations (the eternity of Rome, the connection with the origins) into the picture. To take another example, to the unfamiliar reader Livy's account of the establishment of Magna Mater in Rome will have been nothing more than an episode in the centuries-long history of the integration of foreign cults; but one who knew Rome from everyday experience could not but be reminded of the way the hill had been changed by Augustus' restructuring.

Livy seems to exploit such different levels of knowledge by constructing a narrative which, on the one hand, makes sense even without first-hand knowledge of the city (the sketch in Book 1 contributing to set the scene for readers) but, on the other, plays on the knowledge of those who are familiar with it.

CHAPTER 3

The Space of Battle

1   Shaping Military Space in the *Ab Urbe Condita*

The space of the city finds its counterpart, in the *Ab Urbe Condita*, in the space of war. As I have shown in the previous chapters, the narrative repeatedly evokes the spectre of war within the city as a subversion of basic spatial categories; and tensions within the city are often solved by transferring the violence of war outside, by turning it into an instrument for conquest. The very structure of Livy's history, with its spiralling movement from the city outward and back toward the city every consular year, reflects the basic duality of *domi* and *militiae*, of city space and military space, without and within the city, and sets Rome as the ideal centre to a peripherical space of war and conquest.

The narrative shaping of the settings of military events involves issues and challenges which are different from those involved in cityscaping. Livy probably had no personal experience of most places where the events he narrated had occurred and mainly based his account on the works of previous historians, whose accuracy and detail will have varied.[1] As for his audience, we may surmise that the extent of their geo-topographical knowledge differed; but even for readers who had travelled widely several locations mentioned in the *Ab Urbe Condita* will have been little more than names. Moreover, as I mentioned in my Introduction (p. 17), the use of maps as supports for the writing or reading of history was virtually unknown in the Roman world.[2] Therefore, Livy's readers might have been left with nothing but their own imagination to put together the pieces of information provided by the historical narrative.

In his study of Caesar's *Bellum Gallicum*, Rambaud (1974) notably distinguished between three modes of spatial representation, all of them concerning military space: 'geographic space' ('espace géographique'), that is, the synthetic representation of extended areas, usually in the context of digressions; 'strategic space' ('espace stratégique'), that is, the linear space along which armies on the march move from one place to the next; and 'tactical space' ('espace

---

1 On Livy's geo-topographical inaccuracy and his lack of first-hand experience cf. e.g. Walsh (1961, pp. 138–139, 154–157); Girod (1982). Walsh (1961, pp. 157–163) also argues that Livy lacked military expertise, which led to inaccuracies and mistakes in his battle narratives; *contra* Koon (2010, pp. 23–26).
2 Cf. e.g. Janni (1984); Brodersen (1995).

tactique'), that is, the bi-dimensional space of smaller areas which function as the settings for fighting. The latter is, according to Rambaud, organised according to a system of perpendicular axes, thus revealing the influence of Roman practices of land surveying (*agrimensura*).[3] Strategic space, on the other hand, is strictly hodological and consists of a series of location names and distances between locations. This feature is connected to the fact that Roman armies on the march would generally use lists of stations (*itineraria*) rather than maps; strategic space, therefore, reproduces the actual experiences of commanders and soldiers. Geographic space is, to the contrary, based mainly on works of scientific geography written by previous authors. The juxtaposition of a linear mode based on personal military experience (strategic) and a two-dimensional mode implying the use of cardinal directions but based on second-hand knowledge (geographic) explains why even someone with such a deep knowledge of the terrain as Caesar can occasionally commit geographical inaccuracies.

Rambaud's distinction into three modes of space representation is applicable, in its main lines, to the *Ab Urbe Condita*, if with some further specifications.

'Geographic' space is the least frequent mode in the work, as is consistent with its more general tendency to present space dynamically rather than through extended descriptive passages.[4] Moreover, among the few geographic digressions of the *Ab Urbe Condita* some only appear to aim at providing useful information for understanding the narrative;[5] more often, just as I have shown to be the case with descriptive passages in general (cf. Introduction, pp. 24–26), an excursus signals a moment or a theme of special importance.

The discussion of the ancient power of the Etruscans in Italy at 5.33.7–11, for example, is part of the great narrative concerning the Gallic invasion of 390 BCE: it introduces the account of how the Gauls first migrated to Italy at the time of the Etruscan hegemony in the peninsula, about two hundred years before their war with Rome. The narrator introduces it through the words 'Before Roman dominance, the power of the Etruscans extended widely on land and sea' (*Tuscorum ante Romanum imperium late terra marique opes patuere*, 7). He goes on to explain that the very names of the Tyrrhenian and Adriatic Seas bear proof of the ancient Etruscan power: *Tyrrhenum* means 'Etruscan'

---

3 Riggsby (2006, pp. 21–45) has further developed Rambaud's observations, arguing for additional similarities between the representation of space in the *Bellum Gallicum* and the writings of Roman *agrimensores*.
4 Cf. Introduction, pp. 19–26.
5 For two examples cf. the descriptions of Acarnania and Leucas at 33.17.5–8 and of Scodra and the nearby regions at 44.31.2–5 (both certainly of Polybian origin: cf. Briscoe, 1973, pp. 1–2; 2012, p. 2).

and *Atriaticum* derives from Atria, an Etruscan colony. He then shows how the Etruscans expanded first to the west of the Apennines, then colonised the lands to the east and north as far as the Alps (8–11).

By emphasising the strength of the Etruscan people the Romans eventually conquered, this digression precedes Rome's even broader *imperium*. Significantly, the passage is recalled at the end of Book 5, in the last part of Camillus' great speech against abandoning Rome in favour of Veii.[6] As evidence of Rome's excellent position, Camillus mentions the city's military successes against much older peoples, among which 'the whole of Etruria, so powerful on land and sea and extending over the whole width of Italy between the two seas' (*universa Etruria, tantum terra marique pollens atque inter duo maria latitudinem obtinens Italiae*, 5.54.5). Such an intratextual allusion at a prominent point of Book 5, and the First Pentad, signals that, on the eve of its rebirth after the Gallic sack, Rome has come to take on the hegemonic role destiny has allotted to it. The geographic excursus at 5.33 should be interpreted as part of the same discourse on Roman power as a successor to Etruscan might.[7]

Similarly, the very brief and vivid description of the Isthmus of Corinth at 45.28.2, placed within the narrative of Aemilius Paullus' tour of Greece after the victory of Pydna, evokes the future destruction of the city in 146 BCE and in so doing becomes part of a broader reflection about Rome's conquest of Greece.[8] Finally, digressions on Gaul and Germany were contained in the lost Books 113 and 114, which narrated, among other things, Julius Caesar's campaigns (cf. *Per.* 103: *situm Galliarum*; 104: *situm Germaniae moresque*). It is very likely that the insertion of extensive geo-ethnographical sections in these two books was meant as an intertextual reference to Caesar's own work.

Strategic space, on the other hand, is pervasive. As Pausch (2011, pp. 130–131) remarks, this mode fulfils a crucial function in the *Ab Urbe Condita*: by bringing foreign territories to the readers' attention and by structuring them according to the hodological perspective of armies on the march, or of Roman magistrates reaching their field of operations, the strategic presentation of space incorporated such territories into the chronological and spatial dynamics of Roman expansion.

At the same time, Livy's presentation of strategic space appears more complex than Caesar's. The *Ab Urbe Condita* contains numerous military narratives

---

6 Cf. above, pp. 112–116.
7 In Book 5, of course, the opposition between Rome and Etruria plays a major role, since the first part of the book is devoted to the siege and conquest of Veii (5.1–22).
8 Cf. Clark (2014, pp. 238–239).

and a much greater variety of landscapes and terrains than the *Bellum Gallicum*. Moreover, strategic and tactical spaces are often mixed more flexibly within the same account. Strategic and tactical space are deeply merged, for example, in narratives in which armies march through a rough and difficult terrain which becomes an object of interest in its own right: one need only think of the famous account of Hannibal's crossing the Alps in Book 21 or the Romans' crossing Lower Olympus at 44.3–5.[9] In such cases, the notion of 'strategic space' does not seem entirely satisfactory.

'Tactical space', that is, the space of battle, is my main concern in this chapter. Battle accounts often constitute dramatic episodes, and some figure among the narrative highlights of Livy's work. Some major battles constitute the turning-points of war and the climatic narratives of individual books; they might be crucial in portraying the strengths and weaknesses of the opposing armies and the personalities of their commanders. Moreover, whereas spatial information in 'strategic' sections usually keeps to the essentials, the settings of battles often display much more literary elaboration, and thereby allow a fuller appreciation of the narrative strategies at work.

In shaping 'tactical spaces', Livy uses three main spatial information sets. The first serves to locate the battle site within the geography of a country: this is usually achieved by indicating the name of the nearest town or locality. Information of this sort is quite cursory, and its insertion marks the shift from 'strategic' to 'tactical space' since the locality, near which the battle takes place, is usually the arrival point of a previous march.[10]

The other two sets of information are strictly relative to the bi-dimensional space of battlefields. One refers to what I will call 'standard military space', that is, the space created by the deployment and manoeuvring of fighting armies, as well as by the relative positions of camps and fortifications;[11] I use the term 'standard' to indicate that these are basic forms of military space that are applicable in any campaign. The second concerns the topography of a battlefield, that is, the physical features of the terrain. Most battle narratives include a mix of both types of information, but the relative importance of the former or latter varies from case to case.

---

9 For space and landscape in the account of Hannibal's march, see Fabrizi (2015); for the march through Lower Olympus, Clark (2014, pp. 205–207).
10 Cf. Rambaud (1974, p. 120).
11 Cf. van Gils (2019), who understands camps and sectors of armies as a category which lies between 'locations' and 'objects', since they share features of both.

On the other hand, the reference system based on the cardinal points is notably absent.[12] There are only a few exceptions to this rule, and they mostly concern explanations of specific details that could not have been understood without reference to cardinal orientation[13] or belong to contexts in which geographic descriptions are embedded in battle narratives.[14]

In what follows, I analyse how these different types of spatial information structure the mental model of *Ab Urbe Condita* battlefields. I shall focus mainly on the semantic values that standard military space and topography can take on in battle accounts: I will look at how narrated space shapes thought about military ethics, victory, conquest, and Roman identity. I first examine how the text constructs standard military space (2). Secondly, I consider the role of topography (3): I ask what kinds of topographic features appear most prominent in battle accounts and enquire into the functions such features can play. In the final section (4), I draw some conclusions and reflect on the constant anxiety about with control and the imposition of Roman space on foreign territories that the *Ab Urbe Condita* displays.

2 Standard Military Space

2.1 *Camps and Sectors of Armies as Spaces*

An easily recognisable pattern, which applied to virtually all battles, is provided by the typical organisation of military space, which has its main reference points in camps and sectors of deployed armies. It can be assumed that some of Livy's readers were familiar with such a pattern from personal experience on military service; others will have perceived it as familiar because it belonged to the conventions of battle descriptions in the ancient historical tradition.[15] So, the standard organisation of the space of battle could provide a

---

12 This probably corresponded to a general feature of Roman military imagery: cf. Rambaud (1974, p. 123) on Caesar.

13 Cf. 22.46.8–9 (the orientation of the Roman and Carthaginian armies at the battle of Cannae, which Livy mentions in order to explain why the Romans were blinded by the dust raised by the wind: see below, p. 186).

14 Cf. e.g. 26.42.6, 8; 26.44.2 (the siege of New Carthage, where Livy extensively describes the position of the city); 33.17.7; 37.31.9. The reference to cardinal points is normal in the 'geographic space' mode, as well as in descriptions of towns and cities. Further instances of the use of cardinal points in military contexts ('tactical space') in Livy are 29.35.14 (again in the context of a coastal landscape); 38.20.4, 7; 38.21.1.

15 On the conventional features of battle descriptions in ancient historiography see Koon (2010, p. 27, pp. 35–36); Lendon (1999, 2017a and b).

basic form of orientation for readers, even in cases where the text gave virtually no clue about the topography of a battlefield.

Camps are omnipresent landmarks in military narratives in the *Ab Urbe Condita* and are important in defining the bi-dimensional space of battle, especially when topography is very vague. While camps can relate to topographical features (e.g. when a camp is placed upon a hill), this is not necessarily the case. The approach of battle is usually signalled by the fact that armies set up camp, and relative distances between the camps of the two opponents may be stated; commanders lead their armies out of their camps before a battle, and victorious armies typically end their pursuit of the enemy by attacking and plundering their camp. Thus, in a way, camps are spaces that mark the beginning and end of battles.[16]

On some occasions, camps may even work as battlefields, for example, when they are stormed or put under siege. When Livy reports combats, or other kinds of events, which take place within Roman camps, he often makes explicit reference to their internal arrangement – a standard structure that at least some of his readers would have been familiar with.[17] A Roman camp was typically a square (or, later, rectangular) space surrounded by a palisade (*vallum*) and a mound (*agger*). Its main axis was the *via principalis*, its main landmarks the *praetorium* (the general's tent) and the *forum*; two gates (*portae principales*) were placed in line with the *via principalis* on either side of the camp, and two more on the two remaining sides (*porta praetoria* and *porta quaestoria*).[18]

---

16   For armies conquering camps after battles as a recurring element if historical narratives cf. Oakley (1997, pp. 622–623).

17   The most detailed description of a Roman camp of the Mid-Republican period is provided by Polyb. 6.27–42, on which cf. Fabricius (1932); Walbank (1967, pp. 709–723). On the structure and characteristics of Roman camps more generally, see e.g. Rüpke (2019, pp. 169–174); Richardson (2004). The arrangement of Roman camps seems to have changed over time, but the basic principles remained the same, at least in the first centuries of the Empire.

18   In 2.45, for example, the camp is the setting for the events prior to the battle against the Etruscans (cf. below, pp. 168–170) and the *praetorium*, the rampart and the gates are mentioned; at 2.47.5 during the Etruscans' attack to the camp, the Roman *triarii* fight near the *praetorium*. In 34.46.7–47.8, in the account of an assault on a Roman camp by the Boi (a Gallic tribe) in 194 BCE, Livy mentions, among other things, the two *portae principales* (34.46.9) and the *porta quaestoria* (34.47.2–3). Camps, and their standard deployment, also appear as settings for events other than fighting: cf. e.g. 8.31.1–33.2 (the dispute between Papirius Cursor and Fabius Rullianus; Livy repeatedly mentions the *tribunal*, a raised platform placed by the *praetorium*); 30.14–15 (Massinissa scolded by Scipio for marrying Sophoniba and, later, honoured by Scipio; the actions are set outside the praetorium, in Masinissa's tent, then again outside the *praetorium*, where Scipio summons the soldiers from the *tribunal*).

On two occasions, Livy elaborates on the significance of such orderly, structured camps as outposts of Roman space. At 31.34.8, the historian describes Philip of Macedon's reaction when first seeing a Roman camp in 199 BCE:

> ac subiecta cernens Romana castra, admiratus esse dicitur et universam speciem castrorum et discripta suis quaeque partibus cum tendentium ordine tum itinerum intervallis, et negasse barbarorum ea castra ulli videri posse.

> and it is said that, as he saw the Roman camp lying below him, he admired the look of the camp as a whole and its sections assigned to specific areas, both for the methodical arrangement of the tents and for the regular intervals at which streets lay; no one, he said, could think it a camp of barbarians.

This passage of the text powerfully delineates the link between the rational arrangement of the camp and Roman (non-barbaric) identity through the words of an enemy who was the heir to the glorious tradition of ancient Greece. Moreover, Philip's admiration of the orderly nature of his enemy's camp resonates with one recurring theme in Livy's narrative of Roman wars (and one I shall repeatedly touch upon in this chapter), namely the Romans' ability to impose their control on foreign spaces.[19]

Even more significant is the second reflection about the space of camps that Livy introduces in the *Ab Urbe Condita*. At 44.38–39, the historian reports a speech allegedly pronounced by Lucius Aemilius Paullus in front of his troops shortly before the battle of Pydna of 168 BCE.[20] The Roman soldiers were eager to fight and blamed their general for having them set up camp first instead of attacking the enemy on the spot. Among the other arguments that Paullus used to defend his sensible conduct, he reminded his men of the importance of a well-kept camp (44.39.2–5).

Considerations of a practical nature – a camp is a resting place for the victor and a refuge to the defeated (2–3) – give way, in section 5, to the recasting of the camp as a second Rome through the correspondences between the rampart and city walls and between individual tents and houses:

---

19 Cf. e.g. Clark (2014, p. 157 n. 49).
20 Polybius, Livy's main source for the battle of Pydna, might have also introduced a speech at this point, but Livy's speech will have been, as ever, his own re-elaboration: cf. Briscoe (2012, pp. 588–589).

> Patria altera militaris est haec sedes, vallumque pro moenibus et tentorium suum cuique militi domus ac penates sunt.

> This place is a second military fatherland; the rampart stands for the city walls and to each soldier his own tent is like his house with his household gods.

This 'Rome' is the space whence armies go out to fight (*unde ad pugnam exirent*) and whither they eventually come back (*quo iactati tempestate pugnae receptum haberent*, 2). In a way, the well-ordered structure of the Roman camp allows the imposition of Roman space onto hostile territories[21] and reproduces the very framework of Livy's *Ab Urbe Condita*, with the city as the beginning and the end of each year of campaign.

Apart from camps, the deployment of armies, too, provides a standard spatial pattern that creates a sense of order and regularity out of the various circumstances and terrains the Romans encounter. Several battle accounts in the *Ab Urbe Condita* begin with, or at least include, a detailed description of the array of the two opposing forces.

This was a conventional element of ancient battle accounts, but ancient historians show a significant degree of flexibility in using it. For example, the description of the array is not necessarily functional to the understanding of the ensuing battle: in several cases, contingents mentioned by a historian during the array section do not appear at all in the combat section. In some cases, the function of arrays can be to provide an enticing narrative through the presentation of different types of troops and weaponry – some of them foreign and exotic – as well as to stress the tactical acumen of commanders.[22]

In the *Ab Urbe Condita*, array sections at the outset of battle narratives play a variety of functions. In several cases, the description of the deployments of troops is relevant to the understanding of what follows: either because the main sections of the armies mentioned in the array section are, indeed, recalled in the account of the fighting[23] or because the array section draws an explicit connection between certain contingents in one army and the ones

---

21 Cf. Clark (2014, pp. 218–219).
22 Cf. Lendon (2017, esp. pp. 58–62).
23 Cf. e.g. Ticinus (218 BCE), 21.46; Trebia (218 BCE), 21.54–56 (array at 21.55.2–4); Cannae (216 BCE), 22.45.5–49.10 (array at 22.45.6–46.10); Metaurus (207 BCE), 27.48.1–49.4 (array at 27.48.4–8); Zama, 30.32.1–35.3 (array at 30.33.1–7); Cynoscephalae (see Philip's array at 33.8.12–14 and how the effect of deployment of the phalanx is mentioned later, at 33.9.5); Callinicus (171 BCE), 42.58–59 (array at 42.58.6–14).

they directly face.²⁴ In other cases, the deployment is not described in full at the outset but, rather, is selectively sketched in the course of the account of the fighting.²⁵ Most importantly, the text can use the standard array section creatively to express ideas about the political or moral character of the forces involved in the fighting or the reasons for victory and defeat.²⁶

The space of several Livian battles is mainly constructed along two perpendicular axes: on the one hand, the one constituted by the ranks of two armies; on the other, the axis along which one army advances into its enemy's ranks and the other army retreats. Encircling manoeuvres can occur, and skirmishing between cavalry corps on the wings is frequent. The outcome of combat is generally represented, as we shall see, as the steady advance of one army vs. the scattering of the other.²⁷

Standard military space is enough to make sense of a battle in spatial terms. In the *Ab Urbe Condita*, many battle accounts contain virtually no mention of topography, and the reader can only locate the narrated events with reference to the space shaped by the fighting armies and their respective camps.²⁸ Standard military space also provides a useful organisational principle for ordering the chaotic battle experience into a consistent storyline. By shifting the spotlight from one sector of the battle to the next, for example, the narrator can relate contemporaneous events in sequential order and in so doing convey the collective battle experience in an understandable way.²⁹

---

24 At Cannae, for example, Hannibal is said to deploy his Gallic and Spanish horsemen 'on the left wing, near the riverbank, and facing the Roman cavalry' (*prope ripam laevo in cornu adversus Romanum equitatum*, 22.46.2); and this detail is later recalled at the beginning of the account of the fighting, at 22.47.1 (*deinde equitum Gallorum Hispanorumque laevum cornu cum dextro Romano concurrit*). Note also that at 22.48.1 the text again recalls the disposition of troops described in the array-section: *Iam et sinistro cornu Romano, ubi sociorum equites adversus Numidas steterant, consertum proelium erat* (cf. 22.45.7; 46.3). See also 27.48.4–8 (Metaurus; recalled at 48.9–10); 30.33.2 (Zama).

25 Cf. 31.21.7–8 (quoted below, pp. 159–160), where only the right wing of the army is mentioned.

26 For an example of such a use of the array section see Fabrizi (2021a, pp. 51–54).

27 Cf. e.g. 30.35.1–3 (Zama), 34.15.2 (Emporiae).

28 Cf. e.g. the battles of Zama (30.32.1–35.5); Emporiae (34.14–15); and the narratives examined below. This is especially frequent for battles that were fought on plains since Roman historians tended (as I show below) to think of plains as indefinite spaces. However, there are also cases in which more complex topographies are overlooked by Livy. Sometimes, information about the terrain was absent in Livy's source (as, for example, in Polybius' account of the battle of Zama at 15.9–14); elsewhere it is possible that Livy omitted topographical information that he found in others' accounts.

29 On the structuring function of space in battle narratives cf. van Gils (2019, pp. 255–256, with specific reference to the battle of Cannae). On Livy's fondness for organising battle

This is not the only way, however, in which standard military space can play a structural role in battle accounts. In some narratives, as I now intend to show, standard military space can also work as a bearer of specific notions and themes. In what follows, I examine two such themes: the contrast of order vs. disorder and the inner workings of political communities.

2.2 Order and Disorder

A recurrent motif in military narratives across Livy's history is the contrast between order and disorder.[30] Working as a compact and disciplined body of soldiers guarantees an advantage. At the same time, the inability to keep ranks can result in disaster: battles often end when one of the two armies is scattered across the field. Moreover, a set of moral qualities (discipline, courage, respect for authority) is involved in preserving order, and such qualities often appear as important reasons for victory in Livy.[31]

Often in the *Ab Urbe Condita*, the contrast between order and disorder is linked to a discourse about Roman versus foreign (and especially 'barbarian') identity. At 31.21, for example, Livy narrates how, in 200 BCE, the praetor Lucius Furius Purpureo went to the rescue of Cremona, which the Gauls were then besieging. The lack of discipline among the enemy is immediately evident on Furius' arrival: the barbarians 'roamed here and there as they dispersed across the fields, leaving no strong garrison' (31.21.4: *palate passim vagabantur per agros, nullo satis firmo relicto praesidio*). The actual battle takes place on the following day and highlights the contrast between the Romans' well-organized army and the Gauls' disordered way of fighting (31.21.5–12).

As soon as the two forces descend into the field, the Gauls rush to the attack. The Romans barely have time to deploy their line, but still, they *do* deploy it (6), and Livy provides some details about their battle formation (7–9):

> Dextra ala – in alas divisum socialem exercitum habebat – in prima acie locata est, in subsidiis duae Romanae legiones. M. Furius dextrae alae, legionibus M. Caecilius, equitibus L. Valerius Flaccus – legati omnes erant – praepositi. Praetor secum duos legatos, C. Laetorium

---

narratives by army sectors cf. Walsh (1961, pp. 161–162). Walsh sees it as a sign of the historian's rigidity and ignorance of the complexity of military matters; I argue that, on the contrary, this kind of organisation is often functional to Livy's overall interpretation of a battle.

30 On order and disorder as a frequent subject of ancient military narratives cf. Lendon (2017, pp. 55–57).
31 For the role of courage (*virtus*) cf. Levene (2010, pp. 281–283); and below, pp. 179–184.

et P. Titinium, habebat, cum quibus circumspicere et obire ad omnes hostium subitos conatos posset.

7. The right wing – the commander had the army of allies split into wings – was located in the first row, two Roman legions were located in reserve; 8. Marcus Furius was set in command of the right wing, Marcus Caecilius of the legionaries, Lucius Valerius Flaccus of the cavalry (these were all legates). 10. The praetor had two legates, Gaius Laetorius and Publius Titinius, near him, so that with them he could survey and go to meet any sudden assault of the enemies.

Such details, derived from the annalistic source Livy was following,[32] are incomplete (we only know, for example, about the right wing of the allies, while we receive no information about the left wing). Still, they are enough to understand the course of the battle.[33] On the other hand, the Gauls fight without any ordered arrangement: first, they charge the allies *en masse* (10); it is only when they realize that this is not working that they attempt to encircle the Romans (11). Furius reacts to their attempt by redeploying his army. As a result, the Gauls are killed by the cavalry on the flanks and the infantry in the centre, who eventually penetrate the enemy line (31.21.12–13). The Gauls turn and flee towards their camp; the Roman cavalry pursues them and conquers it (31.21.15–16). The whole course of the battle graphically portrays the ethnic character of the Gauls, as the *Ab Urbe Condita* repeatedly describes them:[34] fierce but unable to bear discipline and prolonged fatigue.[35]

A more complex representation of ethnic differences is provided by the account of the battle fought by Marcus Porcius Cato's soldiers against the Spaniards at Emporiae in 195 or 194 BCE, which shall be my focus in the

---

[32] For Livy's source here cf. Plathner (1934, p. 53); Briscoe (1973, p. 110).

[33] Cf. Plathner (1934, pp. 54–55). Briscoe (1973, pp. 110–114), on the contrary, sees the incompleteness of Livy's information about the Roman deployment as problematic, and thinks that the historian 'has taken his account from an annalistic source, and has not worked it up with usual care' (p. 110).

[34] For such a characterization of the Gauls see Livy 5.48.3; 7.12.11; 22.2.4; 27.48.16; 33.36.8; 34.47.5; 38.17.7–8; and cf. Oakley (1998, pp. 158–159, with references to further ancient passages on this stereotype). On ethnic stereotypes in general in Livy, see e.g. Walsh (1961, pp. 108–109); Luce (1977, pp. 276–294); Levene (2010, pp. 214–260); Bernard (2015). Some aspects of Gallic warfare, which are expounded by Goldsworthy (1996, pp. 53–60), might explain the origins of such an image of the Gauls.

[35] Of course, Romans can also fail to fight in an orderly fashion: se e.g. 6.24.3–4, where the Romans first recklessly pursue the Volscians, then rush back to their own camp after falling into the enemy's ambush.

remainder of this section.[36] The battle itself is narrated at 34.14–15, but to fully understand its implications one should read it within the wider narrative context of Cato's campaigns in Spain in 195–194 BCE (34.8.4–21.8). It is now generally assumed that the main source for this section of Book 34 was Cato himself – most likely the *Origines*, even if one cannot rule out that Livy also drew on Cato's speeches – and that Livy's account was, at least in its structure, quite close to that of his 2nd century predecessor.[37]

After reporting the arrival of Cato and his fleet at Emporiae (34.8.4–7), the narrator introduces a brief excursus on the topography of the town and its inhabitants (34.9.1–10). As he explains, Emporiae was, in fact, made up of two towns, a Hispanic and a Greek one, the latter a loyal Roman ally and inhabited by Phoceans (1–2).[38] This information is likely to have been present in the *Origines*, which had a well-known interest in geo-ethnographical material, but the *Ab Urbe Condita* integrates it with material concerning more recent developments of the town: Julius Caesar added a third community of Roman citizens after his victory in Spain and, by Livy's times (*nunc*), the three communities had been 'lumped into one body' (*in corpus unum confusi*) thanks to the awarding of the Roman citizenship (3).[39] The narrator then expands on the exposed position of the 2nd century Greeks between the open sea and the bellicose Spaniards. One might have wondered, he writes, what kept them safe. His answer is 'discipline' (*disciplina*), 'the guardian of the weak, which fear preserves at best among stronger peoples' (*custos infirmitatis, quam inter validiores optime timor continet*, 4). Through this remark, the text introduces one of the leading themes of the following narrative, the value of discipline, which, together with valour (*virtus*) emerges as a reason for Roman success in the account of the battle at 34.14–15.

Cato, as any good commander, devotes special attention to the choice of terrain: he occupies the site he deems most appropriate before the enemy realises, brings his soldiers around the enemy camp during the night, and at the break of dawn, 'after arraying of army' (*acie instructa*), sends three legions against the Spaniards' defensive palisade (34.14.1). The sudden appearance of the Roman soldiers at their rear (*a tergo*) surprises the enemies, who 'run here and there' (*discurrere*) to take up arms (2). The prefix *dis-*, with its implication

---

36   For the chronology of the battle cf. (with opposing views and further bibliography) Astin (1978, pp. 308–310); Briscoe (1981, pp. 65–66).
37   Cf. Astin (1978, pp. 302–307); Briscoe (1981, pp. 63–65); Cornell (2009, esp. pp. 19–27).
38   For the history of Emporiae see e.g. Almagro (1951 and 1956).
39   On the historical facts see Briscoe (1981, pp. 68–69 with further bibliography).

of scattered movement, suggests a stark contrast between the Spaniards and the well-arrayed Roman army.

Cato then briefly harangues the troops, reminding them that 'there is no hope but in valour' (*Nusquam nisi in virtute spes est*, 3). The very location of the battlefield – which Cato himself has carefully chosen – makes *virtus* unavoidable: 'The enemies lie between us and our camp, and behind us there is enemy country' (*Inter castra nostra et nos medii hostes et ab tergo hostium ager est*, 4). Cato orders his cohorts to simulate a flight to lure the enemies out of their camp (34.14.4–5). The trick works: the Spaniards 'sally forth from the gate and fill the space between their own camp and the enemy line with armed men' (*porta erumpunt et quantum inter castra sua et aciem hostium relictum erat loci armatis complent*, 5). The narrator once more emphasises the contrast between the Spaniards' hasty deployment of their line and the orderly disposition of the Roman army (6):

> Dum trepidant acie instruenda, consul iam paratis ordinatisque omnibus incompositos adgreditur.
>
> While they bustled about arraying the army, the consul attacked them, as they were still disarranged, with his prepared and orderly troops.

Up to this point, the text provides hardly any topographical information. All the reader gets to know is the relative positions of Romans and Spaniards with reference to the two camps and the fact that the armies come to fight behind the Spanish camp, in what one can imagine as an extended open space. In what follows (the account of the combat itself) the only spatial references are provided by the sectors of the Roman army. This, I argue, further enhances the narrative focus on *virtus*, and on the opposition between order and disorder.

Cato first sends the cavalry from both wings into the fight, but those on the right are pushed back, causing fear in the infantry, too (6). The consul then orders two cohorts to encircle the enemies' right wing (7). The Spaniards now find the Romans at their back again and are also thrown into panic; but on the Roman right cavalry and infantry are still so scared that Cato himself has to grab some of them and turn them against the enemy (8). Cato, in other words, intervenes to re-establish order in his battle line. The two forces fight for some time with missiles: the combat is uncertain on the (Roman) right, while on the (Roman) left the Spaniards are pressed between the Romans in the front and those at the back (9).

When it comes to fighting with swords, however, the battle starts anew: now, 'with soldiers fighting foot to foot, all hope was in valour and strength' (*pede conlato tota in virtute ac viribus spes erat*, 10). The alliterating syntagm *virtute ac viribus*, together with the reference to Roman soldiers fighting in close ranks ('foot by foot') reinstates the main theme of the account: only through valour and discipline – the latter epitomised by the ranks of the Roman army – can one achieve victory. Seeing that his men are tired, Cato sends forth some cohorts from the second line (34.15.1) and 'a new line is formed' (*nova acies facta*). The fresh Roman troops attack their exhausted enemies in a wedge-like formation and set them to flight since they are 'scattered' (*dissipatos*): the Spaniards now spread all over the field (*effuso per agros cursu*) and rush to their camp (2).

The remaining part of the account reports the storming of the Spanish camp (34.15.3–8). Cato's effort to re-establish order when it is imperilled comes once more to the fore when he launches the assault on the camp: 'if someone ran forth out of the ranks in excessive eagerness, Cato rode up and beat him with his javelin and gave tribunes and centurions the order to punish him' (4).[40]

Apart from the constant focus on the importance of an orderly army (and on Cato's role in preserving such order), the narrative displays another significant feature: almost all spatial references concern the structure of the Roman, not the Spanish, army (with the exception of the mention of the Spanish right wing at 34.14.7). Hence, the reader receives the impression of one orderly force (the Roman one), with its ranks and sectors, fighting against a much less orderly force of barbarians. While disorder threatens both at different points of the battle, the Romans succeed in falling back into line, while the Spaniards do not.

It is possible, or even likely, that Livy derived such a representation from Cato himself. The repeated stress on the consul's role in preserving order in his army, of his energy and skill as a commander, certainly point to a significant influence of the *Origines*. Also, the detailed portrayal of the actions of different sectors of the army at various phases of the combat probably derive from the commander's personal experience. Thus, it may well be that the contrast between Roman military discipline and barbarian disorder was also crucial in Cato's account of the events.

Yet, there is a further slant to Livy's narrative. One should not forget that the theme of discipline is first introduced in the geo-ethnographical digression at the beginning of the narrative of Cato's campaigns, at 34.9. There, discipline is a feature of the Greeks of Emporiae, who must defend themselves against their neighbours the Spaniards. The narrator soon makes clear, however, that things have changed from Cato's times: now Greeks, Spaniards and Romans are

---

40   *Si quis extra ordinem avidius procurrit, et ipse interequitans sparo percutit et tribunos centurionesque castigare iubet.*

'lumped into one body'. The ambiguity of the participle *confusi* is worth noticing here. While the verb *confundo, -ĕre* has the primary (and neutral) meaning of 'mixing', some of its other usages are decidedly negative. It can mean, for example, 'to upset' (both in a material and in an emotional sense), 'to scatter' (an army) in military contexts, or when applied to body parts, 'to disfigure, to defile'.[41] In the passage under examination, the narrator is clearly saying that the three ethnic groups are 'mixed up', but his choice of words might suggest the ideas of 'defilement' (of the new 'body' of citizens) and of military disorder. At the very least, the reader will draw the conclusion that, if fear (*timor*) of a stronger enemy makes people disciplined, then discipline will have declined as a result of the ethnic mixing.

The notion of mixed ethnicities as a potential weakness for an army is, after all, prominent elsewhere in the *Ab Urbe Condita*. To take a well-known example, Livy's account of the battle of Zama in Book 30 represents the mixed ethnic composition of the Carthaginian army and its consequent lack of coordination as an important reason for its defeat; and, as Levene (2010, pp. 239–244) argues, such a representation evokes the complexities of Roman armies of Livy's times, with their ethnically diverse contingents.

In the account of the battle of Magnesia, as well (37.39.7–44.1), the long and detailed array section (37.39.7–41.1) presents a strong contrast between the Romans' homogeneous army and Antiochus' oversized battle line, which is made up of many contingents of various ethnic origins.[42]

When read against such a background, the account of the battle of Emporiae seems to confound the distinction between Roman order and 'barbarian' disorder. The Romans owe their success (not just in the Spanish campaign but in many conflicts) to their ability to fight with valour and discipline; but what will be of valour and discipline in an increasingly mixed empire? Will Romans remain 'Roman' in their outlook? Also, the theme of fear cannot but remind the reader of the Sallustian notion of *metus hostilis*.[43] If fear is a guarantee of discipline, how can one maintain discipline in the absence of enemies who can seriously threaten Rome?

Livy, as is often the case, provides no definite answers. At the very least, however, his account invites his readers to think about how to preserve the values that made Rome successful. Such values (*virtus, disciplina*) find their embodiment in the battle space, or rather, in the standard military space that successful Roman armies create and strive to preserve.

---

41   Cf. *TLL* 4, coll. 259–267.
42   Cf. Fabrizi (2021a, pp. 51–54).
43   Cf. Sall. *Iug.* 41.

2.3 Army and Political Community

The ability of an army to act as an orderly, compact body presupposes the integration of the individual soldier or leader within the collective structure of the army. Apart from expressing ideas about the political relationships between ethnic elements within an imperial system, the space of an army can also, therefore, embody notions about other kinds of relationships, such as those between different social components of a community.[44] I will conclude my analysis of Livy's construction of the space of armies by examining two accounts from Book 2 in which standard military space works as a means for representing shifting power relationships within the Roman citizen-body: the narrative of battle of Lake Regillus in 499 BCE (2.19–20) at that of a battle against the Etruscans in the vicinity of Veii in 480 BCE (2.45.1–47.9).[45]

Scholars have read these narratives, which are usually assumed to derive from the first-century annalist Licinius Macer,[46] as resulting from the application of Homeric modules to early Republican material, with the occasional insertion of anachronisms drawn from later warfare techniques.[47] Both accounts consist largely of single combats in the Homeric style between aristocratic leaders. As I argue, the spatial arrangement of the events reinforces the focus on individual heroes while at the same time integrating the single

---

44 Cf. Goldsworthy (1996, pp. 40–41) on the relationship between 'an army organization' and 'the socio-political organization of the people that produced it' (p. 41).

45 Parallel narratives are provided by Dion. Hal. *Ant. Rom.* 6.3–13 (Lake Regillus, on which see Sautel, 2010 ad 2014) and 9.5–12 (Veii).

46 Since Livy and Dionysius' narratives share a general outline, but also display a number of significant differences, it is likely they followed different annalists as their main sources for the episode (and that their two sources ultimately went back to the same common tradition). Since one piece of information reported by Livy and criticized by Dionysius is said by the latter to have been present in Gellius and Licinius Macer (Dion. Hal. *Ant Rom.* 6.11.2: cf. below, n. 53), and since it is usually assumed that Livy did not use Gellius in his First Decade, scholars have identified Licinius as Livy's main source for the battle (cf. Ogilvie, 1965, p. 286). At the same time, it should be borne in mind that both Livy and Dionysius will have read other accounts of the same battle besides the one on which they based, as is evident by the fact that both know about variant versions of the events (for Livy's working methods, see Luce, 1977; more recently, Levene, 2010 has argued that Livy's approach to his sources may have been more flexible than scholars used to assume).

47 Cf. e.g. Pareti (1959); Ogilvie (1978, p. 353). However, Burck (1934, pp. 60–61) pointed out that, in the narrative of Lake Regillus, Livy appears more interested in the moral and psychological aspects of the fighting with respect to Dionysius of Halicarnassus, who devotes considerable attention to technical details of the duels, as well as to elements aimed at inspiring wonder in the reader (for the miraculous intervention of the Dioscuri, and the consequent foundation of the temple of Castor in Rome, cf. Chapter 1, p. 39). Burck interpreted Dionysius' technique as more 'Homeric' and Livy's as closer to Virgil's. Of course, one cannot rule out the influence of earlier Roman epic (above all Ennius' *Annales*).

combats within the collective structure of the army; more to the point, the passage from the first battle to the second shows a significant shifting of the balance between the individual and the collective, which corresponds to the political development of the Roman citizen-community.

As Livy writes, the battle of Lake Regillus was fought against a confederacy of Latin peoples, who had allied themselves with the exiled Tarquins, in 499 BCE.[48] This event constitutes an important turning point in Book 2 since it marks the shift from the first part of the book, which centres upon the Tarquins' attempts to regain their power in Rome,[49] to its second part, where the main theme is the beginnings of the Struggle of the Orders.[50] Livy begins his account *in medias res*, with no word about the preliminary movements of the two armies or the terrain, apart from the short statement that the opponents fought 'at Lake Regillus in the territory of Tusculum' (2.19.3: *ad lacum Regillum in agro Tusculano*).[51] Whether the scantiness of topographical information was due to Licinius Macer or whether it was the result of Livy's adaptation of him, is impossible to state with any confidence. Certainly, details about the hilly countryside where the events took place were present in the annalistic tradition because they are extensively transmitted by the other main source we possess about the battle, Dionysius of Halicarnassus.[52] However, the terrain is irrelevant to Livy's narrative, and no mention of it is made after that.

After an emphatic statement of the importance of the events he is about to relate (2.19.3–5), the narrator begins his account of the actual battle at 2.19.6. He does not describe the deployment of the two armies in advance; instead, he starts by narrating the assault brought by the former king Tarquinius Superbus against the dictator Postumius, who was himself encouraging his soldiers 'in the front line' (2.19.6: *in prima acie*). Tarquinius was wounded and brought to safety away from the field.[53] The reader gets no clue of where, exactly,

---

48 The annalistic tradition did not agree on the dating of the battle; as Livy explains in 2.21.3, other historians dated the battle to 496 BC; the latter is the version followed by Dion. Hal. *Ant. Rom.* 6.2.1.
49 Cf. Burck (1934, p. 60).
50 Cf. Ogilvie (1965, p. 233); Forsythe (2015, p. 316).
51 For the localisation of the historical battle, see e.g. Pareti (1959); Ogilvie (1965, p. 287).
52 For the events leading up to the battle and their topography, see Dion. Hal. *Ant. Rom.* 6.3.3–5.2.
53 This is the detail that Dion. Hal. *Ant. Rom.* 6.11.2 attributes to Licinius Macer and 'the ones who follow Gellius' (οἱ περὶ Γέλλιον), and which he dismisses on the grounds that Tarquinius was too old to be fighting. Instead, Dionysius has Titus, one of Tarquinius' sons, fight against Postumius. As Plathner (1934, p. 26) noted, Livy's explicit remark that

Postumius and Tarquinius are fighting until the narrator shifts his attention to the attack led by the master of the horse Aebutius against the Latin dictator Octavius Mamilius (Tarquinius Superbus' son-in-law), which he locates 'on the other wing' (2.19.7: *ad alterum cornu*). Now the reader is led to imagine Postumius and Tarquinius on one side of the field and Aebutius and Mamilius on the other; this is virtually everything one gets to know about the space of the battle.[54] Consequently, the reader is led to think of the combat as having two main spatial focuses, corresponding to the two main areas where heroic action is performed.

The remaining part of the account concentrates mostly on the sector where Aebutius and Mamilius are fighting against each other. Both are wounded, but whereas the master of the horse is forced to leave the battle, the Latin dictator fights and calls the cohort of Roman exiles, led by Lucius Tarquinius, to his aid (2.19.8–10). When the Romans start giving up terrain 'on that side' (*ea parte*), Marcus Valerius[55] launches himself against Tarquinius. The latter retreats into the lines of his army, and the pursuer, surrounded by enemies, is mortally wounded (2.20.1–3).

At this point, the dictator – who, as we know, is in the other sector of the army – realises that the Romans are in trouble and orders his *manipulus* of chosen men to force their army comrades to fight the enemy. Consequently, the Romans make a stand, and Postumius' men, who enter the battle for the first time, have no problems cutting the exhausted Latins to pieces (2.20.4–6).

Then the final act of the battle begins. Mamilius runs to the first line to help the exiles, who are being surrounded by Postumius' men. The Roman *legatus* Titus Herminius attacks Mamilius and kills him, only to be mortally wounded in turn while he is stripping Manilius' body of its arms (2.20.7–9). Postumius now launches the final charge: following his command, his cavalry dismount from their horses and run up to the first lines to fight alongside the infantry.

Tarquinius Superbus charged Postumius *quamquam iam aetate et viribus gravior* seems to suggest that he knew about the critiques to this version of events.

54   Livy's version is different from Dionysius': according to the Greek historian, who introduces a detailed description of the two deployments before his account of the battle (*Ant. Rom.* 6.5.4–5) Postumius and Titus Tarquinius occupied the centre of the respective armies, Aebutius the Roman left against the Latin right wing commanded by Mamilius, and the consul Titus Verginius the Roman right against Sextus Tarquinius on the Latin left wing. Livy (possibly following Macer) leaves Dionysius' Roman right and Latin left completely out of his account, and with good reason: as Verginius was the consul of 496 BCE, the year in which Dionysius, but not Livy, dated the battle, he could not appear in the narrative of the *Ab urbe condita*; and Sextus Tarquinius was already dead according to Livy 1.60.2.

55   Livy introduces him as 'the brother of Publicola'.

The Latin line wavers under their joint attack; it is finally routed when the cavalrymen remount their horses and, followed by the infantry, pursue them up to their camp (2.20.10–13).

Throughout the narrative of the battle, space remains very much indefinite. Whereas Dionysius moves in an orderly fashion from the centre of the field to one flank, then to the next, Livy moves his spotlight through a series of individual duels and fights. Only in the end are individual displays of heroism eventually subsumed into the victorious collective attack of the Roman army.

The narrative of the battle of 480 BCE against the Etruscans, in Livy 2.45.1–47.9, is, in several respects, similar. I will not consider in detail the first part of the account (2.45), where Livy relates how the Roman soldiers, who at the beginning were refusing to fight in protest against the patricians, became increasingly eager for battle due to the enemy's provocations. The main setting for such events is the Roman camp, with its gates, palisade, and *praetorium*; and the camp appears as a sort of second Rome, where the discord between patricians (the consuls) and plebeians (the soldiers) is re-enacted, only to be overcome by hatred of the common enemy.

I will focus, instead, on the account of the actual battle (2.46.1–47.9). As in the Lake Regillus narrative, the battlefield is divided into two sectors. One is dominated by the exploits of the Fabii (2.46.4–7): Quintus Fabius, a former consul, is killed by an Etruscan while leading the charge against the closely packed enemy line; the consul Marcus Fabius and the former consul Caeso Fabius make a stand in front of the corpse, and in so doing rekindle the spirits of their soldiers. In the other sector of the battlefield, the leading role is played by the second consul, Gnaeus Manlius (2.47.1–3):

> 1. Proelio ex parte una restituto, nihilo segnius in cornu altero Cn. Manlius consul pugnam ciebat, ubi prope similis fortuna est versata. 2. Nam ut altero in cornu Q. Fabium, sic in hoc ipsum consulem Manlium iam velut fusos agentem hostes et impigre milites secuti sunt et, ut ille gravi volnere ictus ex acie cessit, interfectum rati gradu rettulere; 3. cessissentque loco, ni consul alter cum aliquot turmis equitum in eam partem citato equo advectus, vivere clamitans collegam, se victorem fuso altero cornu adesse, rem inclinatam sustinuisset.

> 1. As the fighting was revived on one side, on the other wing the consul Gnaeus Manlius roused the battle just as vigorously; there, an almost similar fortune reigned. 2. In fact, just as happened on the other wing with Quintus Fabius, so on this wing the soldiers energetically followed the consul Manlius as if he were driving away the enemies while they were scattered but, when he was gravely wounded and left the field, they

thought him dead and retreated 3. They would have abandoned their place if the other consul, riding fast to that part of the field with some squadrons of cavalry, had not cried out that his colleague was alive and that he was there to aid after victoriously setting the other wing to flight; he thus checked their wavering.

Livy creates a strong parallelism between the two 'wings' and stresses it repeatedly through the expressions *ex parte una ... in cornu altero ... altero in cornu ... in hoc ... in eam partem*. Again, spatial information is scanty, and no further hint at the deployment of the two forces is made, although Livy mentions at the very outset that they were deployed (2.46.1 *Instruitur acies* ...; 2.46.3: *vix explicandi ordines spatium Etruscis fuit*). Compared to the battle of Lake Regillus, however, the actions of the leaders are more tightly integrated into the overall dynamics of the fight. The correspondence of the events happening on the two 'wings', or 'sectors', is forcefully stressed through the *ut ... sic* structure.

Moreover, the collective movement of the soldiers, and their reactions to the *proceres*' actions, receive more emphasis. At the very beginning of the battle, for example, Livy reports that the Roman soldiers attacked forcefully and quickly – arguably, even too enthusiastically, since in their anger and fury, they threw their javelins rather randomly (2.46.3). Such fury, however, is only spontaneous in appearance, as it is actually part of the consuls' psychological manipulation; the assault is soon reabsorbed into the collective dynamics of the army.

This happens, among other things, because the aristocratic leaders are aware of their function as role models for common soldiers. At 2.46.7, for example, after the death of Quintus Fabius, his kinsman Marcus Fabius rebukes the soldiers for retreating (2.46.5–6). His brother Caeso then intervenes to exhort him to set an example by fighting rather than to spur on the soldiers with words (2.46.6–7); 'thus, the two Fabii flew forth to the front line with their spears outstretched and carried the whole army with them' (*Sic in primum infensis hastis provolant duo Fabii, totamque moverunt secum aciem,* 7). Just as the soldiers had previously been upset by the death of a prominent man (*unius viri casum,* 5), two other *proceres* now literally move the entire fighting line along with them. The same happens, as we have seen, in the other fighting sector, where the soldiers first follow the consul Manlius, then retreat after he is wounded, only to be encouraged again when both consuls reappear before their eyes.[56]

---

56 The last part of the account (2.47.4–9) narrates the attack to the Roman camp brought by a part of the Etruscan troops. The Romans are ultimately able to drive away and slaughter the enemy, but not without losses, among them the consul Manlius.

Rather than a sequence of individual duels, this battle appears more decidedly as an interplay between individual aristocrats and the mass of Roman fighting men.[57] The reason for this is probably to be found in the different historical circumstances that characterise the second part of Book 2. While its first part is still steeped in the history of the monarchic period, in the second, the historian's main concern is with the political struggles within the Republic. In the narrative of the battle against the Etruscans, Livy emphasises how the conflicting components of Roman society, patricians and plebeians, momentarily overcome their enmities for the sake of the common good, that is, the victory over an external foe. As my analysis in previous chapters has suggested, this is a central theme in the First Pentad, where war against foreign enemies repeatedly saves Rome from internal dissolution.

It will by now be clear how standard military space is not only one of the main organisational criteria for action during a battle but can also embody significant themes of the narrative, such as the ethnic character and political values of combatants. Of course, arrays, manoeuvring and camp-building do not always play such a significant function as in the examples I have shown. In other cases, they simply provide the reader with an easily recognisable spatial pattern, making it possible for them to imagine events even without topographic information. At the very least, however, they convey the idea that battle (and war) is about imposing that standard spatial pattern upon the variety of topographies one could encounter.

3 Topography

3.1 Introduction

In most of Livy's battle narratives, the space formed by the deployment of military forces comes together with topography to shape a mental model of the battlefield. But what does topography look like in a battle account? Which features does a battlefield usually contain? How detailed are battle topographies, and how conventional?

To answer these questions, I shall first ask what topographical features are more likely to recur on battlefields in the *Ab Urbe Condita*. Once more, scholarship about space in Caesar's *Commentarii* is useful for singling out some narrative tendencies in Livy, too. Riggsby (2006, pp. 21–45) recognises a limited number of topographical features that appear in tactical spaces in

---

57   Note also that, while the Roman *proceres* play a central role, their opponents are not identified by name.

Caesar' *Bellum Gallicum* (plains, hills, mountains, rivers, marshes, forests, and the Ocean) and argues that the way Caesar constructs battle topographies out of them constitutes a way to impose control upon the conquered space of Gaul within the text.[58] Things are certainly much more complex in the *Ab Urbe Condita*, where one finds more battles, military operations, and natural environments, than in Caesar's work. However, it is still possible to single out some topographic features that recur with particular frequency. I am particularly concerned with the functions that such features play, both from a strategic and a narrative perspective. I argue that while certain features could play various strategic roles in the reality of warfare, the *Ab Urbe Condita* tends to associate recurrent topographic features with specific aspects of war and their ethical implications (3.1 and 3.2).

Secondly, I will investigate how the narrative arranges information about such features (3.3). As I shall show, the *Ab Urbe Condita* tends to convey simplified topographies by selecting functional elements, not only to understand the dynamics of a certain battle, but also to interpret the events in historical and ethical terms. Ultimately, I argue that, in the *Ab Urbe Condita*, the narrative construction of military topography works as a way of making sense of an alien world in Roman terms.

3.2 Topographic Features and Their Functions

Despite the great number of battle narratives the *Ab Urbe Condita* contains, topographic features appearing in tactical spaces can be grouped into a few types.

Plains are – unsurprisingly – frequent settings for battles. Major military engagements, which required the manoeuvring of armies of several thousands of men, were best fought on even ground. As I have mentioned above, the *Ab Urbe Condita* does not usually give specific information about battlefields of this kind, which tend to function as featureless, implicit backdrops to battles. Exceptions are constituted by accounts in which features of a plain play a specific role in the action. At the battle of the Trebia, for example, the steep riverbanks covered in shrubs are crucial to the setting of Hannibal's ambush and of his first display of *fraus Punica* (21.54.1–2).[59] In some cases, plains appear as elements of more detailed tactical spaces: they are often, for example, bordered by mountains or hills, interrupted by hills, or traversed by rivers and roads.

---

58 For the singling-out of some recurring types of topographic features, cf. also Rambaud (1974, pp. 121–123).
59 Cf. Chapter 1, p. 23. On the theme of *fraus Punica* in the *Ab Urbe Condita* see e.g. Levene (2010, pp. 228–236); Pausch (2019).

Rivers appear mainly as boundaries, providing a basic criterion for orientation in the context of (usually) simplified topographies: they can work as boundaries separating two opposing armies or as lines which an army must cross to reach its enemy;[60] often, camps are set close to a river. In the account of the battle of Cannae (216 BCE),[61] for example, the only physical landmark in the plain[62] is the river Aufidus, the crossing of which, first by the Romans and then by the Carthaginians, marks the start of the battle. And, in the battle of Magnesia, the river Meander delimits the Roman line on one side (37.39.11; 42.7–8).[63] Here and in similar cases, a river works as a natural protection for an army, preventing encircling manoeuvres on the enemy's part. In some cases, rivers can play more important roles: in 44.35.16–22, for example, Roman and Macedonian soldiers fight in the riverbed of the Elpeus, while their comrades watch the combat from their camps placed on the opposing riverbanks.[64]

Other water features, such as lakes or the sea, occur less frequently. The sea is the setting for naval battles, but one can hardly speak of a 'tactical space' in such cases since the sea tends to be an indefinite space. The siege or storming of cities lying on the coast constitutes a separate category. Here, the sea can play a more substantial role: the most famous example is possibly constituted by Publius Cornelius Scipio's conquest of New Carthage in Book 26, where the ebb of the tide in the lagoon surrounding the city is a crucial element of Scipio's plan.[65] Otherwise, seas or lakes appear as bordering features for battles fought on land. Lake Trasimene is an obvious example: in 217 BCE, the Roman army commanded by Gaius Flaminius ended up squeezed between the lake and the mountains so that Hannibal's men could easily fall upon it (22.4.1–5).[66] Finally, swamps make the occasional rare appearance in the *Ab Urbe Condita*, although

---

60 See e.g. 33.18.9–18; 39.30.10–31.1. Östenberg (2017, pp. 248–249) stresses the function of rivers as obstacles to be crossed in Roman historiography.
61 The problems involved in the localisation of the historical battle are discussed below, pp. 185–187. The ancient town of Cannae stood on the hill now called Monte di Canne, on the right side of the Aufidus.
62 Cf. Livy 22.44.4: *locis natis ad equestrem pugnam*.
63 Cf. also the battle of Metaurus in 27.47–49; here, Hasdrubal's failed attempt at crossing the river is related in a fairly detailed way during the account of the preliminary movements, at 27.47.10–11. A different situation is described in 32.5.10–13, where Philip sets up camp near the river Aous, which flows in a valley between two mountains.
64 Similarly, at 44.40.5–9 a fight in the bed of a stream (identified by Hammond, 1984, pp. 44–45 as the stream now known as Ayos Dimitrios) between Romans and Thracians marks the beginning of the battle of Pydna.
65 Livy 26.42–46. Cf. also 44.9.2; 44.11.1–12.7.
66 For the sea as bordering a tactical space, see e.g., 41.2.8; 44.10.8–11.

they account for some graphic narratives of military events – one need only think of Hannibal's adventurous crossing of the Arno marshes at 22.2.[67]

After plains, hills and mountains are the most frequent topographic features in battle accounts across the *Ab Urbe Condita*. Hills can appear as bordering features of a tactical space – e.g. when hills surround a plain or a plain has hills on one side – or, more often, as features within it. In the latter case, battlefields are often constituted by even ground interrupted by isolated reliefs;[68] few consist of extensively hilly terrain.[69] A 'hill' (*tumulus* or *collis*) can also be a minor peak within a mountain range.[70] Mountains, too, can be features within a tactical space;[71] in other cases, a battle can take place on the flanks of a mountain,[72] or, again, mountains can border a tactical space.[73] Other topographical elements that recur with a certain frequency – and which are usually part of a mountain or hill – are crags, rocks (*rupes*, *saxum*), valleys or hollows (*vallis*), and gorges (*saltus*, *angustiae*).

Forests, too, appear, principally, as elements of mountainous or hilly landscapes and only rarely as independent features.[74] One of the most frequent terms (alongside *silva, -ae*) that the *Ab Urbe Condita* uses to speak about forests is *saltus, -us*, which designates a mountainous *and* forested area. Among the exceptions to the tendency to imagine woods as parts of mountains or hills are the narratives of ambushes set by Gauls in woodlands in Northern Italy at 21.25.8–9 and 23.24.6–10.[75]

Given the frequency of hills and mountains as elements of tactical spaces, it is worth considering their strategic functions in battle accounts in *Ab Urbe Condita*.

Hills can afford natural protection against enemy attacks. Therefore, they often figure as places where armies set up camp or place garrisons.[76] An army

---

67 For swamps in a military context, see also 31.37.8–11 (where the Macedonians and their king Philip flee through the swamps after being routed by the Romans); 44.46.5–7 (the swamps surrounding Pella).
68 Cf. e.g. 31.34–35; 31.42; 42.57–59; 42.65–67.
69 Cf. e.g. 32.10.9–12.10 (Aous); 33.6–10 (Cynoscephalae).
70 Cf. e.g. 21.32.8, 10, 13; 32.10.8.
71 Cf. e.g. 38.18–23; 41.18.9–13.
72 Cf. e.g. 44.1–6.
73 Cf. e.g. 43.19.8.
74 For forests in Roman historiography see Östenberg (2017, pp. 241–248).
75 The fact that the Gauls liked using forests as cover for their assaults amounts to an ethnographic topos: cf. e.g. Polyb. 3.71.2.
76 Cf. e.g. 4.17.11; 7.29.6; 23.26.10; 27.2.4; 27.48.2; 29.28.1; 31.41.8; 33.7.3–5; 33.36.4; 37.18.11; 39.30.10; 40.22.2 (*sub colle*, 'at the foot of a hill'); 44.3.4–6. Low, gentle-sloped hills were ideal for setting up camps; cf. Rüpke (1990, p. 165).

or a contingent can also take up a defensive position upon a hill during a battle or a march or during intervals between combats, for example, to fight from a favourable position or escape an enemy's charge.[77] Hills – just like rivers – can also function as natural defences for the sectors of an army that are deployed close to them,[78] can be used to fight from a favourable position,[79] or can affect the manoeuvres of troops during battles.[80]

Hills are frequently used for blocking access to a pass or road or setting ambushes. Fighting men can be hidden on the flanks of hills or behind hills so they can unexpectedly fall upon enemies positioned on lower ground.[81] Similarly, detachments of soldiers can take advantage of hills to make encircling manoeuvres.[82] While, in such cases, hills (especially thickly forested ones) hid troops from sight, hills can also work as places where soldiers make themselves visible to the enemy to intimidate them.[83] Of course, hills are also places from which soldiers or generals can enjoy an extensive view of the landscape and thus see what is happening on the battlefield.[84] Moreover, because fighting against enemies who are positioned on the higher ground is a disadvantage, climbing a hill can occasionally be represented as an act of valour;[85] this is especially the case when soldiers who are ambushed are eventually able

---

77 Cf. e.g. 2.50.10–11 (Cremera); 4.39.4–8; 5.18.8; 5.28.7–10; 22.6.8; 24.16.6; 25.36; 27.15.8; 27.18; 27.28.1; 28.15.8–10; 28.16.6–7; 28.33.16; 33.7.8 (Cynoscephalae. In this case, the fact that fighting is taking place on a hill higher than the others also isolates the main action from the rest and directs the gaze of King Philip – who is watching the scene –as well as of the reader towards it; cf. Fabrizi, 2021a, pp. 46–51); 38.2.13–14; 42.65.6–66.9.
78 Cf. e.g. 27.48.7–8, 12 (Metaurus); 42.58.5 (Callinicus).
79 Cf. e.g. 1.27.10 (where the attack is only feared, not actually carried out); 7.23.5–10; 8.24.4; 10.26.8–9; 32.25.5; 42.64.7–10 (Perseus tries to provoke the Roman column to battle by appearing on hills bordering the road, but the Romans refuse to fight).
80 This is especially the case with the battle of Cynoscephalae (33.7–10), where Romans and Macedonians clashed in 197 BCE around a range of hills of the same name. The two sides are affected by, and make use of, the terrain in various ways. Philips places garrisons on some hills. Later, he is repeatedly described as watching the battle from different vantage points of the range. The Macedonians are shown taking advantage of their more elevated position twice, but eventually the phalanx is hindered by the uneven terrain.
81 Cf. e.g. 6.24.2–3; 22.4.1–6; 25.15.10–13; 27.26.7–27.7; 27.41.3–42.8; 28.2.1; 28.13.6; 29.34.9–13.
82 Cf. e.g. 28.33.8–13; 36.18.8 (Thermopylae).
83 Cf. e.g. 10.40.6 (where a visual trick is involved); 22.24.4 (Hannibal occupies a hill visible to Marcus Minucius Rufus, so that he knew he would protect his foragers in case of a skirmish); 24.1.6 (the Carthaginians appear on the hills surrounding Locri, in order to sway the city's inhabitants to break the alliance with the Romans); 32.5.13; 34.29.11.
84 Cf. e.g. 31.34.7 (Philip of Macedon looks down on a Roman camp: cf. above, p. 156); 33.10.1 (Philip sees the rout of his men at Cynoscephalae from a hill higher than the others).
85 See e.g. 28.15.8–11.

to fight their way up to the spots originally occupied by the enemy.[86] Finally, mention must be made of the numerous instances of combat taking place by or in cities, whereby hills can be elements of a cityscape; in some cases, the narrative provides brief topographic sketches.[87]

To summarise, hills appear to play two main functions: on the one hand, they provide protection for soldiers positioned upon them or set challenges to those who attempt to climb them; on the other hand, they are involved in manipulations of vision. In many respects, the role of mountains is analogous, but the fact that mountains are higher than hills lends them further connotations, which Livy's narrative usually exploits to produce pathos and tension.

Mountains often appear as places where people – not only combatants but also, in several cases, entire tribes or the inhabitants of a town – take up a well-defended position[88] or where combatants are placed to be able to fight from a favourable position[89] or where they (attempt to) escape when pursued by enemies.[90] On the contrary, attacking an enemy positioned on the flanks of mountains can be seen as brave, if sometimes reckless.[91] Mountains, like hills, can protect the back or the flanks of deployed armies;[92] they can also be used for ambushes, encircling manoeuvres, or generally for hiding.[93] Garrisons are

---

[86] Cf. e.g. 7.34–36 (a sortie led by Publius Decius Mus saves for the day for the Romans ambushed by the Samnites; recalled at 22.60.11 together with an analogous episode from the First Punic War); 27.18 (the Romans fight their way up a hill where the Carthaginians have set up fortifications); 31.39.13–15 (the Macedonians seize a pass through which they know the Roman army will march, but the Romans fight bravely and eventually climb up a hill garrisoned by the Macedonians).

[87] For hills as elements of cityscapes, or as topographic features of which one can take advantage of in besieging a town, see e.g. 1.12.1; 3.7.2; 5.40 (Rome); 26.42.8; 26.44.2, 6; 26.46.8–9; 26.48.4 (New Carthage); 29.35.7; 30.4.10 (Utica); 32.18.7 (Daulis); 36.25.3 (Lamia); 38.4.1–4 (Ambracia); 43.22.8 (Stratum); 44.46.5 (Pella).

[88] Cf. e.g. 2.30.9; 4.39.6; 9.44.7; 22.14.1; 22.24.2; 22.30.8 (Quintus Fabius Maximus; the whole account of Fabius' dictatorship forcefully stresses the fact that he consistently kept to higher ground in order to avoid direct combat with Hannibal. Cf. Fabrizi 2017a); 25.32.6; 27.28.2; 28.8.9; 31.33.5; 39.2; 39.32.3; 39.53.13; 40.22.14; 40.58.2; 41.18.1–3.

[89] Cf. e.g. 9.35.1–2; 36.18.3; 38.20–23; 38.25–27.

[90] Cf. e.g. 1.37.4; 7.15.6; 9.35.7; 9.43.20; 23.27.8; 26.6.11; 29.31.2; 39.31.13.

[91] Cf. e.g. 3.31.4–6; 10.30.7; 41.18.9–13. See also, for the ambiguity between courage and recklessness, the debate between Manlius Vulso and his adversaries on his conduct in the battles of Mts. Olympus and Magaba against the Gauls (38.44.9–50.3; and for the account of the battle, in which the Romans attacked the Gauls who had taken up positions on the mountains, see 38.21–23 and 25–27).

[92] Cf. e.g. 4.32.8.

[93] Cf. e.g. 4.32.9–33.12; 7.14.6–15.7 (not really an ambush, but a stratagem); 9.2.6–9; 9.3.1–3 (the Caudine Forks); 10.14.13–21; 22.4–6 (Trasimene); 22.15.3–18.4; 22.41.6; 27.46.4; 28.33.2–4; 29.32.4–5; 40.31.

often stationed on mountain passes to block the passage of enemy armies or supplies.[94] Moreover, mountains can be part of the topography of cities under siege.[95]

Unlike hills, mountains can also provide an extremely harsh, in some cases openly hostile terrain for armies on the march. This is the case, for example, with Hannibal's crossing the Alps in Livy 21.32.6–37.6, his subsequent attempt to cross the Apennines at 21.58, or the Romans' march through the massif of Lower Olympus in 169 BCE, related at 44.3–5. Accounts of this kind appear to put the distinction between 'strategic space' and 'tactical space' into question: although the narrative relates the movement of an army through space, such a space is hardly ever linear, and the three-dimensional landscape plays an ongoing role in the narrative – in fact, the report of the march is occasionally interrupted by the narrative of skirmishes or ambushes taking place in 'tactical spaces'.

Such tactical spaces are usually located on the flanks or (more rarely) at the summit of a mountain or in valleys enclosed between mountain peaks. For example, the Carthaginians' march across the Alps comes to a temporary halt as Alpine people block the way at 21.32.8. And, at 44.4.4–6, the Romans, on the march across Lower Olympus, fight against a Macedonian garrison guarding a pass. In the latter case, the nature of the tactical space – a mountain peak – makes it impossible to fight a conventional battle because of the narrowness and roughness of the battleground.

Accounts of armies proceeding through mountainous terrain usually stress the heroism of the soldiers who conquer such difficult landscapes. They can also precede an army's conquest of an enemy country – or the latter's resistance to the invader. For example, Hannibal's march through the Alps can be viewed as an effective means of characterising Hannibal himself – an exceptional general and one bold enough to attempt the epic crossing – as well as a representation of his claim to mastery of the Italian landscape. Such mastery is powerfully evoked by the vista of Italy that Hannibal shows his soldiers from the top of the Alps (21.35.6–9). As Clark (2014, pp. 202–209) has recently shown, extensive views of this kind precede conquest, or – as in Hannibal's case – its possibility,[96] while incapacity of gaining a panoramic view can symbolise the

---

94 Cf. e.g. 36.15–16 (Thermopylae); 37.4.7; 40.41.2 (in this case, the Romans block the passes of the mountains where the Ligurians have settled in order to cut off their supplies).
95 Cf. e.g. 36.22–24 (Heraclea); 43.19.7 (Oenaeum); 44.13.2 (Meliboea).
96 Cf. Clark (2014, p. 207): 'The possibilities that opened up along with the view seem to last only as long as the view itself, a momentary vision into the future that is dampened by the danger and loss the Carthaginians experience as soon as they begin to descend'. For further discussion of and bibliography on the idea that the Italian landscape might be resisting Hannibal, cf. Fabrizi (2015, p. 139).

failure of hegemonic ambitions. Other similar scenes mentioned by Clark are the description of Thermopylae at 36.15 (although this is made in the narrator's voice), the view of Macedon that the army of Quintus Marcius Philippus enjoys from (probably) Mt. Metamorphosis at 44.3.7–8,[97] and Philip's failed attempt to see the Adriatic, the Alps, the Danube and the Black Sea from the summit of Mt. Haemus at 40.21.[98]

It will by now be clear how, in the *Ab Urbe Condita*, hills and mountains fulfil two main sets of functions. On the one hand, they constitute natural obstacles or – depending on the side one is fighting on – natural defences. In this capacity, they are often represented as hindrances to open fighting, as topographic features one can take advantage of to mitigate one's inferior numbers, skills, or courage – but also as providing the chance for displays of valour on the part of combatants who are ready to conquer them. On the other hand, hills and mountains are often involved in controlling and manipulating vision. A mountain or hill is a place from which one can obtain a wide-ranging view and thus exert control of military events. One can, besides, use mountains or hills to hide something – typically, men lying in ambush.

Of course, these functions of mountains and hills belonged to the reality of warfare. The *Ab Urbe Condita*, however, frequently elaborates on that reality. One of the ways in which it does so is by representing rough landscapes, and mountains in particular, in a highly rhetorical way, stressing their impassability, steepness, and narrowness.[99] Adjectives like *invius*, *devius*, and *avius* ('impassable') – often found in the substantivised neutral plural ('impassable places') – are quite frequent in Livy as applied to mountainous or hilly topographies.[100] *Angustus* ('narrow', in one case intensified in *perangustus*),[101]

---

97 Note that the Romans' panoramic view provides a strong contrast to King Perseus' sudden 'blindness' of the mind as he panics at the news of the Romans' arrival in Macedon in 44.6 (cf. *caecata mens subito terrore*, 17). For Perseus' characterization in this narrative sequence see Clark (2014, pp. 209–214).

98 On this famous episode cf. Introduction, pp. 21–22.

99 Cf. Todaro (2023a).

100 *Invius, -a, -um*: 9.14.9; 9.24.5; 9.38.4; 21.25.13; 21.30.9; 21.35.4; 21.36.3–4; 22.15.10; 27.39.7; 31.2.10; 31.37.11; 32.11.7; 38.2.13; 38.20.4; 38.21.1; 38.22.1; 38.23.1, 7; 39.2.2; 40.22.2; 40.27.12; 40.53.1; 42.16.1; 42.55.1; 43.23.2; 44.4.11; 44.5.2, 12; 44.20.2. *Devius, -a, -um*: 21.33.3; 22.14.8; 34.16.8; 34.20.2 (in the latter two cases, the adjective is referred to peoples who inhabit rough or forested countries; on this usage, cf. Briscoe, 1981, p. 79); 35.30.10; 38.45.9 (here, too, applied to people); 39.49.5; 40.17.6; 40.27.13; 41.19.8. *Avius, -a, -um*: 9.9.15; 9.31.7; 25.32.6.

101 *Angustus, -a, -um*: 7.39.7; 9.2.7; 9.23.7; 9.24.7; 21.35.12; 22.17.2; 27.46.5; 28.5.8; 28.11.13; 28.33.8–9; 31.27.2; 32.5.11; 32.14.1; 35.11.1; 35.30.1; 38.40.6; 38.49.7; 39.1.5; 40.41.2. *Perangustus, -a, -um*: 22.4.2.

arduus ('steep'),[102] *altus* ('high'),[103] *artus* ('narrow'),[104] *praeceps* ('steep, precipitous'),[105] *confragosus* ('uneven, rough'),[106] and *cavus* ('hollow')[107] are also relatively common.

Moreover, one can observe a tendency in the text to cluster adjectives to enhance the rhetorical effect of scenic descriptions of mountainous landscapes. At its most effective, this stylistic device involves the use of *tricola* in either asyndeton or polysyndeton;[108] more often, the historian introduces pairs of adjectives that express the impassability, harshness, and steepness of mountains and hills.[109] Furthermore, one can observe the recurrence of almost formulaic expressions, as with *iuncturae,* in which the noun *saltus* is joined to the adjectives *invius* or *devius*.[110] Such stylistic devices can enhance

102 Cf. e.g. 2.65.3; 4.61.8; 5.26.5; 9.24.5, 7; 10.9.8; 23.26.10; 25.13.13–14; 28.20.4; 38.19.4; 38.20.4; 38.21.3; 38.49.7; 39.1.5; 42.16.1; 44.3.3.

103 Cf. e.g. 21.30.7; 21.48.3; 22.12.8; 22.14.11; 22.18.5; 22.19.6; 24.34.3; 25.16.22; 27.18.14; 27.28.2; 27.46.5; 33.10.1; 36.18.3; 36.22.5; 38.2.13; 40.22.4; 44.3.7.

104 Cf. e.g. 5.26.5; 21.35.3; 22.6.5; 22.15.11; 26.17.8; 29.32.3; 31.39.7; 32.10.10; 34.28.2; 37.27.7.

105 Cf. e.g. 10.9.8; 21.33.7; 21.35.3, 12; 21.36.2; 27.18.9; 28.6.10; 36.22.5; 42.66.7.

106 The adjective *confragosus, -a, -um* appears ten times in Livy, out of its thirty-eight occurrences in the whole of classical Latin literature. Before Livy, it is only used twice by Varro in its proper meaning (*Rust.* 1.18.4 and 1.20.5) and, metaphorically, twice by Plautus (*Cist.* 614; *Men.* 591) and once in a Ciceronian fragment quoted by Lactantius Placidus (*Ad Stat. Theb.* 1.306–307). The occurrences of the adjective in the *Ab Urbe Condita* are the following: 5.26.5; 21.32.9; 28.2.1; 32.4.3; 32.10.9; 35.27.16; 35.29.7; 38.40.6; 38.41.5; 44.3.3. On Livy's preference for this term see Briscoe (2012, p. 473).

107 See Oakley (2005, p. 53). There are thirteen occurrences of *cavus* referring to elements of landscape in the *Ab Urbe Condita*, and in all of such cases the adjective refers to *vallis, rupes* or *via*: see Livy 3.8.9; 7.34.1; 9.2.9; 22.28.6; 23.1.6; 23.37.5; 23.47.7; 25.16.22; 25.39.1; 26.10.5; 28.2.2; 38.40.12; 44.5.10.

108 Cf. e.g. *Saltus duo alti, angusti silvosique sunt*, 9.2.7; *Omnis enim ferme via praeceps, angusta, lubrica erat*, 21.35.12; *A Cypselis via decem milium fere silvestris, angusta, confragosa excipiebat*, 38.40.6; *itinera ardua angusta, infesta insidiis*, 39.1.5; *ardua et aspera et confragosa* (...) *via*, 41.3.3. *Avius*: 9.9.16; 9.31.7; 25.32.6.

109 Cf. e.g. *asperis confragosisque* (...) *partim artis partim arduis viis*, 5.26.5; *per ardua ac prope invia*, 9.24.5; *invia atque horrenda*, 9.36.1; *arduus atque in parte una praeceps*, 10.9.8; *e saltu invio atque impedito*, 21.25.13; *inter confragosa omnia praeruptaque*, 21.32.9; *praecipites deruptaeque utrimque angustiae*, 21.33.6; *per artas praecipites vias*, 21.35.3; *per invia circa nec trita antea*, 21.36.4; *per omnia arta praeruptaque*, 22.6.5; *arduo ac difficili ascensu*, 25.13.13; *per artas semitas ac difficiles*, 26.17.8; *in arta et confragosa loca*, 32.10.10; *per angustam et proclivem viam*, 35.30.1; *loco alto et undique praecipiti*, 36.22.5; *in altiorem deruptioremque undique tumulum*, 38.2.13; *per tam ardua atque iniqua loca*, 38.19.3; *arduas et rectas prope rupes*, 38.20.4; *loca montana et aspera*, 39.1.5; *silvestria et pleraque invia loca*, 40.22.2; *per invia atque ardua*, 42.16.1; *asperi ac prope invii soli*, 42.55.1.

110 Cf. e.g. *in saltus invios*, 9.38.4; *se aperuisse Ciminiam silvam viamque per devios saltus Romano bello fecisse*, 10.24.5; *e saltu invio atque impedito*, 21.25.13; *nos hic pecorum modo per aestivos saltus deviasque callis exercitum ducimus conditi nubibus silvisque*, 22.14.8 (a

the pathos of the account, stress the hardships combatants endure and the heroism of their feats, or, as is the case with ambush narratives, emphasise the uncertainty provoked by the fear of deception.

3.3 Locus, virtus, *and* arma: *Landscape and Military Ethics*

Another way the *Ab Urbe Condita* elaborates on the strategic functions of mountains and hills is by setting 'position' (*locus*), as a factor in battle, in opposition with terms like *virtus*, *arma*, or – less frequently – *multitudo*. In other words, the text repeatedly emphasises that an elevated position can counterbalance an army's numerical inferiority or the lack of spirit of its soldiers.

At 2.30.9, for example, the Aequians take up position on the mountaintops to avoid fighting against a Roman army sent against them: 'The Aequians left the plain and defended themselves on the mountain peaks, confiding more on position than on arms' (*Cessere Aequi campis, locoque magis quam armis freti summis se iugis montium tutabantur*). At 3.42.3–4, it is the survivors of a Roman army who set up camp on a height (*loco edito*) and 'by nowhere offering themselves to direct combat, defended themselves through the nature of the land and the rampart, not through valour and arms' (*nusquam se aequo certamine committentes, natura loci ac vallo, non virtute aut armis tutabantur*). Similarly, at 31.45.6, the inhabitants of Gaurium take refuge on their citadel 'trusting position more than arms' (*loci se magis quam armorum fiducia*). The Ligurians occupy well-defended positions on the mountains at 41.18.1, 'with the intention of defending themselves against the violence they had unfortunately experienced more through the protection offered by the place than through arms' (*locorum magis praesidio adversus infeliciter expertam vim quam armis se defensuri*). When mention is made of combatants fighting from lower ground, the motif can also be reversed in that *virtus* is displayed as overcoming an unfavourable *locus*. This is the case with the Romans fiercely resisting a Volscian ambush at 6.30.5: 'There, as the soldiers, who resist in an unfavourable position with only their valour, kill and are killed (...)' (*Ibi dum iniquo loco sola virtute militum restantes caedunt caedunturque ...*).[111]

---

variation; cf. *deviis callibus medio saltu recipiebant se*, 25.30.10); *per saltus prope invios*, 31.2.10; *in devios saltus*, 40.17.6; *fugientes per saltus invios*, 40.27.11; *quem scrutantes ante devios saltus abditum et latentem vix inveniebamus*, 40.27.13; *devio saltu*, 41.19.8; *per invios saltus*, 44.20.2.

111 Cf. also Liv. 2.65.3, where the Roman consul hesitates to give the order to attack, because he confides more in his soldiers' valour than in their position (*dum cunctatur consul virtute militum fretus, loco parum fidens ...*).

The *locus/arma* opposition is more extensively expressed at 32.10.11, where Livy reports the beginning of the battle of Aous (198 BCE).[112] Skirmishes had first taken place in an expanse of flat terrain (*in planitie satis ad id patenti*, 32.10.9) at the entrance of the so-called Stena, a gorge in the vicinity of Antigonea where Philip of Macedon positioned his garrisons.[113] Then the Macedonians retreated onto higher ground (*in arta et confragosa loca*, 32.10.10), and the Romans pursued them there. This is how Livy presents the ensuing combat, comparing the various factors that affected the course of the fighting (32.10.11):

> Pro his ordo et militaris disciplina et genus armorum erat, aptum tegendis corporibus; pro hoste loca et catapultae ballistaeque in omnibus prope rupibus quasi in muro dispositae.

> The Romans were favoured by their order, their military discipline, and the fashion of their weaponry, which was suited to covering their bodies; the enemies were favoured by their position and by the catapults and hurling engines, which had been arranged on all the crags as if on a wall.

The usual 'military skill' (*arma*)-factor is further specified to include military discipline and appropriate weaponry. Conversely, the *locus* has the Macedonians using the kind of devices one would use from the walls of a besieged city.

To have an idea of how the *loco non armis*-motif can significantly colour the account of a battle, one can consider some passages of Livy's narrative of Cynoscephalae – the battle which finalised the Roman victory over Philip V of Macedon in 197 BCE – in Book 33. Livy's here follows Polybius (18.24–27), whose military competence is evident in the accuracy with which he portrays the phases of the battle and the features of the terrain. The Roman narrative is quite close to the Greek one, but its emphasis is slightly different. As scholars have remarked, for example, Polybius' focus is on strategy, while Livy's is on morality and gripping action; moreover, Livy' account is peculiar in its graphic portrayal of vivid scenes (*enargeia*) and in its interest for the emotions of characters (especially King Philip, whose fear and instability are presented as a cause for his ultimate defeat).[114]

---

112 Cf. Plut. *Vit. Flam.* 4.2. On the battle of Aous cf. also Zon. 9.16.1; Hammond (1966); Chaplin (2010a); Clark (2014, pp. 161–162 and 171–173).
113 Cf. Liv. 32.5.8–13. For the topography of the battle see Hammond (1966).
114 For comparisons between Livy's and Polybius' narratives of Cynoscephalae, cf. e.g. Walsh (1961, pp. 151–152, 186–187); Luce (1977, pp. 39–41); Tränkle (1977, pp. 99–102); Carawan (1988); Eckstein (2015, pp. 411–416); Fabrizi (2021a, pp. 46–51). For Livy's creative use of Polybius more generally, Tränkle (1977); Levene (2010).

During an early phase of the battle, Romans and Macedonians fight on a lofty hill (33.7.9):

> Deinde, postquam nuntii instabant, et iam iuga montium detexerat nebula, et in conspectu erant Macedones in tumulum maxime editum inter alios compulsi loco se magis quam armis tutantes ...

> The messengers urged the king and the mist had already uncovered the mountain peaks; one could see the Macedonians, who had been driven onto the highest peak of all, as they defended themselves more through their position than their arms.

The remark according to which the Macedonians defended themselves *loco magis quam armis* constitutes a departure from Livy's source, Polybius. Indeed, the Greek historian states that 'the Macedonians defended themselves nobly but, in turn, pressed hard and utterly overwhelmed, they fled to the heights and sent messengers to the king to ask for help' (18.21.8).[115] Thus, whereas Polybius has the Macedonians fighting bravely against the Romans' advance, the *Ab Urbe Condita* suggests they withstood the enemy because of their favourable position.

The same idea returns later in the portrayal of the final stage of the battle when the two sides clashed in full battle array (33.9.3–4):

> 3. Dextro cornu rex loci plurimum auxilio, ex iugis altioribus pugnans, vincebat; sinistro, tum cum maxime adpropinquante phalangis parte quae novissimi agminis fuerat, sine ullo ordine trepidabatur; 4. media acies, quae propior dextrum cornu erat, stabat spectaculo velut nihil ad se pertinentis pugnae intenta.

> 3. On the right wing, the king was victorious due to the great advantage of his position, since he fought on higher peaks. On the left, there was confusion and no order at all, as in that moment the part of the phalanx which had been in the rear was coming near. 4. The centre of the line, which was closer to the right wing, remained still, watching eagerly as if the battle did not involve them at all.

---

115   Οἱ δὲ Μακεδόνες ἠμύνοντο μὲν γενναίως, πιεζούμενοι δὲ πάλιν οὗτοι καὶ καταβαρούμενοι τοῖς ὅλοις προσέφυγον πρὸς τοὺς ἄκρους καὶ διεπέμποντο πρὸς τὸν βασιλέα περὶ βοηθείας.

Here, again, Livy's narrative is biased quite differently to the corresponding passage of Polyb. 18.25.2. The Greek historian reports that 'Philip's right wing had splendid success in the fighting because they launched the attack from higher ground, prevailed due to the weight of their formation and, due to the different nature of their weaponry, had a great advantage in the present combat'. But Livy omits the military superiority of the Macedonian right wing, suggesting, once more, that they were only successful because they fought from higher ground.

The stress upon the aid the terrain provided the Macedonians on these two occasions is quite interesting in this context since, at Cynoscephalae, the rough terrain constituted, in fact, a crucial disadvantage for the Macedonian phalanx. Not that Livy fails to mention this: at 33.9.8–11, the inability of the rigid Macedonian formation to manoeuvre as it is encircled by a Roman contingent, which is now coming down from the hilltop, is presented as the reason for the final massacre of the king's army (and this time, as stated at section 11, the Macedonians are hard pressed by *locus*, too). However, the relevance of this fact is counterbalanced by the presence of the *loco non armis*-motif twice in the previous part of the account.

Moreover, Livy has nothing like the excursus on the advantages of the Roman legionary army over the phalanx, which Polybius inserts at the end of his account of the battle (Polyb. 18.28–32). Here, the Greek historian points out that, among other factors, the phalanx can only achieve its full potential on level ground with no obstacles of any kind (18.31.5–6), but 'in war the times and places of combat are uncertain' (18.31.2). In fact, the interpretation of the role of military technology in Polybius and Livy is similar, but the difference resides in the nuances. In both authors, the Romans win thanks, among other things, their ability to conquer a difficult terrain through their superior military organisation.[116] While this is mainly a matter of strategy for Polybius, in the *Ab Urbe Condita* the emphasis lies on Roman discipline as an integral part of that organisation versus the Macedonians' (failed) attempts to use the terrain as a substitute for valour (and Philip's incapacity to effectively react to the events of the battle).

The opposition between *locus* and *virtus/arma* is also an effective topic for commanders haranguing their troops. At 9.31.12–13, the consul Gaius Iunius

---

[116] Clark (2014, pp. 162–165) interprets the narrative of Cynoscephalae as part of a 'discourse over Roman technology and armour' (p. 165) that is prominent in the Fourth Decade: in her reading, through their discipline and technology the Romans can overcome the landscape of Greece, which is their real enemy in this battle.

Bubulcus spurs his men to fight back as they are being ambushed by the Samnites in 311 BCE:

> 12. Coniterentur modo uno animo omnes invadere hostem victum acie, castris exutum, nudatum urbibus, ultimam spem furto insidiarum temptantem et loco non armis fretum. 13. Sed quem esse iam virtuti Romanae inexpugnabilem locum? Fregellana arx Soranaque et ubicumque iniquo successum erat loco memorabantur.

> 12. They should only, all with one and the same spirit, put forth all of their strength to attack an enemy defeated in battle, driven away from his camp, despoiled of his cities, who was testing his last hope with a deceitful ambush, trusting position, not arms. 13. But what position could be unconquerable for Roman valour? The citadels of Fregellae and Sora, and the places where they had been victorious even in an unfavourable position were brought to their minds.

Interestingly, the opposition works in two ways here. On the one hand, the Samnites rely 'on position, not arms' (*loco non armis*). On the other, the courage (*virtus*) of the Romans can conquer any position. Thus, *locus* can compensate a lack of *virtus*, but *virtus* – specifically, Roman *virtus* – can prove victorious over an *iniquus locus*.

Similarly, in 27.18.8–9, Scipio encourages his soldiers to attack the Carthaginians, who have settled upon a hill near the Spanish town of Baecula (208 BCE):

> 8. Scipio circumvectus ordines signaque ostendebat hostem, praedamnata spe aequo dimicandi campo captantem tumulos, loci fiducia non virtutis aut armorum, stare in conspectu. Sed altiora moenia habuisse Carthaginem quae transcendisset miles Romanus; 9. nec tumulos nec arcem, ne mare quidem armis obstitisse suis. Ad id fore altitudines, quas cepissent, hostibus ut per praecipitia et praerupta salientes fugerent; eam quoque se illis fuga clausurum.

> 8. Scipio, riding around the ranks and standards, showed that before their eyes was the enemy, who, having given up beforehand the hope of fighting on even ground, occupied the hills trusting in his position, not in in his valour or his arms. But New Carthage had higher walls, which Roman soldiers had climbed; 9. neither hills nor citadel – and not even the sea – had hindered their arms. Those heights that the enemies had taken up

would have the effect that they would flee leaping through steep and broken land; but he would make even that flight impossible for them.

Scipio suggests that the enemies should not be feared since they are not brave enough to risk an open battle. Their only strength is constituted by the height of the hill they have occupied, but even this cannot prove a match for Roman courage, which can overcome hills, city walls – even the sea. Indeed, the very heights the Carthaginians have occupied will end up proving a disadvantage to so cowardly an enemy in that their flight will be hindered – thus proving that *locus* is, in the end, nothing without *virtus*. Scipio proves right: his soldiers attack the enemy by climbing the hill and with this act of valour achieve a clear victory (27.18.10–20).

Of course, *locus* and *arma/virtus* are not always opposed. In some cases, they work together to bring advantage to one side. In 7.23.8, for example, the Romans are aided by their *virtus* and their position (*praeter virtutem locus quoque superior adiuvit*) as the Gauls attack them while they are building fortifications on a hill. And, in 29.33.4, Masinissa is said to have both *locus* and *virtus* on his side, while his enemy Syphax can only count on numbers, *multitudo*. Passages of this kind, however, do nothing but confirm the general tendency of the *Ab Urbe Condita* to think of *locus*, *virtus*, *arma*, and in some cases *multitudo*, as distinct factors in battle, which each side of a battle may make good use of or not. While, theoretically, more than one of such factors may favour the same side, *locus* – which usually means an elevated position – is often seen as opposed to *virtus* or *arma*.

It will hardly have escaped attention that, when the text draws such opposition, it usually locates *virtus* and *arma* on the Romans' side and *locus* on the enemy's. A contrast thus emerges in the *Ab Urbe Condita* between 'Roman' martial prowess, which can take control of even the harshest landscapes, and 'foreign' reliance on position and ambush. More to the point, the text delineates two approaches to landscape. For the enemies of Rome, this works as a natural protection that can be used to avoid direct confrontation or to compensate a lack of martial prowess or military technology. For the Romans, instead, landscapes, and especially harsh or hostile landscapes, are something to conquer through valour. By the repetition of the *loco non armis* motif, the narrative constructs a Roman approach to landscape, which, as I argue, is an integral part of what it presents as the Roman approach to fighting.

3.4 Basic and Complex Topographies

In the previous paragraphs, I showed that the *Ab Urbe Condita* tends to work with a limited set of topographic features and that some of these features recur with particular frequency associated with specific functions. How, however, does the text build complex topographies from such features? How complex can topographies be in the *Ab Urbe Condita*? And how integral are they to battle narratives?

Once more, there is no straightforward answer to such questions. The complexity and detail of battle topographies, as well as the degree to which topography plays a role as a structural element of the action, varies greatly from episode to episode. Therefore, one must be content with singling out some general tendencies.

Often, the topography is reduced to basic elements, which are strictly necessary for understanding the course of a battle. In several cases, individual features of the terrain, which are functional to the narrative of specific actions or events, are mentioned in isolated remarks and are not embedded in an organic representation of the physical battlefield; the latter is largely left to the reader's imagination.

In the account of the battle of Cannae (216 BCE),[117] for example, the only physical landmark within the otherwise featureless plain[118] is the river Aufidus, which plays an important role at the outset of the fighting. The positions of the Carthaginian and Roman camps are described at 22.43.10–44.3;[119] it is especially interesting how the narrator introduces topographical elements here. He initially writes that Hannibal made camp by the village of Cannae, 'so that it faced away from the Volturnus wind, which carries clouds of dust in the fields parched from drought' (*aversa a Volturno vento, qui campis torridis siccitate nubes pulveris vehit*, 22.43.10). As van Gils (2019, p. 258) notes, this piece of information serves to stress Hannibal's strategic skill and his concern for the choice of a convenient terrain, a quality his adversary Varro definitely lacks; however, no mention is made of the Aufidus, which is not relevant at this point (22.43.10–11).

Then the narrator reports the Romans' arrival: their forces are divided into two camps, a smaller and a larger one, in the same manner that they were at Gereonium before the consuls moved to Cannae (22.44.1; cf. 22.40.5–6). After that, one learns that both Roman camps have access to the river, but the smaller one is more conveniently located because it lies 'on the far side' of the

---

117 The problems involved in the localisation of the historical battle are discussed below. The ancient town of Cannae stood on the hill now called Monte di Canne, on the right side of the Aufidus.
118 Cf. Livy 22.44.4.
119 A recent study on spatial reference in Livy's account of Cannae is van Gils (2019).

Aufidus (*scil.* with respect to the direction the Romans have come from),[120] where the Carthaginian camp, one now learns, is *not* placed. Since the Romans have come from North-West,[121] the 'far side' must be the right (South-Eastern) bank of the Aufidus; this is also confirmed by information which Livy provides later, during his account of the battle, and which I shall soon mention. This means that the Carthaginians and the larger Roman camp are on the left bank, and the smaller Roman camp is on the right bank. It is significant, however, that none of this is made explicit in the historian's description. Moreover, Livy does not provide all the information at the outset but introduces parts of it if and when they become necessary for understanding the events.

The Aufidus is an object of interest for Livy because the fighting starts when it is crossed. At 22.45.1–2, Hannibal sends some of his Numidians across the river (i.e. to the right bank) to attack the Romans *aquatores* from the smaller camp. Aemilius Paullus, the consul in command of the army on that day, keeps his troops within the (larger) camp (22.45.4–5). The following day, his colleague Gaius Terentius Varro crosses the river and reunites the soldiers from the larger camp with their comrades from the smaller one. In this way, he deploys his army so that the right flank is closest to the river (22.45.5–8).

Hannibal crosses the river, too (22.46.1). After describing the Carthaginian deployment (22.46.2–7), Livy explains the advantages and disadvantages of the two armies' positions. Both, he says, were favourably placed with respect to the sun – the Romans facing South and the Carthaginians North – but the Romans had the Volturnus wind blowing dust in their eyes (22.46.8–9). This is, as I have mentioned above (p. 154), one of the very few passages in the *Ab Urbe Condita* where reference to the cardinal points is made in descriptions of 'tactical space': cardinal orientation here is strictly functional to the mention of such a distinctive phenomenon like the raising of the dust.

Now Livy's text offers a fairly consistent picture. The battle takes place on the right bank of the Aufidus, which is imagined as running more or less South to North.[122] The Romans, facing South, have the river to their right and the Carthaginians to their left. However, this is a picture that one can only put together gradually and with a good deal of effort; indeed, the topography of the historical battle of Cannae has been a major issue of debate for modern

---

120   Van Gils (2019, p. 165) mentions *trans flumen* as an example of a 'relative frame of reference' as defined in cognitive linguistics. A relative frame of reference is tied to a specific standpoint, in this case the Romans'.
121   Cf. Kromayer (1924–31, pp. 616–617); Walbank (1970, p. 437); Daly (2002, p. 17). *Contra* De Sanctis (1968, pp. 134–135).
122   As it is in Polybius: cf. Walbank (1970, p. 436); Lazenby (1978, p. 77).

scholarship, for which the most hotly contested point has been precisely whether the battle was fought on the left or the right bank of the Aufidus. While a positioning on the right bank is the one that fits best with the accounts of both Livy and Polybius, objections to such a localisation have been raised based on various strategic and topographical considerations, and attempts have been made to reconcile Polybius' and Livy's texts with a left-bank topography.[123]

The debate over the topography of Cannae is symptomatic of the problems posed to modern scholarship by ancient approaches to space and topography.[124] When reading a historical narrative, we automatically try to locate the tactical space of a battle within a geo-topographical framework, usually by checking the information in our source against a map. An ancient reader of Livy, however, would have read the narrative of Cannae by aligning themselves with the perspective of the Roman army: the reader knew that the Romans encountered a river, that a part of them crossed it to pitch camp on the other side, and that, eventually, Hannibal and the main body of his army crossed, too. This was virtually all that one needed to know to make sense of the battle account. When the reader received the additional information that the Romans were facing South, that did not substantially change their mental model of the battlefield; the statement that the Romans had the Aufidus[125] to their right was more important, because this would once more be relevant in the combat narrative.[126] The apparent imprecision in topographical details

---

123 It was pointed out, for example, that the left bank of the river is level, while the right one is hilly, which would seem to run counter to Livy and Polybius' statements that the battlefield was perfect for cavalry combat. See, in particular, De Sanctis (1968, pp. 131–138, with further bibliography). The influential treatments of the issue by Kromayer (1912, pp. 280–307, with further bibliography), and Kromayer and Veith (1924–1931, pp. 610–625), demonstrated that the terrain is almost level on the right bank just east of Cannae, where the site of the clash should be located; and today this theory is, with occasional modifications, the most widely held by scholars (see e.g. Walbank, 1970, pp. 435–438; Lazenby, 1978, pp. 77–79; Daly, 2002, pp. 32–35).

124 Cf. Introduction, pp. 13–14.

125 The river is mentioned once more at 22.47.2, where Livy reports that the fight between the Roman right flank and the Carthaginian left was made particularly congested by the fact that the armies were hemmed in by the river. After this, no further hint to topography is given: the space of combat is, from this point onwards, the one shaped by the armies.

126 Further examples of battle narratives in which elements of the terrain are only mentioned with reference to specific moments of the combat include e.g. the battle against the Volsci at 6.23.12–24.11 (a hill that the Volscians use for ambush is mentioned at 6.24.2); the battle of Metaurus in 27.47–49 (Hasdrubal's failed attempt to cross the river is related in a fairly detailed way during the account of the preliminary movements, at 27.47, 10–11; later there is mention of a hill that dominated Hasdrubal's left wing, and which prevented him from extending his line further, at 27.48.7; and the same hill reappears at 27.48.12, to

derives, at least in part, from the fact that Livy's narrative, as argued by Van Gils (2019), often provides spatial information from the spatial standpoints of characters: in this way, it presents the reader with their different perceptions and uses of the space of battle, and alerts them to the main theme of the narrative, namely the contrast between Hannibal's strategic control of the terrain and Varro's rashness.

In other accounts, a comprehensive bi-dimensional model of a battlefield is more easily recoverable from the text. Still, such a model appears as a simplified sketch rather than a fully-fledged topography. At 7.7.6, for example, a battle between Romans and Hernicans is introduced by the words:

> Duum milium planities castra Romana ab Hernicis dirimebat; ibi pari ferme utrimque spatio in medio pugnatum est.
>
> A plain two miles long lay between the Roman camp and the Hernicans; there they fought in the middle, with roughly as much space from both sides.

This is all the reader knows about the battlefield's topography, but it is still enough to shape a consistent model.[127] Similarly, at 39.30–31, Livy reports a military engagement in Spain (185 BCE).[128] The battle is fought by the river Tagus (39.30.9–10; 31.5) in an open plain (39.30.12: *campum apertum*) extending between the river and a hill, where the Spanish camp is located (39.30.10). When, in the end, the Romans conquer the Spanish camp, some of the enemies flee to occupy a nearby mountain (39.31.16: *montem propinquum*). All in all, the spatial development of the battle is quite clearly mapped onto this basic model, with the Romans moving from the river to the middle of the plain where fighting takes place and then to the hill.

Finally, there are some (rarer) cases in which topography is more detailed, and its role in a battle's development is crucial. In what follows, I would like to examine one such example of complex topography. I have selected a narrative which constructs tension between standard military space and landscape, by showing how the latter can be disruptive to the former, and how

---

account for the fact that the Romans were not able to launch an attack in that direction); the battle of Magnesia in 37.38.–44 (where the river Phrygius is the only landmark: see 37.39.11; 42.7–8).

127 The brief description of the battlefield here sets the scene for a battle which will be developed as a major episode: cf. Oakley (1998, pp. 102–104).

128 There is no certainty on Livy's source here, although Calpurnius Piso is a candidate: cf. Briscoe (2008, p. 324).

victory and defeat are strictly tied to an army's ability to impose the former upon the latter: namely, the famous account of the battle at Lake Trasimene in 217 BCE (22.4–8).

Much recent scholarly work has focused on this narrative, and this is no surprise given its literary effectiveness and its importance in the account of the turbulent early years of the Second Punic war. The clash at Trasimene – the major episode of the first part of Book 22 – belongs in a series of almost proverbial Roman setbacks following Hannibal's invasion of Italy: it comes after the battles of Ticinus and Trebia, which Livy reports in Book 21, and before the catastrophe of Cannae at the end of Book 22. The *Ab Urbe Condita* turns the account of these events into a complex reflection on strategy, defeat, and the Roman capacity for reacting to adversities. Scholars have stressed the role of Trasimene (and its landscape) in the theme of Punic deceit (*Punica fides*), a crucial explanation for Hannibal's victories over the Romans:[129] at Trasimene, the Carthaginian commander achieves victory by using the landscape to set a trap for the reckless consul Gaius Flaminius.[130] Moreover, attention has been devoted to the text's treatment of causality,[131] to Livy's use of *enargeia*, and to the symbolic implications of its pervasive theme of vision and blindness.[132]

The narrative starts with an unusually long and detailed description of the site chosen by Hannibal for his ambush (22.4.2–3):

> 2. Et iam pervenerat ad loca nata insidiis, ubi maxime montes Cortonenses †inTrasumennum submit†. Via tantum interest perangusta, velut ad ⟨id⟩ ipsum de industria relicto spatio; deinde paulo latior patescit campus; inde colles adsurgunt. 3. Ibi castra in aperto locat, ubi ipse cum Afris modo Hispanisque consideret; Baliares ceteramque levem armaturam post montes circumducit; equites ad ipsas fauces saltus tumulis apte tegentibus locat, ut ubi intrassent Romani, obiecto equitatu clausa omnia lacu ac montibus essent.

> 2. Already they had reached a place that was naturally suited to an ambush, where the mountains of Cortona reach closest to the Trasimene. There is only a very narrow path in between, as if space had been left

---

129 Pausch (2019).
130 This belongs in a broader pattern at work in Books 21 and 22, whereby Roman defeats are explained through the recklessness of ambitious and demagogic generals, who are usually opposed by a wiser (and more politically conservative) colleague or superior: cf. Östenberg (2017). On Flaminius see also Chapter 2, pp. 91–93.
131 Levene (2010, pp. 281–295, considering various battle accounts, Trasimene among them).
132 Feldherr (2021).

there specifically for that purpose; then the plain becomes a little wider; then the hills begin. 3. There he pitched camp in the open, so that he, with only the Africans and the Spaniards, could settle there; he led the Baleares and the rest of the light infantry around and behind the mountains; he placed the cavalry by the very entrance to the gorge on heights that conveniently hid them, so that, as the Romans would enter, the whole space between the lake and the mountains could be closed once the cavalry barred the way.

All the events that follow are quite clearly mapped in this space. Flaminius leads his army into the stretch of flat terrain between the mountains and the lake without realising the presence of the men lying in ambush; the Carthaginians attack the Romans simultaneously from all directions (22.4.4–5). The Romans are now trapped and are further hindered by the rising of a mist, which does not, on the other hand, affect the Carthaginian assault since the various contingents of the latter are positioned on the hilltops and are thus able to see one another while they fall upon their enemies (22.4.6–7).

One consequence of the Romans' diminished vision[133] is their incapacity to keep their ranks. The battle starts before they can deploy their line or wield their swords (22.4.7). In the confusion that follows, things get even worse (22.5.3):

> Ceterum prae strepitu ac tumultu nec consilium nec imperium accipi poterat, tantumque aberat ut sua signa atque ordines et locum noscerent ut vix ad arma capienda aptandaque pugnae competeret animus, opprimerenturque quidam onerati magis iis quam tecti.
>
> But because of the dim and bustle no advice or command could be heard; they did not recognize their own standards, ranks, and positions, to the point that their spirits were hardly enough to grab their arms and put them on. Some were killed because their arms weighed them down rather than protected them.

Standards, ranks, and the place (*locus*) each man is supposed to occupy are the fundamental elements of standard military space, which the effects of mist

---

133 The Romans' failure is auditory as well as visual: cf. 22.5.3–4 (the first part of which is quoted below), with Levene (2010, p. 269). The theme of perceptual failure is investigated in detail by Feldherr (2021).

and landscape disrupt. Eventually, the men find a way to fight even in such conditions (22.5.6–8):

> 6. Deinde, ubi in omnes partes nequiquam impetus capti et ab lateribus montes ac lacus, a fronte et ab tergo hostium acies claudebat apparuitque nullam nisi in dextera ferroque salutis spem esse, 7. tum sibi quisque dux adhortatorque factus ad rem gerendam, et nova de integro exorta pugna est, non illa ordinata per principes hastatosque ac triarios nec ut pro signis antesignani, post signa alia pugnaret acies nec ut in sua legione miles aut cohorte aut manipulo esset: 8 fors conglob<ab>at et animus suus cuique ante aut post pugnandi ordinem dabat.

> 6. Then, as their useless charges in all directions were broken and they were blocked by the mountains and the lake on the flanks and by the enemies' army on the front and back, it became evident that there was no hope of safety but the weapons in their right hands; 7. at that moment, each one became his own commander and encouraged himself to fight. The fighting then started anew – but not in an orderly fashion with *principes*, *hastati*, and *triarii*, nor one in which the *antesignani* fought before the standards and the rest of the army behind them, or in which each soldier was in his own legion or cohort or *manipulus*. 8. Chance led them together and each one's courage gave him his battle rank in front or behind.

Again, the text underlines the disappearance of the usual 'Roman' way of organising the space of battle, with the three lines of *principes*, *hastati*, and *triarii*, and with the distinction between the different units of an army. The landscape, in its durable and ephemeral components (topography and the mist), escapes Roman attempts to control it and controls the course of the battle in its turn (or better, Hannibal controls the course of the battle by controlling the landscape).

After Flaminius is killed (22.6.1–4), the flight of the Roman soldiers begins. Some of them run through the mountains (*per omnia arta praeruptaque velut caeci evadunt, armaque et viri super alium alii praecipitantur*, 22.6.5);[134] others seek refuge in the waters of the lake, only to drown or be killed by the enemy (22.6.6–7). Six thousand manage to escape to a hill and, when the mist finally lifts, see the defeat of their army (22.6.8–10).

---

134 'They run off blindly through the rugged landscape and its narrow passages, arms and men tumbling over each other.'

The narrative constructs an opposition between Hannibal, who can use and control the landscape through his deceitful strategy, and the Romans, who fail to control it by imposing the standard spatial structure of the Roman army on it. Flaminus' recklessness and his disregard for the actual conditions of the terrain can be seen as the opposite of the behaviour of a wise Roman commander such as Cato at Emporiae, who reconnoitres before setting up camp and deploying his army. Hannibal is peculiar among Rome's enemies in his relationship to the landscape – here and elsewhere. While other foreign peoples tend to identify with their landscapes, to use them as natural defences to compensate their lack of valour and discipline,[135] Hannibal, just like the Romans, controls it. His strategy of control is, however, based on deceit, which the *Ab Urbe Condita* portrays as essentially un-Roman,[136] while the Roman way of controlling foreign landscapes is, for Livy, conquering them through valour, order, and discipline. Of course, landscape can sometimes disrupt order and discipline – and that is when Roman defeats occur.[137]

4   The Spatial Vocabulary of Battle: War, Conquest, and Control

This chapter has examined the space of battle, in the *Ab Urbe Condita*, as an integral part of the imagery of war. The space of battle emerges, as I have shown, from the interaction of two main components: on the one hand, the topographies where battles are fought; on the other, human attempts to control them through standard military ways of organising space.

The space formed by armies and camps is at work in virtually all battle narratives. Sometimes it is only briefly sketched, while on other occasions it functions as the main reference system in a narrative; and, in some cases, it reflects the main theme(s) of a battle account.

The role of topography and landscape, too, varies greatly from battle to battle. Most topographies are simplified: the text usually concentrates on a few landscape features, weaves the action around them, or sometimes mentions

---

135   Cf. e.g. Fabrizi (2017b).
136   This basic difference between Romans and Carthaginians is, however, complicated in the narrative of the dictatorship of Quintus Fabius Maximus, which follows the defeat at Trasimene at 22.12–18, 23–30. For Livy's reflections on how Romans should learn from the enemy without, however, losing their own identity, see Levene (2010, pp. 79–81, 228–231); Fabrizi (2017a).
137   On landscape and treachery as justifications for defeat in Livy and other Roman historians see Östenberg (2017).

a topographic feature only in connection with a specific action. At the same time, some features of Livian topographies tend to recur in association with specific functions, which are not merely strategic but – in some cases – directly address aspects of military ethics (e.g. the roles of valour and discipline, the uses of ambush and military technology). What emerges from Livy's history is what one might call a vocabulary of military space, in which each feature is associated with specific semantic values. The reader learns to recognise such features and their meanings, which the text can, in some cases, re-activate to construct even lengthier, and more symbolically charged, topographies (as in the example of the battle of Lake Trasimene). So, just like the space of the city of Rome participates in the political thought that the *Ab Urbe Condita* develops, so the space of battle is an integral part in its reflections on war, conquest, and Roman identity.

At the core of such reflection lies a constant anxiety about bringing a potentially hostile world under control through war and conquest. As I have suggested, the *Ab Urbe Condita* constructs what it presents as a Roman approach to both war and the natural environment. Such an approach includes open fighting rather than ambush, and mastery of the landscape, often seen almost as an enemy force, rather than the strategic use of it. While foreign landscapes often seem to act against the Romans (and thus can serve to justify Roman defeats), Roman valour – so the text implies – is ultimately able to conquer any landscape.

Conquering landscapes usually involves subjecting them to the structures of Roman space. Roman armies, in the *Ab Urbe Condita*, bring their own (Roman) space along with them: this can be the well-ordered structure of Roman camps – which reproduces the inner structure of the city, thus bringing 'Rome' into the foreign world –, or the well-ordered space of Roman armies, with their sectors and ranks. The core military values that Livy's history outlines, such as *virtus* and *disciplina*, are functional in preserving such a spatial structure in the whole variety of landscapes the Romans encounter.

This resonates with a broader discourse at work in the *Ab Urbe Condita* about the relationships between peoples and their environments. Foreign landscapes can be dangerous in different ways. They can, of course, be harsh, impassable, or deceitful, and thus hinder Roman armies; this is the kind of danger which is most relevant to battle narratives, and as a consequence the one I have focused on in this chapter. Foreign landscapes can, however, also be dangerous because their climate and abundance is so welcoming as to entice their conquerors into softening their morals. This is a major and well-investigated theme in Livy's narrative of the Asian campaigns: the riches brought home from victorious commanders catalyse, in the historian's view, the beginning of the Roman moral decay which will reach its nadir in the age of civil wars.[138]

Indeed, the *Ab Urbe Condita* shows the corrupting effects of foreign landscapes as acting not only on the Romans but also on other peoples.[139] At 38.17, for instance, the Roman general Gnaeus Manlius Vulso portrays the Gauls of Asia Minor as a people who has lost its original fierceness due to the attractiveness of the country they migrated to (*degeneres ... mixti et Gallograeci vere*, 38.17.9; *Uberrimo agro, mitissimo caelo, clementibus accolarum ingeniis, omnis illa cum qua venerant mansuefacta est feritas*, 17);[140] moreover, he mentions the inhabitants of the Spartan colony of Tarentum and the Macedonians of Syria, Egypt, and Babylonia as further instances of originally martial peoples who degenerated due to the influence of more agreeable lands and climates (13).[141] Manlius, of course, has every interest in portraying the Gauls of Asia Minor as weak, since he is haranguing his soldiers who are about to fight against a Gallic people in that region. The theme, however, has wider ramifications: at 38.46.1, two of the Roman envoys who accuse Manlius of misbehaviour in the campaign in Asia Minor, argue that he had only been able to defeat the Gauls because the latter's bodies and souls were 'mixed and tainted' (*mixti ac vitiati*). An earlier speech, that of the Rhodian ambassadors at 37.54.18–19, develops an opposing argument: the Greeks of Asia Minor – the speakers say – have *not* changed their Greek nature and mores. The Rhodians, however, do not appear very reliable in this respect, since Livy's narrative tends to represent them as bearing the typical 'Asiatic' traits of untrustworthiness and a tendency towards overblown rhetoric.[142] And, at the very least, the fact that they feel the need to deny their degeneration alerts the reader to the fact that degeneration resulting from contact with foreign landscapes is an issue.

---

138 On ideas about Roman decadence in Livy and other ancient authors, see e.g. Bringmann (1977); Luce (1977, pp. 270–275); Walter (2004, pp. 319–329); Fabrizi (2017c).

139 On environmental determinism in the *Ab Urbe Condita* see esp. Luce (1977, pp. 276–284); Bernard (2000, pp. 39–51); Mineo (2006, pp. 32–45).

140 On the discourse about the corrupting effect of Asia in Books 37–39 (including the speeches of Manlius, the Roman envoys, and the Rhodians) see Luce (1977) and Mineo (2006), quoted in the previous note; Clark (2014, pp. 186–199); Fabrizi (2017b). In these and the following paragraphs I summarise some of their observations and mine.

141 Vulso also mentions the Massiliotes as an instance in which the change was apparently for the best, since the Greek colonists 'drew some courage from the inhabitants' of Gaul (39.17.12). His summarising remark at 39.17.13, however, suggests that migration usually produces degeneration rather than improvement (*Generosius in sua quidque sede gignitur; insitum alienae terrae, in id quo alitur natura vertente se, degenerat*). Cf. Fabrizi (2017b, p. 137).

142 Cf. Chapter 1, p. 84.

Manlius himself states what is ultimately at stake in these circumstances when, at 38.17.18 (i.e. at the end of the above-mentioned speech) invites his soldiers to beware the *amoenitas* of Asia, the influence of 'foreign pleasures' (*peregrinae voluptates*) and of the 'discipline and customs' (*disciplinae atque mores*) of the locals. His soldiers will conspicuously fail to be wary of such things, since, as Livy writes in 39.6.6–9, it is the very booty of Manlius' Asiatic campaigns that marks the beginning of 'foreign luxury' (*luxuriae peregrinae*, 7) in Rome, which is a major sign of Roman moral decay. At the beginning of the same book (39.1), the external narrator powerfully anticipates such a historical turning point by comparing the wars in Liguria, where a harsh landscape, scanty resources, and fierce inhabitants provide an ideal training ground for Roman *diciplina*, and those in Asia, where *amoenitas* mollifies the Romans.

Another prominent instance of a warlike people softened by an overwelcoming landscape is provided by Hannibal's Carthaginians, who are corrupted in body and mind by their sojourn in the beautiful town of Capua in the winter of 216 BCE and the various pleasures they enjoy there (23.18.9–15). Hannibal's failure at foreseeing the effects of Capua's *amoenitas*[143] on his men's spirits is all the more striking[144] because, up to this point, Livy's narrative has shown him as a master in taming or controlling the Italian landscape.

It seems, therefore, that in the *Ab Urbe Condita* adaptation to, or lack of control of, foreign landscapes is problematic; but what about foreigners' use of foreign landscapes? As we have seen, most enemies of Rome tend to use their own landscapes as allies. The identification between people and landscape appears strongest with 'barbarians' like the Ligurians or the Gauls, whose warfare techniques mostly involve ambushes set in mountainous landscapes or forests. Do Romans, too, identify or ally themselves with their own landscape?

In book 5, as we have seen, Camillus powerfully affirms the deep bond between the Romans and their land: Rome's position close to the Tiber is a reason for her success and the land itself, with its hills and river, is like a mother to her inhabitants. Apart from allowing for Rome's initial birth and growth, however, the natural features of the countryside near the Tiber never seem to be the main force shaping the Romans' interaction with their space. Rather,

---

143 The term does not occur in this passage, but the *amoenitas* of Capua is almost proverbial; therefore, even if the Carthaginians' corruption is especially attributed to banqueting, sexual intercourse with prostitutes, and inactivity (*otium*), the beauty of the landscape and the mildness of the climate are implicitly the causes of such a lifestyle.

144 Cf. Livy 23.18.13.

the space of Rome is, from its very beginning, a political and sacral space far more than a natural one.

Romulus' founding of Rome involves a quintessential act of control in the establishment of a boundary; and the Forum, as I have shown in Chapter 1, ceases to be just a valley between two hills the very moment Romans and Sabines form a new political community there. It is also telling that Livy does not normally show Romans taking advantage of their natural landscape, even in the early books when wars are fought close to the city. Indeed, the text gives very little information about the physical features of the countryside outside of the city: the Romans identify primarily with their city, as a humanised space, rather than with their natural landscape.

The relationship with the natural environment that the *Ab Urbe Condita* represents as quintessentially Roman is thus one of control rather than identification, adaptation, or collaboration. Roman armies win by imposing their Roman space during acts of expansion into the rest of the world; when they fail to do that, defeat or ruin ensues. In this respect, the space of battle can be seen as a microcosm, epitomising the issues involved in conquest and empire.

CHAPTER 4

The Semantics of Space and Gender

1 Space, Gender, and Narrative

As geographers and sociologists have shown, power relationships between genders shape the organisation of space, and, conversely, the organisation of space shapes gender roles.[1] A society can, for instance, determine that certain kinds of spaces or places are either 'feminine' or 'masculine', or spaces and places to which such binary categories do not apply. Socioeconomic structures are involved in the shaping of both gender and space:[2] 'space is not a neutral entity; rather, it is culturally constructed, creating symbolic meanings with regard to gender relations, roles, and values' (Fenster, 2005, p. 468). Literary narratives can draw on and elaborate upon such symbolic meanings to develop their semantics of space.[3] For example, narratives can attribute 'masculine' or 'feminine' connotations to specific types of spaces, such as 'wilderness', 'the city', or 'the home'. Moreover, socially defined spaces can take on different meanings depending on the gender of the focaliser. Therefore, how characters act with space can be an effective way of characterising them.[4]

Recent years have witnessed a surge of interest in the spatiality of gender in Roman society.[5] Many of these studies – especially those written in the 2010s and 2020s–focus on women's uses of space, often with the aim of revising traditional assessments of gender roles and space in the Roman world. For a long time, studies about space and gender tended to attribute a crucial role to the dichotomy of 'public' vs 'private space'. 'Public' space – the space of social interaction outside the household, of business and politics – is supposedly marked off as masculine, 'private' or domestic space as feminine.[6] Studies of urban space in ancient Greece and Rome have been no exception, but more recently scholars have shown that the degree of spatial segregation between

---

1 On space and gender see e.g. Spain (1992); Massey (1994); Fenster (2005).
2 Massey (1994) provides several examples.
3 Cf. Würzbach (2004), from whom I derive the following observations.
4 The significance of space in characterization is famously discussed in Lotman (1973 and 1974).
5 Cf. e.g. Milnor (2005); Allison (2006 and 2007); Boatwright (2011); Cenerini and Rohr-Vio (2016); Russell (2016b); Rohr Vio (2019); Degl'Innocenti Pierini (2022–2023); Cornwell and Woolf (2023); Flower and Osgood (2024).
6 Cf. Fenster (2005, pp. 468–470); Russell (2016b, pp. 167–169).

© VIRGINIA FABRIZI, 2025 | DOI:10.1163/9789004733213_006

the genders in ancient societies was probably lower than used to be assumed. While our literary sources – mostly written by elite male authors – tend to ignore women's presence in non-domestic spaces, archaeological findings suggest a very different reality:[7] women, for example, participated in a variety of cults, both private and public, and could be highly visible on such occasions. Moreover, even the literary sources, if read with an eye to what they implicitly reveal, rather than to the explicit statements they contain, yield a more nuanced picture: some women at least, who belonged to the highest strata of Roman society, enjoyed significant power, which they exerted, and were expected to exert, through webs of interpersonal connections. On an even more fundamental level, the notion of 'public' and 'private' spaces, as applied to the ancient world, has been questioned, as scholars have shown that some of the most important sites in ancient cities included aspects of both.[8]

Livy is among the most frequently quoted ancient sources in studies of this kind, and episodes such as the debate about the Oppian Law in Book 34 or the discovery of the Bacchanalian conspiracy in Book 39 have sometimes been read as showing women's political agency in the *Ab Urbe Condita*. I believe caution is needed here: it is important to carefully consider the broader narrative strategies at work in Livy and, especially, be attentive to the gap between reality and narrative. It is certainly true that women were not confined to their homes in ancient Rome, that they were normally visible in public space and could play active roles in politics; it is also true that the distinction between 'public' and 'private' space was more fluid than in later epochs. Is that, however, what the *Ab Urbe Condita* shows? How does *the text* express the distinction between 'public' and 'private'? When it portrays women outside their homes, does it present it as a normal or as unusual situation? And how could this interact with ancient readers' experiences of space and gender?

These questions, of course, are part of a broader inquiry about the narrative construction of gender (and space) in the *Ab Urbe Condita*. How does the text negotiate notions of femininity *and* masculinity? How does it treat, if at all, non-binary concepts of gender, or intersections between masculinity and femininity? And how does narrated space take part in such negotiations?

Recent studies of gender in Livy have laid the foundations for such an investigation. Here too, close attention is mostly paid to women and notions of

---

7 Cf. e.g. Allison (2006 and 2007); Trümper (2012). On women's changing role in Roman society see also Keegan (2021, pp. xvi–xix).
8 Cf. e.g. Zaccaria Ruggiu (1995); Allison (2006, p. 345); Trümper (2012, p. 291); Russell (2016a). For a more general discussion of the terms 'public' and 'private' as referred to ancient Rome see Milnor (2005, pp. 16–27, with further bibliography).

femininity.[9] In her by now classic study of Augustan ideas about gender and domesticity, Milnor (2005) argues that the importance of domestic life and the emphasis of women's sexual morality in Augustan discourse was tied to the *princeps'* realigning the *res publica* around one man and one family. Drawing from these insights, Helmke (2023) analyses exemplary concepts of femininity in Livy's crisis narratives. He argues that women, in the *Ab Urbe Condita*, are especially prominent at moments of crisis, which can be interpreted as a crisis of masculinity:[10] women momentarily transgress gender norms, appropriating some actions and features the text normally considers as masculine, in order to fill the gap left by men's inability at solving a crisis. Such interventions, however, are temporary and their aim is to catalyse masculine action, ultimately reinstating a socio-political system dominated by men. The idea that women's presence in Livy's history tends to be connected to moments of historical changes and crisis is also prominent in Keegan's (2021) monograph on female characters in the *Ab Urbe Condita*. His analysis, however, devotes more attention to the social differences between the women in the narrative and argues for the presence of a more nuanced representation of women's participation in public matters in the text. These observations are a counterpart to Albrecht's (2016) investigation of the construction of masculinity, and specifically 'hegemonic masculinity',[11] in the *Ab Urbe Condita*; in Albrecht's reading, Livy's narrative constructs a set of values and behaviours that shape the concept of the 'great men' ruling the state.

In what follows, I look at narrated space as an element in the construction of gender norms in Livy. I argue that, in the narrated world, the duality of public and private space appears to be not only present but also fundamental to the way the space of cities is imagined. I also argue that the disparity between public and private space is crucial to the narrative's construction of gender.

As the preceding chapters suggest, the *Ab Urbe Condita* styles some places within the city of Rome as prevalently masculine. Above all, the Forum appears as a political space, where magistrates and senators go about their institutional activities and the people assemble in their role as Roman (male) citizens in *contiones*. In the case of more informal crowds, one might wonder whether the reader is supposed to imagine women alongside men; but, in most cases, the text tends to ignore women's presence in the Forum for religious, commercial, or other reasons. As my analysis will show, when Livy explicitly introduces

---

9   For a review of Livian episodes in which women appear and a discussion of the roles they play see Kowalewski (2002).
10 For a similar thought cf. Fuhrer (2020).
11 For this concept, see e.g. Connell (1987); Connell and Messeschmidt (2005).

one or more women into the Forum (which happens on a few occasions), he presents their presence as unusual; on the contrary, he introduces many male characters as acting in the Forum as part of normal city life.

The Capitol, too, often appears as either a location for politics or as the place where a triumphant general offers his thanks to the god. Its symbolic role as the core of Roman identity is more inclusive; however, when people look at it or talk about it (as is often the case in the *Ab Urbe Condita*), men are always the speakers or focalisers. As for the Campus Martius, its very function as the assembly place of the people in arms provides it with masculine connotations throughout the text. This is also true of military settings such as battlefields and camps, where the narrative usually features no female characters except for (occasionally) prisoners of war (cf. below, p. 242). War, as I have shown in Chapter 3, appears in the *Ab Urbe Condita* as a means for imposing Roman space on foreign landscapes; and that space is the space of the military divisions of the Roman army, an embodiment of Roman (male) valour and discipline.

Since norms are especially visible when they are transgressed, my analysis will focus on episodes that involve transgressions of gender norms and that present them as violations of spatial norms. In most cases, the latter involve breaching the ideal boundary between 'public' and 'private' spaces within a city. In some cases, the text explicitly represents an action in terms of crossing a boundary, in others the notion is implicit but still evident from the language used or the narrative organisation of an account.[12]

Essentially, there are two main types of spatial transgression, which recur throughout the work. The first, which I investigate in section 2, involves men invading other men's private spaces, which can be constituted by a house or by a woman's body (and usually by both simultaneously). This kind of transgression imperils the fundamental solidarity between freeborn male citizens on which the political stability of the State ultimately rests. The second kind of transgression, which is the object of section 3, takes place when one or more women invade or appropriate public space. For the sake of analysis, I distinguish between collective appearances of women in public spaces – which constitute a recurring *topos* in the *Ab Urbe Condita* – and the appearance of individual female characters. However, in section 4, I show that while the text does not grant women a formal right to act independently in public spaces, it suggests that women can play an active role in Roman society if they can move in the liminal space between private and public, without crossing the

---

12　On boundary crossing and gender in Livy see also Fabrizi (2018).

boundary. Sections 5 and 6 focus on two episodes that Livy constructs as general subversions of spatial (and gendered) boundaries, namely the Decemvirate of 450/449 BCE and the Bacchanalian scandal of 186 BCE. Finally, in section 7, I attempt to contextualise the significance of Livy's semantics of space and gender within the overall ideology of his work.

2   Spatial Transgressions 1: Men in (Other Men's) Private Spaces

Feminist readings of Livy have emphasised the role of women as spaces, separating men from each other and defining relationships between men within the community.[13] Since the community relies on solidarity among its male citizens, it is paramount that each male citizen respects the boundaries between himself and others. Consequently, ancient writers often represent tyrannical ambitions and political violence in terms of a transgression of fellow citizens' private spaces – not only the physical space of their household but also the bodies of their wives or children.[14]

Most famously, the space of the house and its transgression plays a major role in Livy's account of the rape of Lucretia and the fall of the Tarquins (1.57–59).[15] The reader first sees Lucretia sitting and spinning wool 'in the heart of her house' (*in medio aedium*, 1.57.9); later, Sextus Tarquinius first enters her house and then her bedroom, the most private room of the house, to rape her (1.58.1–4). Livy never has Lucretia leave her home for the whole duration of the narrative. While Dionysius of Halicarnassus, who was writing at about the same time as Livy and probably relied on the same set of sources, recounts that Lucretia rode to her father's house in Rome after her rape (*Ant. Rom.* 4.66.1–67.2), Livy has her summon her father and husband to her (husband's) house; the men find her in her bedroom (*sedentem maestam in cubiculo*, 1.58.6), where she tells them about her rape, exhorts them to avenge her, and then commits suicide.[16]

---

13   See especially Joplin (1990); Joshel (1992); Matthes (2000). On the Sabine women as spaces, see also Jaeger (1997, pp. 48–49).

14   For lust as a stock character-trait of tyrants in ancient literature, cf. Vasaly (2015, pp. 68–70 and n. 41, with further bibliography; and, on the tyrannical temperament in Livy more generally, pp. 55–76).

15   On the tale of Lucretia see e.g. Joplin (1990); Joshel (1992); Feldherr (1998, pp. 194–202); Kowalewski (2002, pp. 107–137); Langlands (2006, pp. 80–96); Freund (2008); Keegan (2021, pp. 35–44); Helmke (2023, esp. pp. 51–57 and *passim*).

16   On Lucretia's 'fixity in space' see Joshel (1992, p. 122). Ogilvie (1965, p. 219) connects the unity of space with the theatrical quality of Lucretia's story in the *Ab Urbe Condita*.

Feldherr (1998, pp. 194–203) reads Sextus' violation of Collatinus's house and wife as an instance of a more general confounding of the boundary between the private and the public sphere, between domestic life and the state, which characterises the whole reign of Tarquinius Superbus. More recently, Helmke (2023, pp. 51–57) argues that Sextus' incapacity to regulate his own emotions and Lucretia's active role in stirring her menfolk to rebellion signal the inability of men under the monarchy to perform masculine roles as is expected of them: a woman must take the lead to re-establish order by undertaking a temporary transgression of the gender code.[17] It appears significant that, after Lucretia's death, her body is finally brought out of her home to be exposed in the Forum of Collatia (*Elatum domo Lucretiae corpus in forum deferunt*, 1.59.3), where its exposure incites the people to rebel against the Tarquins. In this way, Sextus' private crime is made 'public', that is, turned into a reason for collective action, and this time men take the lead.[18]

I believe one can fully understand the spatial dynamics at work in the text if one considers the crucial role of women in patriarchal societies, which I mentioned at the outset of this paragraph (connecting and separating men through bonds of marriage): as Joshel (1992, p. 27) puts it, 'under patriarchy the ability to control the exchange of women is important because it guarantees the certainty of paternity', on which the patriarchal system is based. The point is that Sextus violates the private space of another man belonging to the same community. In so doing, he shows he has no respect for the bonds of reciprocity that should tie members of a community together: indeed, he is laying claim to the main social capital of another citizen, namely his ability to act as a *pater familias* and produce a genuine offspring.[19] This is the typical behaviour of a tyrant, who holds himself above even the most basic rules of socio-political interaction.

A comparable spatial pattern has been recognised in the tale of Verginia, the plebeian maiden whose attempted rape by the patrician Appius Claudius brings about a popular insurrection and the fall of the Decemvirate in 449 BCE (3.33–48). The story is very similar in its structure to the story of Lucretia (violation of a woman by a powerful man catalyses a change in regime) and scholars have noted that Livy's narrative considers Verginia as an extension of her

---

17 On Lucretia's straddling gender roles cf. Glendinning (2013, pp. 64–65); Benoist (2015).
18 On the significance of the public display of Lucretia's corpse see also Joplin (1990, pp. 64–65).
19 See, again, Joplin (1990, p. 28): 'Thus, Sextus Tarquin's rape of Lucretia is designed, at least in part, to prevent the legitimate paternity of the Collatine line, a lineage thwarted from the onset of the Tarquin reign'.

father's house.[20] Political violence (in this case, the violence of the patrician Decemvirs against the plebeians) is again conceived in terms of violating a private space. As I argue in section 5 below, however, such a transgression is part of a broader and more complex pattern of spatial subversion. Therefore, at present I do not examine it in detail but leave analysis for later.

A spatial dynamic involving male transgressions of private spaces is at work in two other episodes, worth considering in detail. The first is the tale of the maid of Ardea at 4.9–10, which provides the legendary background for the Romans' intervention in an Ardeatine civil conflict in 443 BCE. Livy's narrative starts with harsh criticism of factional strife (4.9.2–3), presented as the cause not only of Ardea's conflict with Rome, but also, more generally, of ruin for 'many peoples' (*multis populis*, 3). The universalising remark suggests the story to follow is to be read in parallel with the narrative of Roman internal conflict, which is among the main themes of the Pentad (and also with an eye to Rome's more recent civil wars).[21]

Book 4 opens, just a few chapters earlier, with a significant instance of discord between factions, the much-debated approval of the Canuleian Law about the right of intermarriage between patricians and plebeians (4.1.1–6.4). While the victory of the tribune Gaius Canuleius is a success of the plebeians, it also constitutes an important symbolic step toward amalgamating the two orders into one; and, as Milnor (2007, pp. 16–17) shows, Canuleius' famous speech advocates the substitution of the boundaries internal to the Roman citizen-body with the boundary that separates the city from the external world. It is worth noting that the above-quoted passage, too, stresses the boundary between internal and external space through the opposition between *intestina arma* and *bella externa*.

In Ardea, like in Rome, marriage is at the centre of a controversy between the aristocracy and the plebs. Two young men, a plebeian and an aristocrat (*nobilis*) ask for a beautiful plebeian girl's hand in marriage. The former has the support of the girl's tutors, who were plebeians themselves and, as Livy writes at 4.9.5, 'mindful of their own faction' (*partium memores*); the latter is favoured by the girl's mother, who wishes for an advantageous marriage (4.9.4–5). The matter soon becomes the focus of factional conflict. The aristocrats support their man (5):

> Adiuvabant eum optimatium studia, per quae in domum quoque puellae certamen partium penetravit.

---

20 Cf. Chapter 1, pp. 60–61.
21 Cf. Weissenborn and Mueller (1896, p. 24).

The zeal of the nobles supported him; thus, factional strife penetrated even into the girl's house.

Once more, the political has entered the domestic sphere, embodied by a house and a woman (in this case, an unmarried girl). This is how, in what immediately follows, Livy relates the breakout of hostilities (4.9.6–8):

> 6. Cum res peragi intra parietes nequisset, ventum in ius est. Postulatu audito matris tutorumque, magistratus secundum parentis arbitrium dant ius nuptiarum. 7. Sed vis potentior fuit; namque tutores, inter suae partis homines de iniuria decreti palam in foro contionati, manu facta virginem ex domo matris rapiunt; 8. adversus quos infestior coorta optimatium acies sequitur accensum iniuria iuvenem.

> 6. Since the matter had proved impossible to settle within the walls of the house, they went to court. After hearing the mother's and the tutors' requests, the magistrates gave the mother the right to decide about the marriage. 7. But violence prevailed; the tutors, after haranguing the people of their own faction openly, in the Forum, about the injustice of the verdict, put together a host of men and abducted the maiden from her mother's house. 8. Against them the throng of noblemen rose even more fiercely and followed the young man, who was enflamed by the outrage.

First, the private matter concerning the girl's marriage cannot be solved within its natural space (*intra parietes*) and is brought before a tribunal (*in ius*). This is the first disturbance of the spatial order. The tutors, outraged for what they see as an *iniuria* (7), make public their grievances in the Forum, thereby making the whole matter even more public (note the adverb *palam*); eventually, they resort to violence, kidnapping the girl from her mother's house. Political conflict has now literally penetrated the house.

What follows is outright war: the *optimates*, who believe they have been wronged (*iniuria* again, 8), move in an army (*acies*) against their fellow citizens. The battle, Livy goes on to write, was bloody. The plebs, 'not at all like the Roman plebs' (*nihil Romanae plebis similis*),[22] marched in arms out of the city, occupied a hill, and launched plundering expeditions into the aristocrats' lands. After that, they besieged the city, a fact which prompts one more grim comment from Livy (4.9.10):

---

22   Livy often remarks on the restraint of the Roman plebs on such occasions as the First and Second Secession: cf. 2.32.4; 3.52.3.

> Nec ulla species cladesque belli abest, velut contacta civitate rabie duorum iuvenum funestas nuptias ex occasu patriae petentium.

> And no appearance or calamity of war was absent, as if the state had been seized by the frenzy of the two young men, who looked for a deadly wedding in the ruin of their fatherland.

The vocabulary of civil war runs deep throughout this passage. *Rabies*, a term whose meanings include 'ferocity', 'rabies', and 'frenzy', is often found concerning civil wars in Latin writers of late republican and imperial times (cf. *TLL* 11.2, coll. 42–51). In the *Ab Urbe Condita*, it appears twice more in contexts of this kind (3.66; 7.40.2), although it is more often used in purely military contexts.[23] In the passage under consideration, the noun implies the metaphor of illness, as is clear from *contacta*. Such a metaphor recurs in the *Ab Urbe Condita* to describe the weakening of the *res publica* through inner conflict or moral decay (or both, since these two factors are often connected).[24]

Occasu patriae is a powerful image of the ruin caused by civil conflict. At 3.52.8, Livy similarly uses *occasu* (...) *urbis* to evoke the spectre of a plebeian invasion of Rome after the death of Verginia and the Second Secession.[25] So, the story of Ardea provides a negative version of Roman civil tensions. The behaviour of the Ardeatine plebs contrasts with the moderation shown by the Roman plebs during both the First and the Second Secession. And yet, Livy's contemporaries will have been reminded that Romans would one day go down the same path.

In what follows (4.10), the text recounts that the plebs and the aristocrats of Ardea called for the help of, respectively, the Volscians and the Romans, that

---

[23] *Rabies* can designate the fury of soldiers or armies against their enemies (e.g. 6.33.4; 28.8.10; 31.17.10), the folly of breaking one's allegiance (e.g. 21.48.3; 28.34.4; 45.36.7), or of committing collective suicide, in the face of enemy conquest (e.g. 31.17.4; 31.18.7).

[24] On Livy's use of sickness and healing as metaphors for the condition of the State see e.g. Moles (2009, pp. 67–73); Scafuro (2009, pp. 339–343). The basis for such metaphors is a concept of the State as a living organism, for which see Mineo (2006, pp. 19–67).

[25] At 26.12.9 *patriae occasum* occurs in a properly military context, where the idea of civil war is absent. However, the notion of a disruption of civil life is active here, too. Livy tells of the Capuan nobles, who, fearing the imminent conquest of their town by the Romans, lost any interest in the administration of the State (*rem publicam deseruerant*, 8) and 'could not be summoned to the Senate' (*neque in senatum cogi poterant, ibid.*). Indeed, they did not even show up in 'in the Forum, or in a public place' (*foro ... aut publico loco*, 9), but rather 'shut themselves in their houses and waited each day for the ruin of their fatherland' (*domibus inclusi patriae occasum ... in dies exspectabant*). Again, the confusion between private and public spaces signals the downfall of a city.

the Romans defeated the Volscian army; and that they eventually re-established order in Ardea by executing the troublemakers. The maid of Ardea disappears from the story after her kidnapping, nor do we know what came of her in the end (did she eventually marry her noble suitor?). Her role is merely to be the catalyser of political violence, like Lucretia before her.[26]

However, things are more complex in this story than in the previous one. In the tale of Lucretia, Sextus Tarquinius's breaching of Collatinus' private space expresses the tyrant's disrespect for the prerogatives of other citizens. In the case of the maid of Ardea, the point is that the girl does *not* have a father or a husband. No 'man of the house' could logically claim control over it as his private space. The ensuing conflict can be read as a struggle for control over that space.

Of course, such a struggle entails a fundamental legal dimension. Ogilvie (1962) argues that the whole tale originated as an exemplification of the right of *conubium* between patricians and plebeians and of some technical issues of the tutorship legislation contained in the Twelve Tables. The fact that the judging magistrate favoured the girl's mother over the tutors affirms the right for a plebeian to marry a patrician and that a tutor's consent was not required for the marriage to be valid.

This may very well be true. On a more general level, however, how different actors deal with boundaries also represents how the forces at work in the state interact with one another – more to the point, how they solve their issues regarding contested prerogatives. Both *optimates* and plebs notably fail to deal with space acceptably in this episode. The *optimates* are the first to turn a private concern into a matter of factional politics by supporting, as a body, the noble suitor and bringing the dispute from the house to the tribunal. The plebs originate a second, much more serious, spatial anomaly in that they substitute violence for legal procedure. After all, the judgement passed by the magistrate represents the capacity of the institutions to take over when a space is contested. For a faction to counter such a judgement by physically violating the girl's (or better, her mother's) house is tantamount to a violent assault on the state itself. In the end, it takes Roman intervention to re-establish order.

There is another much more famous foreign city that functions as a distorted mirror of Rome in the *Ab Urbe Condita*. In Books 24 and 25, Livy narrates the turbulent events that led to the defection of Syracuse during the Second Punic War, which resulted in the Roman siege and conquest of the city. As scholars

---

26   For Lucretia and Verginia's disappearance from Livy's history after the revolt has been set in motion, cf. Joshel (1992, pp. 398–405). Of course, in both cases their disappearance is quite literal, since it coincides with their death.

have noted, the unusually long and detailed narrative that Livy devotes to the political turmoil in Syracuse in Book 24 can be read as an exploration of the damage wrought by tyranny, civic discord, and the lack of suitable leaders.[27]

After the death of the Syracusan king Hiero, a long-time ally of Rome, in 251 BCE, the throne passed to his fifteen-year-old grandson Hieronymus (24.4). As Livy explains, the boy indulged in every possible cruelty and depravity and started negotiations with the Carthaginians (24.5–6). A conspiracy eventually killed him (24.7.1–7), and a republican government replaced him (24.21.1–23.4). Hippocrates and Epicydes, the envoys Hannibal had sent to negotiate with Hieronymus,[28] asked for permission to leave but secretly stirred discontent in the hope of taking power themselves (24.23). In the meanwhile, the husbands of Hiero's daughters and granddaughter made a show of supporting the new government but plotted to re-establish the monarchy; when their plans were discovered, the Syracusan Senate had them killed, and the ruling magistrates decreed that their families be killed, too (24.24–25). However, the ruthless slaughter of one of Hiero's daughters, Heraclia, and her maiden daughters alienated the people (24.26), who elected the Carthaginian envoys Epicydes and Hippocrates among the higher magistrates (24.27.1–4). At first, it seemed that the ruling board of magistrates and the Senate would nonetheless renew the alliance with Rome (24.27.5–28.9), but Hippocrates and Epicydes eventually succeeded in overthrowing their colleagues, taking power, and establishing an alliance with the Carthaginians (24.29–32).

The murder of Heraclia and her daughters, which Livy relates in chapter 26, constitutes one of the dramatic high points of the narrative. Knowing that assassins were coming for her, Heraclia took refuge with her young daughters in the shrine of her house (*in sacrarium ad Penates*, 24.26.2). When the assassins arrived, she begged for mercy – if not for her, at least for her children (24.26.3–11). The men, however, paid no heed to her plea; instead, they 'dragged her from the sanctuary and slit her throat' (*abstractam a penetralibus iugulant*, 24.26.12). The tragic climax of the episode follows immediately (24.26.12–14):

> In virgines deinde respersas matris cruore impetum faciunt, quae alienata mente simul luctu metuque velut captae furore eo cursu se ex sacrario proripuerunt ut si effugium patuisset in publicum, impleturae urbem tumultu fuerint. 13. Tum quoque haud magno aedium spatio inter

---

27 Cf. Jaeger (2003). For yet another type of parallelism between Syracuse and Rome, cf. Rossi (2000).
28 As Livy explains in 24.6.2, Hippocrates and Epicydes has been born in Carthage but were the grandsons of a Syracusan exile.

> medios tot armatos aliquotiens integro corpore evaserunt tenentibusque, cum tot ac tantae validae eluctandae manus essent, sese eripuerunt. 14. Tandem volneribus confectae, cum omnia replessent sanguine, examines conruerunt.
>
> Then they assaulted the maidens, stained as they were with their mother's blood; out of their minds and conquered by both grief and fear, these ran out of the shrine in such a frenzy that, had they had the chance to escape into public space, they would have caused a commotion in the whole city. 13. Even at that moment, although the space of the house was not big, they got away several times unharmed among so many armed men and broke away from those grasping them even if they had to fight against such numerous and strong hands. 14. In the end they were killed by their wounds and, after covering everything with blood, they fell.

In the episode, the emphasis lies upon the unbounded violence that contaminates even the most intimate and sacred place of the house, the *sacrarium*. Indeed, the scene of the girls' murder stresses how the narrow space of the house turns from a haven to a deadly trap.

Jaeger (2007, p. 213) points out the analogies between this episode and the story of Lucretia. In both cases, a woman is assaulted in her house; in both cases, the death is 'a sacrifice (…) to the change in regime'. The Syracusan mob is thus characterised as a tyrant, just as the Tarquins are (p. 226).

Jaeger goes on to argue that there is a notable difference between the tale of Lucretia and that of Heraclia, which she sees as connected to the 'interiority' to which the text assigns the events (p. 227):

> Unlike Lucretia's body, which, brought into the forum, made her rape and death a part of the collective Roman experience, the bodies of these women remain indoors, the end of a strand of covert female influence running from Hiero's last days. Most important of all, no one interprets their deaths so as to harness the emotions of the mob for a purpose beyond immediately satisfying its anger. (…) Neither the political assassination of Hieronymus, Adranodorus, and Themisto, nor the 'sacrifical' [sic] deaths of Heraclia and her daughters become the moral and political beginning from which a free *res publica* can grow.

To fully understand such a difference, one should consider the dissimilar kind of 'tyranny' the two episodes expose. In Book 1, the Tarquins are a royal family which exercises tyrannical rule; the rest of Roman society does not seem to be contaminated by their lust for power. When their tyranny goes too far, invading a man's private space, society rebels against them. In Book 24, the tyrant (Hieronymus) has been dead for some time when Heraclia is killed. What follows Hieronymus' murder is a period of instability in which the people seem unsure of whose side to take. It is the people that murder Heraclia and the very same people that regret it just a moment later. The responsibility for ordering the killings lies with the magistrates, but they are yielding to the mob's bloodlust as much as they are leading it. Shortly before the Heraclia-episode, Livy has Sopater, one of the Syracusan magistrates, address the people to persuade them that the killing of the conspirators has been just. His words so move the crowd that they start shouting that the royal family should be killed. The historian bitterly comments on the 'nature of the crowd', which 'either (…) serves humbly, or dominates with arrogance' and often finds someone to stir its more violent spirits (24.25.8–9).[29] In such a condition, it can hardly be a surprise that no Brutus steps in to transform the woman's violation into a sacrifice for liberty: after all, the crowd cannot rebel against itself.

It is probably more rewarding to think of 'political violence' rather than 'tyranny'. Political violence is a broader concept, which includes tyranny – the single-handed invasion of citizens' property or rights by a powerful ruler – but also other disturbances of the social order, such as factional strife or mob rule. Invading private spaces can stand for all these types of political violence. The Heraclia-episode exemplifies the violent excesses arising in politically unstable situations when the worst instincts of the mob are given free rein.

A similar pattern of boundary transgression can even express disturbance of the political order on the larger scale of international politics. A famous episode from Livy's account of the Second Punic War shows how the patriarchal spatial structure outlined intersects with other aspects of the Roman spatial order. In 30.12–15, the historian relates the tragic death of Sophoniba, daughter to the Carthaginian general Hasdrubal, son of Gisgo, and wife to the Numidian king Syphax, an ally of Carthage.[30] After Syphax is defeated in battle by the joined forces of Gaius Laelius and his Numidian ally Masinissa (30.11), the latter rides to Syphax's capital, Cirta, to take possession of it (30.12.1–10). There, in Syphax's palace, he finds Sophoniba, who, reminding him of their

---

29 8. *Ea natura multitudinis est: aut servit humiliter aut superbe dominatur; libertatem, quae media est, nec †stuperet† modice nec habere sciunt; 9. et non ferme desunt irarum indulgentes ministri, qui avidos atque intemperantes suppliciorum animos ad sanguinem et caedes inritent.*

30 The story of Syphax' wedding with Sophoniba and of his subsequent shift of allegiance from Rome to Carthage is narrated at 29.23.

shared African origins, begged him not to give her up to the Romans – if in no other way, then at least by allowing her to die (30.12.11–16). Masinissa was moved by her prayers and instantly fell in love with her; he thus decided to marry her, a move which – as he thought – would protect her from Roman punishment (30.12.17–22). On hearing the news, Scipio was dismayed; when Masinissa arrived, he reproached him for taking such an initiative and depriving the Roman people of their captive (30.13–14). Masinissa recognised his mistake and sought a way to keep his loyalty to Rome and his promise to his wife. After long and painful ponderings, he sent her a poisoned drink so that death could free her from Roman hands; Sophoniba drank it without even flinching (30.15.1–8). Scipio consoled the heartbroken Masinissa by naming him king and lavishing various honours upon him (30.15.9–14).

The episode has been read, among other things, as reflecting modules of tragic historiography;[31] as using a female character to underline male characters' strength and weaknesses, and thereby contrasting Roman ideals of self-control and Numidian weakness;[32] and as alluding to the personality of another foreign queen, Cleopatra.[33] In what follows, I take a different perspective by analysing the narrative in terms of gendered space.

In fact, the space where the episode develops is crucial. The scene is first set at 30.12.5:

> Cirta caput regni Syphacis erat, eoque se ingens vis hominum ex fuga contulerat.
>
> Cirta was the capital of Syphax's kingdom, and there a great mass of people had gone in their flight.

Masinissa persuades Laelius to let him go ahead and take possession of the city. Having reached Cirta, he summons the leading citizens to a parley and shows them the captive Syphax in shackles. The text now leads the reader along Masinissa's pathway into Cirta (30.12.9–10):

> 9. Tum ad spectaculum tantum foedum comploratio orta, et partim pavore moenia sunt deserta, partim repentino consensu gratiam apud victorem quaerentium patefactae portae. 10. Et Masinissa, praesidio circa

---

31   Cf. the discussion in De Franchis (2015), who criticises this line of interpretation.
32   E.g. Helmke (2023, pp. 187–211).
33   Cf. e.g. Haley (1990); De Franchis (2015); Fabres-Serris (2021).

portas opportunaque moenium dimisso ne cui fugae pateret exitus, ad regiam occupandam citato vadit equo.

9. Then laments broke out at such an awful spectacle: the city walls were abandoned by some out of fear and the gates were opened by the sudden unanimous decision of those others who sought the victor's favour. 10. And Masinissa, after sending garrisons around the gates and convenient spots on the walls, so that nobody could leave the town and flee, rode swiftly to take possession of the palace.

The narrative creates suspense by leading the reader, step by step, from the city walls to the heart of the city, the royal palace. It is at his very entry into the palace that Masinissa (and the reader) first encounters Sophoniba (30.12.11–12):

11. Intranti vestibulum in ipso limine Sophoniba, uxor Syphacis filia Hasdrubalis Poeni, occurrit; et cum in medio agmine armatorum Masinissam insignem cum armis tum cetero habitu conspexisset, regem esse, id quod erat, rata, genibus advoluta eius 12. 'Omnia quidem ut possis' inquit 'in nos di dederunt virtusque et felicitas tua'.

11. As he was entering the vestibule, on the very threshold Sophoniba, wife of Syphax and daughter of the Carthaginian Hasdrubal, rushed to meet him. After she saw Masinissa amongst the throng of armed men, notable as he was both for his armour and for his overall appearance, she rightly inferred that he was the king. Throwing herself at his knees, she said: 'The gods and your own valour and fortune have granted you full power over us'.

There follows the woman's eloquent plea to Masinissa. After promising not to let her fall into Roman hands, the king finally enters the palace (*Data dextra in id quod petebatur obliganda fidei, in regiam concedit*, 30.12.18).

Livy's narrative strongly emphasises the liminality of the setting.[34] Masinissa is entering a royal palace and the private space that once belonged

---

34   Polybius' narrative of these events, which is likely to have been Livy's source, is unfortunately lost. App. *Pun.* 27.111, whose narrative appears to be largely independent from the Polybian tradition (cf. Goukowsky and Lancel, p. 2002), has Sophoniba send messengers to Masinissa, to explain that she had been forced to marry Syphax. Zonar. 9.13 simply states that Sophoniba 'was also there', namely in Cirta and then recounts how Masinissa (who, in this version of the story, had once been her fiancée) rushed to embrace her and married her on the spot; given the brevity of his account, however, we cannot know

to his enemy – a space to which Sophoniba is integral. Of course, that act per se is not problematic: he is entering as a victor and on behalf of the Roman people. Problems arise, however, as the continuation of the narrative shows, when it comes to deciding who that space now belongs to.

After reporting the wedding, Livy writes of Laelius' arrival in Cirta and his indignant reaction to the news. The Roman general tried 'to tear her from the wedding couch and send her off to Scipio, along with Syphax and the other prisoners' (30.12.21). Masinissa, however, obtained that judgement on the matter be left to Scipio. Syphax was thus sent to Scipio's camp, while Laelius and Masinissa remained behind to subdue the other cities of the kingdom.

Chapter 13 describes Syphax's arrival at the camp. When Scipio asks him the reason for his breach of loyalty towards Rome, the king, torn by jealousy, shifts the blame for his folly onto his wife (30.13.11–13): the moment he had forsaken all 'private bonds of hospitality and public treaties' (*hospitia privata et publica foedera omnia*, 11), he states, had been when he had 'welcomed a Carthaginian wife into his house' (*cum Carthaginiensem matronam domum acceperit, ibid.*). Syphax represents Sophoniba as a destructive force (*furiam pestemsque*, 12) lurking within his house and palace, ultimately devastating it: 'Those wedding torches had set his palace aflame' (*Illis nuptialibus facibus regiam conflagrasse suam*). Once again, the woman is associated with the space of the house, although, in Syphax's words, her influence extends from the house to the public domain. However, the king continues, she has now passed into Massinissa's 'house' (*domum ac penates*, 13), which, in his hopes, she will also destroy. Clearly, *domus ac penates* here indicates the household in a metaphorical way since Sophoniba has, in fact, not moved. The *regia* has passed into Masinissa's hands – thus becoming his *domus*. But, one should ask, did Masinissa have any right to make Syphax's house his own?

Scipio's rebuke of Masinissa provides a clear answer to this question. In the first part of the speech (30.14.4–8), the Roman general invites his ally to beware of the greatest possible danger for a young man, namely 'the pleasures that are everywhere around us' (*ab circumfusis undique voluptatibus*, 6). 'The man who has curbed and subdued them through his self-control has won a much greater glory and a greater victory than we have after defeating Syphax', Scipio states (7). He sets up his own 'moderation and restraining of his own passions' (*temperantia et continentia libidinum*, 5), of which he gave proof by not violating any of his captives in Spain, as an example for Masinissa.

---

whether Cassius Dio's version was more similar to Livy's. Be that as it may, the particular emphasis the *Ab Urbe Condita* places on the threshold of the palace remains notable.

In the second part of the speech, Scipio shifts from a broader moral discourse to their present situation (30.14.9–10):

> 9. Syphax populi Romani auspiciis victus captusque est. Itaque ipse coniunx regnum ager oppida homines qui incolunt, quicquid denique Syphacis fuit praeda populi Romani est. 10. Et regem coniugemque eius, etiamsi non civis Carthaginiensis esset, etiamsi non patrem eius imperatorem hostium videremus, Roman oporteret mitti, ac senatus populique Romani de ea iudicium atque arbitrium esse, quae regem socium nobis alienasse atque in arma egisse praecipitem dicatur.

> 9. Syphax was defeated and taken prisoner under the auspices of the Roman people. Therefore, he, his wife, his kingdom, his lands, his towns, the people who inhabit them, in short, all things that belonged to Syphax are the spoils of the Roman people. 10. Even if Sophoniba had not been a Carthaginian citizen, even if we did not see her father as the enemy commander, it would still be proper that the king and his wife be sent to Rome; the Roman Senate and people have the right to judge and decide over the woman who, as they say, has alienated an allied king from us and launched him headlong into war.

Scipio's explanation has much to do with control over space. Since Syphax is a king, such control extends well beyond that exercised by individual Roman citizens over their households. Syphax himself and 'all things that belonged to Syphax' – so Scipio's reasoning goes – are now the spoils of war of the Roman people, by whom he was defeated. By taking Syphax's wife, Masinissa has invaded a space that belongs to Rome.

Strictly speaking, of course, it is not the crossing of the physical threshold of the palace that subverts the order. Masinissa would have crossed it anyway, as he had already entered Syphax's kingdom and city, which were also, according to Scipio, spoils of the Roman people. However, the way Livy describes the scene makes that gesture a symbol of another kind of boundary-breach, which endangers Roman control over the conquered space. If the text can make the gesture symbolic, this is – I argue – because the narrative has already set up the transgression of gendered boundaries as such a convincing way to talk about power relationships.

Here, as in similar stories, transgression is the result of an incapacity to tame sexual desire. Livy explains Masinissa's sudden passion for Sophoniba through the Numidians' being particularly prone to lust (*ut est genus Numidarum in venerem praeceps*, 30.12.18); this constitutes a subversion of the relations between victor and defeated, since, in the historian's words, 'the victor was conquered by passion for his prisoner' (*amore captivae victor captus, ibid.*). Levene (2010, pp. 255–260) stresses the importance of this ethnic stereotype[35] and argues that, here as elsewhere, Livy was pointing to the dangers implicit in Rome's incorporation of foreign peoples. The notion of sexual desire as a force endangering the Roman spatial order, however, is clearly apparent from almost the beginning of the *Ab Urbe Condita* and extends beyond anxieties about mixed ethnicities. In Lucretia's story, the transgressive force is *libido*,[36] the opposite of the *temperantia* that Scipio sees as the cardinal virtue. It is true that, as Haley (1990) shows, Livy's characterisation of Numidians remains quite distinct, among other things, in using the noun *venus*, rather than *libido* or *amor*, to denote lust. Still, Livy probably built upon a contemporary stereotype as a cue for an overarching moral discourse.[37] In his speech, Scipio pairs *temperantia* with *continentia libidinum* (30.14.5) – which leads us back to the core of Roman moral discourse.[38] Interestingly, too, in the Heraclia-episode, in which sexual desire does not play any role, the narrator defines the mob as *avidos atque intemperantes suppliciorum* (24.25.9; see above). They also lack *temperantia*, being moved by desires they cannot control.

Such inability is dangerous because it puts in doubt those bonds of solidarity, or hierarchical structures, on which (patriarchal) society rests. The episode of Sophoniba shows the reader that a proper way of dealing with space and boundaries, and above all, awareness of who those spaces ultimately belong to, is crucial not just to civic life but also to the broader political order of the Roman world.

---

35   On this stereotype see Haley (1990); on ethnic stereotypes in general in the *Ab Urbe Condita*, Bernard (2015). Livy also mentions the Numidians' lustfulness at 29.23.4, with reference to Syphax' passion for Sophoniba.
36   Cf. *mala libido*, 1.57.10; *victrix libido*, 1.58.5; *de vi ac libidine Sex. Tarquini*, 1.59.8; and for the same theme in the similar tale of Verginia, *Ap. Claudium virginis plebeiae stuprandae libido cepit*, 3.44.2; *regnum vestrae libidini*, 3.45.8; *decemvir alienatus ad libidinem animo*, 3.48.1. *Amor* is also used in a similar way: *amore ardens*, 1.58.2; *amore amens*, 3.44.4; *tanta vis amentiae verius quam amoris animum turbaverat*, 3.47.4. See also Haley (p. 1990, 376).
37   See Haley (1990, p. 376): 'The characterization of the Numidians as a passionate people clearly suited the moral purposes of the *Ab Urbe Condita*. (...) Masinissa must be passionate *in order* to highlight Scipio's restraint'.
38   For the inclination towards bodily passions as a trait of tyrants see Mineo (2006, p. 64); on *temperantia* as one of the cardinal virtues of Livy's political philosophy, *ibid*. pp. 67–71.

3 Spatial Transgressions II: Women in Public Space

A second, and potentially even more subversive, transgression occurs in the *Ab Urbe Condita* when women step out of the private spaces where they belong and into a public or semi-public spaces. As I have argued in a previous study (Fabrizi, 2018b), the motif is developed throughout the work through the repetition of scenes in which groups of women are shown leaving their homes and invading the streets, the temples, and, in some cases, the Forum in Rome. I shall briefly summarise that argument in the following paragraphs since it is crucial to my subsequent discussion.

In the *Ab Urbe Condita*, groups of women appear in Roman public space for a rather restricted number of reasons: as a reaction to events of public interest, such as military victories, defeats, or plagues (for instance, by crowding the temples and streets to supplicate the gods, or by asking for news about their loved ones);[39] as participants in publicly decreed religious ceremonies;[40] and, in two cases, in an attempt to influence public deliberations that directly affect them.[41] Crucial to Livy's representation of such scenes is a concern about the public control of women's movement through the city's space. In the context of religious ceremonies, such as the reparatory rituals in honour of Juno Regina in 207 BCE (27.37) or the arrival of the Magna Mater in 204 BCE (29.14.5–14), the text stresses that the women were part of well-orchestrated state pageants: their movement through the city is portrayed as orderly and dignified. When it comes to spontaneous appearances in public space, on the other hand, the narrative emphasises the disorderly and transgressive nature of women's actions through some recurrent textual strategies. First, the text tends to present such episodes as exceptional, even in cases in which the women's appearance actually followed an established pattern of behaviour. Secondly, the narrative sets up a contrast between the space of the home and the 'public' one of the city.[42] Finally, it presents women's movement as chaotic and emo-

---

39 Cf. e.g. 4.40.2–3; 5.18.11–12; 22.7.7; 26.9.6–8; 27.50.5. The archetype of this kind of intervention is the plight of the Sabine women, who throw themselves between the warring lines of their husbands and fathers, at 1.13.1–2.
40 See, in particular, 23.37; 29.14.5–14.
41 One is the pleading of the women in Forum for their relatives who were taken prisoners at Cannae, at 22.60.1–2; the second is the account of the demonstrations for the repeal of the Oppian Law, in 195 BCE (34.1.1–8.3; see below).
42 Cf. e.g. *ex maestis paulo ante domibus … procurreretur in vias*, 4.40.2; *matronarum, quae ex domo conciverat publicus pavor*, 5.18.11; *matronas publico arceant continerique intra suum quamque limen cogant*, 22.55.6; *ploratus mulierum non ex privatis solum domibus exaudiebantur, sed undique matronae in publicum effusae circa deum delubra discurrunt*, 26.9.7.

tional, their physical appearance as dishevelled. All the scenes concerning the public appearances of women in the *Ab Urbe Condita* can be read as being on a spectrum that ranges from rigidly supervised ceremonial activities to spontaneous and potentially problematic ones. What is common to all these episodes is that women's public appearance signals a political or social crisis. Even the above-mentioned religious ceremonies are to be read as efforts to re-establish the *pax deorum* at critical moments of the Second Punic War: a temporary and controlled boundary breach allows the reconstitution of order.

The pattern of crisis, spatial transgression, and reconstitution is particularly prominent in a famous episode which does not play out within the city, but does stage the breaching of two boundaries: that of gender norms, and that between the space within and the space without the city. At 2.39–40, Livy narrates how the patrician Gnaeus Marcius Coriolanus, whose opposition to the plebs had led to his trial and exile, waged war on Rome at the head of a Volscian army.[43] Three embassies sent by the Roman Senate to convince him to desist met with no success (39). In the end, the Roman *matronae* asked Coriolanus' mother Veturia and his wife Volumnia to intercede; an embassy of women, led by Veturia reached the Volscian camp. The view of his mother and wife in distress, together with the old woman's reproaching words, finally bent Coriolanus' proud will (40).

The story is one of many showing the dangers of inner discord for the safety of the Roman community as a whole.[44] The struggles between patricians and plebs lead to Coriolanus' trial, and Coriolanus' concern for his own wounded honour turns him into a traitor to his fatherland. Once more, the fundamental boundary between inner and outer space, between citizen and enemy, is imperilled, so women must temporarily step into a normally male realm to re-establish order.[45]

Livy starts by saying that 'the matrons went *en masse* to Veturia, Corionalus' mother, and Volumnia, his wife' (2.40.1).[46] While the parallel narratives by Dionysius of Halicarnassus (*Ant. Rom.* 8.39–43) and Plutarch (*Vit. Cor.* 33) attribute the initiative to a woman named Valeria and describe her plea to the two women in detail, Livy's text omits this information, thus focusing on Veturia and Volumnia. This also has some effects on the spatial dynamics of the episode. Dionysius opens his account with a portrayal of women's

---

43   On Coriolanus' tale see e.g. David (2001); Kowalewski (2002, pp. 34–41); Cornell (2003); Mustakallio (2011 and 2012); Dubosson-Sbriglione (2021, with further bibliography).
44   Se e.g. Ogilvie (1965, pp. 314–315).
45   On crisis resolution in this episode, see e.g. Mustakallio (2012).
46   *Tum matronae ad Veturiam matrem Coriolani Volumniamque uxorem frequentes coeunt.*

interventions in public space of the kind frequent in the *Ab Urbe Condita*: the women, he writes, 'abandoned the sense of propriety that confined them at home and ran to the temples of the gods' (8.39.1), in particular to that of Jupiter on the Capitol.[47] This allows the Greek historian to have Valeria undertake an act which, on the obverse, women do *not* usually perform in the *Ab Urbe Condita*:[48] namely, the holding of a public speech (to the other women) in public space – indeed, on the very steps of the Capitoline temple.[49] By summarising the women's deliberations in just one sentence and by focusing on the following scene of the story, Livy highlights a different kind of spatial transgression, in which women step into the (usually male) space of war outside the city. He even expresses uncertainty as to whether the *matronae*'s visit to Veturia and Volumnia was spontaneous or the result of a public deliberation; what matters is the ensuing embassy.[50]

Veturia and Volumnia, followed by the other women, go to the enemy camp (*in castra hostium*, 2.40.2), emphasising that 'since the men could not defend the city, the women [may] defend it with prayers and tears' (*quoniam armis viri defendere urbem non possent, mulieres precibus lacrimisque defenderent, ibid.*). A significant kind of inversion is at play here: the consequence of Coriolanus' stubbornness is that men are unable to defend the boundaries of the city, so that women have to breach those very same boundaries to defend them in another way.

The idea of inversion and the opposition between the space within the walls and that without is prominent in Veturia's speech to her son, too. The old woman starts by emphatically asking him whether she should consider herself as a mother or a prisoner in his camp (*captiva materne castris tuis sim*, 2.40.5). Then, in a series of direct questions, she vividly describes Coriolanus' boundary-breach (2.40.7):

> Non tibi, quamvis infesto animo et minaci perveneras, ingredienti fines ira cecidit? Non, cum in conspectu Roma fuit, succurrit: intra illa moenia domus ac penates mei sunt, mater coniunx liberique?

> Did not your wrath abandon you as you were entering our territory, although you had come with a hostile and threatening spirit? Did it not come into your mind, as Rome appeared before your eyes: 'Within those

---

47   καταλιποῦσαι τῆς οἴκοι μονῆς τὸ εὐπρεπὲς ἔθεον ἐπὶ τὰ τεμένη τῶν θεῶν. Cf. Plut. *Vit. Cor.* 33.1.
48   Cf. below, section 4.
49   Dion. Hal. *Ant. Rom.* 8.39.2.
50   *Id publicum consilium an muliebris timor fuerit, parum inuenio*, 2.40.1.

walls are my house and my household gods, my mother, my wife, and my children'?

Not only has Coriolanus confused city space and outer military space by entering the Roman *fines*; a related aspect of spatial disorder is that women now appear out of place. In Veturia's words, the logical place for women is 'within the walls' and in the house; but now they are in the camp, where logically they could only be prisoners of war – and if they are in the camp, it is precisely because Coriolanus was unable to stop at the boundary of his fatherland, of recognising his city as a space which cannot be the object of military conquest.

It is probably the evidence of such a mislocation of his womenfolk which makes Coriolanus abandon his war on Rome (*retro ab urbe castra movit*, 'he moved the camp back and away from the city', 10). In this way, the women's boundary-breach has rectified a much more dangerous transgression on Coriolanus' part. The Senate, as Livy writes at 2.40.11–12, gave the women their due for their courageous intervention: the temple of Fortuna Muliebris ('Women's Fortune' on the Via Latina, that is, on the site where the women had met Coriolanus) was built and dedicated as a reminder of it (*monumento quoque quod esset*, 12).

Episodes of the kind hitherto considered expose the fundamental contradiction that characterises any patriarchal society: on the one hand, women are required to actively contribute to the stability of the society and, in so doing, to act as a well-defined group within it; on the other, the relationships between women that thereby come into being are potentially dangerous for the system, and have to be constantly kept in check. Such a contradiction is most clearly at work in the famous account of the debate about the repeal of the Oppian Law (*Lex Oppia*) in 34.1.1–8.3. The matter under contention was a sumptuary law passed in 215 BCE during the Second Punic War, which limited women's display of certain luxury items. In 195 BCE, the tribunes of the plebs Marcus Fundanius and Lucius Valerius proposed repealing the law, which the regained prosperity of the Roman State had made anachronistic. Some senators, however, chief among them the consul Marcus Porcius Cato, opposed the repeal on moral grounds. Matrons from Rome and neighbouring towns demonstrated in the streets of Rome, pressuring the senators into voting for the repeal. In the end, the law was abrogated despite Cato's staunch opposition.

Livy's narrative of the episode emphasises the matrons' invasion of the entrances to the Forum, where they pleaded with the senators going to the Curia to vote. The two contending speeches of Valerius and Cato, which form the bulk of the narrative, provide two diverging interpretations of the women's behaviour. Valerius sees the matrons as an integral part of Roman society: they have a right to participate in the benefits of conquest as well as to intervene publicly for the welfare of the State. Conversely, Cato underlines the dangers of the women's transgression of their spatial, moral, and social boundaries.[51] The text sets Valerius as the winner in the debate by giving him the most effective speech,[52] but the ensuing events might suggest that some of Cato's arguments were not so far off the truth. At 34.8.1–2, the external narrator reports that 'on the next day an even greater crowd of women poured out into the open' (*aliquanto maior frequentia mulierum postero die sese in publicum effudit*) and 'besieged the doors' (*ianuas obsederunt*) of the tribunes who had vetoed the repeal, until the latter were all but forced to capitulate. This intervention on the women's part causes a paradoxical, if temporary, inversion: now it is women who force the tribunes into their homes.[53] The reader thus receives the impression that Roman society is changing and that the increasing involvement of matrons in the life of the State is part of that change – but also that that change itself implies potential threats to social stability.[54]

The episodes I have recalled concern groups of women who act collectively. Their behaviour is consistent from one episode to another, and their appearance is a structural motif through which the text expresses some fundamental concepts about space and gender. In the remaining part of this section, I analyse an episode in which the *Ab Urbe Condita* represents an individual female character in the public space.

The narrative under examination concerns Tullia, daughter to King Servius Tullius and wife to Tarquinius Superbus, who, according to Livy, played a major role in Servius' assassination and Tarquinius' rise to power. The story is told at 1.46–48. Servius Tullius had two daughters, that he married to the two sons (or grandsons)[55] of his predecessor Tarquinius Priscus. One of the daughters was good-natured; the other was ambitious and cruel; the same was true

---

51 For a comparison of the logic and rhetoric of both speeches, see Milnor (2005, pp. 154–179).
52 Cf. McClain (2021).
53 Cf. Riggsby (2009, pp. 161–164); Fabrizi (2018, pp. 39–42).
54 On the Oppian Law episode and its significance in Livy's discourse on change and morality, see also e.g. Luce (1977, pp. 251–253); Russell (2016b, pp. 169–170); Keegan (2021, pp. 85–93).
55 Livy 1.46.4 expresses doubts whether the two Tarquins were the sons or the grandsons of Tarquinius Priscus, but he states that, according to most historians, they were his sons. Dion. Hal. *Ant. Rom.* 4.7 and 4.30.2–3 criticizes Fabius Pictor and other unnamed historians for considering them Tarquinius Priscus' sons despite the chronological implausibility of it.

of the Tarquin brothers. Chance had it that the evil Tullia married the good Tarquinius and the evil Tarquinius the good Tullia. However, the two ambitious natures were soon attracted to each other; after killing their respective spouses, they got married and started plotting against Servius. Tarquinius, soon to be known as Superbus ('the Proud'), declared himself king; when Servius Tullius intervened to protest the coup, his son-in-law first threw him down the steps of the Curia and then sent his men to finish him off as the old man attempted to flee. Far from showing any remorse, Tullia rode to the Forum in her carriage to hail her husband as king.

Here again, as in the tale about Lucretia, a defining feature of Tarquinius' monarchy is a subverted relationship between family concerns and the state's interests.[56] From the outset, the plot to assassinate Servius Tullius develops within the private space of Tarquinius' house.[57] Livy sees Tullia as the real originator of the plot (*initium turbandi omnia a femina ortum est*, 1.46.7). Tarquinius was a 'young man of fierce spirit' (*iuvenis ardentis animi*); still, it was his wife who, at home, constantly urged him to conquer the throne (*domi uxore Tullia inquietum animum stimulante*, 1.46.2). One can add that Tullia's enflaming speech to Tarquinius at 1.47.1–6 strongly stresses the role of the *domus* (4):

> Non tibi ab Corintho nec ab Tarquiniis, ut patri tuo, peregrina regna moliri necesse est: di te penates patriique et patris imago et domus regia et in domo regale solium et nomen Tarquinium creat et vocat regem.[58]

> You do not have to strive for a foreign kingdom from Corinth or Tarquinii, as your father did; your paternal and household gods, the portrait of your father, the royal palace and, within the royal palace, the throne and name of Tarquin make and name you king.

The domestic setting of this part of the story has a counterpart in Tullia's appearance in the Forum at 1.48.5–7:

> 5. Creditur, quia non abhorret a cetero scelere, admonitu Tulliae id factum. Carpento certe, id quod satis constat, in forum invecta nec

---

56 Cf. Feldherr (1998, pp. 187–193).
57 As Feldherr (1998, p. 191) puts it, '[s]ince the more intimate bonds of family now determine the course of public affairs, Livy's narrative is continually pulled away from the public spaces of the city into the private, unseen realm of the domus'.
58 Cf. *Si sibi eum quo digna esset di dedissent virum, domi se propediem visuram regnum fuisse quod apud patrem videat*, 1.46.8. Moreover, it is later said that Tarquinius *domesticis consiliis rem publicam admnistravit* (1.49.7).

reverita coetum virorum evocavit virum e curia regemque prima appellavit. 6. A quo facessere iussa ex tanto tumultu cum se domum reciperet pervenissetque ad summum Cyprium vicum, ubi Dianium nuper fuit, flectenti carpentum dextra in Urbium clivum ut in collem Esquiliarium eveheretur, restitit pavidus atque inhibuit frenos is qui iumenta agebat iacentemque dominae Servium trucidatum ostendit. 7. Foedum inhumanumque inde traditur scelus monumentoque locus est – Sceleratum vicum vocant – quo amens, agitantibus furiis sororis ac viri, Tullia per patris corpus carpentum egisse fertur, partemque sanguinis ac caedis paternae cruento vehiculo, contaminata ipsa respersaque, tulisse ad penates suos virique sui, quibus iratis malo regni principio similes propediem exitus sequerentur.

5. It is believed, since it is not inconsistent with the rest of her crimes, that it was done at Tullia's suggestion. What is certain is that she rode into the Forum on a carriage – this is well attested – and, in no awe of the crowd of men, she called her husband out of the Curia and was the first to hail him as king. 6. He ordered her to go away. She rode back home from such a great commotion and reached the top of the *Cyprius vicus*, where the shrine of Diana was until not long ago; as her carriage turned right into the *Urbius clivus* to ride to the Esquiline, the driver stopped in fear, held the bridles back, and showed his mistress the massacred corpse of Servius lying on the earth. 7. An abominable, inhuman crime is then reported and the place bears memory of it: they call it *Sceleratus vicus*. It is said that Tullia, out of her mind and impelled by the furies of her sister and her husband, drove the carriage over her father's body; the carriage was covered in blood and she herself was stained and sprinkled with it; so she carried part of her father's blood and murder to her and her husband's household gods, due to whose wrath the evil beginning of the reign would be prematurely followed by a similar end.

The episode was no invention of Livy's since we also find it in Dionysius of Halicarnassus (4.39), who followed the same sources;[59] however, Livy's narrative brings out the breach of gendered boundaries in a way that the Greek historian does not.[60]

---

59 Varro *Ling.* 5.159 also mentions Tullia's ride over her father's corpse as an explanation of the noun *vicus sceleratus*.
60 Note also that there is nothing like Livy's insistence on the *domus* in Dionysius' account of the events leading to Servius' assassination (Dion. Hal. *Ant. Rom.* 4.28–38).

Tullia has something in common with other women who appear in public space in the *Ab Urbe Condita*. First, the text emphatically casts the space of the Forum where Tullia enters as a masculine space through the repetition and polyptoton of the noun *vir* at 1.48.5: *in forum invecta nec reverita coetum virorum evocavit virum e curia*. Similarly, at 22.60.2, the women who enter the Forum to plead for relatives who have been taken prisoners at Cannae are said to have joined 'the crowd of men' in the Forum because of fear and necessity (*Feminas quoque metus ac necessitas in foro turbae virorum immiscuerat*): while the presence of women in the Forum was probably normal in Roman everyday life, Livy's phrasing constructs it as exceptional. Moreover, if not in the scene of her appearance in the Forum, at least in the following account of her riding over Servius Tullius' corpse, the narrative emphasises her emotional condition: Tullia is out of her mind (*amens*) and prey to the furies of her sister and first husband. Thus, she displays the irrational element that pertains to most public appearances of women and to men's transgressions of boundaries in the *Ab Urbe Condita*.[61]

However, the episode is unique in one respect: it is the only passage in the surviving books where an individual woman consciously enters the Forum to express a political point. The collective scenes I have considered above draw on the same notions concerning gendered boundaries but are fundamentally different for several reasons. First, when groups of women enter the Forum – as with the women in Book 22 or the Sabine women, who rush onto the battlefield that will become the Forum to separate their fathers and husbands, at 1.13.1–2 – they do so to plead on behalf of their male relatives, or on behalf of concord between their male relatives. While their presence signals an existing crisis, it is not – in itself – deviant behaviour (indeed, it can be functional to solving the crisis). Even the matrons who support the repeal of Oppian Law in Book 34 do not physically enter the Forum but rather occupy its entrances.[62]

Secondly, the very collective nature of such interventions means that they constitute acts or claims that pertain to women as a distinct component of Roman society. Tullia, on the other hand, claims public recognition of her role as a kingmaker. While the collective role of women in the *res publica* can, to some degree and under specific conditions, be accepted – indeed, it can even be beneficial to the state – the *Ab Urbe Condita* casts a woman's wielding of

---

61 The expression recalls 1.47.7, where Tarquinius is *mulieribus instinctus furiis*, i.e. spurred by Tullia's entreaties and reproaches; although, as Ogilvie (1965, p. 190) comments, *furiis* here means 'frenzy' rather than the actual furies, the two passages create a consistent portrait of Tullia.

62 Cf. Riggsby (2009); Fabrizi (2018).

personal power as inherently disruptive. Livy's narrative does not just happen to relate Servius' death, Tullia's appearance in the Forum, and her ride over her father's corpse together in a closely woven episode: Tullia's breaching of the masculine space of the Forum finds a counterpart in her transgression of the ultimate boundary – her father's body. It should be noted that in this episode Tullia is not, like other women in the *Ab Urbe Condita*, addressing Tarquinius in a supportive role as a pleading wife (or even as a reproaching mother) but is appropriating the prerogative of bestowing, or at least validating, her husband's royal power by hailing him as king.

In other words, women's active role in the State is justified by – and limited to – the crucial function they fulfil, as wives and mothers, in the reproduction of the patriarchal system itself. A woman's agency as a person wielding power for herself has no place in Livy's narrated Rome.

4   Liminal Spaces

While the *Ab Urbe Condita* denies women a direct claim to agency in public spaces, it leaves the door open for more subtle forms of influence exercised at the boundary between the 'private' and the 'public'. In this section, I argue that women are represented as successfully wielding power by acting in liminal spaces, without breaching the boundary, in at least two episodes in the surviving books.

The first episode concerns the rise to power of the sixth Roman king, Servius Tullius, through the manoeuvring of his mother-in-law, queen Tanaquil (1.41). According to Livy, Servius Tullius was born in Tarquinius Priscus's palace, the son of a prisoner of war from Corniculum who Tanaquil had spared from slavery because of her noble origins. Another version of the story, which Livy mentions only to discard it, considered Servius the son of a slave of the royal household (1.39.5–6). Tanaquil singled Servius out for kingship when he was still a child because of an omen that she had interpreted as portending his royal destiny;[63] following Tanaquil's advice, Tarquinius gave Servius an education worthy of a prince and later married him to his daughter (1.39.1–4). The preference the royal couple showed for Servius exasperated the sons of the previous king, Ancus Marcius, who Tarquinius had excluded from their father's succession years earlier. They had hoped to regain the throne at Tarquinius'

---

63   While the boy was sleeping, his head burst into flame without any harm coming to him; the flame suddenly went away as soon as Servius woke up. For this prodigy see also e.g. Cic. *Div.* 1.121; Dion. Hal. *Ant. Rom.* 4.2.4; Plin. *HN* 2.241.

death, but now they saw their birthright once more denied them – and by a prisoner's son to boot. Therefore, they plotted against the king and had him murdered in his palace (1.40).

In the turmoil that ensued – as Livy goes on to narrate in 1.41 – Tanaquil ensured that the throne was handed down to Servius Tullius without bloodshed. She had the palace doors shut, thereby cutting off communication between the space within and that without the *regia*, and hid her husband's death from the Roman people. By pretending that Tarquinius was recovering from his wounds, she made it possible for Servius to act in the king's stead. Only after his authority had been established was the news of Tarquinius' death announced to the people – and in the same breath, Servius was presented as his successor.

The climactic point of the narrative is constituted by the two speeches through which the queen handles the crisis. In the first, which she delivers privately to Servius (and which Livy quotes in direct speech at 1.41.3), she exhorts her son-in-law not to let his chance at royal power slip away; she reminds him of the signs of divine favour bestowed on him, and of the importance of individual merits, not ancestry, in making a good king. This brief address, which displays Tanaquil's rhetorical ability and energetic character, corresponds to a widespread motif in Livy's history – that of strong and power-driven women pushing their men to pursue their political ambitions.[64]

The second speech, which Tanaquil pronounces before the multitude assembled outside the palace, is more unusual: here, the queen does not speak as an exhorting mother-in-law but as a person endowed with public authority (1.41.4):

> Cum clamor impetusque multitudinis vix sustineri posset, ex superiore parte aedium per fenestras in Novam Viam versas – habitabat enim rex ad Iovis Statoris – populum Tanaquil adloquitur.

> Since the uproar and the crush of the crowd could hardly be endured, Tanaquil spoke to the people from the upper section of the palace, from the window which faced the Nova Via (the king lived near the temple of Jupiter Stator).

The ensuing speech, reported in *oratio obliqua* in section 5, aims at inspiring confidence in the crowd through its matter-of-fact, paratactic sequence of reports and the medical knowledge it displays.[65]

---

64 Cf. Keegan (2021, *passim*).
65 Cf. Ogilvie (1965, p. 161).

THE SEMANTICS OF SPACE AND GENDER   225

The strikingly active role played (not only in Livy, but also in Dionysius) by Tanaquil as a kingmaker has long attracted the attention of scholars, who have attempted to account for it in different ways: for example, by identifying the queen with various deities of archaic Rome, or by linking her character to Roman stereotypes about 'assertive' Etruscan women. I will not discuss the possible origins of the Tanaquil-legend since my concern here is with Livy's narration, especially with the space in which the events are set.[66]

Feldherr (1998, pp. 212–217) stresses the symbolic role of the *regia* in this episode. He reads the prominence of the inner space of the palace, where Tanaquil manoeuvres to let Servius ascend to the throne and whence she speaks to the assembled people as part of the general blurring of boundaries between the public and the private sphere which characterises the Tarquins' monarchy. In this reading, Tanaquil might be an antecedent for Tullia (*ibid.*, p. 192). Feldherr emphasises, among other things, the ambiguity inherent in Tanaquil's appearance at the window of the *regia*. Her appearance from the 'upper part' of the house may be read as a 'sign of a woman's usurpation of authority both within the state and within the home' (p. 216).[67] However, Tanaquil's intentional construction of a deceptive appearance ultimately saves the state; her claims 'are not only based on omens sent by the gods' but are proven true in that Servius proves to be a 'true' king (p. 217).

I suggest that one can better understand such ambiguity by considering the spatiality of Tanaquil's actions more closely. The queen delivers her speech at the interface between 'public' and 'private' space: while she speaks to people assembled in the street, she does so from the inner space of the palace, which is also her house. This fact, which has generally gone unnoticed, is significant to Tanaquil's role in 'mediating between the public and the private' (Feldherr, 1998, p. 216).

Tanaquil certainly pushes and tests the boundaries separating 'private' and 'public', 'feminine' and 'masculine' space; however, she never crosses them. Herein, I argue, lies the fundamental difference between her and Tullia. The latter's intervention in the Roman Forum represents her transgression of the domestic role she is supposed to play. Tanaquil, on the other hand, wields and directs power within the limits of her role as a wife and mother-in-law and within the spatial boundaries of her household. Her ability to influence public life seems to lie in her ability to move on the very boundary – to exploit the

---

66   See e.g. Bonfante Warren (1973a and 1973b); Martin (1985, pp. 10–15).
67   For the ambiguities inherent in women's political interventions in Livy cf. Stevenson (2011), who, however, in my opinion, reads Livy's representation of Tanaquil in too negative a way.

opportunities the boundary offers as the interface between the two spheres of Roman life.

The second episode I now examine is perhaps less famous than Tanaquil's story but just as significant from the perspective of space and gender. At 10.23.3–10, Livy reports the founding of the cult of *Pudicitia Plebeia* in 296 BCE. *Pudicitia* was a divine personification of the virtue of the same name, which is usually translated in English as 'modesty' or 'chastity'.[68] According to Livy's account, a woman called Verginia, born into a patrician family but married to a plebeian consul, was denied participation in the cult of *Pudicitia Patricia* ('Patrician *Pudicitia*') because she had married a plebeian man. Indignant at the slur, Verginia reacted by founding a new shrine of *Pudicitia Plebeia* ('Plebeian *Pudicitia*', 10.23.6–8):

> 6. Facto deinde egregio magnifica verba adauxit. In vico Longo ubi habitabat, ex ⟨extrema⟩[69] parte aedium quod satis esset loci modico sacello exclusit aramque ibi posuit et convocatis plebeiis matronis conquesta iniuriam patriciarum, 7. 'Hanc ego aram', inquit, 'Pudicitiae Plebeiae dedico; vosque hortor ut, quod certamen virtutis viros in hac civitate tenet, 8. hoc pudicitiae inter matronas sit detisque operam ut haec ara quam illa, si quid potest, sanctius et a castioribus coli dicatur'.

> 6. She then strengthened her high-minded words through an excellent act. In the *vicus Longus*, where she lived, at the furthest end of her house she shut off enough space for a small shrine and set an altar there. Then she summoned the plebeian matrons and, after deploring the patrician women's slur, 7. she said: 'This altar I consecrate to Plebeian *Pudicitia*; 8. and I exhort you to the effect that in this city matrons compete in *pudicitia* in the same way as men compete in valour, and to strive that this altar may be said to be venerated, if it is possible, even more piously and by even more virtuous women than that other one'.

The new shrine, Livy adds, became the seat of a cult that was subject to the same rules as the one in the older temple: only women of proven *pudicitia* and who were *univirae* (i.e. had been married to only one man in their lives) could

---

68　Cf. Palmer (1974, p. 113). Quoting Langlands (2006, p. 31), *pudicitia* is 'a moral virtue (…) that pertains to the regulation of behaviour (either of oneself or of other people) specifically associated with sex'.

69　On this integration, which is not in Conway and Walters's (1919) text, see Oakley (2005b, p. 256).

take part in the cult (10.23.8–9). Later, however, the cult was opened to women of less unsullied reputation, some of whom were not even *matronae,* and eventually it fell into oblivion (10.23.10).

The story poses several problems. We possess no other explicit testimony about the shrine of *Pudicitia Patricia* (which, according to Livy 10.23.2, was 'in the Forum Boarium, close to the round temple of Hercules', *in foro bovario ad aedem rotundam Herculis*), and the only evidence of a shrine of *Pudicitia Plebeia* is a lacunose passage in Festus (Festus, *Gloss. Lat.* 270; Paul. Fest. 271), which seems to transmit a partially different tradition.[70] The problems concerning the historical validity of Livy's account, or its possible origin, lie beyond the scope of the present discussion; my concern is the spatial dimension of this episode within the narrative of the *Ab Urbe Condita*.

Such an intervention in Roman cultic activity on the part of a woman is unique in Livy's extant books. Moreover, Livy inserts Verginia's speech to a crowd of matrons who assemble there *as* matrons, that is, as a distinct component of the community involved in Roman religion. Together with Tanaquil's speech to the crowd, this is the only other public speech delivered by a woman that the *Ab Urbe Condita* reports – that is, the only other speech which is not addressed to a relative or a person in a private contest, but to a collective of people on a matter of common interest. That both the speech and the founding of the cult are political statements is clear not only from the position of this episode within the framework of the patricio-plebeian struggles of the early 3rd century BCE but also from the tribunician rhetoric that Verginia uses against the patrician matrons at 10.23.6 (*conquesta iniuriam patriciarum*: 'she then condemned the insulting behaviour of the patrician women').

But *where* does Verginia make such a political statement? Like Tanaquil, she acts in a space at the intersection of 'private' and 'public'. According to Livy, she made room for the shrine in 'the furthermost end of her house' (*ex ⟨extrema⟩ parte aedium,* 6), a phrase which curiously echoes *ex superiore parte aedium* in the account of Tanaquil's speech (1.41.4). It is the private space of her house, which she turns into a cultic place; as a woman, she would not have the authority to consecrate a sacred building in a public space. As soon as the space of her house becomes a shrine, however, it ceases to be exclusively – or mostly – 'private': the cult it hosts, while not 'public' in a strict sense but rather 'corporate' (cf. Palmer, 1974, 122 and *passim*), has clear communal implications, since it pertains to a specific component of Roman society (plebeian matrons).

---

70 On these problems see Palmer (1974); Oakley (2005b, pp. 247–250), with further bibliography.

The liminal character of the shrine thus reflects the nature of the cult it was dedicated to. *Pudicitia* was closely related to the domestic sphere; at the same time, it possessed a deep public relevance. The regulation of sexual behaviour was one of the ways through which relationships between citizens were organised – which is why virtually all exemplary tales about *pudicitia* that we know from Latin literature concern power relations within Roman society. As Langlands (2006) suggests, *pudicitia* was also a field of Roman politics and society in which women could be active moral agents. In other words, preserving sexual morality constituted a field in which women's status as an integral component of the Roman civic community was displayed, and in which their importance for communal well-being was vital.

The shrine of *Pudicitia Plebeia* was built in this liminal space, which lay between the domestic sphere and the struggles animating the city's political life and presented women some chances to display their semi-public role. The responsibility of women to uphold *pudicitia* also resonated with Augustan discourses on marriage and morals. The stress that Livy lays on Verginia's deed and words also points to a possible role for (free, married) women within the community of citizens and its space.

Thus, the narratives about Tanaquil and *Pudicitia Plebeia* suggest that women can exercise a form of influence not only – as they repeatedly do in the narrative – on their male kin but also on the broader community of citizens, or parts thereof; they can do so by exploiting the chances offered by the liminal space between the 'public' and the 'private', without overstepping the boundary. Even in such cases, their action has a certain degree of ambiguity: Tanaquil is depicted as an ambitious queen, and Verginia's indignation at the patricians' offence is partly due to 'female irascibility' (*iracundia muliebris*, 10.23.4). Both women, however, do something beneficial to the state's welfare (an 'excellent act', *factum egregium*, in Verginia's case). Once more, Livy's narrative recognises the integral role of women in recomposing the crises and fractures within the community of their male counterparts.

5 Subverting Roman Space I: Verginia and the Decemvirate

The previous sections have focused on spatial transgressions and spatially subversive acts, as well as acts which play out at the very boundary between private and public spaces. In this section and the next, I end my discussion by looking at two episodes in which breaching gendered and spatial boundaries is cast as an aspect of the total subversion of Roman civic space.

THE SEMANTICS OF SPACE AND GENDER   229

The first episode concerns the tragic death of Verginia, which catalyses the fall of the Decemvirate in 449 BCE (3.44–48).[71] The story is famous. Appius Claudius, the tyrannical leader of the second board of Decemvirs,[72] is seized by a passion for the beautiful plebeian maiden Verginia. After trying in vain to seduce her with gifts and promises, he devises a plan to bring the girl into his power by taking advantage of the absence of her father, a centurion named Lucius Verginius. Appius instructs one of his clients, Marcus Claudius, to claim the maiden as his slave: she was born – Marcus is to allege – from one of his slaves and then abducted and taken to Verginius' house when still an infant.

Since Appius is the magistrate who is to pass judgement on the matter, Verginia's case seems hopeless. However, the plebeians rally to her defence, and her fiancée Icilius, a former tribune and popular leader, delivers a harsh speech against Appius. The latter, therefore, has to concede that Verginius be recalled from Mount Algidus, where he is on campaign, and the trial be adjourned to the following day. The next morning, Verginius appears with his daughter at the trial, but Appius decrees in Marcus' favour without bothering to hear his case. Amidst the general shock and indignation, Verginius asks for a last private conversation with his daughter. With this pretext, he takes the girl aside, snatches a knife from a butcher's shop, and stabs her to death, thus rescuing her – as he says – from Appius' violence in the only way he could. Verginia's tragic death stirs the plebs to revolt and bring down the Decemvirate.

We possess a parallel narrative of the same events in Book 11 of Dionysius of Halicarnassus' *Roman Antiquities* (11.28–37). Dionysius' account is, as ever, lengthier and richer in pathos but very similar to Livy's in both the scenes' sequence and the description of the characters' actions and motives. Clearly, either both historians followed the same main source, or their common sources presented a consolidated account. Livy consulted more than one source, as his remark at 3.47.5 suggests.[73] Here, the historian admits his inability to find a convincing account of the arguments that Appius used to justify his final verdict; however, he hints that some 'ancient authors' might have preserved part of the truth.[74] My analysis of Livy's narrative, therefore, is based on the

---

71   On this narrative see e.g. Joplin (1990); Joshel (1992); Feldherr (1998, pp. 202–211); Kowalewski (2002, pp. 142–175); Langlands (2006, pp. 97–109); Freund (2008); Helmke (2023, esp. pp. 74–79 and *passim*).
72   For the complete story of the Decemvirate see Chapter 1, p. 56.
73   Other sources for the story are Cic. *Rep.* 2.63; *Fin.* 2.66; 5.64; Diod. Sic. 12.24; Val Max. 6.1.2; Pompon. *Dig.* 1.2.2.24; Eutr. 1.18; [Aur. Vict.] *De vir. ill.* 21; Oros. 2.13.1–7; Zonar. 7.18.
74   Livy is probably referring to versions such as the one in Dion. Hal. *Ant. Rom.* 11.36: according to the Greek historian, the Decemvir cut off discussion by stating that he himself, as

assumption that he worked with an already fully-fledged story the main lines of which were well-established before him but upon which he exerted his critical judgement and artistic freedom.

The Forum is the setting for the two main scenes of the tale, corresponding to the two days of the trial (3.44.6–46.8 and 3.47.1–49.8). Livy's account preserves the unity of action in a way that Dionysius' does not.[75] At the end of the first scene, Livy relates that Verginia's defenders sent messengers to recall her father from the camp on Mount Algidus (3.46.5–6). Then he turns to Appius, who, after remaining a while longer in the Forum, went home and wrote to his colleagues on the Algidus not to let Verginius go – a failed attempt, since Verginius had already left the camp before the arrival of the letter (3.46.9–10). The change of setting is brief and works as an interlude separating the first scene from the next. Dionysius, in contrast, recounts the messengers' mission and the events that occurred during the night at length. Thus, in Livy, the Forum acquires a central role unparalleled in the Greek account.

Each scene opens with an explicit mention of the Forum. At 3.44.6, Verginia's arrival in the Forum sets the following events in motion:

> Virgini venienti in forum – ibi namque in tabernaculis litterarum ludi erant – minister decemviri libidinis manum iniecit, serva sua natam servamque appellans.
>
> As the maiden was going into the Forum – for there, in tents,[76] was the school – the servant of the Decemvir's lust lay his hand upon her, calling her born from his slave and a slave herself.

From the location in the Forum where Marcus Claudius first claims Verginia as his slave, everyone then moves to Appius's dais (*tribunal*), which one should imagine as being located in the Comitium; the rest of the scene will develop there (3.44.9).[77] Livy's remark that Verginia was going to school in the Forum

---

Marcus' guardian, had been informed of the girl's real origins years before, and therefore knew Marcus' claim to be right.

75   Cf. Ogilvie (1965, p. 478).
76   Ogilvie (1965, p. 480 and pp. 487–488) seems to interpret *tabernacula* as a synonym of *tabernae* here. However, *tabernaculum* usually indicates a tent; therefore, it is more likely that Livy means a movable structure of some sort. Cf. Kowaleski (2002, p. 147).
77   For the location of the *tribunal* of the praetor, the magistrate that normally administered justice (and whose role Appius is here fulfilling) cf. Chapter 1, p. 45. Ogilvie (1965, p. 482) remarks that it is not possible to gauge whether Livy had in mind the original site of the praetor's dais in the Comitium or its later one (from the 2nd century onward) on the

is anachronistic.[78] Still, since Dionysius (11.28.3) reports the same, one must conclude that the detail appeared in the two historians' common source(s).

This is one of the occasions on which the text gives its readers a glimpse of everyday life in the Forum, which conflicts in part with its overall ideological constructs. The apparently casual remark suggests that it would be normal (if not in the 5th century, in later times) to see children, among them girls of marriageable age, attending school in the Forum. Since the *Ab Urbe Condita* does not normally mention the presence of women (of any age and status) in the Forum if not to stress its exceptionality, this passage stands out as an exception. One possible explanation for this seeming contradiction is that the space that Livy takes as masculine is not the Forum in its entirety but rather its political core (Curia and Comitium). On a deeper level, however, Verginia's presence in the Forum appears consistent with Livy's overall semantics of space in broader narrative terms. While it is true that her arrival in the Forum is not, per se, a subversive or even a problematic act, in the text, it is in the moment that she appears in the Forum that the crisis begins. From that moment, the scene moves to the political core of the Forum and, more specifically, to Appius' *tribunal*, the location where justice is administered.[79]

Indeed, as Feldherr (1998, pp. 202–211) shows, Livy's narrative is dominated by the idea that the Decemviral tyranny, just like the Tarquins' reign, blurred the boundary between political and private space, *forum* and *domus*. Icilius, for example, promises at 3.45.7 that he will not allow his betrothed to remain a night 'outside her father's house' (*extra domum patris*). Later, when Verginius,

---

eastern site of the Forum. As I have shown in Chapter 1, however, Livy usually displays a good knowledge of the changing architecture of the Forum over time; therefore, it is likely that a position in the Comitium is implied in the story about Verginia.

[78] See Ogilvie (1965, pp. 480–481); Kowalewski (2002, p. 148).

[79] Verginia is not the only female character to be summoned to the Forum in the context of a legal procedure in the *Ab Urbe Condita*. The historian also reports the trials of women convicted of poisoning their husbands. The most detailed narrative is found at 8.18.1–10: in 331 BCE, a female slave revealed that several matrons had caused the deaths of their husbands by concocting poisonous potions. The matrons were summoned to the Forum (8.18.8). When two of them, the patricians Cornelia and Sergia, tried to exculpate themselves by stating their potions were medicinal, the slave proposed they should drink of them. The two patrician women briefly consulted with the other matrons involved; by common decision, they all drank the potions and fell dead on the spot. On this episode see e.g. Oakley (1998, pp. 594–602); Kowalewski (2002, pp. 298–301); Padilla Peralta (2023); Todaro (2023b). Another case of poisoning is reported at 40.37.1–7, but here the Forum as the location for the trial is left implicit; cf. also *Per.* 48. The accounts of poisoning also represent moments of crisis in the State and the explicit mention of the matrons' trial and death in the Forum at 8.18.1–10 might stress such crises. However, this crisis is more limited in its scope than the more general one provoked by the Decemvirate.

after killing his daughter, flees to his comrades-at-arms on the Algidus, he tells them that 'there is no more a place for Appius' lust in his house' (*non esse iam Appi libidini locum in domo sua*, 3.50.9).[80] Through his assault on Verginia, Appius attempted to violate Verginius's house. Verginia, who logically belongs in her father's house, is thus exposed to the most public space in the city, the area in the Forum around Appius' dais – a space which, contrary t its public nature, the Decemvir is using to fulfil his private desires.[81]

The second scene, too, starts when Verginius, on the following day, leads his daughter into the Forum, where the Roman people stand in expectation of the trial (3.47.1):

> At in urbe prima luce cum civitas in foro exspectatione erecta staret, Verginius sordidatus filiam secum obsoleta veste comitantibus aliquot matronis cum ingenti advocatione in forum deducit.
>
> But in the city, at first light, as the citizens stood in the Forum in the excitement of expectation, Verginius in shabby clothes led his daughter, also wearing worn out clothes, with some matrons accompanying her, into the Forum with a great crowd of assistants.

It is important to note that Verginia appears and moves in the Forum, throughout the story, not as a person with her agency but as the object of other people's actions.[82] While Tullia claims political power by entering the Forum, Verginia is at the mercy of a political power that does not respect its boundaries. Even her eventual death does not happen, as Lucretia's, by her own hand, but by the hand of her father.

Langlands (2006, p. 108) sees in Lucretia and Verginius two different 'models of heroic *pudicitia* (…) the defence of one's own body and the protection of the vulnerable body of another'. Helmke (2023, pp. 74–79) explains Verginia's passivity through the effects of the passage from monarchy to Republic: while men under the monarchy seem unable to solve crises without the input provided by women, under the Republican system men have full access to the knowledge and skills necessary to defend the value of *pudicitia*.[83] Such an explanation,

---

80 Cf. Joshel (1992, p. 122).
81 Cf. also Kowalewski (2002, p. 147).
82 On this point see e.g. Kowalewski (2002, pp. 171–172); Langlands (2006, p. 102 and pp. 108–109); Freund (2008, pp. 320–321).
83 Cf. also Freund (2008, p. 320). For the stories of Lucretia and Verginia as exemplars of *pudicitia*, Freund (2008); Langlands (2006, pp. 97–109).

however, does not consider the active role that some women play, in Livy's narrative of Republican times, in upholding *pudicitia* as a central value: the story about the other Verginia, the founder of the shrine to *Pudicitia Plebeia* provides an excellent example.

I suggest the crucial difference between Lucretia and Verginia resides in their respective statuses. Lucretia is a *matrona*, and thus a full member of the Roman citizen community, involved with its reproduction: this means she has her own agency, albeit limited to the domestic sphere. Verginia, as a freeborn unmarried girl, is still under her father's control. In this respect, she is like other young girls who appear in the *Ab Urbe Condita* as vulnerable subjects and as potential or actual victims of the violence of the powerful. I have already mentioned the maid of Ardea and the daughters of Heraclia; the Spanish prisoners that Scipio treats with honour at 26.49.11–50.14 are another example. In all these cases, one or more adults speak and act on behalf of the girl(s): the maid of Ardea is under her mother's and the tutors' care; Heraclia pleads (if unsuccessfully) for her daughters; and the elderly wife of the Spanish noble Mandonius pleads with Scipio to spare the honour of the captive maidens. In such cases, the text does not represent unmarried girls as subjects; rather, they play roles as touchstones of men's behaviour in wielding power.[84]

Consistent with her role as the terrain upon which political relationships are negotiated, Verginia's movements across the Forum are passive throughout the story. Even when, in the beginning, she 'comes' (*venienti*) into the Forum, she is not alone but – as the reader later finds out – escorted by her nurse. In what follows, she is usually the object of action verbs rather than the subject.[85] Marcus Claudius lays his hand on her (*manum iniecit*, 3.44.6) and threatens to drag her away by force (*vi abstracturum, ibid.*) should she hesitate; he then summons her to trial (*Vocat puellam in ius*, 3.44.9). When she and her nurse go to Appius' dais (*tribunal*), it is on the advice of bystanders; even there, the verb of movement is impersonal passive (*perventum est, ibid.*). The following day, Verginius leads his daughter (*deducit*) into the Forum for the trial (3.47.1). After Appius has pronounced his sentence, Marcus tries to get hold of Verginia, but the matrons and her defenders push him away (3.47.6–8). Appius eventually orders his lictors to disperse the mob and take the girl; when her protectors give way, Verginia, who has nobody left to act or speak for her, can do nothing but stand 'alone, prey to violence' (*desertaque praeda iniuriae puella stabat*,

---

84 While Appius, the factions in Ardea, and the Syracusan mob overstep their boundaries in their yearning for political power, Scipio acts as a wise and restrained statesman: cf. Helmke (2023, pp. 198–210).
85 Cf. again Langlands (2006, p. 102).

3.48.3).⁸⁶ Compared to Dionysius' description of Verginia desperately clinging in tears to her father and fiancée, Livy's narrative suggests an idea of thorough passivity and immobility. Finally, Verginius leads (*seducit*, 3.48.5) his daughter and her nurse to a spot near the shrine of Cloacina, for which Livy provides a precise topographical indication (*prope Cloacinae ad tabernas, quibus nunc novis est nomen*, 3.48.5)⁸⁷ and stabs her. Even after her death, Verginia's body is used by men (her uncle and fiancée) to rally the people against the Decemvirs (*Icilius Numitoriusque exsangue corpus sublatum ostentant populo; scelus Appi, puellae infelicem formam, necessitate patris deplorant*, 3.48.7).⁸⁸

Verginia is also notably silent throughout her story. Men speak on her behalf or about her (or the political issues connected to her story), and the matrons who escort her to the Forum on the day of trial lament her destiny, but the reader never hears the girl's voice. In Dionysius' *Roman Antiquities*, Verginia at least shows various emotions (although she does not speak there either) and is an altogether more realistic character; in the *Ab Urbe Condita*, the only glimpse the reader gets of her emotional state is at 3.44.7, when she is said to be scared and shocked by Marcus Claudius's claim on her (*pavida puella stupente*). After that, the reader loses sight of her as a person.

Such a lack of agency, both in spatial and more general terms, highlights Verginia being out of place in the Forum. In this space, men should debate and fight over politics, not women's bodies. I argue that her displacement is in agreement with the overall representation of the Decemvirate as the moment in which all aspects of Roman space are subverted. As I showed in Chapter 1, the tyrannical rule of the Decemvirs disrupts the various patterns and relationships that constitute the Roman spatial order. The Curia and Forum are empty; the Decemvirs make decisions at home rather than in the public space; Roman soldiers in the field behave in an un-Roman way, thus making the danger of an enemy attack a real threat; and, after Verginia's death, the plebs move away from the city, endangering the very existence of Rome both as a material place and as a community space. Indeed, the senators even imagine the spectre of a plebeian attack on Rome, which would turn citizens into enemies – the ultimate subversion of boundaries.

It is no chance that the high point of this set of subversions comes with a breaching of gendered boundaries: gender relationships are such a fundamental element of a society that their disruption can stand for the other disruptions

---

86 On the implications of the noun *praeda* here, see Langlands (2006, p. 204).
87 Cf. Chapter 1, p. 34.
88 'Icilius and Numitorius lift up the bloodless body and show it to the people; they lament Appius' crime, the maiden's wretched beauty, the inevitability of her father's act.'

THE SEMANTICS OF SPACE AND GENDER   235

to Roman stability. Appius Claudius threatens, as a quintessential tyrant, the very *domus* of a free citizen; and the young girl who belongs to that domestic space is dragged into the space of politics and the law. Indeed, Appius prepares the treatment usually reserved for captured enemies, enslavement and physical violation, for a freeborn maiden:[89] the disruption of gendered boundaries brings about a disruption of the boundary between 'inner' and 'outer' space. Only through the Decemvirs' demise can Roman spatial order be restored.

6 Subverting Roman Space II: the Bacchanalian Scandal

The second episode I intend to examine is the famous account of the so-called Bacchanalian scandal of 186 BCE in Livy 39.8–19.[90] Livy's account of the affair is as follows: sometime around the beginning of the 2nd century BCE, a Greek priest introduced the Bacchic rites to Etruria.[91] These were nocturnal ceremonies performed by men and women and characterised by every possible kind of depravity. The rites eventually reached Rome but remained secret (39.8.3–8). In 186 BCE, however, the consul Spurius Postumius Albinus learnt about their existence. After a young man named Aebutius had been left under his mother's and stepfather's guardianship, after his own father's death, the stepfather, who had dishonestly managed the youth's finances, was looking for a way to either get rid of him or bind him to silence by involving him in illicit activity. So, he resolved to lure him into the Bacchic rites; Aebutius' mother, eager to please her husband, persuaded her son to be initiated (39.9.2–4).

---

89 Cf. again Langlands (2006, p. 204) on Verginia as *praeda* ('prey', but also 'booty').
90 Historians have long attempted to separate fictional elements from historical facts in Livy's account and to provide explanations for the Roman Senate's repression of the Bacchic cult in Rome and Italy. Some of the information provided by Livy coincides with the contents a bronze tablet found in Tiriolo (Calabria), reporting the contents of one of the relevant *senatus consulta* (*CIL* I² 581) and it is generally agreed that at least the core of the events concerning the repression of the cult is authentic. Scholars, however, have stressed the similarities between some aspects of Livy's account and Graeco-Roman comedy. Walsh (1996), Wiseman (1998, pp. 43–48), and Scafuro (2009) go as far as to think of a play as a possible source for the unmasking story in Livy; *contra* Flower (2000b and 2024); Briscoe (2008, p. 243). For some influential treatments and surveys of previous scholarship see e.g. Pailler (1988); Gruen (1990, pp. 34–78); Briscoe (2008, pp. 230–250). A recent reconsideration of the evidence is Gallo (2017).
91 On the historical background for this detail cf. Walsh (1996, pp. 190–191).

Aebutius had a relationship with a courtesan of libertine status, Hispala Faecenia,[92] who was – as Livy remarks – much more virtuous than the life she had been forced into as a young slave. The girl dissuaded her lover from becoming a Bacchic initiate; she told him that, when still a slave, she had escorted her mistress to the rites and witnessed how young people were sexually abused by participants in the cult (39.9.5–10.9). When Aebutius consequently refused to be initiated, his mother cast him out. The young man moved to his paternal aunt Aebutia's and she advised him to report what he had heard to the consul Postumius (39.11.1–3). In turn, the consul consulted his mother-in-law, Sulpicia, and had her summon first Aebutia, then Hispala, to her house. The courtesan, who feared revenge from the initiates, was initially reluctant to speak but then, prompted by the consuls' mixed chidings and reassurances, told him everything she knew. Hispala was lodged in a protected attic above Sulpicia's house, and Aebutius found hospitality at one of the consul's clients' (39.11.4–14.3).

Postumius reported to the Senate, who ordered further investigations, prohibited the rites in Rome and Italy, and commanded the Bacchic priests to be captured and questioned (39.14.4–10). The consul then summoned the people to inform them about the great danger the *res publica* faced (39.15.1–16.3). Heavy repression in Rome and Italy followed: more than seven thousand people were said to have taken part in what Livy calls a *coniuratio*; most were sentenced to death, and the others were imprisoned. Bacchanalian rites were prohibited in Italy, save for exceptional cases. Aebutius and Hispala were rewarded with money and other distinctions; the woman was allowed to marry a freeborn man (39.17.1–19.).

Recent treatments of the episode by Albrecht (2016, pp. 100–110) and myself (Fabrizi, 2018c, pp. 42–46) point to the importance of the notion of breaching boundaries. I have argued that the narrative constructs the setting of the Bacchic rites as an indefinite, chaotic space threatening orderly, regulated Roman space from within. The Bacchanalia are said to take place in a 'grove of Stimula', or 'Semele';[93] Hispala describes matrons throwing torches into

---

92 The name Hispala may indicate her origin from Hispalis in Spain, while Faecenia probably derives from her former master (cf. Walsh, 1996, p. 197). Livy introduces her with her full name at 39.9.5, then he calls her simply Hispala in the rest of his account; I will follow his usage.

93 At 39.12.4 the manuscripts have *in luco Similae*, but this is almost certainly a corruption. Stimula was an Italian deity identified with Semele (cf. Walsh, 1996, 188) and the *lucus Stimulae* or *Semelae* (also mentioned by Ov. *Fast.* 6.503) was close to the Aventine.

the Tiber (39.13.9).[94] Later, the consul Postumius states that the rites occur 'in many places throughout the city' (*per urbem … multis locis*, 39.15.6).[95] Descriptions of the rites conjure up the image of dark, indefinite spaces, which are evoked through auditory rather than visual sensations.[96] Special emphasis lies on the abolition of gendered boundaries within this dark and indefinite space: both the external narrator and the characters repeatedly stress that the promiscuity of the rites led to the abolition of moral boundaries as well (e.g. 39.8.5–6; 39.13.10).

I would like to build on such observations by focusing on how the narrative constructs the other pole of the opposition, that is, the regulated space of the Roman city. In particular, I will consider two aspects: the setting of the tale concerning Hispala and Aebutius; and the ideas about Roman space expressed in Postumius' speech (39.15–16).

Livy's historical setting is firmly anchored in Rome's urban space through the mention of the Aventine as the district where Aebutius, Aebutia, and Hispala live. The account of the consul's investigations, too, is remarkable for its insistence on the characters' use of space. Sulpicia first summons Aebutia to her house and learns the details of Aebutius' story from her. She then summons Hispala; when the girl arrives, the consul, who comes to meet her 'in the entrance' (*in vestibulo*, 39.12.2), leads her 'into the inner part of the house' (*in interiorem partem aedium*, 39.12.3), where he questions her in the presence of his mother-in-law. Afterwards, he arranges for the courtesan to be hosted at Sulpicia's, in a *cenaculum* in the highest storey of the house and he shuts off access to the street to protect Hispala from possible retaliation. Aebutius, too, moves to the house of a client of Postumius for security reasons.[97]

As recent scholarship stresses, Sulpicia plays a crucial role in the investigation: thanks to her social connections and her ability to summon other women to her house, she masks the hearing of important witnesses as casual visits and thereby avoids the investigation being exposed. In this way, Livy's account

---

94   As Jaeger (2105) points out, in this context, the mention of the Tiber, the revered river of the Roman foundation legend, was bound to be 'shocking' to readers.
95   On the contradiction between this remark and Livy's previous statement that the cult had remained hidden until that moment, see Walsh (1996, pp. 194–195); Briscoe (2008, p. 234).
96   For darkness as a typical element of the Bacchic rites cf. Plaut. *Bacch.* 53–56, where mention is made of a *latebrosus locus* (56). Cf. Walsh (1996, p. 192).
97   Scafuro (2009, pp. 340–342) argues that these details resonate with the theme of quarantine and isolation connected to Livy's representation of the Bacchic rites as a disease spreading at the heart of the state.

reveals the importance of women's networks and the potential influence of informal political activity by powerful women.[98]

At the same time, the stress on these manoeuvres leaves the reader with an impression of propriety in maintaining the boundaries between genders and between public authority and individual citizens.[99] It is crucial that the communication between women and Sulpicia's mediation between the consul and other women takes place within the space of a house. Therefore, one can interpret Sulpicia's action as that kind of feminine action which is successful and beneficial to the State because it is performed within established boundaries.

The space of this part of narrative is an unofficial, everyday space. It is populated by characters like Aebutius, a young man of equestrian status, and Hispala, a foreigner, freedwoman, and prostitute – i.e. a person living at the intersection of several boundaries of Roman society.[100] At the same time, it is a space where the fundamental boundaries governing Roman life remain valid and in force.

In Postumius' speech to the people, the climax of the whole story, the reader gets to see another aspect of orderly Roman space, as opposed to the chaotic space of the Bacchic rites. The location for the speech is, as the narrator explicitly remarks at 39.15.1, the Rostra,[101] the very heart of Roman political space. The consul starts by drawing an opposition between the city and the threatening outside world, comparing the ancestral gods of the Roman people and those 'who lead spirits ensnared by evil and foreign superstitions to undertake every crime and lust as if spurred on by the Furies' (*religionibus captas mentes velut furialibus stimulis ad omne scelus et ad omnem libidinem agerent*, 39.15.3). The focus then moves to the city itself: now, the Bacchanalia are not only in Italy but 'also in many places across the city', as the people have certainly heard 'from the nocturnal noises and wailings that resonate in the whole city' (*crepitibus etiam ululatibusque nocturnis, qui personant tota urbe*, 39.15.6).

---

98 Keegan (2021); Flower (2024).
99 Cf. Albrecht (2016, p. 110): 'Allen im Kontext der Bacchanalien agierenden Frauen gemeinsam ist jedoch, dass sie ausschließlich in geschlossenen Räumen auftreten. Nur dem Konsul als hegemonialem Mann und Repräsentanten der *res publica* ist es möglich, auf allen Feldern gleichermaßen zu agieren, im eigenen Haus ebenso wie im Senat und vor dem Volk'.
100 On this characterisation of Hispala, cf. Albrecht (2016, pp. 103–104); Keegan (2021, pp. 109–121).
101 *Ad haec officia dimissis magistratibus, consules in Rostra escenderunt, et contione advocata cum sollemne carmen precationis, quod praefari priusquam populum adloquantur magistratus solent, peregisset consul, ita coepit.*

The lack of boundaries of this space within the city finds a correspondence in the absence of gendered boundaries characterising participants in the cult. In Postumius' words (39.15.9):

> Primum igitur mulierum magna pars est, et is fons mali huiusce fuit; deinde simillimi feminis mares, stuprati et constupratores, fanatici vigili⟨i⟩s vino strepitibus clamoribusque nocturnis attoniti.

> First, then, the majority is constituted by women, and this was the source of this evil; moreover, there are males who are in all similar to females, abused and abusers, fanatical and stunned by sleeplessness, wine, and the nocturnal shouts and noises.

The consul contrasts these clandestine meetings with the regulated assemblies of the Roman people, those *contiones* that can only take place when 'the banner is placed in the citadel, the army had been led out for elections, or the tribunes had decreed an assembly of the plebs, or someone of magistrates had called them to an assembly' (39.15.11).[102] His words are as follows (39.15.12–14):

> 12. Quales primum nocturnos coetus, deinde promiscuos mulierum ac virorum esse creditis? 13. Si quibus aetatibus initientur mares sciatis, non misereat vos eorum solum, sed etiam pudeat. Hoc sacramento initiatos iuvenes milites faciendos censetis, Quirites? His ex obsceno sacrario eductis arma committenda? 14. Hi cooperti stupris suis alienisque pro pudicitia coniugum ac liberorum vestrorum ferro decernent?

> 12. What do you think? What kind of meetings are those which, first, take place by night and, secondly, involve promiscuity of women and men? 13. If you knew at what age the males are initiated, you would feel not only pity but also shame for them. Do you think, Quirites, that young men who have been initiated through such an oath should be turned into soldiers? Or that one should entrust weapons to them, who have come out of such an abominable shrine? 14. Will these men, who are buried deep in their own and others' shameful violation, fight in battle for your wives and children's chastity?

---

102 (...) *cum aut vexillo in arce posito comitiorum causa exercitus eductus esset, aut plebi concilium tribuni edixissent, aut aliquis ex magistratibus ad contionem vocasset.*

Proper use of space, as Postumius suggests, implies control from public authority, specific procedures, visibility, and respect of the boundaries separating men and women. When such boundaries – and, by inference, the differences between the genders – are erased, a crucial danger arises: men might, just like women, become exposed to sexual violation. By turning into (potential or actual) victims of sexual violation, men lose their ability to act as men, that is, as soldiers and defenders of the physical integrity of their women and children.

This also means that Roman men lose their ability to act as members of the political community of citizen-soldiers.[103] Hispala has previously spoken of the conspirators as a 'second (Roman) people' (*alterum ... populum*, 39.13.14). Postumius now evokes the spectre of an alternative Roman *contio*, one that the true Roman people have no choice but to face publicly, that is, as a community (39.16.3–4):

> Crescit et serpit cotidie malum. Iam maius est quam ut capere id privata fortuna possit: ad summam rem publicam spectat. 4. Nisi praecavetis, Quirites, iam huic diurnae, legitime ab consule vocatae, par nocturna contio esse poterit. Nunc illi vos singuli universos contionantes timent; iam ubi vos dilapsi domos et in rura vestra eritis, illi coierint, consultabunt de sua salute simul ac vestra pernicie: tum singulis vobis universi timendi erunt.

> The evil grows and penetrates deeper each day. It is already too great for it to be faced with private means: it concerns the very welfare of the state. 4. If you do not take precautions, Quirites, that nocturnal assembly might soon be equal to this one which is lawfully summoned by a consul by daylight. Now those people fear you as you are all convened in the assembly; soon, when you are scattered in your homes and your fields, they will meet and debate over their own safety and your ruin; then you, as individuals, will have to fear them all.

The opposition between public and private spheres, individual and community, is crucial here. One of the main reasons the Bacchic rites were deemed dangerous was that they were secret meetings and thus beyond the control of public authority. Once more, confusion between those two realms emerges as a crucial danger to the community's welfare. The stress Livy places on sexual promiscuity – and especially upon the erasure of gendered boundaries – throughout his narrative does not merely belong in a tradition of Roman

---

103 Cf. Albrecht (2016, p. 108).

moralising of political issues. The narrative also, and crucially, takes once more the gendered use of space as the touchstone of the health of the State.

In the account of the Bacchanalian scandal, both women and men act in a space that is neither public nor private – a space that is outside the normal categories governing the space of the city. For this reason, such a space represents a dangerous alternative to Roman space, a space of chaos and instability lurking at the heart of the *res publica*.

7   Gender, Power, and Space in the *Ab Urbe Condita*

In this chapter, I have argued that the gendered semantics of narrated space is crucial to the *Ab Urbe Condita* because it works as an overarching framework for the narration of social and political instability. Relationships of power within a community (usually the Roman *res publica*, but in some cases, foreign communities, too) are often represented as a transgression of spatial boundaries that separate the community members based on their gender and social status.

The unduly, excessive, or tyrannical exercise of political power is often represented by one or more men penetrating the private space belonging to another man – a space often embodied by one or more women. The underlying idea is that a political community comprises a group of free adult males whose hierarchy is regulated by specific rules and responsibilities. Such free adult males, in turn, exercise control, responsibility, and protection over their freeborn women and children and their slaves. Political violence or tyranny is both the appropriation, on one man's part, of prerogatives that belong to one of his fellow citizens and endangers the physical inviolability of the most vulnerable part of the (freeborn) community, that is, women and children. Such acts are subversive to socio-political stability because they endanger the very relationships among community members on which the community rests.

A different kind of subversion occurs when women attempt to invade or appropriate public space. This can endanger the fabric of social relationships based on freeborn adult men's control over women. At the same time, transgressions of this type appear more complex, their range broader and more nuanced. Even within the highly idealised portrayal of gender and space that the *Ab Urbe Condita* paints, ambivalence characterises women's use of space.

Women seem to have a significant degree of spatial agency for what pertains to their houses (as the examples of Tanaquil and Verginia, the founder of the shrine of *Pudicitia Plebeia*, have shown). An important question needs to be addressed at this point: what does 'their houses' mean? Is it 'their houses' or 'their husbands' houses'? As my analysis has shown, the fundamental spatial semantics of the *Ab Urbe Condita* implies an asymmetrical notion of space: men own their private spaces, while women belong to them. In some tales, especially those about early Rome, this pattern is very clear: Lucretia and Verginia, for example, are presented as parts of their menfolk's houses. In Livy's later books, however, things appear more complex. Women could certainly own houses and, at least from the 2nd century BCE onwards, they often did. In the account about the Bacchanalian scandal, for example, Sulpicia is most probably a widow and might well be the owner of her house.[104] The general spatial pattern holds nonetheless, as does the prevalent association of women with domestic space in the *Ab Urbe Condita*. It is possible, however, that, here as elsewhere, Livy's representation of a woman endowed with spatial agency over her own domestic space reflects historical change: boundaries can be renegotiated, only to be ultimately reaffirmed.

Moreover, women's agency has evident limits; in particular, women's movement in public space appears problematic in the *Ab Urbe Condita*. By 'movement in public space' I mean a presence of women outside their homes which implies a meaningful interaction with 'public' or 'semi-public space'; to the contrary, the simple act of leaving one's home to go somewhere else (typically, to visit a relative or a female friend) is clearly assumed to be normal in the narrative. While women do, in several cases, appear in public space in the *Ab Urbe Condita*, this is usually in moments of crisis or political instability. The very disorderly quality of women's appearance and movement through the city and their highly emotional state embody the idea of crisis. Exceptions are public ceremonies – which also tend to take place at moments of crisis – in which women's movements are supervised by political authority. Significantly, Livy's narrative tends to ignore other kinds of religious activities performed by women in public space, unless as reactions to crises or their resolutions. Thus, the reader is left with the idea that freeborn women are an integral part of the community, but their public appearances as members of the community must be kept under male control.

Such observations apply to adult, freeborn married women whose relative agency in the narrative can be explained through their integral role in the reproduction of the community. In the narrative of the *Ab Urbe Condita* the reader rarely gets a glimpse of other women. One important and often overlooked category is constituted by unmarried (freeborn) girls. Livy's maidens – from Rhea Silvia to the maid of Ardea, from Verginia to the daughters of Heraclia and Scipio's Spanish prisoners – appear in a condition of vulnerability, as

---

104   Cf. Flower (2024).

potential victims of violence; they are mostly passive characters, over whose bodies powerful men exercise and negotiate their power.

The only virgin girl who is granted spatial agency in the *Ab Urbe Condita* is Cloelia, whose story is narrated at 2.13.6–11. Cloelia is among the hostages given by the Romans to the Etruscan king Porsenna in exchange for his promise to move his camp from the Janiculum. The girl escapes the Etruscans' surveillance and leads the other hostage girls across the Tiber and back to Rome. Porsenna, indignant at first, is later filled with admiration for her courage, frees her of his own will, and grants her the choice over which hostages should be freed – at which Cloelia chooses the youngest (*impubes*, 2.13.9) and most vulnerable. The Romans celebrate Cloelia's courage through an equestrian statue, an exceptional honour for a woman; Livy relates that the monument was once placed 'at the top of the Sacra Via', *in summa Sacra via* (2.13.11; it no longer existed in the historian's lifetime). It is worth noting that Cloelia exercises her spatial agency on a space that is not the city's space and that her transgression is performed against Rome's enemies. In other words, her act does not endanger the community but contributes to protecting its most vulnerable elements from external violence. Still, she constitutes a striking exception to Livy's pattern; while other girls in Livy's history generally depend on someone else's assistance, Cloelia successfully protects herself and the other hostage maidens from the men who hold them captive.

Not surprisingly, the narrative repeatedly stresses the exceptional character of her feat. At 2.13.6, the narrator introduces the episode by stating that, after Mucius Scaevola had been rewarded for his heroic attempt at killing Porsenna, 'having valour been so honoured, women, too, were roused to public glory' (*ita honorata virtute, feminae quoque ad publica decora excitatae*). The association of *publica decora* with women is, of course, highly unusual. The novelty of a woman's heroic deed is brought out once more at the end of the tale (2.13.11):

> Pace redintegrata Romani novam in femina virtutem novo genere honoris, statua equestri, donavere; in summa Sacra via fuit posita virgo insidens equo.

> After the re-establishment of the peace, the Romans rewarded such unusual valour in a woman with an unusual kind of honour, an equestrian statue: at the top of the Sacra Via there was once was a statue of a maiden on a horse.

Significantly, Cloelia's statue is placed in the Forum, that is, precisely in that 'public' space which, throughout his narrative, Livy represents as improper for women to enter. In a way, Cloelia's presence in the Forum in the form of her statue is the only instance, in the *Ab Urbe Condita*, of an individual woman's successful presence in the most political and public space in Rome. Just as significantly, however, it is the male governing elite which decides on the statue's placement as an exception due to exceptional circumstances.

Traces of non-freeborn women are even scantier in the *Ab Urbe Condita*. The only prominent character in these categories is Hispala Faecenia in Book 39. Although, as a freedwoman courtesan of foreign origins, she does not participate in the community's reproduction in the same way as matrons do, her use of space is not substantially different from that of other women in Livy's history. Her identity lies at the intersection of social and ethnic boundaries; still, like other women in Livy, she proves aware of Roman space's fundamental boundaries and does not overstep them. Ultimately, through her role in unveiling the Bacchanalian conspiracy, she becomes a Roman citizen who can marry a Roman citizen. In a way, through her narrative arc, she represents the very process by which external elements are integrated into the Roman community in a way that renegotiates but also re-affirms its basic boundaries.

People whose gender identity does not fit the strict binary pattern of the *Ab Urbe Condita* are also virtually absent from Livy's history. Indeed, the text represents the blurring of the boundary between binary gender identities as a dangerous act. Livy's account of the Bacchanalian scandal has both space and gender as significant elements of the threatened subversion of the *res publica* by the hand of Bacchic initiates. The space where the Bacchic rites are performed is a space where every boundary regulating the life of the community ceases to exist: the 'public' and the 'private' lose their meaning, women and men are together, men become similar to women, and the external world penetrates the heart of the city. The *res publica* strikes back by reaffirming its orderly space, where both interactions between the genders and political interaction are subject to (spatial) control.

Control of space and of the activities performed in and through space emerges once more as a crucial concern in the *Ab Urbe Condita*. Feminist narratology shows that literary works often construe control over space as 'masculine' and identification with or an emotionally coloured perception of space as 'feminine'.[105] If one applies such observations to Livy's history, one will see how the historian's representation of space and gender is deeply connected to his representation of military and political space. Transgressions of gendered boundaries are failures of control, threatening the structure, hierarchies, and 'Roman-ness' of Roman society.

---

105   Cf. e.g. Würzbach (2004, pp. 64–68).

Conclusions: Livy's Vocabulary of Space

1 Space, Semantics, and Historical Imagination

In the previous chapters I have read Livy's *Ab Urbe Condita* with a focus on the space the narrative shapes (the 'narrated world'). I first examined how the space of the city of Rome (Chapters 1 and 2) and the space of war are constructed within the text, with special reference to battlefields (Chapter 3). I then investigated a broader spatial pattern at work in Livy's history, namely the spatial semantics of gender, and argued that the narrative treats notions of femininity and masculinity by construing certain ways to use space as feminine or masculine (Chapter 4).

My analysis has revealed the presence and importance of what one might name a 'vocabulary of space': in other words, a tendency to attribute specific and recurrent meanings to specific places or topographic features. In some cases, an episode can be woven around the semantic connotations of its setting: instances of such a use of narrated space include, among others, the Curia and Comitium in several episodes of the Struggle of the Orders, the Capitol in the story of Titus Annius from Setia, and the battlefield of Lake Trasimene. I have used the term 'meaningful settings' when referring to narratives of this kind, to stress the centrality of the setting in the narrative design of an episode.

Even when a setting does not play such a prominent role, however, the text can stress some features or aspects of it to activate semantic associations. For example, mentioning the impassability of a mountainous site in association with the *locus non armis*-motif can evoke a whole set of ideas about treachery, valour, and Roman-ness in the reader. Similarly, a cursory remark about the fact that women did not, on a certain occasion, keep to their homes can play into the overall gendered semantics about domestic space and boundaries.

Of course, not every single element of the narrated space is charged with semantic meaning or plays a symbolic role. Sometimes spatial information is just spatial information, which serves to locate an event or clarify its development. However, my analysis suggests that space is an integral part of Livy's historical imagination and that one should be attentive to its meanings if one wants to fully understand the interpretation of Roman history the narrative proposes.

What, then, does the semantics of narrated space (at least with regard to the aspects covered in this study) reveal about Roman history as represented in the *Ab Urbe Condita*? The following sections discuss some significant ideas which, due to their recurrence and importance, have emerged from my analysis.

2   Relational Space, Control, and Emotion

At the outset of this study, I mentioned the relational nature of space and the two-way relationship existing between space and human beings: people and community shape space and, at the same time, space shapes people and communities. The *Ab Urbe Condita* portrays the complexities of that relationship in a strikingly effective manner.

There is, first, a way in which the Romans are bound to their city space. The gods are said to have chosen the site of city and to reside in its most hallowed sites; the omens of the Terminus shrine and the human head mark the Capitol as the predestined centre of human affairs; and the Romans' attempt to move to Veii after the Gallic sack proves a failure, because there are religious and political (or better: religious-political) actions that one can only perform at specific sites. Especially (but not only) the early books provide the reader with a notion of why Rome is where it is, and why it could not be anywhere else.

The gods appear as the crucial actors in determining the bond between the Roman community and the physical space it belongs to. While Livy's narrative does not, as a rule, feature clear divine interventions, it often sets the gods' connection with Roman space as fundamental and unchangeable. Thus, there is a way in which gods and space – or, rather, space in its religious implications – shape the form and features of the Roman community.

At the same time, however, Rome is not 'Rome' until it is founded, until the community of Roman citizens shapes the city by means of its own inner growth. The city's gradual annexation of hill after hill, their associations with the ethnic communities that constitute the Roman citizen-body, and the shaping of the Forum as a political space are further steps in the process of turning natural space (hills, valleys) into communal space. More to the point, those acts shape a new space, which is at the same time political, religious, and social. The space of the city comes to embody the different groups within the community, and the relationships between those groups: patricians and plebeians, *nobiles* and people at large, women and men, Romans and foreigners, slaves and the freeborn.

The shaping of the human and political space of the city also involves setting a boundary, which separates the space within from the space without. This act is fundamental in shaping the narrated world of the *Ab Urbe Condita* and, on the textual level, it accounts for the crucial distinction between events *domi* and events *militiae*, on which the narrative design of the work is based.

The space outside the city is, in turn, constituted through human action. In particular, the space of war results from the interplay of topography and standard military space: Roman armies shape space as they bring Roman

CONCLUSIONS: LIVY'S VOCABULARY OF SPACE   247

space to foreign landscapes. The text, however, shows other possible ways to shape space socially, as my observations about the relationship of 'barbarian' peoples with their native landscapes have shown. Peoples such as the Gauls or the Ligurians appear to have a relationship of quasi-identification with their landscapes, which stands in opposition to the Roman appropriating and controlling approach. Their landscapes, which the text often depicts as wild and impassable, are re-defined as they are conquered by Roman valour and discipline, which superimposes the features of Roman space onto them.

Conquest and expansion thus emerge as processes by which the space of the world is not just changed, but re-shaped and re-constituted through a series of acts of control. In fact, my analysis has shown that concern with control (and with failures of control) is pervasive in the *Ab Urbe Condita* and is tied to anxieties about Roman identity and stability.

Controlling the terrain is crucial for any military expedition, but Livy's narrative stresses such an issue in a special way. To Roman soldiers and generals in Livy's military accounts, the foreign world is often wild and hostile; they strive to impose the orderliness of Roman 'standard military space' on it, but the nature of the conquered world often threatens to escape their control. Thus, the *Ab Urbe Condita* poses the ability to fight in an orderly manner under any circumstances as an important aspect of Roman military ethics and presents the ability to conquer even the harshest landscapes as a quintessential Roman quality.

Control, however, proves crucial when it comes to Rome's city space, too. The explosions of violence within the city can be interpreted as moments in which the control of socio-political elites over the space of the city (and thus over the relationships among its inhabitants) is endangered. This is most obvious in the account of the plebeian revolts but is also apparent in the portrayal of women's appropriations of the city space, or of tyrants' attempts to gain unlimited power, or of the Bacchanalian conspiracy. Livy presents such occasions, when the spatial order embodying the socio-economic order is put into question, as potentially dangerous for the harmonious functioning of the citizen body. At the same time, temporary disruptions of the spatial order can, under some circumstances, produce salutary effects in the long term. The Struggle of the Orders also shapes the institutions of the later Republic; the resulting patricio-plebeian *nobilitas* partially changes Livy's narrated space, with the Curia becoming the centre of political activity. Women's activities in public space, while presented as instances of boundary transgression, can be vital at moments of crisis. The health of the city's spatial form seems to depend on its ability to adapt to changes while maintaining fundamental boundaries; each historical age must find a new balance between these goals, which must be as harmonious as possible for the community to thrive. On the other hand, the text portrays other kinds of disruptions as devastating: this is the case with tyrannical behaviour, and with the promiscuity of the Bacchanalia, which are depicted as aiming to subvert the spatial order.

As my previous observations suggest, Livy's representations of spatial transgressions or failures of control often emphasise the themes of excessive emotion or passion. Rash commanders falling into enemy ambushes fail to exercise rational control over the terrain. Enemies who choose to take advantage of the terrain are often presented as driven by fear (Antiochus), excessive emotion (Philip and Perseus), or near-sighted strategies (the Gauls and other 'barbarian' peoples). One character who does not fall into any of these categories is Hannibal, whose strength lies precisely in his control of the terrain. Livy's narrative of the Second Punic War is, among other things, a narrative of Hannibal and the Romans' conflicting attempts to gain control of the Italian (and eventually African) landscapes: Hannibal, while at first successful, ultimately fails, whereas the Romans learn to unite strategy with bravery and open fighting.

The link between emotions and (spatial) disorder is perhaps even more evident within the space of the city. An inability to control one's passions or ambitions can lead to political violence and to boundaries being breached. One consequence of emotion is disorderly movement through space. The *Ab Urbe Condita* tends to represent the movements of people from subaltern groups (e.g. plebeians or women)[1] as haphazard and undignified unless they take place under state supervision.[2] Thus, the outraged plebeians of the early books often run here and there through the streets while the consuls and Senate try to regain control, women spontaneously walk into public spaces in the grip of their emotions, and the participants in the Bacchic rites of 186 BCE move around in a frenzy. Re-establishment of the social order often requires re-establishment of the proper, state-approved ways to move through space.

My observations so far point to a subterranean theme running through Livy's history: the notion that, while it is the duty of a good statesman to re-establish order through control, control is, by its very nature, never stable. The narrative suggests that Roman (and particularly elite Roman) control over space is

---

1 Of course, 'women' is a vast category, which includes very different socio-economic milieus. The women from the upper echelons of Roman society certainly enjoyed wealth and, in some cases, (political) power, as the critical literature discussed in Chapter 4 shows. However, the *Ab Urbe Condita* constructs an idealised view of Roman society in which women, while occasionally acting as counsellors or authority figures, do not wield power in person, and in which men are expected to control women's behaviour and sexuality. It is in this sense that I speak of women as a 'subaltern' group.
2 On this point cf. Mineo (2006, pp. 49–50).

constantly endangered, both within and without the city. How can one, then, successfully avert those dangers and maintain spatial order?

3 How to Make the State Function: Space and Livy's Political Vision

One can read Livy's *Ab Urbe Condita* as, among other things, a study on how to make a state work properly. The historian himself prompts his readers to interpret the work in this way: at *praef.* 9–10 he famously invites them to focus on the moral causes of Roman growth, decay, and crisis, in order to learn 'what you should imitate for yourself and your state and what you should avoid as being shameful in both its beginnings and its outcome'.[3] The imagined recipients of such prompting are people engaged in the well-being of the Roman state – those endowed with political authority, of course, but also citizens who want to learn the correct way to behave *as* citizens.

Livy's words in the Preface also resonate with the grim reality of the civil wars, which were probably still in full sway when he started writing; at the same time, they open up the possibility of an improvement of the Roman situation in the future, on the condition that one learns from the past. As the historian went on writing, the *res publica* found a new balance, and gradually the reader will have become aware that the time of crisis was over. Therefore, the question how to make peace and safety endure will have been topical.

Examining narrated space has allowed me to stress some crucial points the narrative presents as necessary for a country's well-being: first, a readiness of all components of a community to compromise and adjust their balance to new historical circumstances; second, the stability of a fixed centre; third, the correct distribution of violence between the space within and the space without.

The first point might seem obvious, but the significant emphasis the narrative lays on it prompts a closer consideration. Livy's reflections on political compromise and adjustment to change appears especially productive in his construction and representation of the city space. The narrated space of Rome is not homogeneous; rather, it is a composite space, with inner workings. Some of its parts are connected with specific elements of the Roman population, others embody crucial institutions; moreover, different components of the population are expected to use different spaces in different ways. At the same

---

3 *Inde tibi tuaeque rei publicae quod imitere capias, inde foedum inceptu foedum exitu quod vites* (*praef.* 10).

time, the space of the city changes and expands in time, and its changes cannot but affect the relationships between its parts.

The text suggests that the ideal condition for the efficient functioning of the city space (and of the *res publica*) is not a static one, but one in which a new balance is established from time to time, so as to adjust to change. The establishment of balance between the different components of the state results from effective communication; it implies each side taking steps toward the other(s) – steps which can be metaphorical, but also (as in the episodes of reconciliation between Senate and plebs examined in Chapter 1) material and spatial. The *Ab Urbe Condita* represents the workings of the state as the result of a collective effort, as an integration of new elements into a political, social, and spatial order, and as a constant renegotiation of existing relationships of power (and spatial relationships).

One of the most crucial issues, and one that deeply affects the space of the city, is the relationship between leadership and collective action. Livy's representation of characters' uses of urban space shows two antithetical dangers constantly looming up behind the Roman political system: on the one hand, collective violence; on the other, the tyrannical power of one or few leaders. Paradoxically, these two extremes have very similar effects on the city space: they disrupt or, in some cases, subvert some of its main structures.

The remedy to such dangers seems to lie in a collective effort within a recognised hierarchical structure. As my analysis has shown, numerous episodes from the *Ab Urbe Condita* are about imposing a political and social hierarchy upon an inherently unstable world. The establishment of socio-political hierarchy requires the collaboration of all (even those excluded from power). Its success in recruiting different components of the citizen body depends, among other things, on its flexibility: a hierarchical structure should adapt over time to include new social or ethnic strata and new forms of government, while maintaining its basic order.

The second point of Livy's political meditation, a stable centre, was topical in the triumviral period and at the beginning of Augustus' principate. In fact, concerns that Rome might lose its centrality to other cities, especially in the East, were alive at least from Caesar's times.[4] There had been rumours that Caesar intended to move to Ilium, or even transfer the seat of power to Alexandria, where the Egyptian queen Cleopatra had given him a son.[5] Such worries resurfaced with more force when, based on the arrangements of the so-called Second Triumvirate, Antony received the East as his area of operations and

---

4 Cf. esp. Ceausescu (1976); Kenty (2017).
5 Cf. Nic. Dam. 20; Suet. *Iul.* 79.3.

subsequently established his residence in Alexandria; in time, rumours spread that he intended to donate Rome to Cleopatra – just as he bestowed various Eastern provinces and kingdoms on the sons he had had from the queen[6] – and to turn Alexandria into the capital of the *imperium*.[7] Octavian was skilled in using Antony's actions and the rumours about his intentions as propaganda weapons against his opponent; and, in contrast to Antony, he took pains to stress the centrality of Rome and Italy as a tenet of his own policy. It is no surprise that the spectre of an *altera Roma*[8] (an 'alternative Rome' in the East) and the re-affirmation of the Italic roots of the city are prominent themes in the literature of the Thirties and Twenties BCE.[9] In the *Ab Urbe Condita*, narratives such as that about the proposed move to Veii at the end of Book 5 (culminating in Camillus' great speech)[10] or the account of the Capuan rebellion during the Hannibalic War (Books 23–26) have been found to resonate with Roman fears of alternative centres of power.[11]

More generally, I have shown that the *Ab Urbe Condita* sets the Capitol as the unmoveable centre of the city and the *imperium*, that guarantees Rome's permanence. One aspect of Livy's representation of the Capitol as a centre is especially significant: its ability to remain stable while allowing for change in external space. The Capitol is the beginning and end point of multiple cycles: the year, military campaigns, narrative sections of the *Ab Urbe Condita*, and even the cycle of growth, crisis and rebirth that the First Pentad represents. Most of those cycles entail a spatial dimension that might best be represented as a spiral: while the centre remains the same, the spaces to which Rome power extends widen as the narrative goes on; at the same time, it is precisely the constant going back to the centre that makes such amplification possible. Livy's history suggests the notion that the centre (Rome, the Capitol) must remain where it is, if expansion is to be successful and not lead to implosion.

The third and final point (correct distribution of violence between inner and outer space) is more complex. As I have shown, the idea that violence must be directed outward, so that it does not break out inwardly, is a constant in the

---

6   Cf. Livy *Per.* 131; Plut. *Vit. Ant.* 55.4–5; Dio Cass. 49.41.1–5.
7   Cf. Dio Cass. 50.4.1; 50.50.4.
8   The expression comes from Cic. *Leg. agr.* 286; *Phil.* 12.7.
9   One might mention e.g. the *laudes Italiae* in Verg. *G.* 2.136–176; the *Aeneid*'s notion of the Trojans' Italic origins (cf. e.g. *Aen.* 3.163–171); also, in the same poem (12.791–842) and in Hor. *Carm.* 3.3.14–78, Juno acceptance of Aeneas' establishment in Latium (Vergil), Romulus' deification (Horace) and Rome's thriving (Vergil and Horace) on the condition that Troy must never be reborn.
10   Cf. e.g. Edwards (1996, pp. 45–52).
11   Cf. Kenty (2017).

Ab Urbe Condita. Yet, the very process of expansion that Livy's history portrays has the potential to push that notion to its limits. First, as Rome expands – and thus Roman space is imposed over more and more countries – the boundary between 'inner' and 'outer' spaces shifts and becomes fuzzier. What is now 'inner' space? The city of Rome? Or Rome and Italy? Or the part of the world controlled by Rome? Such a discussion is only visible in glimpses in the surviving books (which concern a time when Rome's empire was just being born), but it is there: the effort to define 'Roman' military ethics, for example, and the reflections about the possible influence of foreign landscapes, or again the discourse about learning from one's enemy without losing one's identity (which is so prominent in the account of Rome's dealings with Hannibal) are all aspects of the narrative's treatment of the problem.

On an even more fundamental level, the idea that Rome's power shall become coterminous with the world puts the very distinction between internal and external space into question. If Rome and the world become one thing, where shall violence be directed? Will it necessarily explode internally again?[12] Such an implicit anxiety runs as an undercurrent throughout Livy's narrative of the conquests of the 2nd century BCE and one can well imagine it to be present in his account of later history, too.

The historian provides no straightforward answers as to how to avert the danger of the implosion of the Roman world, or even as to whether averting it would be at all possible. Rather, his text invites his readers to think about such problems and find their own ways of acting for the common good. Even more so, it prompts them to reflect about what 'Roman-ness' is, and how to reshape and preserve Roman identity in a changing world.

---

12   For this idea cf. Fabrizi (2021b).

Referenced Works

Acharya, I. and Panda, U.K. (2022) *Geographical Imaginations: Literature and the Spatial Turn*. Oxford: Oxford University Press.

Adam, R. (1982) *Tite-Live, Histoire Romaine*, Tome XXVIII: *Livre XXXVIII*. Paris: Les Belles Lettres. Collection des Universités de France L 259.

Adler, E. (2011) *Valorizing the Barbarians: Enemy Speeches in Roman Historiography*. Austin: University of Texas Press.

Akar, P. (2002) 'Camille et la concorde', *Hypothèses*, 5(1), pp. 205–215.

Albers, J. (2013) *Campus Martius. Die urbane Entwicklung des Marsfeldes von der Republik bis zur mittleren Kaiserzeit*. Wiesbaden: Dr. Ludwig Reichert Verlag.

Albrecht, D. (2016) *Hegemoniale Männlichkeit bei Titus Livius*. Heidelberg: Verlag Antike. Studien zur alten Geschichte 23.

Alexander, M.C. (2010) 'Law in the Roman Republic', in Rosenstein, N. and Morstein-Marx, R. (eds.) *A Companion to the Roman Republic*. Malden, MA: Blackwell, pp. 236–255.

Allison, P.M. (2006) 'Engendering Roman Spaces', in Robertson, E.C., Seibert, J.D., Fernadez, D.C. and Zender, M.U. (eds.) *Space and Spatial Analysis in Archeology*. Calgary: University of Calgary Press, pp. 343–354.

Allison, P.M. (2007) 'Engendering Roman Domestic Space', *BSAS*, 15, pp. 343–350.

Almagro, M. (1951) *Las fuentes escritas referentes a Ampurias*. Barcelona: Casa provincial de Caridad. Monografías Ampuritanas I.

Almagro, M. (1956) *Ampurias. Geschichte der Stadt und Führer durch die Ausgrabungen*. German translation by Erich Kukhain. Barcelona: Casa provincial de Caridad.

Alonso-Nuñez, J.M. (2002) *The Idea of Universal History in Greece. From Herodotus to the Age of Augustus*. Amsterdam: Giebel.

Arata, F.P. (2010) 'Nuove considerazioni a proposito del tempio di Giove Capitolino', *MEFRA*, 122(2), pp. 585–624. DOI: https://doi.org/10.4000/mefra.317.

Ashby, T. and Doughill, W. (1927) 'The Capitol, Rome', *The Town Planning Review*, 12, pp. 159–186.

Astin, A.E. (1978) *Cato the Censor*. Oxford: Oxford University Press.

Bal, M. (1981) 'On Meanings and Descriptions', *Studies in 20th Century Literature*, 6(1), *Getting the Message: On the Semiotics of Literary Signification*, pp. 100–148.

Bal, M. (1997) *Narratology. Introduction to the Theory of Narrative*. 2nd ed. Toronto, Buffalo, and London: University of Toronto Press.

Balland, A. (1984) 'La *casa Romuli* au Palatin et au Capitole', *REL*, 62, pp. 57–80.

Barthes, R. (1968) 'L'effet de reel', *Communications*, 11, *Recherces sémiologiques le vraisemblable*, pp. 84–89.

Bartmanski, D. (2024) 'A Dangerous Liaison? Space and the Field of Cultural Production', in Bartmanski, D., Füller, H., Hoerning, J. and Weidenhaus, G. (eds.)

Considering Space: A Critical Concept for the Social Sciences. London and New York: Routledge, pp. 205–230.

Bartmanski, D. and Füller, H. (2024) 'Introduction. An Invitation to Spatial Theorizing', in Bartmanski *et al.* (2024) pp. 2–15.

Bayet, J. (ed.) and Baillet, G. (transl.) (1940) *Tite-Live, Histoire Romaine*. Tome I: *Livre I*. Paris: Les Belles Lettres. Collection des Universités de France L 96.

Beard, M. (2009) *The Roman Triumph*. Cambridge, MA: Harvard University Press.

Beck, H. (2003) 'Den Ruhm nicht teilen wollen: Fabius Pictor und die Anfänge des römischen Nobilitätsdiskurses', in Gotter et al. (2003) pp. 72–92.

Beck, H. and Walter, U. (eds.) (2005) *Die früheren römischen Historiker*. Band I: *Von Fabius Pictor bis Cn. Gellius*. 2nd revised ed. Darmstadt: Wissenschaftliche Buchgesellschaft.

Bell, A. (2004) *Spectacular Power in the Greek and Roman City*. Oxford: Oxford University Press.

Beltramini, L. (2023) 'Le conseguenze della vittoria. Scipione e la riflessione sull'imperialismo romano in Livio', *Histos*, 17, pp. 205–238. DOI: https://doi.org/10.29173/histos9.

Beltramini, L. and Rocco, M. (2020) 'Livy on Scipio Africanus. The Commander's Portrait at 26.19.3–9', *CQ*, 70, pp. 230–246.

Benoist, S. (2015) 'Women and Imperium in Rome: Imperial Perspectives', in Fabres-Serris, J. and Keith, A. (eds.) *Women and War in Antiquity*. Baltimore: John Hopkins University Press, pp. 266–288.

Bernard, J.-E. (2000) *Le portrait chez Tite-Live: Essai sur une écriture de l'histoire romaine*. Brussels: Latomus.

Bernard, J.-E. (2015) 'Portraits of Peoples', in Mineo (2015) pp. 39–51.

Biggs, T. (2016) 'Contesting *cunctatio*: Livy 22.14, Fabius Maximus, and the Problem of Pastoral', *CJ*, 111, pp. 281–301.

Biggs, T. (2019) '*Cicero, quid in alieno saeculo tibi*? The "Republican" Rostra between Caesar and Augustus', in Loar, Murray and Rebeggiani (2019) pp. 27–44.

Boatwright, M. (2011) 'Women and Gender in the Forum Romanum', *TAPhA* 141, pp. 105–141.

Bonfante, L. (1998) 'Livy and the Monuments', in Lubetsky, M., Gottlieb, C. and Keller, S. (eds.) *Boundaries of the Ancient Near Eastern World: A Tribute to Cyrus H. Gordon*. Journal for the Study of the Old Testament Supplement Series 273, pp. 480–492.

Bonfante Warren, L. (1973a) 'The Women of Etruria', *Arethusa*, 6(1), *Women in Antiquity*, pp. 91–101.

Bonfante Warren, L. (1973b) 'Etruscan Women: A Question of Interpretation', *Archaeology* 26(4), pp. 242–249.

Bonnefond-Coudry, M. (1989) *Le Sénat de la république romaine de la guerre d'Hannibal à Auguste: pratiques délibératives et prise de décision*. Rome: École française de Rome.

Bridgeman, T. (2007) 'Time and Space in Narrative', in Herman, D. (ed.) *Cambridge Companion to Narrative Theory*. Cambridge: Cambridge University Press.

Bringmann, K. (1977) 'Weltherrschaft und innere Krise Roms im Spiegel der Geschichtsschreibung des zweiten und ersten Jahrhunderts v.Chr.', *A&A*, 23, pp. 28–49.

Briscoe, J. (1973) *A Commentary on Livy. Books XXXI–XXXIII*. Oxford: Clarendon Press.

Briscoe, J. (1981) *A Commentary on Livy. Books XXXIV–XXXVII*. Oxford: Clarendon Press.

Briscoe, J. (ed.) (1986) *Titi Livi Ab urbe condita libri XLI–LV*. Stuttgart: Teubner. Bibliotheca scriptorum Graecorum et Romanorum Teubneriana.

Briscoe, J. (ed.) (1991) *Livius Ab urbe condita libri XXXI–XL*. Stuttgart: Teubner. Bibliotheca scriptorum Graecorum et Romanorum Teubneriana.

Briscoe, J. (2008) *A Commentary on Livy. Books 38–40*. Oxford: Clarendon Press.

Briscoe, J. (2012) *A Commentary on Livy. Books 41–45*. Oxford: Oxford University Press.

Briscoe, J. (ed.) (2016) *Titi Livi Ab urbe condita*. Volume 3: Libri XXI–XXV. Oxford: Oxford University Press. Oxford Classical Texts.

Brodersen, K. (1995) *Terra Cognita. Studien zur römischen Raumerfassung*. Hildesheim: Olms.

Buchholz, S. and Jahn, M. (2005) 'Space in Narrative', in Herman, D., Jahn, M. and Ryan, M.-L. (eds.) *Routledge Encyclopedia of Narrative Theory*. London and New York: Routledge, pp. 551–555.

Burck, E. (1934) *Die Erzählungskunst des Titus Livius*. Berlin: Weidmann.

Burck, E. (1962) *Einführung in die dritte Dekade des Livius*. 2nd ed. Heidelberg: Kerle.

Burton, P.J. (2000) 'The Last Republican Historian: A New Date for the Composition of Livy's First Pentad', *Historia*, 49, pp. 429–446.

Burton, P.J. (2008) 'Livy's Preface and His Historical Context', *Scholia*, 17, pp. 70–91.

Carafa, P. (1998) *Il Comizio di Roma dalle origini all'età di Augusto*. Roma: 'L'Erma' di Bretschneider.

Carafa, P., and Bruno, D. (2013) 'Il Palatino messo a punto', *Arch.Class.*, 64, pp. 719–786.

Carandini, A. (2004) *Palatino, Velia e Sacra Via. Paesaggi urbani attraverso il tempo*. Roma: Edizioni dell'Ateneo.

Carandini, A. (2010) *Le case del potere nell'antica Roma*. Roma and Bari: Laterza.

Carandini, A. and Bruno, D. (2008) *La casa di Augusto. Dai 'Lupercalia' al Natale*. Roma and Bari: Laterza.

Carandini, A., and Carafa, P. (1995) *Palatium e Sacra Via I. Prima delle mura, l'età delle mura e le case arcaiche*. Bollettino di Archeologia 31–33.

Carandini, A., Carafa, P. and Ippoliti, M. (2021) *Dal mostro al principe. Alle origini di Roma*. Bari: Laterza.

Carandini, A. and Papi E. (1999) *Palatium e Sacra Via II. L'età tardo-repubblicana e la prima età imperiale (fine III secolo a.C.–64 d.C.)*. Bollettino di Archeologia 59–60.

Carawan, E.M. (1988) '*Graecia liberata* and the Role of Flamininus in Livy's Fourth Decade', *TAPhA*, 118, pp. 209–252.

Casapulla, V. (2024) *Commento al libro XXIX di Livio*. Huelva: Editorial Universidad de Huelva. Huelva Classical Monographs. Exemplaria Classica Supplements.

Ceausescu, P. (1976) 'Altera Roma: Histoire d'une folie politique', *Historia*, 25(1), pp. 79–108.

Cecamore, C. (2002) *Palatium. Topografia storica del Palatino tra III sec. a.C. e I sec. d.C.* Roma: 'L'Erma' di Bretschneider. Bullettino della Commissione Archeologica Comunale di Roma, Supplementi 9.

Cencrini, F. and Rohr Vio, F. (eds.) (2016) *Matronae in domo et in re publica agentes. Spazi e occasioni dell'azione femminile nel mondo romano tra tarda repubblica e primo impero. Atti del convegno di Venezia 16–17 ottobre 2014*. Trieste: EUT.

Chaplin, J.D. (2000) *Livy's Exemplary History*. Cambridge: Cambridge University Press.

Chaplin, J.D. (2010a) 'Historical and Historiographical Repetition in Livy's Thermopylae', in Polleichtner (2010) pp. 47–66.

Chaplin, J.D. (2010b) 'The Livian Periochae and the Last Republican Writer', in Horster, M. and Reitz, C. (eds.) *Condensing Texts – Condensed Texts*. Stuttgart: Franz Steiner Verlag, pp. 451–467.

Chassignet, M. (ed.) (1996) *L'annalistique romaine. Tome 1: Les Annales des pontifes et l'annalistique ancienne (fragments)*. Paris: Les Belles Lettres. Collection des universités de France L 331.

Chassignet, M. (2001) 'La "construction" des aspirantes à la tyrannie: Sp. Cassius, Sp. Maelius et Manlius Capitolinus', in Coudry and Späth (2001) pp. 83–96.

Chatman, S. (1978) *Story and Discourse. Narrative Structure in Fiction and Film*. Ithaca, NY: Cornell University Press.

Claridge, A. (2014) 'Reconstructing the Temple of Apollo on the Palatine Hill in Rome', in Häuber, C., F.X. Schütz, F.X. and Winder, G.M. (eds.) *Reconstruction and the Historic City: Rome and Abroad, an interdisciplinary approach, colloquium October 2012*. München: Ludwig-Maximilians-Universität München, pp. 128–152.

Clark, V. (2014) *Landscapes of Conquest: Space, Place, and Environment in Livy's Ab Urbe Condita*, PhD diss., Princeton University.

Clarke, K. (1999) 'Universal Perspectives in Historiography', in Kraus, C.S. (ed.) *The Limits of Historiography. Genre and Narrative in Ancient Historical Texts*. Leiden, Boston and Köln: Brill. Mnemosyne, bibliotheca classica Batava. Supplementum 191, pp. 249–279.

Coarelli, F. (1968) 'La Porta Trionfale e la Via dei Trionfi', *DArch.*, 2(1), pp. 55–103.

Coarelli, F. (1983) *Il Foro Romano. Vol. 1: Periodo arcaico*. Roma: Quasar.

Coarelli, F. (1985) *Il Foro Romano. Vol. 2: Periodo repubblicano e augusteo*. Roma: Quasar.

Coarelli, F. (1997) *Il Campo Marzio. Dalle origini alla fine della Repubblica*. Roma: Quasar.

Coarelli, F. (2012) *Palatium. Il Palatino dalle origini all'impero*. Roma: Quasar.
Coarelli, F. (2020) *Il Foro Romano*. Vol. 3: *Da Augusto al tardo impero*. Roma: Quasar.
Connell, R.W. (1987) *Gender and Power*. Sidney: Allen and Unwin.
Connell, R.W. and Messerschmidt, J.W. (2005) 'Hegemonic Masculinity: Rethinking the Concept', *Gender and Society*, 19(6), pp. 829–859.
Conway, R.S. and Walters, C.F. (eds.) (1919) *Titi Livi Ab urbe condita*. Vol. 2: *Libri VI–X*. Oxford: Oxford University Press.
Cornell, T.J. (1995) *The Beginnings of Rome. Italy and Rome from the bronze Age to the Punic Wars (c. 1000–264 BC)*. London and New York: Routledge.
Cornell, T.J. (2003) 'Coriolanus: Myth, History and Performance', in Braund, D. and Gill, C. (eds.) *Myth, History and Culture in Republican Rome: Studies in Honour of T.P. Wiseman*. Exeter: The University of Exeter Press, pp. 73–97.
Cornell, T.J. (2009) 'Cato the Elder and The Origins of Roman Autobiography', in Smith and Powell (2009) pp. 15–40.
Cornwell, H. and Woolf, G. (eds.) (2023). *Gendering Roman Imperialism*. Leiden: Brill.
Coudry, M. and Späth, T. (eds.) (2001) *L'invention des grands hommes de la Rome antique = Die Konstruktion der großen Männer Altroms: actes du colloque du Collegium Beatus Rhenanus, Augst, 16–18 septembre 1999*. Paris: de Boccard.
Cugusi, P. and Sblendorio Cugusi, M.T. (2001) *Opere di Marco Porcio Catone Censore*. Volume primo. Torino: UTET. Classici Latini.
Daly, G. (2002) *Cannae. The Experience of Battle in the Second Punic War*. London: Routledge.
Danti, A. (2016a) 'L'*Immobile Saxum* torna alla luce: i ritrovamenti delle demolizioni sul versante meridionale del Campidoglio', in Parisi Presicce and Danti (2016), pp. 181–188.
Danti, A. (2016b) 'Il tempio di Giove Capitolino: contributi per la più recente storia degli studi e degli scavi', in Parisi Presicce and Danti (2016), pp. 209–218.
David, J.-M. (2001) 'Les étapes historiques de la construction de la figure de Coriolan', in Coudry and Späth (2001), pp. 17–25.
De Franchis, M. (2013) 'La figure de Scipion dans la troisième décade de Tite-Live: un idéal pour le princeps?', in Casanova-Robin, H., Boulègue, L. and Lévy, C. (eds.) *Le Tyran et sa postérité dans la littérature latine de l'Antiquité à la Renaissance*. Paris: Classiques Garnier, pp. 143–159.
De Franchis, M. (2015) 'L'episode de Sophonisbe chez Tite-Live, 30.12–15: un morceau d'histoire tragique?', in Naas, V. and Simon, M. (eds.) *De Samos à Rome: personnalité et influence de Douris*. Nanterre: Presses universitaires de Paris Ouest, pp. 303–328.
Degl'Innocenti Pierini, R. (2022–2023) 'Oltre il confine della *domus*: Giulia maggiore e altre donne romane negli spazi urbani e in viaggio', *Storia delle Donne*, 18–19, pp. 205–222.

de Jong, I.J.F. (ed.) (2012) *Space in Ancient Greek Literature*. Leiden: Brill, Mnemosyne Supplements 339.

de Jong, I.J.F. (2014) *Narratology & Classics. A Practical Guide*. Oxford: Oxford University Press.

de Jong, I.J.F. (2018) 'The View from the Mountain (*oroskopia*) in Greek and Latin Literature', *CCA*, 64, pp. 23–48.

Della Calce, E. (2023) *Mos uetustissimus – Tito Livio e la percezione della clemenza*. Berlin and New York: De Gruyter.

Dennerlein, K. (2009) *Narratologie des Raumes*. Berlin: De Gruyter.

Dennerlen, K. (2011) 'Raum', in Martínez, M. (ed.) *Handbuch Erzählliteratur. Theorie, Analyse, Geschichte*. Stuttgart and Weimar: Metzler, pp. 158–165.

De Sanctis, G. (1968) *Storia dei Romani*, 2nd ed. Volume 3: *L'età delle Guerre Puniche*, Part 2. Firenze: La Nuova Italia.

de Souza, M. and Devillers, O. (eds.) (2019) *Le Palatin, émergence de la colline du pouvoir à Rome, de la mort d'Auguste au règne de Vespasien, 14–79 p.C.* Bourdeux: Ausonius Éditions.

Develin, R. (1977) '*Lex curiata* and the Competence of Magistrates', *Mnemosyne*, 30(1), pp. 49–65.

Dillery, J. (2009) 'Roman Historians and the Greek: Audiences and Models', in Feldherr (2009) pp. 77–107.

DiLuzio, M. (2024) 'Women in the Regia and the Republican Imagination', in Flower and Osgood (2024) pp. 89–121.

D'Ippolito, F. (1986) *Giuristi e sapienti in Roma arcaica*. Roma and Bari: Laterza.

Döbler, C. (1999) *Politische Agitation und Öffentlichkeit in der späten Republik*. Frankfurt am Main: Peter Lang.

Dubosson-Sbriglione, L. (2021) 'Veturia: négociatrice et ambassadrice de Rome', *EuGeStA*, 11, pp. 110–130.

Eck, W. (2014) *Augustus und seine Zeit*. 6th revised ed. München: Beck.

Eckstein, A.M. (2015) 'Livy, Polybius, and the Greek East (Books 31–45)'. In Mineo (2105) pp. 407–422.

Edwards, C. (1996) *Writing Rome: Textual Approaches to the City*. Cambridge: Cambridge University Press.

Eigler, U., Gotter, U., Luraghi, N. and Walter, U. (eds.) (2003) *Formen römischer Geschichtsschreibung von den Anfängen bis Livius. Gattungen – Autoren – Kontexte*. Darmstadt: Wissenschaftliche Buchgesellschaft.

Fabres-Serris, J. (2021) 'Identities and Ethnicities in the Punic Wars: Livy's Portrait of the Carthaginian Sophonisba', in Fabres-Serris, Keith, J.A. and Klein, F. (eds.) *Identities, Ethnicities and Gender in Antiquity*. Berlin and Boston: De Gruyter, Trends in Classics – Supplementary Volumes 109, pp. 93–111.

Fabricius, E. (1932) 'Some notes on Polybius's Description of Roman Camps', *JRS*, 22, pp. 78–87.

Fabrizi, V. (2015) 'Hannibal's March and Roman Imperial Space in Livy, *Ab Urbe Condita*, Book 21', *Philologus*, 159(1), pp. 118–155.

Fabrizi, V. (2016) 'Space, Vision and the Friendly Sea: Scipio's crossing to Africa in Livy's Book 29', in Baltrusch, E., Kopp, H. and Wendt, C. (eds.) *Seemacht, Seeherrschaft und die Antike*. Stuttgart: Steiner. Historia Einzelschrift 244, pp. 279–290.

Fabrizi, V. (2017a) '"The Cloud That (…) Sat on the Mountaintops": A Narratological Analysis of Space in Livy's Account of Quintus Fabius Maximus' Dictatorship', *AJP*, 138, pp. 673–706.

Fabrizi, V. (2017b) 'La città e il mondo. Insidie del paesaggio e identità romana in *Ab urbe condita* XXXVIII–XL', in Costa, S. and Gallo, F. (ed.) *Miscellanea Graecolatina VI*. Milano: Biblioteca Ambrosiana, pp. 131–155.

Fabrizi, V. (2017c) 'Livy's Antiquities: Re-thinking the Distant Past in the *Ab Urbe Condita*', in Rocchi, S. and Mussini, C. (eds.) *Imagines Antiquitatis. Representations, Concepts, Receptions of the Past in Roman Antiquity and the Early Italian Renaissance*. Berlin and New York: De Gruyter. Philologus Supplementary Volumes 7, pp. 87–109.

Fabrizi, V. (2018) 'Breaching Boundaries: Collective Appearances of Women Outside Their Homes in Livy's *Ab Urbe Condita*', in Fabrizi, V. (ed.) *The Semantics of Space in Greek and Roman Narratives*. Heidelberg: Propylaeum, 2018. DOI: 10.11588/propylaeum.343.470, Distant Worlds Journal Special Issue 2, pp. 29–52.

Fabrizi, V. (2021a) 'War, Weather, and Landscape in Livy's *Ab Urbe Condita*', in Reitz-Joosse, Makins and Mackie (2021) pp. 38–61.

Fabrizi, V. (2021b) 'La guerra nel foro: analisi e implicazioni di un ricorrente tema liviano', in Baldo, G. and Beltramini, L. (eds.) *Livius noster. Tito Livio e la sua eredità* Turnhout: Brepols, Giornale Italiano di Filologia: Bibliotheca 26, pp. 249–274.

Fabrizi, V. (2023) 'Voice, Silence, and Authority: Two Debates Over the Integration of Latins in Livy's *Ab Urbe Condita*', *AION (filol)*, 45, pp. 140–154.

Falcone, M.J. (2019) 'Filippo sul Monte Emo. Note di lettura a Liv. XL 21–22', in Tauber, M. (ed.) *La montagna nell'antichità – Berge in der Antike – Mountains in Antiquity*. Freiburg, Berlin and Wien: Rombach, pp. 231–241.

Favro, D. (1994) 'The Street Triumphant. The Urban Impact of Roman Triumphal Parades', in Çelik, Z., Favro, D. and Ingersoll, R. (eds.) *Streets. Critical Perspectives on Public Space*. Berkeley, Los Angeles and London: University of California Press, pp. 151–164.

Favro, D. (2005) 'Making Rome a World City', in Galinsky (2005) pp. 234–263.

Feldherr, A. (1998) *Spectacle and Society in Livy's History*. Berkeley and Los Angeles: University of California Press.

Feldherr, A. (ed.) (2009) *The Cambridge Companion to the Roman Historians*. Cambridge: Cambridge University Press.

Feldherr, A. (2021) 'The Challenge of Historiographic Enargeia and the Battle of Lake Trasimene', in Reitz-Joosse, Makins and Mackie (2021) pp. 62–88.

Fenster, T. (2005) 'Space and Cultural Meanings', in Essed, P., Goldberg, D.T., and Kobayashi, A. (eds.) *A Companion to Gender Studies*. Malden, MA: Blackwell, pp. 467–474.

Flower, H.I. (1996) *Ancestor Masks and Aristocratic Power in Roman Culture*. Oxford: Clarendon Press.

Flower, H.I. (2000a) 'The Tradition of the Spolia Opima: M. Claudius Marcellus and Augustus', *ClAnt* 19(1), pp. 34–64.

Flower, H.I. (2000b) '*Fabula de Bacchanalibus*: The Bacchanalian Cult of the Second Century BC and Roman Drama', in Manuwald, G. (ed.) *Identität und Alterität in der frührömischen Tragödie*. Würzburg: Egon Verlag, Identitäten und Alteritäten / Altertumswissenschaftliche Reihe 1, pp. 23–35.

Flower, H.I. (ed.) (2004) 'Spectacle and Political Culture in the Roman Republic', in Flower, H.I. (ed.) *The Cambridge Companion to the Roman Republic*. Cambridge: Cambridge University Press, pp. 322–343.

Flower, H.I. (2017) *The Dancing Lares and the Serpent in the Garden: Religion at the Roman Street Corner*. Princeton and Oxford: Princeton University.

Flower, H.I. (2024) 'Political Conversations in the Houses of Roman Women: Livy's Account of the *Bacchanalia* in 186 B.C.E.', in Flower and Osgood (2024) pp. 11–39.

Flower, H.I., and Osgood, J. (eds.) (2024) *Women in Republican Rome: Space, Religion, and Influence. AJP* 141(1), Special Issue.

Forsythe, G. (1994) *The Historian L. Calpurnius Piso Frugi and the Roman Annalistic Tradition*. Lanham, MD, New York and London: University Press of America.

Forsythe, G. (2015) 'The Beginnings of the Republic from 509 to 390 BC', in Mineo (2015) pp. 314–326.

Freund, S. (2008) '*Pudicitia saltem in tuto sit*: Lucretia, Verginia und die Konstruktion eines Wertbegriffs bei Livius', *Hermes*, 136(3), pp. 308–325.

Freyberger, K.S. (2009a) *Das Forum Romanum. Spiegel der Stadtgeschichte des antiken Rom*, unter Mitarbeit von C. Edel und mit Fotos von Heide Behrens. Mainz: Verlag Philipp von Zabern.

Freyberger, K.S. (2009 b) 'Le basiliche', in von Hesberg, H. and Zanker, P. (eds.) *Storia dell'architettura italiana. Architettura romana: i grandi monumenti di Roma*. Milano: Electa, pp. 164–171.

Freyberger, K.S. (2012) 'Sakrale Kommunikationsräume auf dem Forum Romanum', In Mundt 2012, pp. 49–76.

Fuhrer, T. (2020) '"Weibliche Peripetie": Zur dramaturgischen Funktion der Frauenfiguren in der römischen Geschichtsschreibung', in Plotke, S. and Schierl, P. (eds.) *Gender Studies in den Altertumswissenschaften. De mulieribus claris. Gebildete*

Frauen – bedeutende Frauen – vergessene Frauen. Trier: Wissenschaftlicher Verlag Trier, IPHIS. Beiträge zur altertumswissenschaftlichen Genderforschung, pp. 15–27.

Fuhrer, T., Mundt, F. and Stenger, J. (eds.) (2015) *Cityscaping. Constructing and Modelling Images of the City*. Berlin and Boston: De Gruyter, Philologus Supplementary Volumes 3.

Fuller, M. and Löw, M. (2017) 'Introduction: An Invitation to Spatial Sociology', *Current Sociology Monograph*, 65(4), pp. 469–491.

Gagé, J. (1953) 'La *Rogatio Petillia* et le procès de P. Scipion. Sur une procédure latine archaïque contre l'*hostis Capitolinus*', *RPh*, 27(1), pp. 34–64.

Galinsky, K. (ed.) (2005) *The Cambridge Companion to the Auge of Augustus*. Cambridge: Cambridge University Press.

Gallo, A. (2017) '*Senatus consulta* ed *edicta de Bacchanalibus*: documentazione epigrafica e tradizione liviana', *Boll.Stud.Lat.*, 47(2), pp. 519–540.

Galluccio, F. (2016) 'Il mito torna realtà. Le decorazioni fittili del Tempio di Giove Capitolino dalla fondazione all'età medio-repubblicana', in Parisi Presicce and Danti (2016) pp. 237–256.

Genette, G. (1972) 'Discours du récit', in Genette, G., *Figures III*. Paris: Seuil, pp. 67–282.

Genette, G. (1976) 'Boundaries of Narrative', *New Literary History*, 8.1 (Autumn 1976), *Readers and Spectators: Some Views and Reviews*, pp. 1–13.

Genette, G. (1986) *Narrative Discourse*, translated by J.E. Lewin, foreword by J. Culler. Oxford: Blackwell (original edition Paris: Editions du Seuil 1972).

Girod, M.R. (1982) 'La géographie de Tite-Live', in *ANRW* II.30.2, pp. 1190–1229.

Glendinning, E. (2013) 'Reinventing Lucretia: Rape, Suicide and Redemption from Classical Antiquity to the Medieval Era', *IJCT*, 20(1–2), pp. 61–82.

Goldsworthy, A.K. (1996) *The Roman Army at War. 100 BC–AD 200*. Oxford: Clarendon Press.

Gotter, U. (2009) 'Cato's *Origines*: The Historian and His Enemies', in Feldherr (2009) pp. 108–122.

Gotter, U., Luraghi, N. and Walter, U. (2003) 'Einleitung', in Eigler *et al.* (2003), pp. 9–38.

Goukowsky, P., and Lancel, S. (eds.) (2002) *Appien, Histoire romaine*. Tome IV, *Livre VIII: Le livre africain*. Paris: Les Belles Lettres.

Gruen, E.S. (1990) *Studies in Greek Culture and Roman Policy*. Berkeley: University of California Press.

Gurval, R.A. (1995) *Actium and Augustus. The Politics and Emotions of Civil War*. Ann Arbor, MI: The University of Michigan Press.

Haimson-Lushkov, A. (2010) 'Interextuality and Source-Criticism in the Scipionic Trials', in Polleichtner (2010) pp. 93–133.

Haley, S.P. (1990) 'Livy, Passion, and Cultural Stereotypes', *Historia*, 39(3), pp. 375–381.

Hallet, W. and Neumann, B. (eds.) (2009) *Raum und Bewegung in der Literatur. Die Literaturwissenschaften und der Spatial Turn*. Bielefeld: transcript.

Hammond, N.G.L. (1966) 'The Opening Campaigns and the Battle of Aoi Stena in the Second Macedonian War', *JRS*, 56, pp. 39–54.

Hammond, N.G.L. (1984) 'The Battle of Pydna', *JHS*, 104, pp. 31–47.

Hamon, P. (1972) *Introduction à l'analyse du descriptif*. Paris: Hachette.

Hamon, P. (1993) *Du descriptif*, 4th ed. Paris: Hachette.

Hartog, F. (2010) 'Polybius and the First Universal History, in Liddel and Fear (2010) pp. 30–40.

Harvey, D. (2006) 'Space as a Key Word', in Harvey, D., *Spaces of Global Capitalism. Towards a Theory of Uneven Geographical Development*. London and New York: Verso, pp. 117–148.

Harvey, D. (2009) *Space and place: Cosmopolitanism and the Geographies of Freedom*. New York: Columbia University Press.

Helmke, T. (2023) *Exemplarisches Krisenwissen. Gender in Narrativ und Narration des frühen Prinzipats*. Göttingen: Vandenhoeck und Ruprecht.

Herman, D. (2009) *Basic Elements of Narrative*. Malden, MA: Wiley.

Hoffmann, G. (1978) *Raum, Situation, erzählte Wirklichkeit. Poetologische und historische Studien zum englischen und amerikanischen Roman*. Stuttgart: Metzler.

Hölkeskamp, K.-J. (1995) '*Oratoris maxima scaena*: Reden vor dem Volk in der politischen Kultur der Republik', in: Martin Jehne (ed.), *Demokratie in Rom? Die Rolle des Volkes in der Politik der römischen Republik*, 11–49. Stuttgart: Steiner.

Hölkeskamp, K.-J. (2011) 'The Roman Republic as Theatre of Power: The Consuls as Leading Actors', in Beck, H., Duplá, A., Pina Polo, F. and Jehne, M. (eds.) *Consuls and Res Publica: Holding High Office in the Roman Republic*. Cambridge: Cambridge University Press, pp. 161–181.

Hölkeskamp, K.-J. (2012) 'Im Gewebe der Geschichte(n). Memoria, Monumente und ihre mythhistorische Vernetzung', *Klio*, 94(2), pp. 380–414.

Hölkeskamp, K.-J. (2023) *Theater der Macht. Die Inszenierung der Politik in der römischen Republik*. München: Beck.

Hölscher, T. (2009) 'Denkmäler und Konsens. Die sensible Balance von Verdienst und Macht', in Hölkeskamp, K.-J. and Müller-Lückner, E. (eds.) *Eine Kultur (in) der Krise? Die 'letzte Generation' der römischen Republik*. München: Oldenbourg, pp. 161–181.

Hölscher, T. (2020) 'Das Forum Romanum – die monumentale Geschichte Roms', in Stein-Hölkeskamp, E. and Hölkeskamp, K.-J. (eds.) *Erinnerungsorte der Antike. Die römische Welt*, 2nd ed. München: Beck, pp. 100–122.

Holzberg, N. (2012) 'Der "Böse" und die Augusteer. Cacus bei Livius, Vergil, Properz und Ovid', *Gymnasium*, 119, pp. 449–462.

Horsfall, N. (1982) 'The Caudine Forks: Topography and Illusion', *PBSR*, 50, pp. 45–52.

Horsfall, N. (1985) 'Illusion and Reality in Latin Topographical Writing', *G&R*, 21, pp. 197–208.

Hoyos, D. (2000) 'Maharbal's Bon Mot: Authenticity and Survival', *CQ*, 50(2), pp. 610–614.

Humm, M. (2005) *Appius Claudius Caecus: La république accompli*. Rome: École française de Rome, Bibliothèque des Écoles françaises d'Athènes et de Rome.

Humm, M. (2014) 'Il Comizio del Foro e le istituzioni della repubblica romana', in Corti, E. (ed.) *La città: com'era, com'è e come la vorremmo. Atti dell'Osservatorio Permanente sull'Antico: a.a. 2012/2013, Pavia Sezione di Scienze dell'Antichità*. Firenze: All'Insegna del Giglio. Flos Italiae: Documenti di Archeologia della Cisalpina Romana 13, pp. 69–82.

Humm, M. (2015) 'From 390 BC to Sentinum: Political and Ideological Aspects', in Mineo (2015) pp. 342–366.

Hühn, P., Meister, J.C., Pier, J. and Schmidt W. (eds.) (2014) *The Handbook of Narratology*. Berlin and Boston: De Gruyter.

Iacopi, I. and Tedone, G. (2005–2006) 'Biblioteca e Porticus ad Apollinis', *RömMitt*, 112, pp. 351–378.

Itgenhorst, T. (2005). *Tota illa pompa. Der Triumph in der römischen Republik. Mit einer CD-ROM, Katalog der Triumphe von 340 bis 19 vor Christus*. Göttingen: Vandenhoeck & Ruprecht. Hypomnemata 161.

Jääskeläinen I.P., Klucharev, V., Panidi, K. and Shestakova, A.N. (2020) 'Neural Processing of Narratives: From Individual Processing to Viral Propagation', *Front. Hum. Neurosci.*, 14(253). DOI: 10.3389/fnhum.2020.00253.

Jacobs, P.W. II and Conlin, D.A. (2014) *Campus Martius. The Field of Mars in the Life of Ancient Rome*. Cambridge. Cambridge University Press.

Jaeger, M. (1997) *Livy's Written Rome*. Ann Arbor, MI: The University of Michigan Press.

Jaeger, M. (2003) 'Livy and the Fall of Syracuse', in Eigler *et al.* (2003) pp. 213–234.

Jaeger, M. (2007) 'Fog on the Mountain: Philip and Mount Haemus in Livy 40.21–22', in Marincola (2007a) pp. 397–403.

Jaeger, M. (2015) 'Urban Landscape, Monuments, and the Building of Memory in Livy', in Mineo (2015) pp. 65–77.

Jal, P. (1984a) *Abrégés des livres de l'Histoire Romaine de Tite-Live*, 1re partie: 'Periochae' transmises par les manuscrits (Periochae 1–69). Paris: Le Belles Lettres, Collection des universités de France Série latine 270.

Jal, P. (1984b) *Abrégés des livres de l'Histoire Romaine de Tite-Live*, 2e partie: 'Periochae' transmise par le manuscrits (Periochae 70–142). Paris: Le Belles Lettres, Collection des universités de France Série latine 267.

Janni, P. (1984) *La mappa e il periplo. Cartografia antica e spazio odologico*. Roma: Bretschneider.

Jenkyns, R. (2013) *God, Space, and City in the Roman Imagination*. Oxford: Oxford University Press.

Joplin, P.K. (1990) 'Ritual Work on Human Flesh: Livy's Lucretia and the Rape of the Body Politic', *Helios*, 17, pp. 51–70.

Joshel, S.R. (1992) 'The Body Female and the Body Politic: Livy's Lucretia and Verginia', in Richlin, A. (ed.) *Pornography and Representation in Greece and Rome*. New York and Oxford: Oxford University Press, pp. 112–130.

Kaplow, L. (2012) 'Creating "popularis" History: Sp. Cassius, Sp. Maelius, and M. Manlius in the Political Discourse of the Late Republic', *BICS*, 55(2), pp. 101–109.

Keegan, P. (2021) *Livy's Women: Crisis, Resolution, and the Female in Rome's Foundation History*. Abington and New York: Routledge.

Kenty, J. (2017) 'Altera Roma: Livy's Variations on a Ciceronian Theme', *ICS*, 42(1), pp. 61–81.

Kissel, T. (2004) *Das Forum Romanum. Leben im Herzen der Stadt*. Düsseldorf and Zürich: Artemis & Winkler.

Köb, I. (2000) *Rom – ein Stadtzentrum im Wandel. Untersuchungen zur Funktion und Nutzung des Forum Romanum und der Kaiserfora in der Kaiserzeit*. Hamburg: Verlag Dr. Kovač.

Koon, S. (2010) *Infantry Combat in Livy's Battle Narratives*. Oxford: Archaeopress, BAR International Series 2071.

Koopman, N. (2018) *Ancient Greek Ekphrasis. Between Narration and Description*. Leiden: Brill.

Konstan, D. (1986) 'Narrative and Ideology in Livy: Book I', *ClAnt*, 5(2), pp. 198–215.

Kowalewski, B. (2002) *Frauengestalten im Geschichtswerk des Titus Livius*. Munich and Leipzig: Teubner.

Kraus, C.S. (1994) '"No Second Troy": Topoi and Refoundation in Livy, Book v', *TAPA*, 124, pp. 267–89.

Krebs, C.B. (2012) 'M. Manlius Capitolinus: The Metaphorical Plupast and Metahistorical Reflections', in Grethlein, J. and Krebs, C.B. (2012) *Time and Narrative in Ancient Historiography: The 'Plupast' from Herodotus to Appian*. Cambridge: Cambridge University Press, pp. 139–55.

Kromayer, J. (1912) *Antike Schlachtfelder. Bausteine zu einer antiken Kriegsgeschichte*, Band 3.1: *Italien*. Berlin: Weidmann.

Kromayer, J. and Veith, G. (1924–1931) *Antike Schlachtfelder. Bausteine zu einer antiken Kriegsgeschichte*. Band 4: *Ergänzungsband: Schlachtfelder aus den Perserkrieger, aus den späteren griechischen Geschichte und den Feldzügen Alexanders und aus der römischen Geschichte bis Augustus*. Berlin: Weidmann. DOI: https://doi.org/10.11588/diglit.7384#0003.

Laird, A. (1999) *Powers of Expression/Expressions of Power: Speech Presentation and Latin literature*. Oxford: Oxford University Press.

Lange, C.H. (2009) *Res Publica Constituta. Actium, Apollo, and the Accomplishment of the Triumviral Assignment*. Leiden and Boston: Brill.

Lange, C.H. (2016) *Triumphs in the Age of Civil War: The Late Republic and the Adaptability of Triumphal Tradition*. London: Bloomsbury Publishing.

Lange, C.H. (2020) 'Talking Heads: The Rostra as a Conspicuous Civil War Monument', in Lange, C.H. and Scott, A.G. (eds.) *Cassius Dio: The Impact of Violence, War, and Civil War*. Leiden and Boston: Brill, Historiography of Rome and its Empire, 8, pp. 192–216.

Langlands, R. (2006) *Sexual Morality in Ancient Rome*. Cambridge: Cambridge University Press.

Lazenby, J.F. (1978) *Hannibal's War. A Military History of the Second Punic War*. Warminster: Aris & Phillips.

Lefèbvre, H. (1991) *The Production of Space*. Engl. transl. by D. Nicholson-Smith. Oxford: Blackwell (1991; original French edition 1974).

Leidl, C. (2010) 'Die (Ohn)macht der Rede. Publikumsreaktionen in der Geschichtsschreibung', in Pausch (2010a), pp. 235–258.

Lendon, J.E. (1999) 'The Rhetoric of Combat: Greek Military Theory and Roman Culture in Julius Caesar's Battle Descriptions', *Cl. Ant.*, 18, pp. 273–329.

Lendon, J.E. (2017a) 'Battle Description in the Ancient Historians. Part I: Structure, Array, and Fighting', *G&R*, 64(1), pp. 38–64.

Lendon, J.E. (2017b) 'Battle description in the ancient historians. Part II: Speeches, results, and sea battles', *G&R*, 64(2), pp. 145–167.

Letta, C. (1984) 'L'"Italia dei *mores Romani*" nelle *Origines* di Catone', *Athenaeum*, 62, pp. 416–439.

Letta, C. (2008) 'I legami tra i popoli italici nelle *Origines* di Catone tra consapevolezza etnica e ideologia', in Urso, G. (ed.) *Patria diversis gentibus una? Unità politica e identità etniche nell'Italia antica. Atti del convegno internazionale Cividale del Friuli, 20–22 settembre 2007*. Pisa: ETS, pp. 171–195.

Levene, D.S. (1993) *Religion in Livy*. Leiden, New York and Köln: Brill, Mnemosyne Supplements 127.

Levene, D.S. (2006) 'History, Metahistory, and Audience Response in Livy 45', *Cl. Ant.*, 25, pp. 73–108.

Levene, D.S. (2010) *Livy on the Hannibalic War*. Oxford: Oxford University Press.

Levene, D.S. (2019) 'Monumental Insignificance. The Rhetoric of Roman Topography from Livy's Rome', in Loar, Murray and Rebeggiani (2019), pp. 10–26.

Levene, D.S. (2023a) *Livy: The Fragments & Periochae*. Volume 1: *Fragments, Citations, Testimonia*. Oxford: Oxford University Press.

Levene, D.S. (2023b) *Livy: The Fragments & Periochae*. Volume 2: *Periochae 1–45*. Oxford University Press.

Levick, B. (2015) 'Historical Context of the *Ab Urbe Condita*', in Mineo (2015), pp. 24–36.

Liddel, P. and Fear, A. (eds.) (2010) *Historiae Mundi. Studies in Universal History*. London: Duckworth.

Loar, M.P., Murray, S.C. and Rebeggiani, S. (eds.) (2019) *The Cultural History of Augustan Rome. Texts, Monuments, and Topography*. Cambridge: Cambridge University Press.

Lopes, J.M. (1995) *Foregrounded Description in prose Fiction: Five Cross-Literary Studies*. Toronto, Buffalo, and London: University of Toronto Press.

Loreto, L. (1991) 'La censura di Appio Claudio, l'edilità di Cn. Flavio e la razionalizzazione delle strutture interne dello Stato romano', A&R, 36(4), pp. 181–203.

Lotman, J.M. (1973) *Die Struktur des künstlerischen Textes*, ed. R. Grübel, transl. by Grübel, R., Kroll, W. and Seidel, H.-E. Frankfurt am Main: Suhrkamp.

Lotman, J.M. (1974) 'Das Problem des künstlerischen Raums in Gogols Prosa', in Lotman, J.M., *Aufsätze zur Theorie und Methodologie der Literatur und Kultur*, ed. and transl. by Eimermacher, K. Kronberg Taunus: Scriptor, pp. 200–271.

Löw, M. (2016) *The Sociology of Space. Materiality, Social Structures, and Action*, Engl. transl. by Goodwin, D. New York: Palgrave MacMillan (original German edition Frankfurt a Main: Suhrkamp 2001).

Luce, T.J. (1965) 'The Dating of Livy's First Decade', TAPhA, 96, pp. 209–240.

Luce, T.J. (1977) *Livy. The Composition of His History*, Princeton, NJ: Princeton University Press.

Luce, T.J. (1993) 'Structure in Livy's Speeches', in Schuller, W. (ed.) *Livius: Aspekte seiner Werke*. Konstanz: Universitätsverlag, pp. 71–87.

Luke, T. (2014) *Ushering in a New Republic: Theologies of Arrival at Rome in the First Century BCE*. Ann Arbor, MI: The University of Michigan Press.

Makin, E. (1921) 'The Triumphal Route, with Particular Reference to the Flavian Triumph', JRS, 11, pp. 25–36.

Marincola, J. (ed.) (2007a) *A Companion to Greek and Roman Historiography*, Volume II. Malden, MA: Blackwell.

Marincola, J. (2007b) 'Speeches in Classical Historiography', in Marincola (2007a) pp. 118–132.

Martin, P.M. (1985) 'Tanaquil, la "faiseuse de rois"', *Latomus*, 44(1), pp. 5–15.

Massey, D. (1994) *Space, Place, and Gender*. Cambridge: Polity Press.

Massey, D. (2005) *For Space*. Los Angeles et al.: Sage Publications.

Matthes, M. (2000) *The Rape of Lucretia and the Founding of Republics. Readings in Livy, Machiavelli, and Rousseau*. University Park, PA: The Pennsylvania State University Press.

Mazzei, P. (2019) *Il Campidoglio. Dalle origini fino alla fine dell'Antichità*. Tomo 1. Roma: 'L'Erma' di Bretschneider, Bullettino della Commissione Archeologica Comunale di Roma. Supplementi, 26.

McClain, T.D. (2021) 'Cato vs Valerius/Men vs Women: Rhetorical Strategies in The Oppian Law Debate in Livy's *Ab Urbe Condita*', in Michalopoulos, A.N., Serafim, A., Vatri, A. and Beneventano della Corte, F. (eds.) *The Rhetoric of Unity and*

Division in Ancient Literature. Berlin and Boston: De Gruyter, pp. 351–372. DOI: https://doi.org/10.1515/9783110611168.

McDonald, A.H. (1938) 'Scipio Africanus and Roman Politics in the second century B.C.', *JRS*, 28, pp. 153–164.

Menichetti, M. (2021) *Augusto e la teologia della vittoria*. Roma: Quasar.

Merlin, A. (1960) *L'Aventin dans l'antiquité*. Paris: Fontemoing.

Meunier, N.L.J. (2019) 'Marcus Manlius Capitolinus entre Rome et le Latium. Questions de définition identitaire et de distorsion narrative', *MEFRA*, 131(1), *Tite-Live et la Rome archaïque*, pp. 65–80.

Mignone, L.M. (2016) *The Republican Aventine ad Rome's Social Order*. Ann Arbor, MI: The University of Michigan Press.

Miles, G.B. (1995) *Livy: Reconstructing Early Rome*. Ithaca, NY: Cornell University Press.

Millar, F. (1985) 'Politics, Persuasion, and the People Before the Social War', *JRS*, 76, pp. 1–11.

Miller, J.F. (2000) 'Triumphus in Palatio', *AJPh*, 121(3), pp. 409–422.

Miller, J.F. (2009) *Apollo, Augustus, and the Poets*. Cambridge: Cambridge University Press.

Milnor, K. (2005) *Gender, Domesticity, and the Age of Augustus: Inventing Private Life*. Oxford: Oxford University Press.

Milnor, K. (2007) 'Augustus, History and the Landscape of the Law', *Arethusa*, 40, pp. 7–23.

Mineo, B. (2006) *Tite-Live et l'histoire de Rome*. Paris: Klinksieck.

Mineo, B. (ed.) (2015) *A Companion to Livy*. Malden, MA: Blackwell.

Moles, J. (1993) 'Livy's Preface', *PCPhS*, 39, pp. 141–168.

Momigliano, A. (1942) 'Camillus and Concord', *CQ*, 3–4, pp. 111–120.

Momigliano, A. (1987) *On Pagans, Jews, and Christians*. Middletown, CT: Wesleyan University Press.

Morello, R. (2003) 'Place and Road: Neglected Aspects of Livy 9, 1–19', in Deroux, C. (ed.) *Studies in Latin Literature and Roman History*, Volume 11. Bruxelles: Latomus, pp. 290–307.

Morrell, K. (2019) 'Augustus as Magpie', in Osgood, J., Morrell, K. and Welch, K. (eds.) *The Alternative Augustan Age*. Oxford: Oxford University Press, pp. 12–26.

Morstein-Marx, R. (2004) *Mass Oratory and Political Power in the Late Roman Republic*. Cambridge: Cambridge University Press.

Mosher, H.F. (1991) 'Toward a Poetic of "Descriptized" Narration', *Poetics Today*, 12(3), pp. 425–445.

Mouritsen, H. (2001) *Plebs and Politics in the Late Roman Republic*. Cambridge: Cambridge University Press.

Mundt, F. (ed.) (2012) *Kommunikationsräume im kaiserzeitlichen Rom*. Berlin: De Gruyter.

Mustakallio, K. (2011) 'Representing Older Women: Hersilia, Veturia, Virgo Vestalis Maxima', in Krötz, C. and Mustakallio, K. (eds.) *On Old Age: Approaching Death in Antiquity and the Middle Ages*. Turnhout: Brepols, pp. 41–56.

Mustakallio, K. (2012) 'Women Outside Their Homes, the Female Voice in Early Republican Memory: Reconsidering Cloelia et Veturia', *Index*, 40, pp. 165–174.

Muth, S. (2012) 'Reglementierte Erinnerung. Das Forum Romanum unter Augustus als Ort kontrollierter Kommunikation', in Mundt (2012) pp. 3–48.

Muth, S. (2014) 'Historische Dimensionen des gebauten Raumes – Das Forum Romanum als Fallbeispiel', In Dally, O., Hölscher, T., Muth, S. and Schneider, R.M. (eds.) *Medien der Geschichte – Antikes Griechenland und Rom*. Berlin: De Gruyter, pp. 285–329.

Neel, J. (2015) 'Reconsidering the *affectatores regni*', *CQ*, 65(1), pp. 224–241.

Nicholls, J.J. (1967) 'The Content of the Lex Curiata', *AJP*, 88(3), pp. 257–278.

Nicolet, C. (1991) *Space, Geography, and Politics in the Early Roman Empire*, Engl. transl. Ann Arbor, MI: The University of Michigan Press (original French edition Paris: Fayard 1988).

Niederhoff, B. (2014) 'Focalization', in Hühn *et al.* (2014), pp. 197–205.

Nissen, H. (1863) *Kritische Untersuchungen über die Quellen der vierten und fünften Dekade des Livius*. Berlin: Weidmann.

North, J.A. (2006) 'The Constitution of the Roman Republic', in Rosenstein, N. and Morstein-Marx, R. (eds.) *A Companion to the Roman Republic*. Malden MA: Blackwell, pp. 256–277.

Nünnerich-Asmus, A. (1994) *Basilika und Portikus. Die Architektur der Säulenhallen als Ausdruck gewandelter Urbanität in später Republik und früher Kaiserzeit*. Köln *et al.*: Böhlau.

Nünning, A. (2009) 'Formen und Funktionen literarischer Raumdarstellung: Grundlagen, Ansätze, narratologische Kategorien und neue Perspektiven', in Hallet and Neumann (2009) pp. 33–52.

Oakley, S.P. (1997) *A Commentary to Livy. Books VI–X*, Volume 1: *Introduction and Book VI*. Oxford: Clarendon Press.

Oakley, S.P. (1998) *A Commentary to Livy. Books VI–X*, Volume 2: *Books VII–VIII*. Oxford: Clarendon Press.

Oakley, S.P. (2005a) *A Commentary on Livy. Books VI–X*, Volume 3: *Book IX*. Oxford: Clarendon Press.

Oakley, S.P. (2005b) *A Commentary on Livy. Books VI–X*, Volume 4: *Book X*. Oxford: Clarendon Press.

Oakley, S.P. (2019) 'Livy on Cannae: A Literary Overview', in van Gils, de Jong and Kroon (2019) pp. 157–190.

Ogilvie, R.M. (1962) 'The Maid of Ardea', *Latomus*, 21(3), pp. 477–483.

Ogilvie, R.M. (1965) *A Commentary on Livy. Books 1–5*. Oxford: Clarendon Press.

REFERENCED WORKS 269

Ogilvie, R.M. (ed.) (1974) *Titi Livi ab urbe condita*, Volume 1: *Libri I–V*. Oxford: Clarendon Press.

O' Gorman, E. (2023) 'Embedded Speech and the Embodied Speaker in Roman Historiography', *Histos*, 17, pp. 1–42. DOI: https://doi.org/10.29173/histos522.

Östenberg, I. (2009) *Staging the World. Spoils, Captives, and Representations in the Roman Triumphal Procession*. Oxford: Oxford University Press. Oxford Studies in Ancient Culture and Representation.

Östenberg, I. (2010) '*Circum metas fertur*: an Alternative Reading of the Triumphal Route', *Historia*, 59(3), pp. 303–320.

Östenberg, I. (2017) 'Defeated by the Forest, the Pass, the Wind: Nature as an Enemy of Rome', in Clark, J.H. and Turner, B. (eds.) *Brill's Companion to Military Defeat in Ancient Mediterranean Society*. Leiden and Boston: Brill. Brill's Companions to Classical Studies 2, pp. 240–261.

Padilla Peralta, D.-E. (2023) 'Pharmapolitics and the Early Roman Expansion: Gender, Slavery, and Ecology in 331 BCE', *Cl.Ant.*, 42(1), pp. 159–194.

Pailler, J.-M. (1988) *Bacchanalia. La répression de 186 av. J.-C. à Rome et en Italie: vestiges, images, tradition*. Rome: École Française de Rome.

Palmer, R.E.A. (1974) 'Roman Shrines of Female Chastity from the Caste Struggle to the Papacy of Innocent I', *RSA*, 4, pp. 113–159.

Pandey, N. (2020) 'Shovels out. Excavating Augustus and Partisan Archaeology on the Palatine', *Mnemosyne*, 73(4), pp. 689–701.

Paratore, E. (1971) 'Hercule et Cacus chez Virgile et Tite-Live', in Bardon, H. and Verdière, R. (eds.) *Vergiliana. Recherches sur Virgile*. Leiden: Brill, pp. 260–282.

Pareti, L. (1959) 'Sulla battaglia del Lago Regillo', *StudRom*, 7(1), pp. 18–30.

Parisi Presicce, C. and Danti, A. (eds.) (2016) *Campidoglio: mito, memoria, archeologia*. Roma: Campisano.

Pausch, D. (2008) 'Der aitiologische Romulus. Historisches Interesse und literarische Form in Livius' Darstellung der Königszeit', *Hermes*, 136, pp. 38–60.

Pausch, D. (ed.) (2010a) *Stimmen der Geschichte. Funktionen von Reden in der antiken Historiographie*. Berlin and New York: De Gruyter.

Pausch, D. (ed.) (2010b) 'Einleitung', in Pausch (2010a) pp. 1–13.

Pausch, D. (2010c) 'Der Feldherr als Redner und der Appell an den Leser: Wiederholung und Antizipation in den Reden bei Livius', in Pausch (2010a) pp. 183–205.

Pausch, D. (2010d) '„Und seine Worte waren ungefähr die folgenden;...". Reden in der antiken Geschichtsschreibung zwischen Verwendung und Problematisierung', in Tischer, U. and Binternagel, A. (eds.) *Fremde Rede – Eigene Rede. Zitieren und verwandte Strategien in antiker Prosa*. Frankfurt am Main: Peter Lang, pp. 35–57.

Pausch, D. (2011) *Livius und der Leser. Narrative Strukturen in ab urbe condita*. München: Beck.

Pausch, D. (2018a) 'Livy's Battle in the Forum Between Roman Monuments and Greek Literature', in Sandberg, K. and Smith, C. (eds.), *Omnium Annalium Monumenta: Historical Writing and Historical Evidence in Republican Rome*. Leiden and Boston: Brill. Historiography of Rome and its Empire 2, pp. 279–300.

Pausch, D. (2018b) 'Unkämpfte Erinnerungsorte. Auf der Suche nach Vorbildern für Livius' „Schlacht auf dem Forum" (1.11–13)' in Devillers, O. and Sebastiani, B.B. (eds) *Sources et modèles des historiens anciens*. Bordeaux: Ausonius Éditions. Scripta Antiqua 109.

Pausch, D. (2019) 'Who Knows What Will Happen Next? Livy's *fraus Punica* from a Literary Point of View', in van Gils, de Jong and Kroon (2019) pp. 234–252.

Pelikan Pittenger, M.R. (2008) *Contested Triumphs. Politics, Pageantry, and Performance in Livy's Republican Rome*. Berkeley, Los Angeles and London: University of California Press.

Pensabene, P. (2017a) *Scavi del Palatino 2. Culti architettura e decorazioni. Tomo I: Gli edifici arcaici e repubblicani, i templi della Vittoria e della Magna Mater, i rinvenimenti votivi a 'torre', le iscrizioni*. Roma: 'L'Erma' di Bretschneider.

Pensabene, P. (2017b) *Scavi del Palatino 2. Culti architettura e decorazioni. Tomo II: La 'casa dei grifi', la casa di Ottaviano-Augusto e il tempo di Apollo*. Roma: 'L'Erma' di Bretschneider.

Pensabene, P., and Gallocchio, E. (2011) 'Contributo alla discussione sul complesso augusteo palatino', *Arch. Cl.*, 62, pp. 475–487.

Phillips, J.E. (1974) 'Form and Language in Livy's Triumph Notices', *CP*, 69(4), pp. 265–273.

Pina Polo, F. (1989) *Las contiones civiles y militares en Roma*. Zaragoza: Departamento de ciencias de la Antegüedad Universidad de Zaragoza.

Pina Polo, F. (1995) 'Procedures and Functions of Civil and Military contiones in Rome', *Klio*, 77, pp. 203–216.

Pina Polo, F. (2011) *The Consul at Rome. The Civil Functions of the Consuls in the Roman Republic*. Cambridge: Cambridge University Press.

Plathner, H.-G. (1934) *Die Schlachtschilderungen bei Livius*. Diss. Breslau.

Polito, E. (2017) 'Cosso, Augusto e gli *spolia opima*. Sull'interpretazione di un'emissione monetale augustea', *ArchCl* 68, pp. 175–196.

Polleichtner, W. (ed.) (2010) *Livy and Intertextuality. Papers of a Conference Held at the University of Texas at Austin, October 3, 2009*, Trier: Wissenschaftlicher Verlag. Bochumer Altertumswissenschaftliches Colloquium 84.

Prim, J. (2021) *Aventinus mons: limites, fonctions urbaines et représentations politiques d'une colline de la Rome antique*. Rome: École française de Rome. Collection de l'École française de Rome 571.

Prince, G. (2003) *A Dictionary of Narratology. Revised Edition*. Lincoln and London: University of Nebraska Press.

Purcell, N. (2001) 'The *ordo scribarum*: A Study in the Loss of Memory', *MEFRA*, 113(2), pp. 633–674.

Rambaud, M. (1974) 'L'espace dans le récit césarien', in Chevallier, R. (ed.) *Littérature gréco-romaine et géographie historique, Mélanges offerts à Roger Dion*, Paris: Picard, pp. 111–129.

Reitz-Joosse, B., Makins, M.W. and Mackie, J.C. (eds.) (2021) *Landscapes of War in Greek and Roman Literature*. London *et al.*: Bloomsbury Academic. Bloomsbury Classical Studies Monographs.

Ricchieri, T. (2022) 'Le *Periochae* liviane e le "altre": per la definizione di un genere', *Erga-Logoi*, 10(2), pp. 213–248.

Rich, J. (2011) 'Structuring Roman History: The Consular Year and the Roman Historical Tradition', *Histos*, 5, pp. 1–43. DOI: https://doi.org/10.29173/histos203.

Richardson, A. (2004) *Theoretical Aspects of Roman Camp and Fort Design*. Oxford: John and Erica Hedges. BAR International Series 1321.

Ridley, R.T. (2005) 'Unbridgeable Gaps: the Capitoline Temple at Rome', *BCAR*, 196, pp. 83–104.

Riggsby, A. (2006) *Caesar in Gaul and Rome. War in Words*. Austin: University of Texas Press.

Riggsby, A. (2009) 'Space', in Feldherr (2009) pp. 152–165.

Rohr Vio, F. (2019) *Le custodi del potere: donne e politica alla fine della Repubblica romana*. Roma: Salerno.

Ronen, R. (1986) 'Space in Fiction', *Poetics Today*, 7(3), pp. 421–438.

Ronen, R. (1997) 'Description, Narrative and Representation', *Narrative*, 5(3), pp. 274–286.

Rossi, A. (2000) 'The Tears of Marcellus: History of a Literary Motif in Livy', *G&R*, 47, pp. 56–66.

Rossi, A. (2004) 'Parallel Lives? Hannibal and Scipio in Livy's Third Decade', *TAPA*, 134, pp. 359–381.

Rubincam, C. (1992) 'The Nomenclature of Julius Caesar and the Later Augustus in the Triumviral Period', *Historia*, 41(1), pp. 88–103.

Rüpke, J. (2019) *Peace and War in Rome. A Religious Construction of Warfare*, Engl. Transl. Richardson, D.M.B. Stuttgart: Franz Steiner Verlag (Original German edition Stuttgart: Franz Steiner Verlag 1990).

Russell, A. (2016a) *The Politics of Public Space in Republican Rome*. Cambridge: Cambridge University Press.

Russell, A. (2016b) 'On Gender and Spatial Experience in Public: The Case of Ancient Rome', in Mandich, M.J., Derrick, T.J., Gonzalez Sanchez, S., Savani, G. and Zampieri, S. (eds.), *TRAC 2015. Proceedings of the Twenty-Fifth Annual Theoretical Roman Archaeology Conference*. Oxford and Philadelphia: Oxbow Books, pp. 164–176.

Ryan, M.-L. (2009) 'Space', in Hühn, P., Schmidt, W. and Schönert, J. (eds.), *Handbook of Narratology*. Berlin and New York: De Gruyter. Narratologia 19, pp. 420–433.

Said, E.W. (2000) 'Invention, Memory, and Place', *Critical Inquiry*, 26(2), pp. 175–192.

Sailor, D. (2006), 'Dirty Linen, Fabrication, and the Authorities of Livy and Augustus', *TAPhA*, 136(2), pp. 329–388.

Sautel, J.-H. (2010) 'Un récit de théophanie chez Denys d'Halicarnasse ; l'apparition des Dioscures à la bataille du lac Régille (*Antiquité Romaines* VI, 13). Étude rhétorique', *REA*, 112(2), pp. 375–390.

Sautel, J.-H. (2014) 'Récits de bataille chez Denys d'Halicarnasse : la victoire du lac Régille et la prise de Corioles (*Antiquités Romaines*, VI, 10–13, 91–94 ; Tite-Live, *Histoires*, II, 19–20. 33)', *REA*, 116(1), pp. 145–165.

Scafuro, A.C. (2009) 'Livy's Comic Narrative of the Bacchanalia', in Chaplin, J.D. and Kraus, C.S. (eds.) *Livy*. Oxford: Oxford University Press. Oxford Readings in Classical Studies, pp. 321–352 (first published in *Helios*, 16, 1989, pp. 119–142).

Schmidt, W. (2014) 'Implied Reader', in Hühn *et al.* (2014), pp. 301–309.

Seager, R. (1977) '*Populares* in Livy and the Livian Tradition', *CQ*, 27(2), pp. 377–390.

Sheridan, B. (2010) 'Diodorus' Reading of Polybius' Universalism', in Liddell and Fears (2010), pp. 41–55.

Skutsch, O. (ed., comm.) (1985) *The Annals of Quintus Ennius*. Oxford: Oxford University Press.

Smith, C. (2006) '*Adfectatio regni* in the Roman Republic', in: Lewis, S. (ed.) *Ancient Tyranny*. Edinburgh: Edinburgh University Press, pp. 49–64.

Smith, C. and Powell, A. (eds.) (2009) *The Lost Memoirs of Augustus and the Development of Roman Autobiography*. Swansea: The Classical Press of Wales.

Soja, E.W. (1989) *Postmodern Geography. The Reassertion of Space in Critical Social Theory*. London and New York: Verso.

Soja, E.W. (2009) 'Taking Space Personally', in Warf, B. and Arias, S. (eds.) *The Spatial Turn: Interdisciplinary Perspectives*. London and New York: Routledge. Routledge Studies in Human Geography, pp. 11–35.

Solodow, J.B. (1979) 'Livy and the Story of Horatius', *TAPhA*, 109, pp. 252–268.

Spain, D. (1992) *Gendered Spaces*. Chapel Hill, NC, and London: The University of North Carolina Press.

Spencer, D. (2007) 'Rome at a Gallop: Livy, on not Gazing, Jumping, or Toppling into the Void', in Larmour, D.H.J. and Spencer, D. (eds.) *The Sites of Rome. Time, Space, Memory*. Oxford: Oxford University Press, pp. 61–101.

Stevenson, T. (2011) 'Women of Early Rome as "Exempla" in Livy, "*Ab Urbe Condita*", Book 1', *CW*, 104(2), pp. 175–189.

Syme, R. (1959) 'Livy and Augustus', *HSCP*, 64, pp. 27–87.

Tally, R.T. Jr. (2021) *Spatial Literary Studies. Interdisciplinary Approaches to Space, Geography, and the Imagination*. London: Routledge.

Taylor, L.R. (1966) *Roman Voting Assemblies from the Hannibalic War to the Dictatorship of Caesar*. Ann Arbor, MI: The University of Michigan Press.

Thalmann, W.G. (2011) *Apollonius of Rhodes and the Spaces of Hellenism*. Oxford: Oxford University Press. Classical Culture and Society.

Thein, A. (2014) 'Capitoline Jupiter and the Historiography of Roman World Rule', *Histos*, 8, pp. 284–319. DOI: https://doi.org/10.29173/histos263.

Thiersch, C. (2021) 'Cityscaping – Raumformungsprozesse antiker Städte als Gegenstand aktueller Debatten', *eTopoi. Journal for Ancient Studies*, 9, pp. 105–141. DOI: 10.17169/refubium-29551.

Tilley, C. (1994) *A Phenomenology of Landscape: Places, Paths and Monuments*. Oxford: Berg.

Timpe, D. (1979) 'Erwägungen zur jüngeren Annalistik', *A&A*, 2, pp. 97–119.

Todaro, G. (2023a) 'L'agguato a Marco Minucio Rufo tra geografia reale e topographia letteraria (Liv. 22, 28, 3–7)', *MD*, 91(2), pp. 85–105.

Todaro, G. (2023b) '"Infamem annum pestilentia fecerit": la prima "quaestio de veneficiis" a Roma', *Griseldaonline*, 22(2), DOI: https://doi.org/10.6092/issn.1721-4777/17886.

Tränkle, H. (1977) *Livius und Polybios*. Basel: Schwabe.

Trümper, M. (2012) 'Gender and Space, "Public" and "Private"', in James, S.L. and Dillon, S. (eds.) *A Companion to Women in the Ancient World*. Malden, MA: Wiley-Blackwell, pp. 288–303.

Tsitsiou-Chelidoni, C. (2009) 'History beyond Literature: Interpreting the "Internally Focalized" Narrative in Livy's *Ab urbe condita*', in Grethlein, J. and Rengakos, A. (eds.) *Narratology and Interpretation. The Content of Narrative Form in Ancient Literature*. Berlin: De Gruyter, Trends in Classics Supplementary Volumes 4, pp. 527–554.

Urso, G. (ed.) (2008) *Patria diversis gentibus una? Unità politica e identità etniche nell'Italia antica. Atti del convegno internazionale Cividale del Friuli, 20–22 settembre 2007*. Pisa: ETS.

van Baak, J.J. (1983) *The Place of Space in Narration. A Semiotic approach to the Problem of Literary Space. With an Analysis of the Role of Space in I.E. Babel's Konarmija*. Amsterdam: Rodopi.

van Gils, L. (2019) 'Livy's Use of Spatial References in the Cannae Episode: from Structure to Strategy', in van Gils, de Jong and Kroon (2019) pp. 253–272.

van Gils, L., de Jong, I.F.J., and Kroon, C. (eds.) (2019) *Textual Strategies in Ancient War Narratives: Thermopylae, Cannae, and Beyond*. Leiden: Brill. Amsterdam Studies in Classical Philology 39.

von Haeling, R. (1989) *Zeitbezüge des Titus Livius in der ersten Dekade seines Geschichtswerkes: nec vita nostra nec remedia pati possumus*. Stuttgart: Steiner.

Vasaly, A. (1993) *Representations: Images of the World in Ciceronian Oratory*, Berkeley and Los Angeles: University of California Press.

Vasaly, A. (1999) 'The Rhetoric of Anti-Rhetoric: The Quinctii in Livy's First Pentad', *CW*, 95, pp. 513–530.

Vasaly, A. (2002) 'The Structure of Livy's First Pentad and the Augustan Poetry Book', in Levene, D.S. and Nelis, D.P. (eds) *Clio and the Poets. Augustan Poetry and the Traditions of Ancient Historiography*. Leiden, Boston, and Köln: Brill, pp. 275–290.

Vasaly, A. (2015) *Livy's Political Philosophy. Power and Personality in Early Rome*. Cambridge: Cambridge University Press.

Versnel, H.S. (1970) *Triumphus. An Inquiry into the Origin, Development and Meaning of the Roman Triumph*. Leiden: Brill.

Vout, C. (2012) *The Hills of Rome. Signature of an Eternal City*. Cambridge: Cambridge University Press.

Walbank, F.W. (1967) *A Historical Commentary on Polybius*, Volume 2: *Commentary on Books VII–XVIII*. Oxford: Clarendon Press.

Walbank, F.W. (1970) *A Historical Commentary on Polybius*, reprinted from corrected sheets of the first edition, Volume 1, *Commentary on Books I–VI*. Oxford: Clarendon Press.

Wallace-Hadrill, A. (2005) '*Mutatas Formas*: The Augustan Transformations of Roman Knowledge', in Galinsky (2005) pp. 55–84.

Wallace-Hadrill, A. (2008) *Rome's Cultural Revolution*. Cambridge: Cambridge University Press.

Walsh, P.G. (1961) *Livy. His Historical Aims and Methods*. Cambridge: Cambridge University Press.

Walsh, P.G. (ed.) (1986) *Titi Livi Ab urbe condita libri XXVIII–XXX*. Leipzig: Teubner.

Walsh, P.G. (ed.) (1989) *Titi Livi Ab urbe condita libri XXVI–XXVII*. Leipzig: Teubner.

Walsh, P.G. (1996) 'Making a Drama out of a Crisis: Livy on the Bacchanalian', *G&R*, 43(2), pp. 188–203.

Walter, U. (2003) 'Opfer ihrer Ungleichzeitigkeit. Die Gesamtgeschichten im ersten Jahrhundert v. Chr. und die fortdauernde Attraktivität des "annalistischen Schemas"', in Eigler *et al.* (2003) pp. 135–156.

Walter, U. (2004) *Memoria und res publica: Zur Geschichtskultur im republikanischen Rom*. Frankfurt am Main: Verlag Antike. Studien zur alten Geschichte.

Webb, R. (2009) *Ekphrasis, Imagination and Persuasion in Ancient Rhetorical Theory and Practice*. Farnham: Ashgate.

Weissenborn, W. and Müller, H.J. (eds.) (1896) *T. Livi Ab urbe condita libri*, 6th ed., Volume 2.2: *Buch III–V*. Leipzig: Teubner.

Weissenborn, W. and Müller, H.J. (eds.) (1907) *T. Livi Ab urbe condita libri*, 3rd ed., Volume 8.2: *Buch XXXVII–XXXVIII*. Berlin: Weidmann.

Wiseman, T.P. (1979a) *Clio's Cosmetics. Three Studies in Greco-Roman Literature*. Leicester: Leicester University Press.

Wiseman, T.P. (1979b) 'Topography and Rhetoric: The Trial of Manlius', *Historia*, 28, pp. 32–50.

Wiseman, T.P. (1998) *Roman Drama and Roman History*. Exeter: University of Exeter Press.

Wiseman, T.P. (2007) 'Three Notes on the Triumphal Route', in Leone, A., Palombi, D. and Walker, S. (eds.) *Res Bene Gestae. Ricerche di storia urbana su Roma antica in onore di Eva Margareta Steinby*. Roma: Quasar, pp. 445–449.

Wiseman, T.P. (2009) 'The House of Augustus and the Lupercal', *JRA*, 22, pp. 527–45.

Wiseman, T.P. (2012a) 'A Debate on the Temple of Apollo Palatinus. Roma Quadrata, Archaic Huts, the House of Augustus, and the Orientation of Palatine Apollo', *JRA*, 25, pp. 371–387.

Wiseman, T.P. (2012b) 'Where Did They Live (e.g. Cicero, Octavius, Augustus)?', *JRA*, 25, pp. 656–672.

Wiseman, T.P. (2013) 'The Palatine, from Evander to Elagabalus', *JRS*, 103, pp. 234–268.

Wiseman, T.P. (2014) 'Archaeology and History: The House of Augustus', *JRA*, 27, pp. 544–551.

Wiseman, T.P. (2019) *The House of Augustus. A Historical Detective Story*. Princeton, NJ, and Oxford: Princeton University Press.

Wolf, J.G. (1980) *Die literarische Überlieferung der Publikation der Fasten und Legisaktionen durch Gnaeus Flavius*. Göttingen: Vandenhoeck & Ruprecht. Nachrichten der Akademie der Wissenschaften in Göttingen. I. Philologisch-historische Klasse 2.

Woodman, A.J. (1988) *Rhetoric in Classical Historiography. Four Studies*. London and Sidney: Croom Helm.

Woodman, A.J. (2015) *Lost Histories: Selected Fragments of Roman Historical Writers*. Newcastle Upon Tyne: Histos. DOI: https://doi.org/10.29173/histos679.

Würzbach, N. (2004) 'Raumdarstellung', Nünning, V. and Nünning, A. (eds.) *Erzähltextanalyse und Gender Studies*, unter Mitarbeit von N. Stritzke. Stuttgart and Weimar: Metzler, pp. 49–71.

Yardley, J.C. (transl.) and Heckel, W. (intr., notes) (2000) *Livy, The Dawn of The Roman Empire. Books Thirty-One to Forty*. Oxford: Oxford University Press.

Yarrow, L.M. (2006) *Historiography at the End of the Republic: Provincial Perspectives on Roman Rule*. Oxford: Oxford University Press.

Zaccaria Ruggiu, A. (1995) *Spazio privato e spazio pubblico nella città romana*. Roma: École Française de Rome. Collection de l'École Française de Rome 210.

Zanker, G. (1981) 'Enargeia in the Ancient Criticism of Poetry', *RhM*, 24(3–4), pp. 297–311.

Zanker, P. (1983) 'Der Apollontempel auf dem Palatin. Austattung und politische Sinnbezüge nach der Schlacht von Actium', in De Fine Licht, K. (ed.) *Città e architettura nella Roma imperiale. Atti del seminario del 27 ottobre 1981 nel 25 ° anniversario* dell'Accademia di Danimarca. Odense: Odense University Press. Analecta Romani Instituti Danici Supplementa 10, pp. 21–40.

Zanker, P. (1987) *Augustus und die Macht der Bilder*. München: Beck.

Zink, S. (2008) 'Reconstructing the Palatine Temple of Apollo. A Case Study in Augustan Temple Design', *JRA*, 21, pp. 47–63.

Zink, S. (2012) 'New and Old Archaeological Evidence for the Plan of the Palatine Temple of Apollo', *JRA*, 25, pp. 387–402.

Zoran, G. (1984) 'Towards a Theory of Space in Narrative', *Poetics Today*, 5, pp. 309–335.

Index of Places

Locations and Monuments within Rome

Ad Murciae (or *Admurciae*)   83
Aius Locutius, shrine of   34*n*10, 114, 132, 148
aerarium   43*n*59
Agrippa's baths   137
Apollo, temple of (in the Campus Martius)   46, 46*n*73, 124
Apollo, temple of (on the Palatine)   127–128, 128*nn*129–130, 147
Aqua Virgo   137
Ara Maxima   129, 129*n*136
Ara Pacis   137
area Capitolina   45*n*65, 88, 90, 95
area Vulcani   70
Argei, shrines of   85
Argiletum   85
Arno River   173
arx. *See* Capitol
Asylum   87, 93
auguraculum   89
Aventine   60, 83, 85, 114, 120, 120*n*104, 121–126, 121*n*107, 124*n*116, 130*n*137, 147, 236*n*93, 237
Ayos Dimitrios   172*n*64

basilicas   35, 41
   Basilica Fulvia   41*n*45, 44*n*59
   Basilica Iulia   41*n*45
   Basilica Opimia   41*n*45
   Basilica Porcia   35*n*14, 41*n*45, 44*n*59
   Basilica Sempronia   35*n*14, 41*n*45, 44*n*59
Bellona, temple of   46, 46*n*73

Caelian Hill   83–84, 119
Campus Martius   30, 46, 46*n*73, 47, 70, 83, 85, 87, 89, 110, 133–139, 133*n*149, 134*n*153, 135*n*155, 136*n*156, 147, 200
Capitol   30, 36, 39–40, 42, 44, 46, 46*n*73, 53–55, 67, 70–71, 73–77, 82–119, 87*n*21, 93*n*43, 104*n*63, *n*65, 105*n*69, *n*71, 107*n*79, 110*n*88, 115*n*94, 124, 126*n*120, 128, 130, 132–134, 132*n*146, 133*n*148, 136, 146–149, 200, 245–246, 251
arx (the northern summit of the Capitol)   53–55, 87, 89–91, 104*n*63, 106–107, 106*n*72, 109–110, 112–113, 239, 239*n*101
Capitolium (the southern summit of the Capitol)   87, 89–91, 107, 109–110, 110*n*88, 112–113
   Tarpeian Rock   104*n*64, 107, 109–110, 110*n*88, 119
Capitoline Hill. *See* Capitol
Capitoline Triad, temple of. *See* Jupiter Optimus Maximus, temple of
Capitolium. *See* Capitol
carcer   43*n*59, 85
Carinae   120
Carmenta, shrine of   107
casa Romuli on the Palatine   126, 126*n*120, 132
casa Romuli on the Capitol   126*n*120
Castor, temple of   38–39, 38*n*30, 39*n*37, 43–44*n*59, 45*n*65, 79, 165*n*47
cella Iovis. *See* Jupiter Optimus Maximus, temple of
Ceres, temple of   124*n*116
Cermalus   84*n*12, 126*nn*119–120
Circus Flaminius   45*n*65, 89, 137
Circus Maximus   82–83, 89, 89*n*28, 115*n*94, 121, 126, 126*n*119, 145
Cispius, Mons   84*n*12
citadel. *See* Capitol
clivus Capitolinus   89
clivus Publicius   124
Cloacina, shrine of   34, 34*n*12, 43–44, 234
Cloelia, statue of   43*n*59, 243–244
Comitium   36–40, 36*n*18, *n*19, 37*n*21, 37*n*25, 43–47, 45*n*64, *n*65, *n*68, 49, 53, 63–67, 70, 75–77, 79–80, 79*n*130, 142–144, 230–231, 230–231*n*77, 245
Concordia, shrine (*aedicula*) of   70–71
Concordia, temple of   40, 40*n*41, 41*n*45
   Concordia Augusta, temple of (Augustan renovation of the temple of Concordia)   40
Curia   27–28, 36–39, 36*n*18, 36*n*19, 44, 45*n*68, 46, 49–55, 52*n*81, 57–59, 61–67, 70–71,

Curia (cont.)
    74–80, 142–149, 218, 220–221, 231, 234, 245, 247
    Curia Cornelia   38
    Curia Hostilia   36–37, 46–47, 46n69, 65, 75, 85
    Curia Iulia   38
Cyprius vicus   221

Diana, shrine of (at the top of the *Cyprius vicus*)   221
Diana, temple of (on the Aventine)   85, 121, 147–148
Divus Iulius, temple of   39
domus publica   128

Emporium   121
Esquiline Hill   84, 84n10, 119–120, 120n106, 122–123, 221

Faustolus, hut of   126n120
Ficus Ruminalis (in the Comitium)   129n134
Ficus Ruminalis (in the Lupercal)   34n10, 129, 129n134
Fortuna Muliebris, temple of   218
Fortuna Primigenia, temple of   119
Forum Augustum   42, 42n53
Forum Boarium   82, 89, 89n28, 110, 110–111n88, 121, 124, 129
Forum Iulium   38, 42
Forum Romanum (or simply: Forum)   22, 27–28, 30, 32–81, 41n47, 42n53, 45–46n68, 52n81, 70n115, 83, 85–89, 89n28, 93, 100–102, 104, 108, 108n83, 109, 110n88, 119, 120, 124, 128, 130, 132–133, 133n148, 136, 142–149, 196, 199–200, 215, 215n41, 218, 220, 222–223, 225, 230–234, 231n77, n79, 243, 246

gates   30, 77, 77n127, 139, 141–143, 141n169,
    Porta Caelimontana   119, 142n173
    Porta Capena   35, 85, 85n15, 120, 141n173
    Porta Carmentalis   124, 142n173
    Porta Collina   120, 122, 142n173
    Porta Esquilina   120, 141–142n173
    Porta Flumentana   110, 142n173
    Porta Fontinalis   142n173
    Porta Mugonia (or: *vetus porta Palatii*)   42–43, 83, 141n173
    Porta Naevia   142n173
    Porta Trigemina   142n173
Graecostasis   37, 70, 75
grove of the Camenae   85

Hercules, temple of (in the Forum Boarium)   227
hills (for specific hills see under the name of each, e.g. Capitol, Palatine, etc.)   83, 86, 119, 140, 195, 246
Horatius Cocles, statue of   44
Horologium   137
house of Augustus   127–128
house of Cicero   127
house of Publius Scipio Africanus   44n59

inter duos lucos   87, 87n22, 93n43
Iuventas, shrine (*aedicula*) of   114–115, 115n94
Iuventas, temple of   115n94

Janiculum   30, 84, 86, 130, 139n159, 146, 243
Janus, temple of   11n42, 85
Juno, temple of (adjoining the temple of Jupiter Optimus Maximus)   88
Juno Moneta, temple of   89
Juno Regina, temple of (on the Aventine)   123–125, 147–148
Jupiter Elicius, altar of   85, 121
Jupiter Feretrius, temple of   85, 89, 93, 104n63
Jupiter Optimus Maximus, temple of   40, 45n65, 46, 73–74, 85–89, 88n26, 90–94, 102n61, 104nn64–65, 114, 116–118, 128, 147, 217
    cella Iovis   44
Jupiter Stator, temple of   42–43, 124, 126, 130, 224
Jupiter Tonans, temple of   89

Lacus Curtius   41n49, 42–43, 43n55, 85, 100–101, 101n56, 103
Libertas, temple of   125
Luna, temple of (on the Aventine)   124n116
Lupercal   126, 126n119, 129

INDEX OF PLACES

Magna Mater (or Idean Mother), temple of (on the Palatine)   126, 126*n*122, 132, 147–149
Mars, altar of (in the Campus Martius)   136
Minerva, temple of (adjoining the temple of Jupiter Optimus Maximus)   88, 115, 115*n*94
Mausoleum of Augustus   137
Mulvian Bridge   144

navalia   141*n*167
Navius, Attus, statue of   44
Nova Via   114, 224

Oppius, Mons   84*n*12

Palatium. *See* Palatine Hill
Palatine Hill (or Palatium)   36, 39, 41–42, 82–86, 84*n*12, 89*n*28, 93, 121, 126–133, 126*n*119, 130*n*137, 137, 147–149
Palus Caprae   137, 147
Petelian grove (*lucus Petelinus*)   110, 110*n*88
pila Horatia   33, 33*n*6, 33*n*7, 44
pomerium   46, 46–47*n*74, 75–76, 83, 85–86, 85*n*15, 89, 110*n*88, 121, 124, 133, 137, 147
Pons Sublicius (or Sublician Bridge)   84, 130, 139*n*159
Porta Capena, Porta Caelimontana, Porta Carmentalis, Porta Collina, Porta Esquilina, Porta Flumentana, Porta Fontinalis, Porta Mugonia, Porta Naevia, Porta Trigemina. *See* gates
prata Quinctia   34*n*10
Pudicitia Plebeia, shrine of   226–228, 241

Quirinal   84, 119

regia   39, 39*n*36
Rostra   42, 44, 80, 80*nn*131–132
    Augustan   39–40
    Cesarian   80
    of the Comitium   37–38, 38*n*32, 40, 45, 49, 67–68, 72–74, 79–80, 144, 146, 238, 238*n*101

Sacra Via   43*n*58, *n*59, 89*n*28, 243
Saturn, temple of   39–40, 40*n*38, 43*n*59

Scalae Caci   126, 126*n*120, 129, 130*n*137
Sceleratus vicus   221, 221*n*59
Senate House. *See* Curia
Servius Tullius' palace   120, 224–225
speakers' platform. *See* Rostra
Stimula, grove of   236, 236*n*93
Sublician Bridge. *See* Pons Sublicius
subsellia (seats) of the tribunes of the plebs (in the Comitium)   37, 45, 56

Tarpeian Rock. *See* Capitol
temples (in general)   28, 86, 101–103, 132*n*146, 143–147, 145*n*175, 149, 215
tabernae (shops)   34–35, 34*n*13, 40, 44, 85
    tabernae novae   34
    tabernae veteres   34, 44*n*59
Terminus, shrine of   86, 90, 114–115, 246
Theatre of Pompey   137
Tiber River   30, 83–84, 86, 119, 121, 126, 129*n*136, 135, 135*n*155, 139–141, 139*n*159, *nn*162–163, 146, 195, 237, 237*n*94, 243
tigillum sororium   33, 33*nn*8–9
Tremulus, Quintus Marcius, statue of   43–44*n*59
tribunal (dais) of the praetor or other magistrates (in the Comitium)   37, 45, 45*n*64, 60, 66, 77, 77*n*127, 108, 144, 230–233, 230*n*77

Urbium clivus   221

Vacci prata   130
Velabrum   89*n*28, 124
Velia   34, 41, 84
Vesta, temple of   39, 39*n*37, 43*n*58, 85, 114–115, 126, 132, 132*n*146, 148–149
Vestal Virgins, house of   39
Vica Pota, temple of   34
Victoria Virgo, temple of (on the Palatine)   126, 132, 147–148
vicus Iugarius   124
vicus Longus   226
vicus Tuscus   124
villa publica   134*n*153
Viminal   84, 119
Vortumni signum   44*n*59

walls 30, 55, 84, 85*n*15, 86, 135, 139, 141, 141*nn*168–169, 146–148, 156–157
    Romulus' wall 83
    Servian Walls 83–84, 137

Locations outside Rome

Acarnania 24
Achaea Phthiotis 24
Actium 11*n*42, 128, 128*n*129
Adriatic Sea 1*n*3, 21, 151–152, 177
Aetolia 24
Alba Longa 82–83
Alexandria 251
Algidus, Mount 229–230, 232
Allia River 114
Alps 9*n*28, 21, 28, 135, 152–153, 176–177
Ambracia 175*n*87
Antigonea 180
Aous River 26*n*73, 172*n*63, 173*n*69, 180, 180*n*112
Apennines 24–25, 25*n*72, 152, 176
Ardea 203–206, 233, 233*n*84
    Ardea, Forum of 204
Ariminum 92, 93*n*41
Artemis, temple of (in Ephesus) 121
Asia 78, 194–195, 194*n*40
Atria 152
Attica 24
Aufidus River 171, 172*n*61, 185, 184*n*117

Baecula 183
Beneventum 125
Black Sea 21, 177
Boeotia 24

Callidromon (mountain) 24–25
Callinicus 157*n*23, 174*n*78
Cannae 7*n*23, 106, 118*n*100, 125*n*117, 154*n*13, 157*n*23, 158*n*24, *n*219, 172, 172*n*61, 185, 185*n*117, 189, 215*n*41, 222
Capua 195, 195*n*143
Carthage 9*n*28, 94, 106
Caudine Forks 104*n*64, 175*n*93
Cirta 210, 211*n*34, 212
Collatia, Forum of 202, 208
Corinth 220
Corinth, Isthmus of 152

Corniculum 82, 223
Cortona 189
Cremera 174*n*77
Cremona 159
Cynoscephalae 157*n*23, 173*n*69, 174*n*77, *n*80, *n*84, 180–182, 182*n*116

Danube 177
Daulis 175*n*87
Delphi 7*n*23

Elpeus River 172
Emporiae 158*n*27, *n*28, 160–161, 160*n*38, 163–164, 192
Epirus 24
Etruria 152, 152*n*7, 235
Euboea 24
Europe 78

Fidenae 104*n*63
Fregellae 183
Fundi 130

Gades 2
Gaul 152, 194*n*141
Gereonium 185
Germany 152
Greece 24–25, 129*n*136, 152, 182*n*116
    Continental Greece 24

Haemus, Mt. 21–22, 28, 177
Heraclea 176*n*95
Hispalis 236*n*92
Hister, river 21

Ionian Sea 25
Italy (or: Italian peninsula) 1, 7–8, 9*n*27, 9*n*28, 10, 12, 24, 116, 151–152, 176, 189, 235*n*90, 236, 238, 251–252

Juno, temple of (in Veii) 123

Lamia 175*n*87
Latium 251*n*9
Leucas 24
Liguria 195
Liternum 35, 73
Locri 174*n*83
Locris 24

INDEX OF PLACES

Lower Olympus (mountain range)   153, 153*n*9, 176
Luceria   130

Macedon   7, 78, 98–100, 136, 145, 177, 177*n*97
Maedica   21
Magaba   175*n*91
Magnesia   24, 164, 172, 188*n*126
Malian Gulf   24–26
Meander River   172
Mediterranean Sea
   Western Mediterranean   9*n*28
Meliboea   176*n*95
Metamorphosis, Mt.   177
Metaurus River   115*n*94, 143, 157*n*23, 158*n*24, 172*n*63, 174*n*78
Monte di Canne   172*n*61, 184*n*117

Neapolis   35*n*15
New Carthage   153*n*13, 172, 175*n*87, 183

Ocean   2, 171
Oeneum   176*n*95
Oeta (mountain range)   24
Olympus, Mt.   175*n*91

Padua   1*n*3
Palaepolis   35*n*15
Pallanteum   129
Pella   173*n*67, 175*n*87
Peloponnese   24
Perrhaebia   24
Pessinus   130
Phocis   24
Phrygia   130
Phrygius River   188*n*126
Politorium   83
Praeneste   77
Pydna   152, 156, 172*n*64

Red Sea   2
Regillus, Lake   165–166, 165*n*45, *n*47, 168–169
Rhodes   75, 77

Sabina   121–122
Sacred Mount   59, 91–93, 122–123
Sora   183
Spain (or: Spanish provinces)   8*n*28, 162, 188
Stena   180
Stratum   175*n*87
Syria   7
Syracuse   206–209

Tagus River   188
Tarquinii   220
Thermopylae   24–26, 25–26*n*73, 174*n*82, 176*n*94, 177
Thessalia   24
Thyrrenian Sea   151–152
Ticinus River   157*n*23, 189
Tiriolo   235*n*90
Trasimene, Lake   93*n*41, 142, 172, 175*n*93, 189–193, 192*n*136, 245
Trebia River   157*n*23, 171, 189
Troy   1, 1*n*2, 1*n*4, 251*n*9
Tusculum   55, 166

Utica   175*n*87

Vecilius, Mt.   122
Veii   63–64, 79*n*130, 104*n*63, 112, 114, 123, 123*n*115, 125, 132, 139, 152, 152*n*7, 165, 165*n*45, *n*47, 246, 251
Veseris, River   103*n*61
Via Latina   218

Zama   157*n*23, 158*n*24, *n*27, *n*28, 164

Index of Ancient People

Male Roman characters are mostly listed based on their *cognomina* (if they have one: e.g. Capitolinus, Marcus Manlius), or else their gentilician *nomina* (e.g. Aebutius, Publius). In some cases, though, a character with one or more *cognomina* is listed based on his *nomen* if the latter is the name by which he is usually mentioned (e.g. Quintus Fabius Maximus Verrucosus, the Cunctator, appears as 'Fabius Maximus Verrucosus, Quintus').

Achilles   19
Acidinus, Lucius Manlius   144
Acilius, Gaius (historian)   7n23
Adranodorus   207
Aebutia   236–237
Aebutius, Publius   235–238
Aebutius, Titus (*magister equitum* 499 BCE)   167, 167n54
Aemilius, Mamercus (dictator 437 BCE)   104n63
Aeneas   1, 1n3, 132, 251
Aequians   57, 61, 179
Africans   189–190
Agrippa, Marcus   137
Albans   83
Albinus, Aulus Postumius (historian)   7n23
Albinus, Spurius Postumius (cos. 186 BCE)   72, 235–240
Alexander the Great   99–100
Alimentus, Lucius Cincius (historian)   7n23
Ancus Marcius   82–85, 130, 223
Anicius, Lucius (propraetor in 167 BCE)   94–95, 94n46
Annius Luscus, Titus (cos. 153 BCE)   79
Annius, Titus, from Setia   116–118, 245
Antenor   1n3
Antiochus the Third (King of Syria)   2, 24, 26n73, 72, 73n119, 77, 164, 248
Antipater, Coelius (historian)   9n32, 106
Antony, Mark (Marcus Antonius)   80, 250–251
Aequians   107
Asellio, Sempronius (historian)   9n31, 79
Attalus, king of Pergamum   131
Augustus   9n33, 11n42, 12, 12n43, 12n46, 38–40, 39n33, 42, 85, 115n94, 127–128, 128n131, 132, 137–138, 149, 250–251

Baleares   189–190
Barbatus, Cornelius (pont. max. 304 BCE)   70
Boi. *See* Gauls
Brutus, Lucius Iunius (cos. 509 BCE)   99n52, 113, 209
Bubulcus, Gaius Iunius   182–183

Cacus   82, 126, 126n121, 129, 129n36
Caecilius, Marcus   159–160
Caeninenses, king of   89n29
Caesar, Gaius Iulius   9n33, 10n37, 38, 38n32, 41n45, 58n93, 79, 138, 150–152, 161, 170–171, 250
Camillus, Marcus Furius   40, 64, 108, 112–115, 119, 124, 132, 139, 139n159, 140, 152, 195, 251
Canuleius, Gaius   203
Capitolinus, Marcus Manlius   66–67, 66n103, 94, 104n64, 106–111, 106–107n76, nn78–79, 108n81, 110n88, 119, 134, 136
Capitolinus, Titus Quinctius (cos. 471, 468, 465, 446, 443, 439 BCE)   46n68, 52, 61–62, 62n99, 120, 134n153
Capuans   205n25
Carmenta   129n36
Carvilius, Spurius   118n100
Cassius Dio   212n34
Cassius, Quintus (pr. 167 BCE, cos. 164 BCE)   77, 77n127
Cassius, Spurius   106
Carthaginians   73, 125, 172, 174n83, 175n86, 183–184, 186, 190, 192n136, 195, 195n143, 207
Cato, Marcus Porcius (the Censor, or the Elder)   7, 7n25, 8, 8n27, 8n28, 41n45, 75–76, 76n124, 106, 131n142, 160–163, 192, 218–219

INDEX OF ANCIENT PEOPLE

Cato, Marcus Porcius (the Younger) 9*n*33
Catulus, Quintus Lutatius (cos. 102 BCE) 9*n*33
Cicero, Marcus Tullius 9*n*31, 9*n*33, 12*n*43, 69, 79–80, 80*nn*131–132
Cincinnatus, Lucius Quinctius 34*n*10, 52, 134*n*153, 139*n*161, *n*162, 141*n*167
Cinna, Lucius Cornelius 79
Claudius, Appius (cos. 471 BCE) 45*n*68
Claudius, Appius (Decemvir) 34, 52, 56, 60–61, 202, 214*n*36, 229–235, 229*n*74, 230*n*77, 233*n*84, 234*n*88
Claudius Caecus, Appius (cos. 307, 296 BCE, cens. 312 BCE) 68, 68*n*108, 70–71
Claudius Crassus, Appius (tr. mil. cons. pot. 403 BCE) 63
Claudius, Marcus 229–230, 230*n*74, 233–234, 234*n*88
Cleopatra 210, 250–251
Clodius Pulcher, Publius 38, 79
Cloelia 43*n*59, 139, 243–244
Collatinus, Lucius Tarquinius 202, 206
Coriolanus, Gnaeus Marcius 216–218, 216*n*43
Cornelia 231*n*79
Cossus, Aulus Cornelius (trib. mil. 437 BCE) 104*n*63
Cossus, Aulus Cornelius (dictator 385 BCE) 66, 107
Croesus 98*n*49
Curiatii 33–34, 33*n*5, 33*n*6, 85
Cursor, Lucius Papirius (dictator 325 BCE) 67–68, 102–103, 155*n*18
Curtius (probably Gaius Curtius, cos. 445 BCE) 101*n*56
Curtius, Marcus 101, 101*n*56, 103, 103*n*61, 149
Curtius, Mettius 42, 100–101, 101*n*56

Decemvirs 53, 56–59, 56*n*91, 123, 229, 234–235
Dioscuri 39, 39*n*37
Dionysius of Halicarnassus 165*nn*46–47, 166, 167*n*54, 168, 225, 230, 234

Egeria 85
Ennius, Quintus 35, 152, 165*n*47
Epicydes 207, 207*n*28

Etruscans 104, 119, 130, 151, 155*n*18, 165, 168, 169*n*56, 170, 243
  Etruscan women 225
Evander (king of the Arcadians) 129, 129*n*136

Fabius, Caeso 168–169
Fabius Dorsuo, Gaius 119
Fabius Maximus Aemilianus, Quintus 98*n*50
Fabius Maximus Verrucosus, Quintus (cos. 233, 228, 215, 214, 209 BCE, dictator 217 BCE) 135–136, 192*n*136
Fabius, Marcus (cos. 483, 480 BCE) 168–169
Fabius, Quintus (cos. 485, 482 BCE) 168–169
Fabius Maximus Rullianus, Quintus (cos. 322, 310, 308, 297, 295 BCE, cens. 304 BCE) 67–70, 102–103, 103*n*61, 155*n*18
Fabius Ambustus, Marcus (cos. 360, 356, 354 BCE, father of Rullianus) 67, 68*n*107, 102–103
Flaccus, Quintus Fulvius 120
Flaminius, Gaius (cos. 217 BCE) 91–92, 93*n*41, 172, 189–192, 189*n*130
Flavius, Gnaeus (aedile 304 BCE) 68, 68*n*108, 70–71, 70*n*114
Fundani 130
Fundanius, Marcus 218

Galba, Servius Sulpicius (military tribune in Lucius Aemilius Paullus' army) 95
Galba, Servius Sulpicius (propraetor in Farther Spain in 150 BCE, prosecuted in 149 BCE for treacherously massacring the Lusitanians) 7*n*25
Gauls 64, 107–109, 108*n*82, 110*n*88, 113–114, 119, 139*n*159, 151, 159–160, 160*n*34, 175*n*91, 184, 194–195, 247–248
  Boi 155*n*18
Gellius, Gnaeus (historian) 8*n*30, 165*n*46, 166–167*n*53
Gentius, king of the Illyrians 77, 77*n*126
Geryon 129*n*36
Glabrio, Manius Acilius 2, 2*n*11
Gracchus, Gaius Sempronius (trib. pl. 123, 122 BCE) 38, 40
Gracchus, Tiberius Sempronius (cos. 215, 213 BCE, proconsul 214 BCE) 125

Gracchus, Tiberius Sempronius (trib.pl. 186 BCE, cos. 177, 163 BCE, cens. 169 BCE) 41n45, 73
Gracchus, Tiberius Sempronius (tr. pl. 133 BCE) 79
Greeks 161, 163, 194

Hannibal 23, 23n70, 28–29, 106, 120, 135, 143, 153, 158n24, 171–173, 174n83, 185–189, 191, 195, 207, 248, 252
Hasdrubal (Hannibal's brother) 172n63, 187n126
Hasdrubal, son of Gisgo 209, 211
Hemina, Lucius Cassius (historian) 8n30
Heraclia 207–209, 214, 233, 242
Hercules 82, 126, 126n121, 129, 129n36
Herdonius, Appius 53–54
Herminius, Titus 167
Hernicans 188
Herodotus 98–99
Hesiod 10n35
Hiero (king of Syracuse) 207–208
Hieronymus (king of Syracuse) 207–209
Hippocrates (Carthaginian envoy in Syracuse) 207, 207n28
Hispala Faecenia 236–238, 236n92, 238n100, 240, 244
Homer 10n35, 165, 165n47
Horatia (Horatius' sister) 33
Horatii (the three brothers who fought against the Curiatii) 33, 33n5, 33n6
　Horatius (the one of the Horatii who survived the duel) 33, 33n5, 85
　Horatius' father 33
Horatius Cocles 44, 130, 132, 139
Horatius Barbatus, Marcus (cos. 449 BCE) 59
Hortalus, Quintus Hortensius 127

Icilius, Lucius 123, 229, 231, 234, 234n88
Illyrians 77, 77n126

Laelius, Gaius 209–210, 212
Laetorius, Gaius 159–160
Latins 116, 118n100, 166–168
Lentulus, Lucius Cornelius 104n64
Lepidus, Marcus Aemilius 41n45, 136

Licinius Crassus, Gaius (consul 168 BCE) 145
Licinius Crassus, Publius (cos. 171 BCE) 96–98
Ligurians 195, 247
Ligustinus, Spurius 71n115
Livius Andronicus 124
Lucceius, Lucius (historian) 9n31
Lucretia 51, 201–202, 201nn15–16, 202n17, n19, 206, 206n26, 208, 214, 220, 232–233, 232n83, 242
Lucullus, Gaius Licinius (duumvir 191 BCE) 115n94
Lutatius (author of a *Communis Historia*) 10n36

Macedonians 77, 77n126, 135n154, 172, 173n67, 174n80, 175n86, 180–182
Macer, Licinius (historian) 70, 70n114, 165–166, 165n46, 166n53, 167n54
Maelius, Spurius 106
Mago (Hannibal's brother) 23
Maharbal 106
'maid of Ardea' 203–204, 206, 233, 242
Mandonius 233
Manlius, Gnaeus (cos. 480 BCE) 168–169, 169n56
Manlius, Titus 118n100
Marcellus, Marcus Claudius 135
Masinissa 155n18, 184, 209–214, 211n34, 214n37
Marius, Gaius 58n93, 79
Massiliotes 194n141
Metellus, Quintus Caecilius 136
Minucius Rufus, Marcus (*magister equitum* 217 BCE) 174n83
Mus, Publius Decius (cos. 340 BCE) 103n61, 175n86
Mus, Publius Decius (cos. 312, 308, 297, 295 BCE) 105

Navius, Attus 44
Nepos, Cornelius 9n33, 9n35, 10n36
Nicomedes, son of King Prusias 77
Nobilior, Marcus Fulvius (cos. 189 BCE, cens. 179 BCE) 41n45, 136
Numa Pompilius 11n42, 85

INDEX OF ANCIENT PEOPLE

Numidians   120, 120*n*104, 186, 213–214
Numitorius, Publius   234, 234*n*88

Octavia   39
Octavian. *See* Augustus
Octavius, Gnaeus (propraetor in 167 BCE)   94–95, 94*n*46
Octavius Mamilius   167, 167*n*54
Opimius, Lucius   40, 41*n*45, 70

Papirius, Lucius   67–68
Paullus, Lucius Aemilius (cos. 216 BCE)   186
Paullus, Lucius Aemilius (cos. 182, 168 BCE)   75, 94–95, 94*n*46, 98–100, 105, 141, 141*n*167, 145, 152, 156
Persians   26
Perseus, king of Macedon   75, 77, 77*n*126, 94, 96, 98–99, 145, 177*n*97, 248
Petillii (tribb. pl. 186 BCE)   72–74
Philippus, Quintus Marcius   177
Philip the Fifth (king of Macedon)   21–22, 26*n*73, 28, 156, 157*n*23, 172*n*63, 173*n*67, 174*n*77, *n*80, *n*84, 177, 180–182, 248
Philip the Second (king of Macedon)   10*n*36
Phoceans   161
Pictor, Quintus Fabius (historian)   7*n*23, 7*n*24, 219*n*55
Piso Frugi, Lucius Calpurnius (cos. 133 BCE, historian)   8*n*30, 70, 70*n*114, 101*n*56, 188*n*128
Pollio, Gaius Asinius   9*n*31
Polybius   10*n*38, 25, 75, 77–78, 158*n*28, 180–182, 180*n*114, 186*n*122, 187, 187*n*123, 211*n*34
Pompey (Gnaeus Pompeius Magnus)   58*n*93, 138
Pomponius, Marcus (praet. 217 BCE)   142–143
Porsenna   139, 139*n*159, 243
Postumius, Albius (dictator 499 BCE)   166–167, 166*n*53, 167*n*54
Privernates   130
Proculus, Iulius   1–2
Prusias (king of Pontus)   77–78, 77*n*125
Publilius, Gaius   51
Purpureo, Lucius Furius   159–160

Quadrigarius, Claudius (historian)   8*n*30
Quinctius, Caeso (Cincinnatus' son)   53

Remus   1, 82, 121, 126, 129
Rhea Silvia   242
Rhodians   75–77, 75*n*122, 194, 194*n*140
Romans   1, 26
Romulus   1, 12, 42, 43*n*58, 53, 82–87, 89*n*29, 93, 121, 126, 128–130, 137–138, 196
Rufus, Mugnatius   9*n*33

Sabines   42, 43*n*58, 48, 57, 60–61, 82–83, 85, 87–88, 93, 130, 196
  Sabine women   43, 82–83, 87–88, 130, 215*n*39, 222
Salinator, Marcus Livius (cos. 207 BCE)   115*n*94
Sallust (Gaius Sallustius Crispus)   9*n*31, 9*n*32
Samnites   67, 130, 175*n*86, 182
Scaevola, Gaius Mucius   243
Scaurus, Marcus Aemilius   9*n*33
Scipio Aemilianus, Publius Cornelius   98*n*50
Scipio Africanus, Publius Cornelius   35, 44, 72–74, 73*n*119, 94, 131, 155*n*18, 172, 183–184, 210, 212, 214, 214*n*37, 233, 233*n*84, 242
Scipio, Lucius Cornelius (brother of Africanus)   35, 72
Scipio, Publius Cornelius (historian, son of Scipio Africanus)   7*n*23
Sempronius Longus, Tiberius (cos. 218 BCE)   23
Seneca, Annaeus (the Elder)   79
Sergia   231*n*79
Servilius Geminus, Gnaeus (cos. 217 BCE)   92–93
Servilius, Publius (cos. 495 BCE)   48
Servilius Pulex Geminus, Marcus (cos. 202 BCE)   95–96, 98, 100, 104–105
Servius Tullius   27, 82, 82*n*5, 84–85, 84*n*10, 120, 219–225, 223*n*63
Sisenna, Lucius Cornelius (historian)   9*n*31
Sophoniba   155*n*18, 209–214, 209*n*30, 211*n*34, 214*n*35

Sopater   209
Spaniards   160–163, 189–190
　Spanish prisoners   233, 242
Spartans   26, 26n73
Sulla, Lucius Cornelius (the dictator)   9n31, 9n33, 38, 58n93, 79, 123, 132
Sulla, Faustus (son of the dictator)   38
Sulpicia   236–238, 242
Sulpicius, Publius (cos. 200 BCE)   136
Syphax   184, 209–213, 209n30, 211n34, 214n35

Tanaquil   223–228, 241
Tarpeia   88
Tarquins   113, 134, 166, 201–202, 208, 225, 231
Tarquinius, Lucius   167
Tarquinius Priscus   82, 82n5, 85, 93, 219, 219n55, 223–224
Tarquinius, Sextus   51, 167n54, 201–202, 202n19, 206
Tarquinius Superbus   27, 51, 85–86, 88, 90, 93, 120, 166–167, 166n53, 202, 219–221, 222n61, 223
Tarquinius, Titus   166n53, n54
Tatius, Titus   42, 82
Terentilius Harsa, Gaius   52n83
Thalna, Marcus Iuventius   75
Themisto   208
Thracians   172n64
Tiberius (emperor)   40
Tibullus   128n131
Timaeus of Tauromenius   8n28
Tiro (Cicero's freedman)   9n33
Titinius, Publius   160
Torquatus, Titus Manlius (cos. 347, 344, 340 BCE)   102–103n61, 116–118, 118n100
Tremulus, Quintus Marcius   43–44n59

Trogus, Pompeius   10n36
Tubero, Aelius   8n30
Tullia (daughter of Servius Tullius, wife to Tarquinius Superbus)   27–28, 120, 219–223, 222n61, 225, 232
Tullus Hostilius   36, 36n19, 82–83, 85

Valeria   216–217
Valerius Antias (historian)   8n30
Valerius Flaccus, Lucius   159–160
Valerius, Lucius (trib. pl. 195 BCE)   218–219
Valerius, Marcus (Publicola's brother)   167, 167n55
Valerius Potitus, Lucius (cos. 449 BCE)   59
Valerius Publicola, Publius (cos. suff. 509 BCE, cos. 508 BCE)   34, 119
Valerius, Publius (cos. 460 BCE)   53–55, 62
Varro, Gaius Terentius (cos. 216 BCE)   185–186, 188
Varro, Marcus Terentius   84, 84n11
Verginia (daughter of Lucius Verginius)   34, 56, 59–61, 123, 202, 205, 206n26, 214n36, 228–235, 231n77, n79, 232n83, 234n88, 235n89, 242
Verginia (founder of the cult of Pudicitia Plebeia)   226–228, 233, 241
Verginius, Lucius   34, 60–61, 123, 229–234, 234n88
Verginius, Titus (consul 499 BCE)   167n54
Veturia   216–218
Vergil   128n131, 165n47
Vitruvius Vaccus   130
Volscians   48, 120, 160n35, 179, 187n126, 205–206, 216
Volumnia   216–217
Vulso, Gnaeus Manlius   105, 175n91, 194–195, 194nn140–141

Index of Ancient Sources

Bold page numbers indicate a textual quotation.

Alimentus, Lucius Cincius
   FRHist. 2 T1 (=Livy 21.38.2–5)
      7n23
   FRHist. 2 T2 (Dion. Hal. *Ant. Rom.* 1.6.2)   7n23

Antipater, Coelius
   FRHist. 15 F1 (=Cic. *Orat.* 230)
      9n32

Appian (App.)
The Hannibalic War (*Hann.*)
   27.116   7n23
The Punic Wars (*Pun.*)
   27.111   211n34
The Syrian War (*Syr.*)
   17   25

Augustine, *De Civitate Dei* (August. *De civ. D.*)
   4.23.23   114n94

Augustus, *Res Gestae divi Augusti* (*Mon. Anc.*)
   19   114n94
   25.33   12n47
   26.2   2n11

Aurelius Victor, [*De viris illustribus*] ([Aur. Vict.] *De vir. Ill.*)
   21   229n73

Cato, *Origines*
   FRHist. 5 F84   8n27
   FRHist. 5 FF 87–93   76n124
   FRHist. 5 FF104–107   7n25
   FRHist. 5 F 111   8n27
   FRHist. 5 F 116   8n27

Catulus, Quintus Lutatius
   FRHist 19 T1 (=Cic. *Brut.* 132)   9n33

Cicero (Cic.)
Brutus (*Brut.*)
   112   9n33
   132   9n33

De Amicitia (*Amic.*)
   96   37
De Consulatu Suo
   FRHist. 39 T1   9n33
   FRHist. 39 T2   9n33
De Divinatione (*Div.*)
   1.43   7n23
   1.121   223n63
De Finibus (*Fin.*)
   2.66   229n73
De Lege Agraria (*Leg. agr.*)
   286   251n8
De Natura Deorum (*Nat. D.*)
   2.2.6   39n37
De Oratore (*De or.*)
   3.167   49n78
De Re Publica (*Rep.*)
   2.3–10   140
   2.3.5   **140**n164
   2.17.31   36n19
   2.63   229n73
Epistulae ad Atticum (*Att.*)
   1.19.10   9n33
   1.20.6   9n33
Epistulae ad familiares (*Fam.*)
   5.12   9n31
Orator (*Orat.*)
   230   9n32
Philippicae (*Phil.*)
   12.7   251n8
Pro Sestio (*Sest.*)
   45   69

CIL
   1² 581   235n90

Digesta (*Dig.*)
   1.2.2.24   229n73

Dio Cassius, *Roman History* (Dio Cass.)
   fr. 5.7   43n58
   fr. 57, 61   131
   49.15.5   127n126
   49.41.1–5   251n6
   50.4.1   251n7
   50.50.4   251n7

288 INDEX OF ANCIENT SOURCES

Diodorus Siculus, *Bibliotheca Historica* (Diod. Sic.)

4.21.1–4	129n136
12.24	229n73
15.35.3	66n103

Dionysius of Halicarnassus, *Roman Antiquities* (Dion. Hal. *Ant. Rom.*)

1.6.2	7n23
1.32.4–5	126n119
1.39–40	129n136
1.39.2	129n136
1.79	126n118
1.79.8	126n119
1.79.11	126n120
1.85.6	126n118
2.15.4–5	87n23
2.15.4	87n22
2.38	88n25
3.32.9	33n6, 33n7
3.69.4–6	114
4.2.4	223n63
4.7	219n55
4.28–38	221n60
4.30.2–3	219n55
4.39	221
4.61.4	88
4.66.1–67.2	201
6.2.1	166n48
6.3.3–5.2	166n52
6.3.13	165n45
6.5.4–5	167n54
6.11.2	165n45, 166n53
6.13	39n37
6.36.1	62n99
6.88.1	62n99
8.39–43	216
8.39.1	217
8.39.2	217n49
8.69–79	106
7.71.1	7n23
9.5–12	165n45
11.28–37	229
11.28.3	231
11.36	229n74
12.1–2	106
14.11.1–5	101n56
14.11.1	101n56
16.5.1–3	52n81

Ennius, Quintus, *Annales* (Enn. *Ann.*)

75–76Sk	121n109

Eutropius, *Breviarium ab urbe condita* (Eutr.)

1.18	229n73

Festus, *De Verborum Significatu* (Festus, *Gloss. Lat.*)

270	227
372	43n58
474–476	84n14
496	88n25

Paulus Diaconus, *Excerpta ex libris Pompei Festi de verborum significatione* (Paul. Fest.)

271	227
459	84n14

Florus, *Epitoma de Tito Livio* (Flor.)

1.1.7.8	114n94
1.1.9	87n23

Gellius, Aulus, *Noctes Atticae* (Gell. *NA*)

7.9.1–6	70n114
10.24.6–7	106
17.21.24	66n103

Gellius, Gnaeus

FRHist. 14 F17	129n136

Hemina, Lucius Cassius

FRHist. 6 F3	129n136

Herodotus, *Histories* (Hdt.)

1.86–87	98n49
3.39–43	99n51

Horace, *Carmina* (Hor. *Carm.*)

3.3.17–78	251n9

Lactantius Placidus, *Commentary on Statius' Thebaid* (*Ad Stat. Theb.*)

1.306–307	178n106

Livy, *Ab Urbe Condita* (Livy)
Praefatio

praef. 1	12n48
praef. 3	3
praef. 4	2–3
praef. 7	118n98

INDEX OF ANCIENT SOURCES

Livy, *Ab Urbe Condita* (Livy) (*cont.*)
  Praefatio
    praef. 9–10   249
    praef. 10   97, 249, 249*n*3
  Book 1

1.1.1	1*n*2
1.1.2–3	1*n*3
1.1.2	129
1.1.4–2.6	1*n*3
1.4.1	1*n*7, 2
1.4.1–8.3	1*n*4
1.4.4	83
1.4.5	34*n*10, 129
1.5–9	88*n*25
1.6.4	121, 129
1.7.1–3	83
1.7.3	129
1.7.4–15	129
1.8.4	82
1.8.5	87*nn*22–23, 93*n*43
1.9–13	82*n*2
1.9.1	1*n*8
1.9.5–7	93
1.10.5–7	89*n*29
1.10.5	90*n*34
1.11–13	130
1.12.1–13.5	93
1.12.1	90*n*33, 175*n*87
1.12.3	83, 141*n*173
1.12.9–10	85
1.13.1–2	215*n*39, 222
1.13.5	85
1.16.7	1–2
1.19.2	85
1.19.3	11*n*42
1.20.3	85, 85*n*17
1.20.5	85
1.20.7	85, 121
1.21.3	85, 85*n*19
1.25	33*n*5
1.26.2–4	33*n*5, 85
1.26.2	141*n*173
1.26.10	33, 33*n*6
1.26.11	33*n*6
1.26.13	33, 33*n*8
1.27.10	174*n*79
1.29.1–30.3	82*n*3
1.30.1	83
1.30.2	36*n*19, 85
1.33.1–5	82*n*4
1.33.2–5	121
1.33.2	83, 90*n*31, 130
1.33.5	83, 130
1.33.6	84
1.33.8	43*n*59, 85
1.33.9	85
1.34	82*n*5
1.36.1	85
1.36.5	44*n*59
1.37.4	175*n*90
1.38.6	85
1.38.7	85, 90*n*34, 93
1.39–41	82*n*5
1.39.1–6	223
1.40	224
1.41	223–224
1.41.3	224
1.41.4	224, 227
1.41.5	224
1.40.6	129*n*136
1.44.1–2	85
1.44.2	7*n*23
1.44.3	84–85, 119
1.44.4	85
1.45.1, 3	1*n*8
1.45.3–7	85
1.46–48	219
1.46.2	220
1.46.4	219*n*55
1.46.7	220
1.46.8	220*n*58
1.47.1–6	220
1.47.7	222*n*61
1.48.5–7	120, 220–221
1.48.5	27, 222
1.48.6	120*n*101
1.49.7	220*n*58
1.57–60	52
1.55.1–56.2	93
1.55	86
1.55.1	90
1.55.3–4	86
1.55.5–6	86
1.55.6	1*n*8
1.57–59	201
1.57.9	201

Livy, *Ab Urbe Condita* (Livy) (*cont.*)
  Book 1
    1.57.10   214*n*36
    1.58.1–4   201
    1.58.2   214*n*36
    1.58.5   214*n*36
    1.58.6   201
    1.59.3   202
    1.59.8   214*n*36
    1.59.9   **113*n*92**
    1.60.2   167*n*54
  Book 2
    2.1.1   50
    2.1.5   142*n*173
    2.3.5   99*n*52
    2.5.2–3   139*n*161
    2.5.2   134
    2.5.7   **113**
    2.7.5–12   34
    2.7.10   104*n*62
    2.7.7   45*n*61
    2.7.10   90*n*31
    2.7.12   **34**
    2.8.6–8   94
    2.8.6   90*n*34
    2.9.3   113*n*91
    2.10.1–2   139*n*161
    2.10.3   90*n*32
    2.10.4   130
    2.10.9   113*n*91
    2.10.11   139*n*161
    2.10.12   44
    2.11.1–2   139*n*161
    2.11.5   142*n*173
    2.11.7   142*n*173
    2.11.8–9   142*n*173
    2.11.8   119
    2.12.5   139*nn*160–161
    2.13.5   139*n*161
    2.13.6–11   243
    2.13.11   **243**
    2.13.11   43*n*59
    2.15.4   87*n*22
    2.16.6   139*n*161
    2.19–20   165
    2.19.3–5   166
    2.19.3   **166**
    2.19.6   166
    2.19.7   167
    2.19.8–10   167
    2.20.1–3   167
    2.20.4–6   167
    2.20.7–9   167
    2.20.10   39*n*37
    2.20.10–13   168
    2.21.1   43*n*59
    2.21.3   166*n*48
    2.22.6   90*n*36
    2.23–24   47–51
    2.23.3   **48*n*77, 51**
    2.23.7   **48, 51**
    2.23.8   **51**
    2.23.8–9   51
    2.23.9–11   49
    2.23.11   **51**
    2.23.12–13   49
    2.23.12–15   51
    2.24.1   49
    2.24.3   **49**
    2.24.4   49
    2.24.5   141*n*170
    2.24.6–7   52
    2.28.1–3   120
    2.28.1   122
    2.29.6   45*n*68
    2.30.9   175*n*88, **179**
    2.31.7–33.3   122
    2.32.4   204*n*22
    2.34.4   139*n*163
    2.39–40   216
    2.39.2   141*n*169
    2.40.1   216, **216*n*46, 217*n*50**
    2.40.2   **217**
    2.40.5   217
    2.40.7   **217–218**
    2.40.10   7*n*23, 218
    2.40.11–12   218
    2.40.12   **218**
    2.41   106
    2.42.5   39*n*37
    2.45   155*n*18, 168
    2.45.1–47.9   165, 168
    2.46.1–47.9   168
    2.46.1   **169**
    2.46.3   **169**
    2.46.4–9   169*n*56

INDEX OF ANCIENT SOURCES 291

Livy, *Ab Urbe Condita* (Livy) (cont.)
   Book 2

2.46.4–7	168
2.46.5–6	168
2.46.7	**169**
2.46.7	170
2.47.1–3	**168**
2.47.5	155*n*18
2.49.7	90*n*31
2.49.2	142*n*173
2.50.10–11	174*n*77
2.51	139*n*159
2.51.2	139*n*162, 141*n*170
2.51.6–7	139*n*162
2.56	45–46*n*68
2.56.10	45
2.57.1	45*n*66
2.63.1	134*n*152
2.64.3	141*n*170, 142*n*173
2.65.3	178*n*102, **179*n*111**

   Book 3

3.7.2	175*n*87
3.8.9	178*n*107
3.9.2–5	52*n*83
3.10.1	134*n*153
3.10.3	139*n*162
3.11–13	53
3.11–32	52
3.11.1–2	37*n*21
3.15.4–18.11	53
3.15.5	53, 90*n*31
3.15.6	53
3.15.7	53
3.15.8–16.6	53
3.15.9	53, 90*n*32
3.16.5	90*n*32, 104*n*62
3.17	62
3.17.1	53
3.17.2	45*n*63, **54–55**
3.17.3–8	54
3.17.3–4	**54**
3.17.4–7	104*n*62
3.17.7	90*n*32
3.17.9	55
3.17.9–10	104*n*62
3.17.15	113*n*91
3.18	55
3.18.1	90*n*31

3.18.6	90*n*32, 104*n*62
3.18.10	104*n*62
3.19.4–12	52
3.19.6–8	104*n*62
3.19.12	90*n*32, 104*n*62
3.20.3	90*n*32, 104*n*62
3.21.1	46*n*73, 90*n*36
3.22.4	141*n*173
3.25.9	113*n*91
3.26.1	141*n*170
3.26.8	34*n*10, 139*n*162, **141*n*167**
3.26.11	139*n*163
3.27.3	134*n*153
3.29.9	90*n*34
3.31.3	122
3.31.4–6	175*n*91
3.33–48	202
3.33.1	53*n*84
3.33.1–6	56
3.33.7–35.11	56
3.33.5–8	52, 56
3.34.8	56*n*91
3.36–37	56
3.36.3–4	56
3.36.8	57
3.37.6	56
3.38–43	56
3.38.8–11	57–58
3.41.1–5	61
3.42.3–4	**179**
3.44–49	60
3.44–48	229
3.44.2	**214*n*36**
3.44.4	214*n*36
3.44.6–46.8	230
3.44.6	230, **233**
3.44.7	**234**
3.44.9	230, **233**
3.45.7	231
3.45.8	**214*n*36**
3.46.5–6	330
3.46.9–10	230
3.47.1–49.8	230
3.47.1	**232, 233**
3.47.4	**214*n*36**
3.47.5	229
3.47.6–8	233

INDEX OF ANCIENT SOURCES

Livy, *Ab Urbe Condita* (Livy) (*cont.*)
 Book 3

3.48.1	**214n36**
3.48.3	**233–234**
3.48.5	34, **234, 234n88**
3.48.7	**234**
3.50.9	**232**
3.50.11, 15	60
3.50.13	122
3.51.6–10	122
3.51.10	60, 142n173
3.52.1–4	122
3.52.3	60, 204n22
3.52.5–7	28n78, 59
3.52.8	205
3.53.3	122
3.54.8–11	122
3.54.8	122
3.54.9	123
3.57.2–4	60
3.57.2	45n64
3.57.3	**61**, 113n91
3.57.4	43n59, 61
3.57.7	90n36
3.59–72	52
3.63.6	46n73, 47, 134n152
3.64.6	45n61
3.66	205
3.67–68	52
3.67.3	62
3.67.6	**61**
3.67.11–68.1	120
3.67.11	123
3.68.1	**61**
3.68.6–7	61
3.68.7	90n31, 104n62, 141n170
3.68.13	141n170
3.69.6–8	134n153

 Book 4

4.1.1–6.4	203
4.2.13	104n62
4.2.14	90n31
4.3.10–13	84
4.6.1	45n61
4.7.1	134n151
4.9–10	203
4.9.2–5	203
4.9.5	203–204
4.9.6–8	**204**
4.9.10	**204–205**
4.10–20	104n63
4.10	205
4.11.1	134n152
4.12.2	134n151
4.13	106
4.13.6–7	134n152
4.17.1–6	104n63
4.17.11	173n76
4.18.6–7	104n63
4.19.6	139n162
4.20.4–11	89n29
4.20.4	90n36
4.20.7	11n42
4.21.8	142n173
4.21.9	141n169
4.22.7	134n153
4.23.1	134n152, 142n173
4.31.9	142n173
4.39.4–8	174n77
4.39.6	175n88
4.40.2–3	215n39
4.40.2	**215n42**
4.45.1	90n31
4.52.6	139n163
4.53.5	113n91
4.59.11–60.9	62
4.60.1	62, 64
4.61.8	178n102

 Book 5

5.1–22	152n7
5.2.2	45n61
5.7	63
5.7.6	63
5.7.8	44
5.7.8–11	64
5.7.9–10	**63**
5.18.8	174n77
5.18.11	141n171, **215n42**
5.18.11–12	215n39
5.21.3	123
5.21.5	123
5.21.15	113n91
5.22.3–7	123
5.22.7	**123**
5.23.7	123, 125
5.24.4–25.3	112n89

INDEX OF ANCIENT SOURCES

Livy, *Ab Urbe Condita* (Livy) (cont.)
Book 5

5.26.5	178*n*102, *n*104, 178*n*106, *n*109
5.28.7–10	174*n*77
5.30.4	132, **132***n***146**
5.30.5	104*n*62
5.31.2–4	107
5.31.3	123
5.33	152
5.33.7–11	151
5.32.6	34*n*10, 132
5.36.11	134*n*152
5.39.2–3	141*n*16
5.39.3	113*n*91
5.39.9–13	112
5.39.12	90*n*31, **112**, 114
5.40	175*n*87
5.40.1	90*n*31
5.40.5	139*n*159
5.40.8	139*n*159
5.41.4	142*n*173
5.43.6	113*n*91
5.44.5	90*n*31, 104*n*62
5.46.2–3	90*n*32
5.46.2	119
5.46.8	139*n*163
5.47.1–5	107
5.47.2	107
5.48.3	160*n*34
5.49.1	113*n*91
5.50.8	45*n*61, **64**
5.51–54	**64**, 112
5.51.1–2	**64–65**
5.51.3	104*n*62, **113**, 119
5.51.8–9	113*n*91
5.51.9	104*n*62, **114**
5.51.10	114
5.52.1	114
5.52.2	**113***n***90**
5.52.3	90*n*31, 104*n*62,
5.52.6	90*n*36, 104*n*62, 114
5.52.7	114, 132*n*145
5.52.10–11	114
5.52.10	90*n*32, 123
5.52.11–12	104*n*62
5.52.13	114, 132*n*145
5.52.16–17	114
5.53.5	90*n*32, 104*n*62
5.53.7	132
5.53.9	104*n*62
5.54.2–3	**140**
5.54.2	114
5.54.3	114
5.54.4	140, 140*n*164
5.54.5–7	114
5.5.45	**152**
5.54.7	90*n*34, 104*n*62, **114–115**, 132
5.55	1*n*6
5.55.1	44, 79*n*130
5.55.2	28*n*78
5.55.3–4	114

Book 6

6.4.2, 12	90*n*36
6.11–20	66
6.11.3–10	107
6.11.4–5	104*n*64
6.11.4	90*n*31
6.11.7	**107***n***78**
6.12.2	107
6.14.1–10	107
6.14.4	104*n*64, 107, **107***nn***82–83**
6.14.5	113*n*91
6.14.11–13	107
6.15.1–16.3	107
6.15.1–2	45*n*64
6.15.1	44, 66
6.15.2	**66**
6.15.3	**66**
6.15.11	104*n*64, 107, 107*n*84
6.16.2	104*n*64
6.16.4–17.5	107
6.16.4	43*n*59
6.16.8	109
6.17	107
6.17.4	104*n*64, 109, 110*n*88
6.19	107
6.19.6–7	67
6.20.1–10	107
6.20.8–9	109–110
6.20.9	90*n*31, 104*n*64
6.20.10–11	90*n*34, 110, 132
6.20.10	**110**
6.20.11–12	107

Livy, *Ab Urbe Condita* (Livy) (*cont.*)
  Book 6
    6.20.11 — 142*n*173
    6.20.13–16 — 107
    6.20.13 — 104*n*64
    6.20.16 — 104*n*64
    6.22.1 — 134*n*151
    6.22.8 — 120, 142*n*173
    6.23.12–24.11 — 187*n*126
    6.24.2 — 187*n*126
    6.24.2–3 — 174*n*81
    6.24.3–4 — 160*n*34
    6.28.2–3 — 141*n*170
    6.28.2 — 142*n*173
    6.28.3 — 141*n*169 141*n*171
    6.29.8 — 90*n*36
    6.30.5 — **179**
    6.31.1 — 134*n*151
    6.33.4 — 205*n*23
    6.40.17 — 104*n*64, *n*68
    6.41.3 — 104*n*64
  Book 7
    7.1.1–3.4 — 102*n*61
    7.3.2 — 141*n*165
    7.3.6–9 — 102*n*61
    7.4–5 — 103*n*61
    7.5.1 — 113*n*91
    7.6 — 100–101
    7.6.1 — 100
    7.6.2 — **101**
    7.6.3–4 — **101**
    7.6.3 — 90*n*34
    7.6.4 — 149
    7.6.5–6 — 101
    7.7.6 — **188**
    7.12.3 — 141*n*169
    7.12.11 — 160*n*34
    7.14.6–15.7 — 175*n*93
    7.15.6 — 175*n*90
    7.18.1 — **135**
    7.18.9 — **135**
    7.23.3 — 141*n*173
    7.23.5–10 — 174*n*79
    7.23.8 — **184**
    7.28.1 — 134*n*151
    7.29.6 — 173*n*76
    7.34.1 — 178*n*107
    7.34.36 — 175*n*86
    7.38.2 — 90*n*36
    7.39.7 — 177*n*101
    7.39.16 — 35*n*15
    7.40.2 — 205
    7.40.11 — 123
  Book 8
    8.3.8–6.7 — 116
    8.4.11 — 104*n*64, **116**
    8.5.1–6.7 — 46*n*73
    8.5.1 — 90*n*36, 116
    8.5.2 — **116–117**
    8.5.8 — 104*n*64, 117
    8.6.1–3 — **117–118**
    8.6.4–5 — 118
    8.6.5 — 113*n*91
    8.7 — 103*n*61
    8.9.3–12 — 103*n*61
    8.11.6 — 43*n*59
    8.14.12 — 37*n*23
    8.15.8 — 142*n*173
    8.18.1–10 — 231*n*79
    8.18.8 — 231*n*79
    8.19.4 — 130
    8.20.9 — 130
    8.22.5 — 35*n*15
    8.24.4 — 174*n*79
    8.28 — 47, 50–52, 66
    8.28.1 — 50–51
    8.28.2 — 50
    8.28.2–3 — 51
    8.28.4–6 — 51
    8.28.5 — **51**
    8.28.6–7 — **51**
    8.28.7 — **51**
    8.28.8 — 50*n*79
    8.28.8–9 — 51–52
    8.30–36 — 67
    8.30.1–35.9 — 103*n*61
    8.30.1–33.2 — 67
    8.30.4 — 35*n*15
    8.31.1–33.2 — 155*n*18
    8.33.3–36.9 — 67
    8.33.4 — 67
    8.33.9 — **67**
    8.33.9–22 — 68
    8.33.20–21 — 102
    8.33.21 — 104*n*64
    8.33.9 — 45*n*61, *n*62

INDEX OF ANCIENT SOURCES

Livy, *Ab Urbe Condita* (Livy) (*cont.*)
  Book 8
    8.33.10   68*n*107
    8.34.2–11   68
    8.35.1–8   68
    8.35.1–3   68
    8.35.8   45*n*63
    8.35.9   68
    8.37.6   90*n*31, 141*n*169
  Book 9
    9.2.6–9   175*n*93
    9.2.7   177*n*101, **178*n*108**
    9.2.9   178*n*107
    9.4.7   90*n*32, 104*n*64
    9.4.8–9   104*n*68
    9.4.9   104*n*64
    9.9.2   44
    9.9.15   177*n*100
    9.9.16   178*n*108
    9.14.9   177*n*100
    9.23.7   177*n*101
    9.24.5   177*n*100, 178*n*102, **n109**
    9.24.7   177*n*101, 178*n*102
    9.31.7   177*n*100, 178*n*108
    9.31.12–13   **182–183**
    9.34.4   123
    9.35.1–2   175*n*89
    9.35.7   175*n*90
    9.36.1   35*n*15, **n109**
    9.38.4   177*n*100, **178*n*110**
    9.43.20   175*n*90
    9.44.7   175*n*88
    9.44.16   90*n*34, *n*36
    9.44.22   44*n*59
    9.46   69–71
    9.46.1–7   68
    9.46.3   70*n*114
    9.46.6   70
    9.46.10   68
    9.46.11   **69**
    9.46.10–11   70
    9.46.14   **69–70**
  Book 10
    10.4.2   141*n*169
    10.6.3–9.2   105
    10.7.9   113*n*91
    10.7.10   28*n*78, 104*n*64, 105, **105*n*71**
    10.9.8   35*n*15, 178*n*102, 178*n*105
    10.14.13–21   175*n*93
    10.23.2   **227**
    10.23.3–10   226
    10.23.4   228
    10.23.6–8   **226**
    10.23.6   **227**
    10.23.8–10   227
    10.23.12   90*n*36, 141*n*173
    10.24.5   **178*n*110**
    10.24.18   44
    10.26.8–9   174*n*79
    10.30.7   175*n*91
    10.33.9   131*n*142
    10.37.15–16   130
    10.40.6   174*n*83
  Book 21
    21.16.2, 6   141*n*170
    21.25.8   173
    21.25.13   177*n*100, **178*nn*109–110**
    21.30.7   178*n*103
    21.30.9   177*n*100
    21.30.11   **135**
    21.32   28
    21.32.6–37.6   176
    21.32.8   173*n*70, 176
    21.32.9   178*n*106, **n109**
    21.32 10, 13   173*n*70
    21.33.3   177*n*100
    21.33.6   **178*n*109**
    21.33.7   178*n*105
    21.35.3   178*nn*104–105, **n109**
    21.35.4   177*n*100
    21.35.6–9   176
    21.35.12   177*n*101, 178*n*105, **n108**
    21.36.2   178*n*105
    21.36.3–4   177*n*100
    21.36.4   **178*n*109**
    21.46   157*n*23
    21.48.3   178*n*103, 205*n*23
    21.54–56   157*n*23
    21.55.2–4   157*n*23
    21.54.1   **23**
    21.54.1–2   171
    21.57.1   141*n*170
    21.58   176
    21.62.4–8   124

Livy, *Ab Urbe Condita* (Livy) (*cont.*)
  Book 21
  21.63.7–9   90*n*36, **91–92**, 104*n*65
  21.63.9   98*n*48
  21.63.11   113*n*91
  21.63.13–14   93*n*41
  Book 22
  22.1.4–7   92–93
  22.1.6   90*n*36, 104*n*65
  22.1.8–13   93*n*41
  22.1.8   **93n41**
  22.1.14   46
  22.1.15–16   46*n*71
  22.1.17   124
  22.1.19   43*n*59
  22.2   173
  22.2.4   160*n*34
  22.4–8   189
  22.4–6   175*n*93
  22.4.2–3   **189–190**
  22.4.2   29, 29**n**79, 177*n*101
  22.4.1–6   174*n*81
  22.4.1–5   172
  22.4.4–7   190
  22.5.3–4   190*n*133
  22.5.3   **190**
  22.5.6–8   **191**
  22.6.1–4   191
  22.6.5   178*n*104, **n109, 191**
  22.6.6–10   191
  22.6.8   174*n*77
  22.7.1   141*n*172
  22.7.6–14   **142–143**
  22.7.7   44, 215*n*39
  22.7.8   143
  22.7.11–13   143
  22.7.14   **143**
  22.8.7   141*n*169
  22.12–18   192*n*136
  22.12.8   178*n*103
  22.14.1   175*n*88
  22.14.8   177*n*100, **178n110**
  22.14.11   178*n*103
  22.15.3–18.4   175*n*93
  22.15.10   177*n*100
  22.15.11   178*n*104
  22.17.2   177*n*101
  22.18.5   178*n*103

  22.19.6   178*n*103
  22.23–30   192*n*136
  22.24.2   175*n*88
  22.24.4   174*n*83
  22.28.6   178*n*107
  22.30.10   175*n*88
  22.31.1   91*n*39
  22.36.7   124*n*116
  22.36.8   **135**
  22.37.11, 12   104*n*65
  22.40.5–6   185
  22.41.6   175*n*93
  22.43.10–44.3   185
  22.43.10–11   185
  22.43.10   **185**
  22.44.1   185
  22.44.4   172*n*62, 185*n*118
  22.44.5   113*n*91
  22.45.1–2   186
  22.45.4–5   186
  22.45.5–49.10   157*n*23
  22.45.5–8   186
  22.45.6–46.10   157*n*23
  22.45.7   158*n*24
  22.46.1   186
  22.46.2   158*n*24
  22.46.2–7   186
  22.46.3   158*n*24
  22.46.8–9   **154n13**, 186
  22.47.1   **158n24**
  22.47.2   187*n*125
  22.48.1   **158n24**
  22.51.1   90*n*36
  22.51.2   104*n*65, 106
  22.55.6   **215n42**
  22.55.8   141*n*169
  22.57.2   142*n*173
  22.57.3   44
  22.57.4–5   7*n*23
  22.57.11–12   125*n*117
  22.59.18   44
  22.60.1–2   215*n*41
  22.60.2   **222**
  22.60.11   175*n*86
  Book 23
  23.1.6   178*n*107
  23.11.1–6   7*n*23
  23.18.9–15   195

INDEX OF ANCIENT SOURCES

Livy, *Ab Urbe Condita* (Livy) (*cont.*)
  Book 23

23.18.13	195*n*144
23.22.1–9	118*n*100
23.22.7	104*n*65
23.23	71*n*115
23.23.1	45*n*62
23.24.6–10	173
23.26.10	173*n*76, 178*n*102
23.27.8	175*n*90
23.31.1	46*n*73, 90*n*36
23.31.9	90*n*34
23.32.3	142*n*173
23.32.20	90*n*34
23.37	215*n*40
23.37.5	178*n*107
23.47.7	178*n*107
23.48.10	45*n*61

  Book 24

24.1.6	174*n*83
24.4–6	207
24.6.2	207*n*28
24.7.1–7	207
24.7.10–9.4	135
24.9.6	141*n*165
24.10.1	46*n*73, 90*n*36, 91*n*39
24.10.6	90*n*34
24.14–16	125
24.16.6	174*n*77
24.16.19	**125**
24.20.6	44
24.21.1–23.4	207
24.24–26	207
24.25.9	214
24.26.2–11	207
24.26.12–14	207–208
24.27–32	207
24.34.3	178*n*103
24.47.15	142*n*173

  Book 25

25.1.7	90*n*32
25.4.7–11	71*n*115
25.7.6	142*n*173
25.7.7	90*n*34
25.7.14	44
25.13.13–14	178*n*102
25.13.13	**178*n*109**
25.15.10–13	174*n*81
25.16.22	178*n*103, *n*107
25.30.10	**179*n*110**
25.32.6	175*n*88, 177*n*100, 178*n*108
25.36	174*n*77
25.39.1	178*n*107
25.39.16	90*n*36

  Book 26

26.1.1	46*n*73, 90*n*36, 91*n*39
26.9.6–8	215*n*39
26.9.7	**28, 215–216*n*42**
26.9.9	90*n*34
26.6.11	175*n*90
26.10.1–2	120
26.10.1	141*n*173, 142*n*173, 142*n*173
26.10.2, 6	90*n*31
26.10.3	120*n*105, 142*n*173
26.10.5	120, 178*n*107
26.12.8	**205*n*25**
26.12.9	205*n*25
26.16.9	44
26.17.8	178*n*104, ***n*109**
26.19.4–5	74
26.27.2	**34–35**
26.27.4, 13	132*n*147
26.31.11	90*n*34
26.42–46	172*n*65
26.42.6, 8	154*n*14
26.42.8	175*n*87
26.44.2	154*n*14, 175*n*87
26.46.8–9	175*n*87
26.48.4	175*n*87
26.49.11–50.14	233

  Book 27

27.2–4	173*n*76
27.15.8	174*n*77
27.18	174*n*77, 175*n*86
27.18.8–9	**183–184**
27.18.9	178*n*105
27.18.10–20	184
27.18.14	178*n*103
27.26.7–27.7	174*n*81
27.28.1	174*n*77
27.28.2	175*n*88, 178*n*103
27.36.8	44
27.37	124, 215
27.37.1–7	124

Livy, *Ab Urbe Condita* (Livy) (*cont.*)
  Book 27
    27.37.4–10   124
    27.37.11–15   124
    27.37.11   142*n*173
    27.39.7   177*n*100
    27.41.3–42.8   174*n*81
    27.46.4   175*n*93
    27.46.5   177*n*101, 178*n*103
    27.47–49   172*n*63, 187*n*126
    27.47.10–11   172*n*63, 187*n*126
    27.48.1–49.4   157*n*23
    27.48.2   173*n*76
    27.48.4–8   157*n*23, 158*n*24
    27.48.7–8   174*n*78
    27.48.7   187*n*126
    27.48.9–10   158*n*24
    27.48.12   174*n*78, 187*n*126
    27.48.16   160*n*34
    27.50.1–51.10   143
    27.50.4–5   **143**
    27.50.5   215*n*39
    27.50.6–8   144
    27.50.9   45*n*62, *n*64, **144**
    27.50.11   144
    27.51.1–7   144
    27.51.5   45*n*61
    27.51.8–10   145*n*175
  Book 28
    28.2.1   174*n*81, 178*n*106
    28.2.2   178*n*107
    28.5.8   177*n*101
    28.6.10   178*n*105
    28.8.2   113*n*91
    28.8.9   175*n*88
    28.8.10   205
    28.9.5   46*n*73
    28.11.6–7   132
    28.11.13   177*n*101
    28.13.6   174*n*81
    28.15.8–11   174*n*84
    28.15.8–10   174*n*77
    28.16.6–7   174*n*77
    28.20.4   178*n*102
    28.33.2–4   175*n*93
    28.33.8–13   174*n*82
    28.33.8–9   177*n*101
    28.33.16   174*n*77

    28.34.4   205*n*23
    28.38.2   46*n*73
    28.38.8   90*n*36
    28.38.14   46*n*73, 90*n*36, 91*n*39
    28.39.15, 19   104*n*65
  Book 29
    29.1.7–8   131
    29.11.1–4   131
    29.10.4–8   130
    29.10.4   131*n*143
    29.11.13   141*n*173
    29.14.5–14   215, 215*n*40
    29.16.6   45*n*64
    29.22.5–6   131
    29.23.4   214*n*35
    29.28.1   173*n*76
    29.31.2   175*n*90
    29.32.3   178*n*104
    29.32.4–5   175*n*93
    29.33.4   184
    29.34.9–13   174*n*81
    29.35.7   175*n*87
    29.35.14   154*n*14
  Book 30
    30.4.10   175*n*87
    30.12.5   210
    30.12.9–10   210–211
    30.12.11–22   210
    30.12.11–12   **211**
    30.12.18   **211, 213–214**
    30.12.21   212
    30.13–14   210
    30.13.11–13   212
    30.13.11   **212**
    30.13.12   **212**
    30.14–15   155*n*18
    30.14.4–8   212
    30.14.5   214
    30.14.9–10   **213**
    30.15.1–14   210
    30.17.3   45*n*62
    30.21.5   43*n*59
    30.21.11   46*n*73
    30.22.6–23.1   46
    30.27.1   46*n*73, 91*n*39
    30.32.1–35.3   157*n*23, 158*n*28
    30.33.1–7   157*n*23
    30.33.2   158*n*24

INDEX OF ANCIENT SOURCES

Livy, *Ab Urbe Condita* (Livy) (*cont.*)
  Book 30
    30.35.1–3   158n27
    30.38.9   130
    30.38.10–11   142n173
    30.38.10   141n165
    30.40.1   46n73
    30.45   94
  Book 31
    31.1.1–5   2
    31.2.10   177n100, **179n110**
    31.6–7   136
    31.7.1   136
    31.14.1   90n36, 98n48
    31.17.4   205n23
    31.17.10   205
    31.18.3   205n23
    31.21   159
    31.21.4   **159**
    31.21.5–12   159
    31.21.7–9   **159–160**
    31.21.7–8   158n25
    31.21.10–13   160
    31.21.15–16   160
    31.27.2   177n101
    31.33.5   175n88
    31.34–35   173n68
    31.34.7   174n84
    31.34.8   156
    31.37.8–11   173n67
    31.37.11   177n100
    31.39.7   178n104
    31.39.13–15   175n86
    31.41.8   173n76
    31.42   173n68
    31.45.6   **179**
    31.47.7   46n73
  Book 32
    32.4.3   178n106
    32.5.8–13   180n113
    32.5.10–13   172n63
    32.5.11   177n101
    32.8.1   46n73
    32.8.2   91n39
    32.10.8   173n70
    32.10.9–12.10   173n69
    32.10.9   178n106, 180
    32.10.10   178n104, **n109**, 180
    32.10.11   180
    32.11–12   26n73
    32.11.7   177n100
    32.14.1   177n101
    32.18.7   175n87
    32.25.5   174n79
  Book 33
    33.6–10   173n69
    33.7.3–5   173n76
    33.7.8   174n77
    33.7.9   **181**
    33.7.10   174n80
    33.9.3–4   **181**
    33.9.8–11   182
    33.10.1   174n84, 178n103
    33.8.12–14   157n23
    33.9.5   157n23
    33.17.5–8   151n5
    33.17.7   154n14
    33.18.9–18   172n60
    33.22.1   46n73
    33.24.5   46n73
    33.24.4   45n61
    33.25.7   90n35
    33.26.9   120, 142n173
    33.36.4   173n76
    33.36.8   160n34
    33.47.10   69n113
  Book 34
    34.1.1–8.3   215n41, 218
    34.1.4   90n35
    34.5.8   90n32, 104n66
    34.8.1–2   **219**
    34.8.4–21.8   161
    34.8.4–7   161
    34.9   163
    34.9.1–10   161
    34.9.4   **161**
    34.9.6   131n142
    34.14–15   158n28, 161
    34.14.1–2   161
    34.14.3   **162**
    34.14.4–5   162
    34.14.4   **162**
    34.14.5   **162**
    34.14.6   **162**
    34.14.7   162, 163
    34.14.8   162

Livy, *Ab Urbe Condita* (Livy) (*cont.*)
Book 34

34.14.9	162
34.14.10	**162–163**
34.15.1–2	163
34.15.2	158*n*27
34.15.3–8	163
34.15.4	**163**, 163*n*40
34.16.8	177*n*100
34.20.2	177*n*100
34.28.2	178*n*104
34.39.11	174*n*83
34.44.6–8	43*n*59
34.44.6	113*n*91
34.45.6	44
34.46.7–47.8	155*n*18
34.46.9	155*n*18
34.47.2–3	155*n*18
34.47.5	160*n*34
34.53.2	90*n*35
34.53.5	119
34.56.3–5	71*n*115
34.56.3	45*n*62
34.56.5–6	90*n*35

Book 35

35.5.13	174*n*83
35.9.2	141*n*165
35.9.3	119, 124*n*116, 142*n*173
35.9.6	132
35.10.12	142*n*173
35.11.1	177*n*101
35.30.1	**178*n*109**
35.30.10	177*n*100
35.21.5	142*n*173
35.21.6	90*n*34
35.27.16	178*n*106
35.29.7	178*n*106
35.30.1	177*n*101
35.40.8	141*n*165
35.41.10	90*n*36, 142*n*173

Book 36

36.15	177
36.15–19	24
36.15–16	176*n*94
36.15.6–12	**24–25**
36.15.12	26*n*73
36.16.1, 7	26*n*73
36.17	2
36.17.10–11	26*n*73
36.17.14	2
36.17.15	**2*n*9**
36.18.3	175*n*89, 178*n*103
36.18.8	174*n*82
36.21.8	45*n*61
36.22–24	176*n*95
36.22.5	178*n*103, *n*105, **n109**
36.25.3	175*n*87
36.35.12	90*n*36, 104*n*66
36.36.5–6	114*n*94
36.39.5	46*n*73

Book 37

37.1.1–6	46*n*71
37.1.3	46, 91*n*39
37.3.7	90*n*34
37.4.7	176*n*94
37.18.11	173*n*76
37.27.7	178*n*104
37.31.9	154*n*14
37.36	73*n*119
37.38–44	188*n*126
37.39.7–44.1	164
37.39.7–41.1	164
37.39.11	172, 188*n*126
37.54.18–19	194
37.58.3	46*n*73

Book 38

38.2.13–14	174*n*77
38.2.13	177*n*100, 178*n*103, **n109**
38.4.1–4	175*n*87
38.17	194
38.17.7–8	160*n*34
38.17.9	104*n*66, *n*68, **194**
38.17.17	**194**
38.17.18	195
38.18–23	173*n*71
38.19.3	**178*n*109**
38.19.4	178*n*102
38.20–23	175*n*89
38.20.4	154*n*14, 177*n*100, 178*n*102, **n109**
38.20.7	154*n*14
38.21–23	175*n*91
38.21.1	154*n*14, 177*n*100
38.21.3	178*n*102
38.22.1	177*n*100
38.23.1, 7	177*n*100

INDEX OF ANCIENT SOURCES

Livy, *Ab Urbe Condita* (Livy) (*cont.*)
  Book 38
    38.25–27   175*n*89, 175*n*91
    38.28.4   135*n*155, 141*n*165
    38.36.4   124*n*116
    38.40.6   177*n*101, 178*n*106, **n108**
    38.40.12   178*n*107
    38.41.5   178*n*106
    38.44.9–50.3   175*n*91
    38.44.9   46*n*73
    38.45.9   177*n*100
    38.46.1   194
    38.47–49   105
    38.48.13   90*n*36
    38.48.14–16   105, **105*n*69**
    38.48.15   104*n*66
    38.49.7   177*n*101, 178*n*102
    38.50.5–53.11   72
    38.51.1–2   72*n*119
    38.51.1   90*n*31
    38.51.5–14   73
    38.51.5   **73**
    38.51.6   45*n*62, 73
    38.51.6–11   73
    38.51.8   104*n*66
    38.51.12   45*n*62, 73
    38.51.13   73
    38.52.1–53.7   73
    38.52.11   113*n*91
    38.53.8–11   73
    38.52.11   45*n*62
    38.54.9   45*n*62
    38.55.2   141*n*173
    38.56.3–4   **35**
    38.56.4   141*n*173
    38.56.11   44
    38.56.12   104*n*66
    38.57.4   43*n*59
    38.58.3–59.11   71
  Book 39
    39.1   195
    39.1.5   177*n*101, 178*n*102, **nn108–109**
    39.2   175*n*88
    39.2.2   177*n*100
    39.4.2   46*n*73
    39.6.6–9   195
    39.8–19   125, 235

    39.8.3–8   235
    39.9.5–6   237
    39.9.2–4   235
    39.9.5–10.9   236
    39.9.5   236*n*92
    39.11.1–3   236
    39.11.4–14.3   236
    39.12.2–3   237
    39.12.4   236*n*93
    39.13.9   237
    39.13.10   237
    39.13.12   141
    29.13.14   240
    39.14.4–10   236
    39.15–16   237
    39.15.1–16.3   236
    39.15.1   45*n*62, 238, **238*n*101**
    39.15.3   **238**
    39.15.6   237–238
    39.15.9   **239**
    39.15.11   104*n*66, 239, **239*n*102**
    39.15.12–14   **239**
    39.16.3–4   240
    39.17.1–19   236
    39.17.4–5   141*n*169
    39.17.4   141*n*168
    39.17.12   194*n*141
    39.17.13   **194*n*141**
    39.29.4   46*n*73
    39.30–31   188
    39.30.9–10   188
    39.30.10–31.1   172*n*60
    39.30.10   173*n*76, 188
    39.30.12   188
    39.31.5   188
    39.31.13   175*n*90
    39.31.16   188
    39.32.3   175*n*88
    39.32.11   45*n*64
    39.41.7   43*n*59
    39.44.6   35*n*14, 44*n*59
    39.49.5   177*n*100
    39.53.13   175*n*88
  Book 40
    40.2.2   124*n*116
    40.12.18   113*n*91
    40.16.2   142*n*73
    40.17.6   177*n*100, **179*n*110**

Livy, *Ab Urbe Condita* (Livy) (*cont.*)
  Book 40
40.21	177
40.21–22	21
40.21.1–4	**21–22**
40.22.1	173*n*76
40.22.2	177*n*100, **178***n***109**
40.22.4	178*n*103
40.22.14	175*n*88
40.27.11	**179***n***110**
40.27.12	177*n*100
40.27.13	177*n*100, **179***n***110**
40.29.13, 14	44
40.31	175*n*93
4.32.8	175*n*92
4.32.9–33.12	175*n*93
40.34.4	142*n*73
40.37.1–7	231*n*79
40.41.2	176*n*94, 177*n*101
40.45.3	90*n*34
40.45.6–46.16	136
40.45.8	136
40.51.4	44*n*59
40.51.6	141*n*165, 142*n*173
40.53.1	177*n*100
40.58.2	175*n*88
Book 41
41.3.3	**178***n***108**
41.7.5	45*n*61
41.9.6	142*n*173
41.10.5	98*n*48
41.10.7	90*n*36, 98*n*48, 104*n*67
41.10.11	98*n*48
41.10.13	98*n*48
41.12.21	43*n*59
41.18.1–3	175*n*88
41.18.1	**179**
41.18.9–13	173*n*71, 175*n*91
41.19.8	177*n*100, **179***n***110**
41.27.3	91*n*39
41.27.7	43*n*59, 90*n*34
41.27.8	141*n*165, 142*n*173
41.28	172*n*66
Book 42
42.7–8	172, 188*n*126
42.9.4	**113***n***92**
42.16.1	177*n*100, 178*n*102, **n109**
42.21.6	46*n*73

42.28.2	46*n*73
42.29.1–30.7	78
42.32.5–35.2	71*n*115
42.33.2	45*n*61
42.36.2	46*n*73
42.47.1	46*n*73
42.49.1–6	**96–97**
42.49.6	104*n*67
42.49.1	**98**
42.49.6	90*n*36, **98**
42.55.1	177*n*100, **178***n***109**
42.57–59	173*n*68
42.58–59	157*n*23
42.58.5	174*n*78
42.58.6–14	157*n*23
42.64.7–10	174*n*79
42.65–67	173*n*68
42.65.6–66.9	174*n*77
42.66.7	178*n*105
Book 43
43.6.6	104*n*67
43.15.5	45*n*64
43.16.9	90*n*35
43.19.7	176*n*95
43.19.8	173*n*73
43.22.8	175*n*87
43.23.2	177*n*100
Book 44
44.1–6	173*n*72
44.3–5	153, 176
44.3.3	178*n*102, **n106**
44.3.4–6	173*n*76
44.3.7–8	177
44.3.7	178*n*103
44.4.4–6	176
44.4.11	177*n*100
44.5.2	177*n*100
44.5.10	178*n*107
44.6	177*n*97
44.9.2	172*n*65
44.10.8–11	172*n*66
44.11.1–12.7	172*n*65
44.13.2	176*n*95
44.14.3	90*n*36, 104*n*67
44.16.9	35*n*14, 44*n*59
44.17	**177***n***97**
44.19.1–14	46*n*71
44.19.7	46

INDEX OF ANCIENT SOURCES

Livy, *Ab Urbe Condita* (Livy) (*cont.*)
  Book 44
44.20.2	177*n*100, **179*n*110**
44.22	71*n*115
44.22.1	45*n*61
44.31.2–5	151*n*5
44.35.16–22	172
44.38–39	156
44.39.2–5	156
44.39.2–3	156
44.39.2	**157**
44.39.5	156–157
44.40.5–9	172*n*64
44.46.5–7	173*n*67
44.46.5	175*n*87

  Book 45
45.1–2	145
45.1.1–5	145
45.1.6–10	145
45.2.1–2	145
45.2.3–12	145–146
45.2.3	**145**
45.2.4	**146**
45.2.6	45*n*61
45.15.6	120*n*106
45.20.4–25.6	75
45.20.4–9	75
45.20.5, 11	44
45.20.10	75
45.21.1–8	75
45.22.1–2	76
45.22.1	90*n*34, 104*n*67
45.24.11	76
45.24.12	76
45.25.2–3	76*n*124
45.25.3	**76*n*124**
45.28.2	152
45.32.9	113*n*91
45.35.3	141
45.35.4–42.1	94
45.35.4–9	94
45.36.1	90*n*35, 94–95
45.36.2–5	95
45.36.6–10	95
45.36.6–7	90*n*35, **95**
45.36.7	205*n*23
45.36.39	95
45.39.2	90*n*34, **95**, 104*n*67
45.39.10	95
45.39.10–11	**95–96**
45.39.11	90*n*36, 98, 104*n*67
45.39.12–13	96
45.39.13	90*n*36, 96, 104*n*67
45.40	95
45.40.6	**98–99**
45.41.6–12	99
45.41.7–9	99
45.41.10	99, 104*n*67
45.41.11–12	98*n*50
45.21.12	**99**
45.42.2–3	94*n*46
45.42.4–12	94*n*46
45.42.12	135*n*154
45.43	94*n*46
45.44.1–3	94*n*46
45.44.4	77, 77***n*127**
45.44.4–21	94*n*46
45.44.5	45*n*64, 77, 77***n*126**
45.44.6	77, 77***n*128**
45.44.8	104*n*67
45.44.20	78
45.44.21	77*n*125

  Periochae
Per. 5	79*n*130
Per. 45	77*n*125
Per. 48	231*n*79
Per. 58	79
Per. 74	79
Per. 80	79
Per. 89	79
Per. 103	152
Per. 104	152
Per. 107	79
Per. 116	79, 138
Per. 120	79, 80*n*131
Per. 131	251*n*6
Per. 138	138

  Fragments
| F 61 Levene | 80, 80*n*131 |

Lucan, *Bellum Civile* (Luc.)
| 7.438 | 87*n*23 |

Lucceius, Lucius
  FRHist. 30 T1 (=Cic.
  Fam. 5.12.2)   9*n*31

Macrobius, *Saturnalia* (Macr. *Sat.*)
    3.9.6   123*n*115

Nepos, Cornelius (Nep.)
Chronica
    FRHist. 45 F1a–b (=Gell. *NA* 17.21.3;
        Jer. *Chron.* 77b)   10*n*35
Life of Cato (*Cato*)
    3.3–4   7*n*26
    3.3.4   8*n*27

Nicolaus of Damascus, *Life of Augustus*
    (Nic. Dam.)
    20   250*n*5

Orosius, *Historiae adversus paganos* (Oros.)
    2.13.1–7   229*n*73

Ovid, *Fasti* (Ov. *Fast.*)
    1.261–262   88*n*25
    1.543–586   129*n*136
    1.551   130*n*137
    1.553–554   129*n*136
    1.637–648   40*n*39
    2.411–412   129
    3.430   87*n*22
    6.503   236*n*93

Pictor, Quintus Fabius
    FRHist. 1 T3a
        (=Livy 22.57.4–5)   7*n*23
    FRHist. 1 T3b
        (=Plut. *Vit. Fab.* 18.3)   7*n*23
    FRHist. 1 T3c
        (=App. *Hann.* 27.116)   7*n*23
    FRHist. 1 T4
        (=Livy 23.11.1–6)   7*n*23
    FRHist. 1 T6
        (=Polyb. 3.9.4)   7*n*23
    FRHist. 1 T10
        (=Cic. *Div.* 1.43)   7*n*23
    FRHist. 1 T11a
        (=Livy 1.44.2)   7*n*23
    FRHist. 1 T11c
        (=Livy 2.40.10)   7*n*23
    FRHist. 1 T11d
        (=Dion. Hal. *Ant.*
         Rom. 7.71.1)   7*n*23

Piso, Lucius Calpurnius Piso Frugi
    FRHist. 27 F 24 (=Gell.
        NA 7.9.1–6)   70*n*114

Plautus (Plaut.)
Bacchides (*Bacch.*)
    53–56   237
Cistellaria (*Cist.*)
    614   178*n*106
Menaechmi (*Men.*)
    591   178*n*106

Pliny the Elder, *Naturalis Historia* (Plin. *HN*)
    2.241   223*n*63
    3.5.66   83*n*6
    15.77–78   129*n*134
    15.119   43*n*57
    32.19   70
    33.21   9*n*33
    35.108   114*n*94

Plutarch (Plut.)
Life of Antony (*Vit. Ant.*)
    55.4–5   251*n*6
Life of Camillus (*Vit. Cam.*)
    36.1–9   66*n*103
    42.2   40*n*39
Life of Coriolanus (*Vit. Cor.*)
    33   126
    33.1   127
Life of Gaius Gracchus (*Vit. C. Gracch.*)
    5.4   38
Life of Fabius Maximus (*Vit. Fab.*)
    18.3   7*n*23
Life of Flamininus (*Vit. Flam.*)
    4.2   180*n*112
Life of Lucullus (*Vit. Luc.*)
    1.4   9*n*33
    4.5   9*n*33
Life of Romulus (*Vit. Rom.*)
    3.6   126*n*119
    9.3   87*n*23
    19.7   43*n*58
    20   126*n*120
Life of Sulla (*Vit. Sull.*)
    6.10   9*n*33

INDEX OF ANCIENT SOURCES

Polybius, *Histories* (Polyb.)
3.9.4	7n23
6.27–42	155n17
6.53–54	40n49
15.9–14	158n28
18.21.8	181, 181n115
18.24–27	180
18.25.2	182
18.28–32	182
18.31.2	182
18.31.5–6	182

Propertius, *Elegies* (Prop.)
2.31	128n129
3.3.7	33n6
4.4.93	90n38
4.6	128n129
4.9.1–20	129n136
4.9.10	129n136

Rhetorica ad Herennium (Rhet. ad Her.)
4.43	90n38

Sallust (Sall.)
Bellum Iugurthinum (Iug.)
41	164n43

[*Epistula ad Caesarem senem*] ([Ad Caes. sen.])
1.10.8	62n99

Scaurus, Marcus Aemilius
FRHist. 18 T1a
  (=Cic. *Brut.*112)   9n33
FRHist. 18 T2 (=Val.
  Max. 4.4.11)   9n33
FRHist. 18 T3 (=Plin.
  HN 33.21)   9n33
FRHist. 18 T4 (=Tac.
  Agr. 1.3)   9n33

Seneca the Elder, *Suasoriae* (Sen. Suas.)
6.17	80, 80n131

Servius, *Ad Aeneidem* (Serv. Aen.)
3.46	121n109
6.783	84n14
8.641	43n58

Strabo, *Geography* (Strabo)
12.5.2	131n139, n141

Sulla, Lucius Cornelius (the dictator)
FRHist. 22, T1a (=Plut. *Vit.
  Luc.* 1.4)   9n33
FRHist. 22 T1b (=Plut. *Vit.
  Luc.* 4.5)   9n33
FRHist. 22 T1c (=Plut. *Vit.
  Sull.* 6.10)   9n33
FRHist. 22, T4 (=Suet. *Gram.
  et Rhet.* 12)   9n33

Suetonius (Suet.)
De grammaticis et rhetoribus (Gram. et Rhet.)
12	9n33

Life of Julius Caesar (Iul.)
44	90n38
79.3	250n5

Life of Augustus (Aug.)
5	127n124
7.2	128n128
29.3	127n126
31.1	128n131
72.1	127n125

Solinus, *Collectanea Rerum Memorabilium* (Solin.)
1.18	126n120

Tacitus (Tac.)
Agricola (Agr.)
1.3	9n33

Annales (Ann.)
13.58	129n134

Historiae (Hist.)
3.71.3	87n23

Tibullus, *Elegies* (Tib.)
2.5.17	128n131

Valerius Maximus, *Dicta et Facta Memorabilia* (Val. Max.)
1.8.1	39n37
2.2.9	126n118
4.4.11	9n33
6.1.2	229n73

Valerius Maximus (cont.)

8.15.3	131
9.6.1	88n25

Varro
De Lingua Latina (Ling.)

5.41–54	84
5.41	88n25, 90, 90n38
5.54	126n120
5.148–150	101n56
5.155	36n19
5.159	221n59

De Re Rustica (Rust.)

1.2.9	37
1.18.4	178n106
1.20.5	178n106

Velleius Paterculus, Roman History (Vell. Pat.)

1.8.4	126n118
1.8.5	87n22
2.81.3	127n126

Vergil (Verg.)
Aeneid (Aen.)

3.163–171	251n9
6.69–73	128n131
8.185–275	129n136
8.193–199	129n136
8.231	130n137
8.251–266	129n136
8.342–344	87n23
8.704–706	128n129
8.720	128n129
12.791–842	251n9

Georgics (G.)

2.136–176	251n9

Zonaras, John Epitome Historiarum (Zonar.)

7.18	229n73
7.23.1	66n103
9.13	211n34
9.16.1	180n112